Ninth Edition

Self-Directed Behavior
Self-Modification for Personal Adjustment

David L. Watson
University of Hawai'i at Manoa

Roland G. Tharp
University of California, Berkeley

WADSWORTH
CENGAGE Learning

Australia • Brazil • Japan • Korea • Mexico • Singapore • Spain • United Kingdom • United States

To the memories of
Joyce Frank Watson
and
Dr. Tom Ciborowski

WADSWORTH
CENGAGE Learning

Self-Directed Behavior:
Self-Modification for Personal
Adjustment, Ninth Edition
David L. Watson and
Roland G. Tharp

Publisher: Vicki Knight

Senior Acquisitions Editor,
Psychology: Marianne
Taflinger

Assistant Editor:
Dan Moneypenny

Editorial Assistant:
Lucy Faridany

Technology Project Manager:
Darin Derstine

Marketing Managers:
Sara Swangard, Kim Russell

Marketing Assistant:
Natasha Coats

Marketing Communications
Manager: Kelley McAllister

Project Manager, Editorial
Production: Christy Krueger

Creative Director: Rob Hugel

Art Director: Vernon Boes

Print Buyer: Karen Hunt

Permissions Editor: Joohee Lee

Production Service:
Scratchgravel Publishing
Services

Copy Editor: Marjorie Woodall

Cover Designer and Illustrator:
Andrew H. Ogus

Compositor: Interactive
Composition Corporation

For product information and technology assistance,
contact us
at **Cengage Learning Customer & Sales Support,**
1-800-354-9706.
For permission to use material from this text or product,
submit all requests online at **www.cengage.com/permissions**.
Further permissions questions can be emailed to
permissionrequest@cengage.com.

Library of Congress Control Number: 2006904378

Student Edition:
ISBN-13: 978-0-495-09324-4
ISBN-10: 0-495-09324-6

Wadsworth
10 Davis Drive
Belmont, CA 94002-3098
USA

Cengage Learning is a leading provider of customized learning
solutions with office locations around the globe, including
Singapore, the United Kingdom, Australia, Mexico, Brazil, and
Japan. Locate your local office at: **www.cengage.com/global**.

Cengage Learning products are represented in Canada by
Nelson Education, Ltd.

To learn more about Wadsworth, visit
www.cengage.com/wadsworth.

Purchase any of our products at your local college store or at our
preferred online store **www.ichapters.com.**

Printed in the United States of America
5 6 7 8 9 10 13 12 11

Contents

4   The Principles of Self-Regulation: Theory and Practice   109

5   Antecedents   135

6   Behaviors: Actions, Thoughts, and Feelings   164

7 Consequences   204

8 Developing a Successful Plan   246

9 Problem Solving and Relapse Prevention   271

10 Termination and Beyond   295

Preface

This book is designed to acquaint you with a general theory of behavior, to guide you through exercises for developing skills in self-analysis, and to provide you with concrete information on how to achieve the goals you hold for yourself. The most important goal of this volume is to help you achieve more self-determination, more "willpower," more control over your own life.

The book can serve as a textbook in psychology courses but does not depend on a formal course structure. Any reader can use it for self-instruction; no "prerequisites" are necessary. Clients of therapists or counselors can use it as an adjunct in planning their own self-change.

You should be warned about one possible side effect: You may become interested in the science of behavior. A number of people delve deeper into the subject as a result of studying this material and in response to the experiential learning that can result from the self-change process.

The vehicle for learning will be your own self-analysis, your own program for implementing your values. Throughout the book, you are urged to accompany your reading with your own self-improvement project. In a sense, your daily life will become the laboratory in which you will study and develop your own behavior.

Foreword to the Professional

This book's ninth edition continues the authors' intentions: to provide scientifically based instruction in the principles and practices of self-applied psychology. In the proliferation of self-help manuals, we have defined our niche as the one that offers an opportunity for students to learn principles of scientific psychology in the laboratory that is most important to them—the laboratory of their own life problems. Simultaneously, they will learn verified coping skills for personal problem solving.

To achieve these goals, we have set certain standards: to maintain an up-to-date review of all important literature, including both empirical and theoretical publications relevant to self-managed behavior; to maintain accuracy of summary and interpretation so that instructors can be confident in assigning this text; to be conservative in making recommendations that arise only from a secure data base; and to advance integrative interpretations that offer some coherence to a vigorous and expanding field. In addition, we employ one further screen: first to do no harm. Thus we do not cover emerging therapeutic techniques unless we are confident that readers can safely use them without professional supervision. And finally, we strive to maintain the readability that has characterized our previous editions.

The field of self-directed behavior began as self-behavior modification, but it has expanded in a vortex that has swept in vicarious and observational learning, cognitive behaviorism and verbal self-control, imagery, and information science. It now includes theoretical and empirical concepts of skills analysis, delay of gratification, learned resourcefulness, control theory, relapse prevention, neo-Vygotskian developmental theory, self-efficacy, commitment theory, decision making, attribution theory, self-regulation, behavioral economics, and most recently the study of emotional regulation, health and illness behavior, educational settings, and the general self-regulation of action. This enrichment has provided key conceptual links that have made self-direction more coherent, more understandable, and more integrated.

Recently psychology has generated a proliferation of theoretical studies of self-direction, both directly and indirectly. Theoretical and empirical work move knowledge along like right foot and left foot. During the four years since the previous edition, the left foot of theory has been hopping ahead, while the excitement of empirical studies is provided by evaluation of techniques using sophisticated formal design, including meta-analyses. Self-direction is now a mature field, with reliable and effective theory- and research-based procedures.

Empirical testing of this book has been uniformly positive: Students using this text in courses have achieved their goals for self-change in percentages varying from 66% to 84% (Brigham, 2002; Clements & Beidleman, 1981; deBortali-Tregerthan, 1984; Deffenbacher & Shepard, 1986; Dodd, 1986; Hamilton, 1980; Rakos & Grodek, 1984) and have also reported a general improvement in lifestyle (Castro, 1987).

The organization of the book is designed to make it as useful as possible for students. Reading can be guided by the *learning objectives* at the beginning of each chapter. Key terms are highlighted in italic, and a special section at the end of each chapter identifies the successive steps of the self-direction project throughout the book. The Tips for Typical Topics, included in most chapters, facilitate rapid formulation of self-modification plans.

Acknowledgments

For this edition, we are particularly indebted for the excellent critical analyses provided by David Browning, University of Toledo; Jim Eubanks, Central Washington University; Gerald Harris, University of Houston; Ellen Koch, Eastern Michigan University; Carolynn Kohn, University of the Pacific; Christy Porter, College of William and Mary; Laura Seligman, University of Toledo; A. Robert Sherman, University of California–Santa Barbara; Judith Siegel, UCLA; and Jon Swanson, Benedictine University. Special thanks to Richard Suinn, Jerry Deffenbacher, Jack Kirschenbaum, Richard Rakos, and William Higa for their useful advice and correspondence; Karen Budd and Kelly Chang for new cases from their courses; and Naomi Olson for excellent research assistance.

Our greatest debt of gratitude is to all our students. For 30 years, they have come from the University of Hawaii at Manoa, and now from classes taught nationally and internationally. Students and their self-change projects have taught us much and made the life of this book possible. The current ages of former students who have contributed to this book now range from 20 to . . . well, eligibility for Social Security. We have always disguised their identities; we hope that in this anonymity they will all recognize themselves, accept our thanks, and acknowledge our tribute to the Unknown Student.

David L. Watson
Roland G. Tharp

For Further Research on the World Wide Web

Here are websites full of psychological information that you may want to peruse:

American Psychological Association	www.apa.org
Association for Psychological Science	www.psychologicalscience.org
Association for Behavioral and Cognitive Therapies	www.abct.org
APA Databases	www.psycinfo.com
Psychology Information Online	www.psychologyinfo.com

Some students like to research their topic of change online. The book *Authoritative Guide to Self-Help Resources in Mental Health* (Norcross, Santrock, Campbell, Smith, Sommer, & Zuckerman, 2003) lists and evaluates hundreds of sites on 38 topics. From that book as well as from our experience, here are some of the most recommended sites for the topics we list in our Tips for Typical Topics sections:

- **Anxieties and stress**
  Generalized anxiety disorder
     www.queendom.com/articles/mentalhealth/gad.html
  Panic anxiety education management:
     www.healthyplace.com/communities/anxiety/paems/index.html
  Anxiety panic Internet resource
     www.algy.com/anxiety

- **Assertion**
  Assertiveness
     www.couns.uiuc.edu/brochures/assertiv.htm
  Are you assertive?
     www.queendom.com/tests/minitests/fx/assertiveness.html

- **Depression and low self-esteem**
  Depression
     www.nimh.nih.gov/healthinformation/depressionmenu.cfm
  Wings of madness: depression information, news, and support
     www.wingsofmadness.com
  Self-esteem—what is it?
     www.positive-way.com/stopping%20your%20inner%20critic.htm

- **Exercise and athletics**
  Try searching for "exercise for health" or a specific exercise such as "jogging" on a search engine.

- **Relations with others: social anxieties, social skills, and dating**
  Cooperative communications skills
     www.newconversations.net

- **Smoking, drinking, and using drugs**
  Web of Addictions
    www.well.com/user/woa
  HabitSmart
    www.habitsmart.com
- **Studying and time management**
  Wadsworth College Success Solutions
    www.cengage.com/success
- **Weight loss and overeating**
  Calorie Control Council
    www.caloriecontrol.org
  Weight loss
    http://weightloss.about.com

Learning about other ideas and getting in touch with other people wrestling with the same issues can be a big help. Here are two books that list and evaluate hundreds of web resources dealing with all aspects of mental health, adjustment, and self-help. Just look up the topics of interest to you, and plug into websites devoted exclusively to those topics.

- John M. Grohol (2000). *The Insider's Guide to Mental Health Resources Online.* New York: The Guilford Press.
- John C. Norcross et al. (2003). *Authoritative Guide to Self-Help Resources in Mental Health.* New York: The Guilford Press.

If the instructor chooses to adopt the InfoTrac® College Edition option, the student will have access to a fully searchable, online library of nearly 6000 journals 24 hours a day, 7 days a week through the computer. InfoTrac College Edition can be searched by key term, author, or topic, and it provides both abstracts and full text articles. It's a useful tool, not only for this course, but for all courses that a student may take. It includes such journals as *American Scientist, American Journal of Community Psychology,* and the *Psychological Record* as well as many others.

InfoTrac® College Edition Key Terms

Addiction(s)	Healthy behavior
Anxiety	Healthy habits
Assertion	Panic
Assertiveness (psychology)	Relaxation
Calorie Control Council	Relaxation techniques
Communication skills	Self-esteem
Depression	Social anxieties
Exercise	Social skills
Exercise addiction	Stress
Habit (and all its subtopics)	Stress relief
Health	Weight loss

Chapter 1

The Skills of Self-Regulation

Outline and Learning Objectives

Each chapter begins with a set of learning objectives, in which all the major points in the chapter are listed. The learning objectives are phrased as questions. When you can answer all these questions, you have mastered the chapter. Read these objectives just before reading each section of the chapter. That tells you what to look for in each section.

Self-Regulation

1. What is self-regulation?
2. What is the best way to study this book?
3. What are the implications of thinking of self-regulation as a skill?
4. What are the problems with the idea of willpower?

The Skills of Self-Regulation and the Purpose of This Book

5. What are the two elements of skill? What are the stages in the development of a skill? *KNOWLEDGE + PRACTICE*   *AQUIRE KNOWLEDGE / PRACTICE   SKILL / MAKE SKILL AUTOMATIC*
6. Explain the purpose of this book.

Behavior and Its Context

7. What are antecedents, behaviors, and consequences?
8. How does learning affect them and their relationship to each other?

The Process of Self-Modification

9. What is a target behavior? What are the steps in most self-change programs?
10. How do we use the A-B-C paradigm to understand how we can change?

Does Self-Modification Really Work?

11. Are people able to change themselves when they have a relatively serious problem with their behavior? Give examples.
12. What does the research show about the success of students who use this book?

13. What is the likely main cause when a self-modification plan doesn't work?
14. Give some examples of the uses of self-modification in health and/or educational settings.

For Further Research

Chapter Summary

Your Own Self-Direction Project: Step 1

Self-Regulation

We humans regulate our actions minute to minute. If you're talking too quietly or mumbling and realize others cannot understand you, you make changes before continuing to speak. If you're jogging too fast and are getting out of breath, you slow down. If you are driving over the speed limit and think, "I may get a ticket," you make changes. We often make changes in our personal interactions, too. In a discussion with a friend you might think, "She looks bored. I think I'll change the topic."

To regulate something means that we control it or direct it by a principle—such as the small principles of not getting a ticket or not being boring. We regulate our behavior to act in accord with many different principles. When we regulate we put things in good order. We make adjustments.

Self-regulation means that we put ourselves into good order. Self-regulation implies the ability to control ourselves, to exert control over our acts and inner processes. We self-regulate our thoughts, our feelings, our impulses, and our behaviors. We have the capacity of self-control.[1]

Self-regulation occurs in short time spans, as when we speak more clearly to avoid mumbling, and over long time spans, as when we consciously eat less and exercise more over several months so we can lose weight, or when we engage in time management over an entire college career to help ourselves study more.

Being able to self-regulate allows us to guide our behavior to gain desirable outcomes. We change the topic to avoid boring a friend. We stop drinking to avoid getting drunk. We spend more time studying to improve our grades. We work on our listening skills to better please our partner.

The more people self-regulate, the better it seems to be for them. To say that someone has high self-control means that they can successfully self-regulate in a variety of situations. People who are high in self-control make better grades in school, are less depressed and less anxious, have higher self-esteem, enjoy more satisfying intimate relationships, and are more popular (Tangney, Baumeister, & Boone, 2004). Wow! And, there doesn't seem to be a downside. Such folks are not miserably over controlled (Tangney et al., 2004). They give up control when it's fun to do so, but can use it when they need it.

Where does self-regulation come from? Research and theory point to the idea that it is a learned skill (Peterson & Seligman, 2004), although there may be some inherited

---

[1]Some authors use the term *self-control* only when speaking of impulse control, but in accord with the *Handbook of Self-Regulation* (Baumeister & Vohs, 2004), we define *self-regulation* and *self-control* as the same. In earlier editions of this book, we used the term *self-direction,* but the field now favors *self-regulation,* and we treat those two terms as interchangeable.

Box 1-1
How to Study This Book

At the beginning of each chapter is a set of learning objectives that are phrased as questions. The learning objectives cover all the major points in the chapter. If you can answer them, you have mastered the material. Find the answers to those questions and then learn them.

Here are some steps to follow in learning the material (Robinson, 1970). Research shows that students who follow a procedure like this get better grades, particularly if they have *not* been doing well (Pintrich, McKeachie, & Yin, 1987).

Read just one or two sections of the chapter at a time, and use the following procedure for each section:

1. Read the learning objectives at the beginning of the chapter and the part of the chapter summary that corresponds to the section you are working on.
2. Read the section itself.
3. Reread the summary material.
4. Answer the learning objective questions for the section. To remember the material, tie the ideas to your own life. For example, if you were reading about techniques for relaxation, ask yourself, "How could I use this in my life?"

Repeat this process for each section. Don't move on from one section to the next until you can answer the learning objective questions.

When you are studying for a course exam, give yourself a pretest by answering the learning objectives. Check your answers against the text. Reread the chapter summary and those parts of the chapter you need to review to answer the learning objective questions.

Before a test, read Box 2-6 in Chapter Two for ideas on the most efficient way to take a test.

This method may sound cumbersome compared with your present way of studying, but research has shown that it is the best way to learn the material in a textbook (Kirschenbaum & Perri, 1982). As you practice the method, it will become easier and easier for you.

---

elements (cf. Baumeister & Vohs, 2004). It varies within a person depending upon the situation. You might have wonderful self-control over your eating, and show the world a slim, attractive figure, but have little control over your worrying and feel tense and distracted. You might be a superb student with an easy ability to self-regulate your studying, but less polished and less in control in your social life.

We are better at self-regulating some of our behaviors than others. You may feel that you eat too much and wish you could better self-regulate your eating. But do you have the skill to change? If you don't, then people who do self-regulate this behavior successfully seem a marvel. A slim friend says, "Yes, I decided I was about five pounds overweight, so I just took it off." You listen with mouth agape, you who have been trying to control your eating for years.

All of us have certain goals we cannot reach "just like that." Most of us have skills for certain situations but not for others. You might easily increase studying when that is necessary, while your slim friend needs to do the same thing but lacks the skill. *When we have the ability to change ourselves, we have the skills that make up successful self-regulation.*

The Skills of Self-Regulation

A skill is the ability to do something well, developed through knowledge and practice. If one person practices certain behaviors while another does not, we expect that the person who practices will become more skilled at those behaviors. We may have an aptitude for certain skills—we are able to learn them easily—but in all cases we understand that skills have to be learned. It does not surprise us to learn that our friend who has been practicing the piano 6 hours a day has become a skilled musician. Nor are we surprised to learn that many great musicians come from families in which music is an important part of daily life. The opportunity to develop skill is an important precursor of the development of musical skill.

The idea of skill implies skill in a specific domain, such as playing the piano or tennis, or speaking Spanish. We do not necessarily expect a skilled pianist to be skilled at languages.

We do not learn general skills that apply across a wide range of situations but rather specific ones that apply to specific tasks (Patrick, 1992). The same thing is true of the skills of self-regulation: You might be skilled at controlling your weight but not at avoiding procrastination. You might do a brilliant job of controlling your studying in school, but seem to have little control over certain negative thoughts that depress you.

Being skilled implies that one can perform some action in spite of the fact that the task varies (Fischer, 1980). A soccer player who could kick a goal only from one precise spot on the field would not be considered skilled. It is the ability to kick from any position, through opposing players, having received the ball from various other positions on the field and at different speeds, that makes a player skilled.

If self-regulation, or self-direction, is a skill, we must think about both the behavior we need to perform and the situations in which we will perform it. Our goals for self-regulation are defined in terms of particular behaviors in particular situations. If you can only kick a goal from one spot on the field, but your position on the field keeps changing, then you need to practice kicking from a variety of spots. If self-direction is a skill, we must practice the skill in different conditions, and we know that only with practice will we improve.

What Keeps You from Reaching Certain Goals?

What should you do to change yourself when you want to? The answer to this depends upon your view of what has been keeping you from reaching your goals. For example, if you want to get along better with other people, but have not, what keeps you from reaching your goal?

Consider our student, Calvin, who can't hold a job for more than a few weeks, even though he is 21 and needs the money. Calvin feels something is wrong.

But what? How Calvin thinks about the problem has a strong impact on what he thinks should be done about it. There are different ways to think about a problem in self-regulation, and each has a different implication for Calvin's response. Alternative ways are outlined in Figure 1-1.

Alternative 1: Explanation by the Environment

The causes of behavior are found in the environment—events and forces outside the person—such as the stars, luck, fate, other people, or the situation.

Alternative II: Explanation by the Personal

The causes of behavior are found in the person—in willpower, personality traits, or symptoms of inner disorders.

Alternative III: Explanation by Skills: The Person/Situation Interaction

The person's behavior changes somewhat from one situation to the next, depending on personal skills appropriate to different situations. There is an interaction of person and situation. This is the point of view we will adopt in this book.

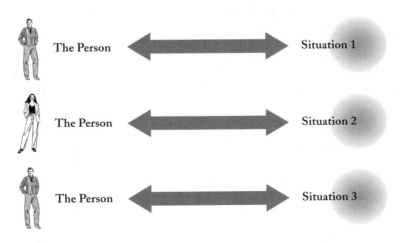

Figure 1-1 Three ways of thinking about the relationship between a person and the environment

We could say, for example, that Calvin has a bad astrological sign, is unlucky in his stars. But then there is nothing to be done but wait to see what happens. Fate will unfold, and the stars will determine if Calvin is to be a failure or not. Some people like to talk about astrology, crystals, or pyramids as party chatter, but should we take these ideas seriously when faced with important life problems? Not if we really want to do something about our lives. As Shakespeare says in *Julius Caesar,* "The fault is not in our stars, but in ourselves."

The Concept of Willpower

People often speak of problems of adjustment such as Calvin's in terms of willpower. He can't make himself get up for work in the morning. He can't resist taking too long for lunch. This is a common way of thinking about our problems in self-regulation. "I want to quit smoking, but I don't seem to have any willpower."

The word *willpower* implies some entity, something in your psychological makeup, something that allows you to do hard jobs, overcome temptations, stick to your goals. But it is merely a word, a label we use to describe how people deal with problems in self-direction. "She could do it because she has lots of willpower. He couldn't do it because he doesn't have much willpower."

This idea of willpower has problems. For example, you may be able to stick to your goals in some situations but not in others. Calvin, for example, is able to get along well with his girlfriend, and they've been together for nearly a year. Most of us find that in certain situations we have adequate "willpower," but in others we do not have enough. You might realize that there are certain things you can do—for example, resist smoking although you used to smoke, or get your assignments done on time—and certain things you can't do—for example, relax on a date or quit biting your fingernails.

A better way of thinking about such strengths and weaknesses is to realize that they are tied to particular situations. In the situation with-girlfriend, Calvin succeeds; in the situation need-to-go-to-work, Calvin struggles. When faced with the situation I-have-to-do-my-assignment, you are able to do what has to be done, but when in the situation I-should-relax-on-this-date, you don't do what has to be done. The simple concept of willpower overlooks important variations in our behavior from one situation to another.

Many people overlook the impact different situations have on them, and instead explain their own behavior by referring to their personality traits (Nisbett & Ross, 1980). This probably stems from the belief that our personality is something we carry around with us, projecting it out onto whatever situation we are in. In fact, modern psychology has learned that our behavior changes from situation to situation (Mischel & Shoda, 1995). We don't project the same personality all the time, but change our behavior as we go from one situation to another. A person who is normally warm and outgoing might find herself suddenly shy in a novel social situation.

Some people who fail to stay on a diet blame their personalities or their weak "willpower," but in fact the blame usually lies in how they react to very specific situations (Jeffrey, French, & Schmid, 1990). Most of the time they control their eating well, for example, but not when they are very hungry. Some diabetic patients go off their special diets even when it leads to poor health, but personality or temperament is not the cause. Situational factors such as feeling stressed or pressured by others to eat are the causes (Goodall & Halford, 1991).

Some people speak as though willpower involves standing in the face of temptation, fists clenched, jaw tight, refusing to do what one shouldn't do, even though one wants to do it. After several decades of practicing chastity, for example, Mahatma

Gandhi sometimes slept with attractive young followers to demonstrate his ability to abstain from sex. But most people with effective self-direction simply avoid that kind of situation. It is far easier to remain chaste while sleeping alone.

People use foresight and planning to avoid temptation. This point can be found in many ethical and religious systems. St. Paul, St. Augustine, and St. Thomas Aquinas, for example, all taught that to avoid sin one should avoid the occasion for sin. Dieters who plan how they will deal with a temptation like Thanksgiving dinner are more likely to deal with it successfully.

If you, like Gandhi, can resist temptation even when it's staring you in the face, then you don't need the techniques in this book. But most of us encounter situations in which we choose a short-term pleasure over our long-run goals, even though we regret it later. We goof off when we know we should be studying; we eat when we know we should not.

How can we make ourselves do things we find so difficult? *Plan ahead.* In Homer's *Odyssey,* written about 800 B.C., Odysseus and his crew sailed through straits where the Sirens sang a song so alluring that it drew sailors to their deaths on the rocks. Odysseus wanted to hear the Sirens' wonderful music, but he wanted to avoid sailing too close. He ordered his men to lash him to the mast and—no matter how much he begged to be set free—to keep him there until they had passed through the straits. Then he plugged their ears with wax so they could carry out his orders and row safely through without hearing the music (Ainslee, 1975).

The same strategy—acting in advance to prevent a behavior we do not want—is used by many of us every night when we set an alarm clock. The crucial element is making the desired choice when we are more likely to choose correctly (Rachlin, 1974). We tell our spouse that we don't want to eat more than one piece of pie at the dinner, and ask to be reminded of this if it looks like we're going for seconds. We might even promise ourselves, "I won't eat the ice cream, either, just that one piece of pie." We plan for temptation before it occurs.

Self-regulation is not just lots of willpower. It is "a skill involving anticipation and cleverness, so that immediate and tempting rewards do not impede progress toward a long-range goal" (Fisher, Levenkron, Lowe, Loro, & Green, 1982, p. 174). Odysseus made sure that the temptations of the Sirens did not lead away from his long-range goal, and you make sure you don't eat too much pie. One of our dieting students said, "You know, I realized that for years I'd been trying the Gandhi approach, staring at tempting food and trying to resist it, but usually failing. Once I realized this, I switched techniques, and did things like distracting myself or distancing myself, so I wouldn't have to stare down temptation."

The Skills of Self-Regulation and the Purpose of This Book

Behavior cannot be explained by the person or by the environment, but behavior is a function of the person in interaction with the environment. We want to explain problems in self-regulation by analyzing people's skills in specific situations. This interactional approach explains behavior in the famous equation of the psychologist Kurt Lewin:

$$\text{Behavior} = f(\text{Person and Environment})$$

Mental skills, such as knowing how to change your behavior, function the same way as other kinds of skills, such as knowing how to serve in tennis. *Skills are based in knowledge. They can be taught. They are developed through practice. You must then rehearse*

(Adams, 1987; Patrick, 1992). In this book it's our task to supply you with the knowledge, and your task to practice using it.

Task/Skill Mismatches

Whatever skills one has, there are always tasks that call for more than one can muster, whether it be the fairly good tennis player matched against the state champion, or the person unskilled in resisting good food faced with a table of tempting morsels. There are times when one's skills at self-direction are not up to the task at hand (Karoly, 1993). Because people differ in their level of skill, an easy task for one person may be difficult for another. Our slim friend takes off five pounds "just like that," but we cannot. Some tasks call for skills that we have not yet learned.

All of us experience times when our usual self-control skills fail us. In these situations, we self-regulate in a more self-conscious fashion (Karoly, 1993; Kirschenbaum & Flanery, 1984; Rosenbaum, 1988). A planned, continuing effort to change behavior to cope with a task we cannot presently master is called *self-modification.*

In specific situations, some people are more skilled at self-modification than others. For example, when a person is in a stressful situation, how much stress the person experiences is less crucial than how the person copes with stress (Schafer, 1992). Learning an active skill to use when faced with anxiety-provoking tasks actually prevents the anxiety (Barrios & Shigetomi, 1980). Students may begin to feel nervous while taking a test, realize that the anxiety will make their performance worse, and deliberately take a couple of minutes out to calm down. They can tell themselves to be calm, think calming thoughts, avoid thoughts that lead to the anxiety, and consciously relax. These are learnable skills that can improve academic success (Rosenbaum, 1983). (If you suffer from text anxiety, see Box 2-6 on taking a test in Chapter 2.)

Walter Mischel (1981) has shown how children learn self-control by increasing the skill with which they deal with tempting situations. Very young children have greater difficulty coping with temptations than do older children. What do older children do that younger ones don't do? Children who successfully resist temptations tend to think about the tempting object—for example, a marshmallow—using "cool" thoughts. "The marshmallows are puffy like clouds." Children who are less successful tend to think about the tempting object with "hot" thoughts. "The marshmallows taste yummy and chewy." "Hot" thoughts make it harder to resist temptation. Children who successfully resist temptation also distract themselves from "hot" thoughts. They avoid thinking about the tempting object altogether and think about other, irrelevant objects.

The ability to resist temptation is a learnable skill (Eisenberger & Adornetto, 1986) tied to specific situations (Barrios, 1985). Many people learn these skills without being aware of it, often in childhood. But as adults we can study the skills necessary to resist certain temptations—for example, what should the chronic overeater learn to do and think?—and then set out to learn these skills. Box 1-2 shows how one of our students learned new coping skills using the ideas in this book.

Purpose of This Book

Our goal in this book is to teach ways to improve your skills in situations where the task is difficult for you. This requires a planned effort at self-modification. We will do this by teaching new actions, coping skills, problem-solving skills, and knowledge to use in generating adequate matches between your skills and the tasks you face.

Box 1-2
Freeing the Captured Mind: Overcoming a Fear of Elevators

A.S. was a small, athletic, middle-aged man who took our course in self-change in night school. At the beginning of the course he told us he wanted to get rid of a strong fear of elevators, but he didn't know how. Here is a summary of his report at the end of the term.

When I was 7, my Dad, the wild pig man, used to scare us to death at bedtime. Snorting loudly, he'd come grunting down the hall to eat us. I used to run into the closet to hide, but once a stick fell onto the tracks of the sliding door and I couldn't get out. The wild pig man kept coming and coming, and I was trapped in the dark with no place to run. The louder I screamed in fright, the closer he came.

My brothers learned that I was afraid of the dark and of being in an enclosed place. Once. to tease me. they locked me in a dark storage room. I felt I was about to die. The more I begged to be let out, the more they laughed. It was like being trapped in a dark coffin in the center of the earth. I began to kick and punch the door, and after a few minutes it began to break. With a burst the door flew open, and I fell on the driveway. From then on I had a strong fear of being in a closed, dark place. By the time I was grown I would never enter an elevator, fearing the closing doors and the chance that the lights would go out. I quit a good job as a telephone repairman when they asked me to work on the phones in elevators.

Flying in an enclosed plane also became a problem. Once on a trip to Disneyland I had to take four sleeping pills and drink a pint of vodka just to get the nerve to get on the 747. I woke up 3 days later at Knotts Berry Farm, with my family very angry at me. They had to wait 10 minutes each time we went up to our room on the sixteenth floor, so I could walk up. My kids thought I was crazy.

So I set out to get over this fear of being in elevators. I wasn't sure how to do this, but I learned in the course. First, I started keeping records of how often I had bad thoughts about elevators and how often I climbed steps to avoid them. I began working on getting rid of bad elevator thoughts, and practiced this every night. I also practiced being relaxed while thinking about elevators.

Second, I began gradually approaching elevators. I worked out a detailed schedule to gradually deal with real-life elevators. In step one I would walk into an elevator, keep one hand on the door, press a button, and then walk out. In step two I would put one hand on the Door Open button, let the doors close, then push the button and exit. I made sure to practice being relaxed while doing these steps. In step three I rode up one floor while practicing relaxing and doing the multiplication tables in my head to distract myself from fearful thoughts.

(continued)

Box 1-2 *(continued)*

I also carried out each practice step in my imagination at least three times each day. I went through 24 steps and rewarded myself each day if I had done the step for that day.

At the end of my project I am riding all the elevators I come into contact with. I'm still not totally comfortable being in one, but I'm not avoiding them either, and I'm no longer embarrassing my family.

Why teach basic skills instead of simply telling you specific things to do for specific problems? "If you want to lose weight, increase your exercise to 60 minutes per day," or "To increase your studying, gradually work up to 8 hours per week." First, you may not be aware of some elements of your current problem. Also, as you change yourself, new problems will appear. You need general skills to deal with these unanticipated problems. If you learn only very specific tactics for specific problems, you will learn nothing to help you deal with different problems in the future.

Our goal is to teach you general skills for coping with problems of self-regulation. The age-old axiom is right: If you give a hungry man a fish, you have fed him for one day. If you teach him how to fish, he can feed himself for life.

Success depends on you. Understanding requires effort and study; perfection requires practice. In fact, developing skills typically go through a set of stages, and this is true whether it's a coping skill for life or skill at a sport (Adams, 1987).

First, you have to acquire knowledge. What is a good backhand? What is a good way to relax? Should you reward your efforts?

Second, you must practice the skill over and over. During this process you expect to make mistakes, but you continue practicing.

Finally, the skill becomes so well practiced that it is automatic.

Specific exercises are suggested at the end of each chapter. It is important that you carry out these practice assignments. Like someone who is learning to ride a bicycle, you must actually ride, be willing to wobble a bit, even take a fall. The only way you can learn to ride "just like that" is through practice.

This book is not like most textbooks. You don't just study it and take a test on it. You need to apply the material to your own case, to see how you can use the various ideas in your plans for self-change.

To begin, you need knowledge, just as the tennis player needs to be shown how to serve. The starting knowledge you need is a point of view, a way of understanding your own behavior. Here's that beginning.

Behavior and Its Context

If you are shy, just seeing a roomful of strangers at a party is enough to make you feel uncomfortable. Nothing bad has actually happened, but you feel nervous. You think, "I don't know anybody here!" Feelings and thoughts of discomfort are set off by the sight of a roomful of strangers. This party isn't for you, you think. Suppose you flee? Immediately

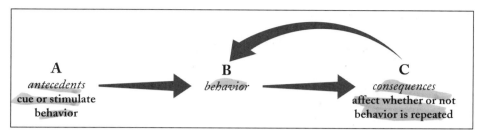

Figure 1-2 Antecedents, behavior, and consequences

your nervousness fades. You feel relaxed, and your thoughts turn to where you will go next. Fleeing has consequences: You feel better.

You have learned a way to deal with that kind of situation—fleeing—but you can see that in the long run this will create other problems. Often we learn things that work in the short run but create other problems later. A.S., in Box 1-2, feared enclosed, dark places and learned that he could avoid the fear by avoiding such places, although later this created problems for him.

What caused his fear to spring up? First came a thought or sight of an elevator, then came the fear. And his flight had consequences: His fear was reduced.

Human behavior and feelings are imbedded in a context, situations that come before and after the behavior. Situations can be divided into two elements: the events that come before a behavior and those that come after it. In psychology these are called *antecedents* and *consequences*. See Figure 1-2.

Antecedents are the setting events for your behavior. They cue you or stimulate you to act in certain ways. They can be physical events, thoughts, emotions, or inner speech.

Consequences affect whether or not you will repeat certain acts. They reinforce behavior or fail to do so. And they affect how you feel.

The antecedent for the behavior of the shy person is seeing the roomful of strangers and thinking, "Get out of here!" The behavior is turning around and walking out of the room. The consequence of fleeing is feeling better, and that is reinforcing.

The effects of situations—antecedents, behavior, and consequences—are influenced by the learning experiences a person has had in similar situations. Entering a roomful of strangers, one person—who has learned to be nervous in this situation—flees. Another who has no experience of fear in a roomful of strangers thinks, "Terrific! A party!"

Different learning experiences produce different behaviors even when we are dealing with the same antecedent or consequence. When you enter an elevator you just think about what floor you want to go to, but A.S., in Box 1-2, used to think, "I'm going to die!" It's clear where he learned to fear elevators: in locked closets and storage bins when he was a child.

Habits are automatic responses to situations (Bargh, 1997). Once we have learned, for example, we can drive a car without thinking about it at all. If we have formed bad habits, we also perform them without much thought, and we need to de-automatize the situation in order to make desired changes.

Thus, in the process of self-modification you set out to produce new learning for yourself in specific situations. To change your own behavior—to bring it under control or determine its course—you will have to learn new skills for particular situations.

"I am . . . when . . ."

You may not have the habit of thinking about yourself in relation to your environment. You may think, "I am . . ." and then fill in particular words that describe your general personality. You might think, "I am . . . shy . . . brave . . . smart . . . insecure . . . happy." There is a very long list of words you could use to describe yourself.

This way of thinking about yourself ignores the effect of the situation on your behavior. You are probably not always shy or always happy or always anything. To think that way ignores the effect of the environment. Most of the time our behavior is an interaction between ourselves and our environment.

You will think more clearly if you think like this: "I am . . . when . . ." For example, "I am shy when dealing with parties." (But not when dealing with my family.) "I am brave when dealing with bullies." (But not when dealing with professors.) "I am self-controlled when dealing with cigarettes." (But not when dealing with desserts.)

Thinking in terms of "I am . . . when . . ." instead of simply "I am . . ." leads to a more fine-grained and accurate understanding of yourself (Mendoza-Denton et al., 2001). Using only "I am . . ." encourages you to think of yourself in global, stereotyped ways, but using "I am . . . when . . . " gives you a more precise understanding of your own behavior.

The Process of Self-Modification

Plan—Monitor—Evaluate

Successful self-modification always contains certain essential elements: self-knowledge, planning, information gathering, and modification of plans in light of new information. There is a definite sequence in deliberate self-modification. Most self-change programs involve these steps:

1. Select a goal, and develop a commitment to change in order to reach that goal. Specify the behaviors to be changed. These behaviors are called *target behaviors.*
2. Make observations about the target behaviors. You may keep a kind of diary describing those behaviors or count how often you engage in them. Try to discover the antecedents that stimulate your acts and the consequences that reward them.
3. Work out a plan for change. Your plan might call for changing a pattern of thought that leads to unwanted behavior, gradually replacing an unwanted behavior with a desirable one, and rewarding yourself for desired behavior. See Figures 1-3 and 1-4.

(A) *Antecedents*	*(B)* *Behavior*	*(C)* *Consequences*
You can change the triggering events for a behavior by building in antecedents that lead to wanted behavior, and removing antecedents that lead to unwanted behavior.	You can change actions, thoughts, feelings, or behaviors by practicing desired acts or substituting desired alternatives for undesired actions.	You can change the events that follow your behavior to reinforce desired acts, and not reinforce undesired actions.

Figure 1-3 The A-B-Cs of self-change

Present situation:

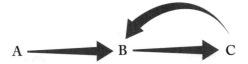

I. To change, you can add new elements:
   1. Add a new Antecedent, which leads to new Bs and Cs:

   2. Add a new Behavior, which will lead to a new Consequence:

   3. Or add a new Consequence, which will affect a new Behavior:

II. To change, you can also take out old, unwanted elements:
   1. Block old Antecedents, wall them off:

   2. Substitute new Behaviors for old, unwanted ones:

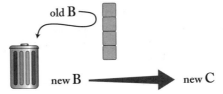

   3. Get rid of Consequences that are reinforcing old Behaviors:

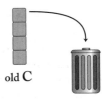

Figure 1-4 Changing target behaviors by adding new A-B-Cs or dropping old ones

4. Readjust your plans as you learn more about yourself. As you practice analyzing your behavior, you will be able to make more sophisticated and effective plans for change.

5. Take steps to ensure that you maintain the gains you make.

A Sample Self-Change Project

Here is the report of one of our students who carried out a self-change project in our class. Her name is Mary, and she is 21 years old. Mary's experience with her self-modification plan is presented largely in her own words, along with our comments.

> I gossip too much. I do it when I'm bored, with friends or family, just about anywhere. I thought this was a terrible habit, and at first I wanted to rid my life of gossip entirely. However, after discussing this idea with several people, I realized that it's really one particular kind of gossip that upsets me—saying negative things, or put-downs, about other people. My goal was to decrease these put-downs.

Mary has taken the first step in self-modification: She has translated a vague sense of dissatisfaction into a concrete goal.

> I began collecting my data on a 3" × 5" card, which I kept with me at all times. On the card I wrote the date, the person I was talking to, and the number of times I said something negative about another person. Sometimes I would forget to mark my card, and I'm sure I missed a few, but I was very shocked and surprised at the outcome. I said something negative about another person approximately 98 times per week—about 14 times each day! I noticed that keeping a record of the number of put-downs cut down on these numbers, so the real figures would have been even higher.

Mary has taken the second step in self-modification: making observations. She was wise to get this record before attempting to change. To begin an improvement program before getting careful information often results in failure. Mary wouldn't have known enough to change successfully unless she first observed herself. Also, her counting record made it possible to measure the success or failure of her self-modification program. We report her story in abbreviated form: Mary actually took several weeks to carry out her project.

> I noticed that these put-downs of other people occurred in particular situations: When I was with my sister or my cousin, and when I was feeling down and out, or depressed. I think I put down others because it made me look better than them. If I saw a pretty girl, for example, I might say, "Oh, she's pretty, but her nose is too big." Or if I saw a handsome guy, I'd say, "He's cute, but he's too short and stubby." It seemed I always found fault with everyone. This somehow made me feel superior to the other person. But I realized I was telling myself, "I really shouldn't be saying this. Well, I'll quit doing it soon." But I never did quit.

Often self-observation results in the realization that the target behavior occurs, or fails to occur, because of specific circumstances. This makes changing easier because you can change the circumstances. And that is what Mary did, as we will see in a moment. Notice that you have to make self-observations in order to discover the circumstances. Mary now took the third step in self-modification: She made a plan for change.

My plan for changing:

First, I decided to decrease put-downs of other people and to increase saying positive things about them. I kept a record of how often I did each of these. I started out at a very low level of saying nice things, about one per day, and gradually increased the number of positive things I said each day.

Second, I gave myself instructions. When I was in one of the tempting situations, I told myself, "I don't need to put down other people in order to look good. In fact, this turns people away from me, and it lowers my self-respect. So, don't do it."

Third, I substituted saying nice things for negative ones. I'd tell myself, "Stop!" if I started saying something negative and would think of something positive to say about the person instead.

Fourth, I used imaginary practice to imagine myself in a situation in which I performed the desired behavior flawlessly. This sounds corny, but it worked beautifully!

Last, I rewarded myself with extra spending money for each day that I did all these steps in my plan.

Mary's plan is a good one, for several reasons:

1. She uses several techniques for change.
2. She deals with the antecedents, the behavior itself, and the consequences.
3. She changes the behavior gradually.
4. She gives herself extra practice, rewards, and instructions to increase the chances that she will be able to change.

All these aspects of her plan are good simply because they increase her chances of success. Mary adds:

The plan really worked! I cut down negative statements from an average of 14 per day to nearly zero, and increased saying nice things from an average of once per day to 7. I can say I have an inner sense of self-worth now. I feel good about myself and others around me. Now that I know a lot more about myself, I feel I can control my thoughts and behaviors. I can say that I really like myself better today!

Applying Principles

What makes a self-modification plan like Mary's different from any New Year's resolution? Is self-modification anything more than a resolution to do better? Sometimes we just make up our minds to change and then do it. "I turned over a new leaf." or "It was time to get my act together." But it is not always so easy. Mary, for example, had intended to stop her bad habit for years, but had not. Something more than just good intentions was needed. That something more was a correct, conscious application of the principles of behavior change.

Mary made changes at three locations: She dealt with the old antecedents differently and inserted new ones. She practiced new behaviors and substituted them for the old acts. And she changed the consequences of her behavior.

Self-modification is a set of techniques that must be learned. To see if you already know some of the major points, evaluate the following report, which is a first effort at a self-modification plan by one of our students. Is it a good plan? What are its weaknesses?

Jack, a 25-year-old senior, writes:

> I used to have an "okay" body, but ever since I have been so swamped with work and school, I've become a bit chubby because I sit around in front of a computer screen or in class all day long. I usually eat three meals a day, and sometimes more. I'm always snacking when I'm doing things around the house—a little here, a little there. I rarely exercise, and when I do, I do it in spurts . . . sometimes I don't for months at a time. I always make up some kind of excuse why I cannot exercise. I am seldom motivated to exercise and eat right because there are always other things to do or other things to eat around the house. I want to lose at least 10 pounds.
>
> I kept a day-to-day journal on what I ate and what I did to exercise. In the journal I covered not only what I did and ate, but also my feelings about how my plan was working. I also went to the bathroom scale to weigh in at the end of every week. My reinforcer was going to be how good I'd feel when I lost the 10 pounds.
>
> I had to get my girlfriend involved in this since she lives with me, and she would like to help shape my behavior. We started buying healthier foods when we went grocery shopping: things like substituting ground turkey for ground beef and buying "lite" products and skim milk. We bought the healthy foods along with our usual snacks and other junk like caramel popcorn, chocolate candy, and potato chips. So I just ate both.
>
> My girlfriend also agreed to come along with me when I jog, so I wouldn't cheat by cutting my time jogging short. The first week went well, and I built up to 20 minutes jogging nonstop. What glitched this program was the very next week it poured! It rained every day for almost 2 weeks, so I stopped jogging.
>
> Pretty soon I stopped all of the program. I looked in the mirror and saw no change.

Jack's plan has some good points and several weak ones. The good points are that Jack kept a record of his eating and exercise and that he enlisted the aid of his girlfriend. One of the weak points of his plan—weak because it decreased Jack's chances of success—is that he made no effort to substitute healthy food for junk food. He didn't really try to change his eating behavior. Also, he didn't try to get the tempting foods, the old antecedents, out of the house. Further, he had no effective plan to reinforce his healthy eating or jogging. Waiting until he has lost the weight to see his slim image in the mirror is just too long delayed. Finally, Jack didn't plan for inevitable problems—such as rain on a jogging day—so when the first difficulty came up, his plan went down.

Adjusting and Changing Plans

If Jack is going to succeed in losing weight, he will have to change his plan as he learns more about self-modification. Often people start with what they think is a sound plan, but as they try it, they find that it needs adjusting. Plans must be changed as one finds parts that are not working. Problems almost always come up. Sometimes an entire plan must be redesigned, as our next case illustrates. Kate felt that she was not studying enough.

> Like a lot of students, I only study just before a test or when some deadline is coming up. I decided to reward myself with some favorite activity—going out for pizza, watching TV, playing with my parakeet—if I completed at least 2 full hours of studying each day. I planned to increase this later to 3 or 4 hours per day, since

actually I think I would like to go to graduate school. If I didn't do the studying, I would play with the bird anyway—he needs the attention—but wouldn't go out for pizza or watch a TV program.

My plan quickly ground to a halt. I didn't do any studying; I just didn't go out for pizza or watch the TV program. After about a week of that, I quit keeping records. So I was pretty much back where I started.

Then you announced in class that we would have to make progress reports on our projects, so I got serious again about keeping records. I realized that my thoughts at the time I was supposed to study were probably keeping me from studying. I was thinking things like, "I don't want to do this now. . . . I really don't have to do it now. . . . It's so boring,"—things like that.

I have decided to begin a new plan. I will schedule study times for myself and will figure out some rewards that are actually worth working for. More important, I will watch myself for those kinds of thoughts that lead me to avoid studying. I really do want to study more, as I feel I'm not living up to my potential, and—let's face it—I won't have a chance to get into graduate school with my present grades. So when those thoughts occur, I will try to spot them and change them.

It often happens that once you begin a plan, you realize that you need to change some of the details, or even that you have to reorient the goal of your plan entirely, as Kate did. *Start with a simple plan that seems to meet your needs. Then find out what interferes with success.* That was Kate's approach: She found that her thoughts at the moment she sat down to study were interfering with her studying. Whatever interferes with your success will tell you what the new, changed plan should be. Thus, Kate worked on changing the thoughts that discouraged studying.

But can you really change yourself?

Does Self-Modification Really Work?

When people have a moderately serious problem with their own behavior, are they able to change themselves? Absolutely. An estimated 29 million Americans quit smoking between 1965 and 1975, following the first surgeon general's report indicating that smoking causes cancer (Prochaska, 1983). Ninety-five percent of the people who quit smoking do it without any professional help (Cohen et al., 1989), and about seventy-five percent of people with serious alcohol problems who learn to control their drinking do so without professional help (Sobell, Cunningham, & Sobell, 1996). A surprisingly large number of veterans who returned from the Vietnam War as heroin addicts were able to stop their habit by themselves (Horn, 1972).

Those who successfully changed on their own employed strategies such as those taught in this book. Surveys of research find that these self-regulation techniques are by and large effective (Febbraro & Clum, 1998).

Even for serious problems such as alcoholism a goodly number of people are successful at self-change. The techniques we teach here are so effective that self-modification procedures are commonly suggested by psychotherapists to help their clients make changes (Keeley, Williams, & Shapiro, 2002). It has been shown that encouraging in-training psychotherapists to use self-modification techniques increases their skill in dealing with clients (Bennett-Levy et al., 2001).

Published Cases of Successful Self-Modification

To illustrate the wide range of applicability of the techniques of self-modification, here is a list of successful cases published in professional medical and psychological journals. These show that people often change as a result of a conscious effort to change. We provide a long list of cases to encourage you to see the relevance of self-regulation techniques to your own life, no matter what issue you may focus on.

Self-modification has been used to:

- cope with panic attacks (Gould, Clum, & Shapiro, 1993; Carlbring, Westling, Ljungstrand, Ekselius, & Anderson, 2001);
- help children cope with fear of the dark (Mikulas, Coffman, Dayton, Frayne, & Maier, 1986);
- improve gymnastic performance (Wolko, Hrycaiko, & Martin, 1993);
- increase creative productivity (Herren, 1989);
- improve study habits (Richards, 1976; Watson, 2001);
- handle anxiety in social situations (Rehm & Marston, 1968);
- control nervous habits such as scratching, nail biting, and hair pulling (Watson, Tharp, & Krisberg, 1972; Perkins & Perkins, 1976);
- overcome depression in college students (Tharp, Watson, & Kaya, 1974; Hamilton & Waldman, 1983, see Box 1-3) and in elders (Rokke, Tomhave, & Jocic, 2000);
- eliminate teeth grinding (Pawlicki & Galotti, 1978);
- encourage speaking in class (Barrera & Glasgow, 1976);
- improve one's writing, reading, spelling, vocabulary, and test-taking skills (Watson, 2001);
- increase exercising (Kau & Fischer, 1974; Sherman, Turner, Levine, & Walk, 1975);
- reduce conflicts with co-workers (Maher, 1985);
- improve the productivity of workers with developmental disabilities (Christian & Poling, 1997); and
- improve self-control in couples' therapy (Halford, Sanders, & Behrens, 1994).

There are many cases of deliberate use of self-modification techniques published in nonprofessional publications as well. Jack Nicklaus, the golfer, used several of the techniques we teach in this book, such as mental practice and use of a model. Self-guiding instruction is taught at the Nick Bolliteri tennis academy. Famous writers such as Proust or Trollope have described how they controlled their behavior so they would write more and better (Zimmerman, 1998). Cases of self-modification are even told in the Bible: Parents are taught how to be good models for their children in Deuteronomy, and relaxation techniques are taught in Philippians (Lasure & Mikulas, 1996).

Case histories, of course, can be good illustrations of an idea, but because each case is unique, we can't be sure the results will generalize to whole groups of people. It is best to know what the scientific evidence is for an idea. Evidence us usually gathered by comparing a treated group, such as a class that learns how to use the techniques of self-regulation, with another that does not learn the techniques. Then we can ask, Is there any difference between them in their ability to self-regulate?

There is a long history of self-help books in the United States, going back as far as 1886 when "Dr. Smiles" wrote *Happy Homes and the Hearts that Made Them* (Rosen,

Box 1-3
Successful Self-Modification of Depression
During a Course in Self-Modification

In the journal *Cognitive Therapy and Research,* Scott Hamilton and David Waldman (1983) report the case of Al, who successfully reduced his moderately severe depression. The case nicely illustrates the process of self-modification.

Al was a 20-year-old student taking a course similar to the one you are taking, in which he was asked to carry out a self-modification project. He chose to attack his depression, which had lasted for 4 years. It was associated with severe family stress, the divorce of his parents and continued criticism from his mother. Al often engaged in self-criticism—"I'm stupid and a total failure because my grades are bad"—and often had negative thoughts about his insufficient studying, poor grades, inadequate time scheduling, and lack of career goals. These negative thoughts sometimes lasted as long as 4 hours, leading to intense depression.

Al began by counting the number of negative thoughts per day—ignoring whether they were long or short—and also rated how depressed he felt each day on a scale from 0 for no depression to 6 for extreme depression. He made this count for 18 days. During this time he averaged 3.2 negative thoughts per day, and his average depression rating stayed at about 3 on his scale.

For the next 14 days Al tried to lift his depression by doing something about the topics that depressed him. He attempted to reward himself for getting information about various careers, meeting daily study goals, and following through with his appointments and deadlines. He continued counting his negative thoughts and rating his moods.

During this period his average number of negative thoughts dropped to 2.8, a slight improvement over his earlier average, but his rated mood actually worsened—to an average of 4 on his scale.

Al now started a second attack, a new self-modification plan in which he worked directly on his negative thoughts. As soon as he began a negative thought, he recorded what set it off, how depressed it made him feel, and rationally reevaluated the situation. He also required himself to review written positive statements about himself daily while engaging in pleasant activities and to imagine himself in a stressful situation but coolly working out the best possible solution to it. This period of working on his thoughts lasted 70 days.

Throughout the 70 days Al's number of negative thoughts per day dropped, and in the last 10 days of the period he had only one. His rated mood also improved, and in the last 10 days he felt no instances of depression. When asked to comment, Al's roommate rated him as much less depressed. Six months later Al again recorded negative thoughts for 2 weeks, during which time he averaged less than one per day, and he was not depressed during that period. He had successfully changed himself.

Glasgow, & Moore, 2002). Many self-help books offer no research support for their ideas. To be sure, some self-help books are better than others (cf. Norcross et al., 2003), but many have never been evaluated.

Is there scientific support for our ideas? Our goal is to present ideas that are supported by scientific research. So we ask, When entire college classes in self-modification are examined and compared to a control group, what is the general success rate of the students? We'll answer that question in the next section.

Research in Self-Modification Courses

Psychologists have run experiments to compare what percentage of students improve after studying the concepts in this book to those who were not taught these concepts. Here are their findings.

For 6 years Jerry Deffenbacher and Jeffrey Shepard (1989) taught a course in stress management at Colorado State University. The course was based heavily on the ideas in this book. After the course the students reported that they felt significantly less anxious generally, became angry less often, and showed fewer physical symptoms related to stress.

Thomas Brigham and his associates (1994) taught a course in academic skills designed to help minority students succeed at a large state university. The researchers adapted the ideas in this book to help the minority students self-modify their own class attendance, studying, speaking to professors outside class, note taking, and other academic activities. A second group of minority students—the control group—were not trained in applying self-modification to their academic problems. The results: Students who learned to self-modify their academic skills earned a grade point average of 2.10 while those who did not had a grade point average of 1.27, quite an improvement.

For several years Felipe Castro (1987) at UCLA conducted a course in health promotion, teaching procedures adapted from this book. Students who learned the procedures, compared with those who did not, increased their amount of exercise and decreased their consumption of high-calorie foods. In addition, students who learned the procedures showed other changes in lifestyle, such as eating more salads, vegetables, or fruits. They were self-regulating in a more healthful way.

David Dodd (1986) at Eastern Illinois University taught a course in self-modification for several years and found that on average about 70% of his students were able to reach their own goals for change by the end of the semester. Scott Hamilton (1980) used this text to teach self-change techniques to 72 students. He reported that 83% of the students met their goals for behavior change. In New Zealand, Gail deBortali Tregerthan (1984) taught self-modification to 100 high school students who had *not* volunteered to learn self-modification but were required to do so as part of a psychology class. She found that 66% of those who learned self-modification were able to change their target behaviors, while only 26% of those who selected a behavior to change but did not learn the techniques were able to change.

Richard Rakos and Mark Grodek (1984) at Cleveland State University used this text in a course in self-modification. Comparing this class to another that did not use the text, they concluded:

> Participants in the class demonstrated improvement in their target behaviors and reported significant positive changes in dysfunctional attitudes, fear of negative evaluation, and general self-control skills. The absence of self-reported change . . . in controls suggests that the gains were a function of the specific class. (p. 160)

Box 1-4
Unsuccessful Self-Modification of a Case
of "Writer's Block"

Not everyone who tries self-modification is successful. There are, however, very few published examples of unsuccessful cases. Here is one paper, in its entirety:

The Unsuccessful Self-Treatment of a Case of "Writer's Block"
Dennis Upper
Veterans' Administration Hospital, Brockton, Massachusetts

REFERENCES

_____

_____

Portions of this paper were not presented at the 81st Annual American Psychological Association Convention, Montreal, Canada, August 30, 1973.

SOURCE: From "Unsuccessful Self-Treatment of a Case of 'Writer's Block,'" by Dennis Upper, 1974, *Journal of Applied Behavior Analysis, 7*. Copyright © 1974 Pergamon Press, Ltd. Reprinted with permission.

Other systematic reports have been presented, with similar results (Barrera & Glasgow, 1976; Clement & Beidleman, 1981; Menges & Dobroski, 1977; Payne & Woudenberg, 1978). Typically two-thirds or more of students who use self-modification techniques are able to change successfully. The question "Can students learn self-modification?" has been answered with a resounding "yes."

Of course, self-modification does not always work (see Box 1-4). When does it, and when does it not? Michael Perri and Steve Richards (1977) studied the differences between people who succeeded at self-change and those who did not. They found that successful self-modifiers used more techniques and for a longer period of time. For smokers, for example, using several techniques helps in quitting (Kamarck & Lichtenstein, 1988).

Similar results have been found for college women taught good dental hygiene—brushing twice and flossing once each day—by the use of self-modification techniques. Three months later the women were interviewed. The ones who were still following good dental hygiene reported using *several self-modification techniques* to control their own behavior, but the women who had given up the rigorous schedule of brushing and flossing were not using any techniques (O'Neill, Sandgren, McCaul, & Glasgow, 1987). Similarly, when schoolchildren were taught self-modification techniques to improve things like the amount of time they focused on their work, the more techniques they used, the bigger the effect on their schoolwork (Fantuzzo, Rohrbeck, & Azar, 1987).

People do not fail at self-modification because the techniques don't work; they fail because they don't use the techniques (Gould & Clum, 1993). For example, in one study a manual was developed for people who have a strong fear of open places—agoraphobia (Holden, O'Brien, Barlow, Stetson, & Infantino, 1983). The manual described the techniques that subjects could use to lessen their agoraphobia. The subjects in one group were simply given the manual and invited to change themselves, but the manual was not effective because the subjects did not use the techniques suggested. Similarly, when therapists gave their depressed patients homework assignments involving self-modification, the only patients who improved were those who actually did the homework (Neimeyer & Feixas, 1990).

These results are not surprising: If you want to develop a skill, you have to practice it, and if you don't practice, you should not be surprised if you don't learn the skill.

This is not to say that all problems are equally easy to deal with. Some are relatively easy to change; some are harder (Polivy & Herman, 2002). Some of most successful targets for permanent change involve social skills, anxiety and fear, study habits, depression, and parenting issues. Those that were less often successful were smoking, drinking, and weight control (Gould & Clum, 1993; Seligman, 1994). But all categories of target behaviors require the work and practice of change, and the more diligently you do the work of change, the more likely change becomes. Even with the more difficult behaviors, those who use the methods in this book report "moderate" success while those who don't use the techniques report little success or none at all (Gould & Clum, 1993).

This book is not a magic bullet: *You must do the work; you must use the techniques.* The particular techniques you use will depend on your targets and goals, but the message is clear: To increase your chances of success,

> use the techniques,
> use as many as you can, and
> use them long enough to have an effect.

The Uses of Self-Modification

Increasingly, some form of self-modification is seen by professionals as an important part of most programs for change (Gould & Clum, 1993), whether in the delivery of psychological services or in medical settings (Karoly, 1991; Marks, 1994; cf. Creer, 2000; Endler & Kocovoski, 2000). Much "treatment" occurs outside the doctor's office, whether it is engaging in exercise or taking pills, and control over that is in the patient's hands. For example, mild cases of diabetes can be treated without medication as long as the patient makes changes in eating and exercise.

In previous editions of this book we expressed amazement at the ingenuity of fellow psychologists in teaching patients to use self-regulation techniques to cope with a variety of medical conditions, and we were delighted to print a long list of such uses. But the list of uses of self-regulation in medical settings has grown too large to include. It is now common to find self-regulation techniques as part of medical treatment. Self-regulation in medical settings is used whenever patients need to make life style changes to cope with their illness, whether the change involves more exercise, relaxation, eating different foods, or less panic when in pain (see Bandura, 2004; Maes & Karoly, 2005; Mithaug, Agran, Martin, & Wehmeyer, 2003; Petrie, Broadbent, & Meechan, 2003).

In psychological settings, self-modification is now used as an effective major component of treatment in all these situations:

- increasing employee efficiency and stress reduction (Godat & Brigham, 1999; Kagan, Kagan, & Watson, 1995);
- treating depression in senior citizens (Rokke, Tomhave, & Jocic, 2000);
- increasing the life satisfaction of individuals suffering with schizophrenic-like problems (Mezo & Heiby, 2004);
- increasing the use of condoms to reduce AIDS risk (Horn & Brigham, 1996);
- teaching teenagers to control their discipline problems (Brigham, 1989);
- promoting physical activity (Saelens et al., 2000);
- improving the social skills and reducing the disruptive behavior of autistic children (Koegel, Koegel, Hurley, & Frea, 1992);
- improving behavior of disturbed adolescents (Ninness, Fuerst, Rutherford, & Glenn, 1991);
- encouraging homework (Olympia, Sheridan, Jenson, & Andrews, 1994);
- teaching children to resist pressures to take up smoking (Gilchrist, Schinke, Bobo, & Snow, 1986);
- ceasing smoking (Curry, 1993) and use of smokeless tobacco (Severson et al., 2000) and smoking during pregnancy (Aaronson, Erschoff, & Danaher, 1985);
- encouraging underachieving children to do better in school (Stevenson & Fantuzzo, 1986);
- helping depressed children (Stark, Reynolds, & Kaslow, 1987);
- treating depression in general (Jamison & Scogin, 1995; Smith, Floyd, Scogin, & Jamison, 1997);
- aiding the hard-core unemployed to find work (Kanfer, 1984);
- helping mentally retarded students to perform at a higher level (Sowers, Verdi, Bourbeau, & Sheehan, 1985);
- treating panic disorder (Gould & Clum, 1995; Febbraro, Clum, Roodman, & Wright, 1999);
- treating binge eating disorder (Carter & Fairborn, 1998; Loeb, Wilson, Gilbert, & Labouvie, 2000);
- treating sexual dysfunction (van Lankveld, 1998);
- treating obsessive-compulsive disorder (Fritzler, Hecker, & Losee, 1997);
- treating specific phobias, such as fear of spiders (Öst, Stridh, & Wolf, 1998); and
- increasing self-control in mentally retarded individuals (Agran & Martella, 1991; Agran & Martin, 1987).

Self-Regulated Learning

There has been an explosion of research by educational psychologists studying self-regulation in the learning process, called self-regulated learning (Zimmerman & Schunk, 2001, 2004). In the process of negotiating their way through school, students have to learn to do many things: focus while in class, do their homework, get ready for tests, or carry out and report on special projects. These are all acts that require much self-regulation—resisting a distraction, for example, when you need to be studying, or checking yourself to be sure you've memorized a formula correctly, or scheduling library time to do research on a term paper. What are the processes that students must learn in order to deal with academic tasks?

Box 1-5
"Me and My Girls": An Example of a Complete Plan for Self-Modification

by Tom Ciborowski and "Adele"
University of Hawaii

Every chapter in this book ends with an added step to take in your plan for self-modification. Here is the final, completed report on a self-modification project by Adele, carried out in a class taught by our good friend, the late Dr. Tom Ciborowski, showing her progress as she worked through this book chapter by chapter. Read this carefully to get an idea of what a good, completed project looks like.

For Chapter 1: Adele wrote, "All my life I've had a problem with yelling. It began when I was a little kid trying to speak to my father. He has poor hearing and tends to speak too loudly, and as a result everyone in my family talks too loudly. And we have the tendency to yell when we're frustrated/stressed. In February I was made head coach of the fifth- and sixth-grade girls' basketball team at the school where I volunteer. The first thing that came to my mind was how my high school coach used to yell at us, and how it brought our spirits down. So, this and my experience with my loud family led me to choose as my project controlling my yelling."

For Chapter 2: "My goal is to eliminate yelling at my players. I have to remember that some of my young girls don't even know how to dribble or shoot. If I can keep my frustration and yelling under control, it will be easier for me to increase my players' motivation and confidence. If I yell they won't learn as much and will disrespect me."

For Chapter 3: Adele kept a daily record of her stress level during basketball practice, which she rated from 1 to 10. "I didn't put a zero on the graph because there's never a day when I'm totally stress-free." She noted reasons why she felt stressed. "I had a lot of studying to do, many papers to write, and my midterms were coming up soon." And, "The girls were just cutting up, and no one seemed to be listening to me."

After each team practice she also wrote a diary entry about her interactions with the girls. Here is her entry from February 10. "Today was frustrating for all of us. We worked on shooting. I got mad at them because they weren't trying hard enough and giving up. I told them if they didn't want to learn to go and sit down on the side. Many of them told me, 'I can't do it,' or 'I can't reach the basket.' I yelled and told them if they weren't willing to try, why even stay on the team? I told them I didn't want to coach those who didn't want to learn, and that I didn't want to waste my time. I totally lost my cool, got a migraine, and completely lost my appetite. Stress level was 10."

Adele's diary entry one week later: "Played a game with my girls. We had fun and they learned to block out and play defense. I didn't stress out as much as I did the past week. Maybe I should think of more games to play. I didn't yell

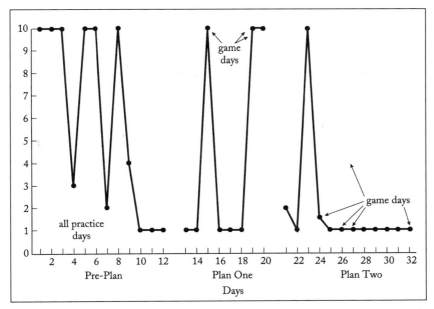

Figure 1-5 Adele's stress level

at them today. We had a team talk to see if there were any problems, and my girls complimented me on being an understanding coach!"

Adele made a diary entry for every practice or game day for 2 months. Whenever something went wrong, she tried to figure out what its antecedents were and what she could do to change her behavior. She also presented a graph of her daily stress level for the 2-month period. See the pre-plan stage in Figure 1-5.

For Chapters 4, 5, 6, and 7: Adele's First Plan for Change. Adele continued observing and recording her own behavior while she read Chapters 4 through 7. She was then in position to design an effective plan. She wrote, "By then I knew what triggered my yelling. It was a combination of different variables. One was being a student. Another was that my mind was always racing around the clock trying to figure out plays/strategies for my players. Also, my players sometimes didn't listen to me when I was trying to explain things. My ill health, migraines, and not eating right added fuel to my fires. But the most stressful variable was feeling stressed, plus having awful referees. All these set off my yelling. Some days at practice were good, but some were awful, and before I thought of my plan I yelled at them until they almost wanted to quit."

Adele has a good grasp of both the long-term and short-term antecedents to her yelling. "I finally thought of a plan to keep myself from yelling. It had five steps:

1. Be aware of my stress and frustration when my girls aren't listening to me;
2. To show my disappointment with them without yelling, ask them calmly to go shoot free throws. Then I will go to the other basket and shoot ten free throws myself before I coach them again;

(continued)

Box 1-5 *(continued)*

3. While shooting my free throws, I will think of the consequences of yelling at them—I'll lose their respect if I yell too much—and of the inexperience my girls are faced with;
4. Before each free throw, do relaxation exercises to relieve my tension;
5. After my free throws, go back to coaching."

Adele's plan allows her to "take a break" before things get out of hand, and to substitute relaxation for yelling. She also reminds herself of the unwanted consequences of yelling.

"This plan worked just fine. My girls were shocked that I didn't yell at them during practice, except when they played around too much. My stress level would start to go up, but when I became aware that it was accumulating, and I was about to yell, I just went off to the side and told the team captain to run the drills while I cooled off.

"I had one big downfall in my plan. I forgot that I couldn't shoot free throws during games. Boy, did I yell a lot during the first games. I yelled at the referees because they called horribly, and I yelled at my girls because they weren't concentrating and working together. I yelled and yelled and couldn't stop myself from yelling. My girls were afraid to talk to me because I was so angry."

Adele's setback is absolutely typical: Something unanticipated comes up, and the plan has to be changed.

For Chapters 8 and 9: Adele's Second Plan for Change. She wrote, "I was finally able to think of another plan to follow while we had games. If I did start yelling, one of my girls would tug on my shirt and tell me I was starting to yell. That reminded me. Of course, it didn't always work because my girls were afraid to tell me, or I was just too angry to calm down. But the times I did follow this plan I calmed down and was a more effective coach. It was funny: Sometimes the girls had to tug on my shirt so hard it pulled me down into my chair. They began making a game out of it and said it was like pulling on a horse's harness. Also, after the games, I played a game with them, and then bought them all ice creams. More and more I got my yelling under control, and I got better at relaxing. On the practice days I continued my plan as I had before, shooting free throws and relaxing."

Adele's records showed that in the period before her first plan she yelled at her players on one-third of the practice days. She yelled on 4 of the 8 days during her first plan—50%—but after beginning the second plan, she yelled only 1 out of 12 days—12.5%. She wrote, "This doesn't mean I didn't start to feel stressed during games. I did. But I was able to bring it under control."

She reduced her stress as well. Look at Figure 1-5. You can see that by the end of her program she significantly reduced her stress level.

Adele concludes, "All of my players, the athletic director, and the players' parents complimented me on my coaching. They never expected my girls to become better players or winners. My girls were second to last during the regular season, but in the post-season tournament we surprised everyone and took third place overall. I was happy about my girls' performance, and they were happy to be winners. And, I was asked to be coach again next year."

Zimmerman and Pons (1986) identified over a dozen skills students need to learn in order to do well in school, and found that, sure enough, the students who were using these skills were doing much better in school than students who were not. Here's our question: How well do you do these skills?

Be honest with yourself. Fill out this little questionnaire to see which skills you are currently performing well, and which could use some work. Think about carrying out a self-modification project in which you try to improve in those areas that could use improvement. Learning these skills will improve your grades in school (Hofer & Yu, 2003).

1. Do you organize well? For example, do you make an outline before writing?
2. Do you set goals and make plans on how to reach them? For example, do you start working on a paper a week or more before it's due?
3. Are you good at seeking out information? For example, do you do library research before writing a paper?
4. Do you try to minimize distractions from studying? When you're studying, do you work on focusing?
5. Do you work on memorizing well when it is needed? For example, do you work on learning vocabulary words in a language class?
6. Do you use peers for assistance? For example, might you talk with a peer about how to do some assignment?
7. Do you use your professors for assistance? Might you talk with your prof about what might be covered on a test?
8. Do you review your tests, that is, go over them to learn what you didn't know when you took the test?
9. Do you study your notes prior to taking a test?
10. Do you review the text before taking a test?

For Further Research

Here are websites full of psychological information that you may want to pursue:

http://www.apa.org (American Psychological Association)
http://www.psychologicalscience.org (American Psychological Society)
http://www.abct.org (Association for Behavioral and Cognitive Therapies)
http://www.psycINFO.com

Chapter Summary

Self-Regulation

Self-regulation means controlling or directing your own behavior according to some principle. We regulate our thoughts, actions, feelings, and impulses. Self-regulation can occur over long or short time periods, and the more one self-regulates the more one is capable of gaining desirable goals.

Self-regulation is learned, a learned skill. We are better at it in some situations than in others.

The Skills of Self-Regulation and the Purpose of This Book

Two important elements of skill are knowledge and practice. You must know what to do, then practice doing it. The purpose of this book is to teach ways to improve your skills in situations where the task is difficult for you.

Behavior and Its Context

One's behavior, thoughts, and feelings are embedded in contexts—the things that go before them (antecedents) and the things that come after (consequences). A shorthand way of expressing this is A-B-C: Antecedents-Behavior-Consequences. The effects of situations (As and Cs) upon our behavior (Bs) are influenced by learning experiences that continue throughout our lives.

The Process of Self-Modification

In the process of self-modification, you produce new learning for yourself in specific situations. You select a target behavior, make observations, work out a plan for change using psychological principles, and readjust your plans as you learn more about yourself.

You accomplish this by inserting new antecedents or avoiding old ones, by inserting new behaviors, or by substituting new ones for old ones, and by insuring you are not rewarded for unwanted acts.

Does Self-Modification Really Work?

Millions of people have successfully changed their behavior to stop unwanted acts such as smoking or overeating, and there are many published case histories of successful self-modification. Self-modification is increasingly used in problems of chronic ill health.

Research has shown that students using this book can learn the principles of self-change and carry out successful projects. You are more likely to be successful if you use a variety of techniques for a long period of time, and if you follow the exercises at the end of each chapter.

Your Own Self-Direction Project: Step 1

There's a difference between knowing ideas well enough to pass a test on them and knowing them well enough to use them in your daily life. To reach this more advanced stage, you must practice self-change.

Make a list of three to five personal goals. These might be expressed as things you want—to study more, to date more, to exercise more, to save money—or things you want to stop—drinking too much, swearing, watching TV, being nervous.

Think over your list for a day or two, perhaps adding some goals to it or changing some. Then select one goal for a learning project. The goal can be a major, long-term one such as overcoming shyness or a minor, short-term one, but it should be important to you. You won't learn much by trying to change something trivial.

Box 1-6
Criteria for a Good Project

What can you do to get a good grade on your self-change project? Success or failure in your self-change project is less important than your sophistication in carrying out the project. What makes a plan sophisticated? Sophistication—or complexity—refers to the number of different techniques you try and to the relationship between the techniques and your self-observation.

If you take on a difficult project, be sure your instructor realizes that the project is a difficult one for you and agrees to grade you on complexity and effort, not just on success.

Here are some tips that we give our students. Your instructor may have additional ones.

1. Make careful observations. If you observe yourself carefully, you will see ways to use more techniques. Learn about the actual A-B-C relationships in your behavior. Figure out the conditions that facilitate or compete with the target behavior. Keep good records throughout the project, even if you change plans.
2. Use a variety of techniques. These techniques for change are grouped under the A-B-C headings in the book. Try to use some techniques from each category.
3. Change your plans as you find out what works and what doesn't work. Tinker with your system. Be creative in your use of the techniques. Deal with problems that come up by changing your plan, as Adele did when she realized her plan for relaxation wouldn't work during a real game.
4. Be persistent. Sheer effort makes a difference. Note that Adele kept extensive records in her diary and tried several things to control her yelling. Keep trying to change, and change your plans as you learn more about yourself and your A-B-C relationships.
5. Be well organized in your final report. Here is a possible outline for the report:
   - The goal you selected (Chapters 1 and 2);
   - Your observations about your behavior (Chapter 3);
   - Your first plan for change. Use several techniques (Chapters 5, 6, and 7);
   - Your results (Chapter 8). Your second plan for change (Chapters 8 and 9);
   - If the first plan is not successful, readjust. Draw on ideas from Chapters 5, 6, and 7, tinker with the system, or draw up a new system altogether (Chapters 8 and 9);
   - Your plans for the future—what you will do to maintain your gains (Chapters 9 and 10).
   - Your final conclusions.

The ideal choice is a project that (1) is interesting enough to be a challenge, but (2) has some chance of success.

A project that will require changing several aspects of your life, such as losing weight and keeping it off or improving your study habits, may take longer than one semester. If you are overweight, for example, you will have to change several different things about your pattern of overeating and underexercising. Select important aspects of the overall goal for your learning project.

Tackle a project on which you feel you have some chance of success (Kanfer & Schefft, 1987). Failure is discouraging, and you might give up efforts at self-change prematurely. As you learn the ideas in this book your skill level will increase, and later you may realize that in fact you do have a chance to make those changes.

Some of the things we will suggest doing will be new to you. For any important, challenging project, you may have to do things you have not done before. An overweight woman in a slimming class said, "If you want something you've never had, you have to do something you've never done."

Chapter 2

Forethought: Planning for Success

Outline and Learning Objectives

Specifying Targets for Change

1. What are three tactics for specifying behaviors-in-situations?
2. Explain how your goal should be to increase what you want to do in certain situations.
3. What tactic should you use when your goal is to eliminate some undesirable behavior?
4. What two tactics should you use if you are not sure what to do? Explain brainstorming.
5. Explain how even if your goal is not a behavior change, you can reach it by changing behaviors.
6. Why should you expect your targets to change as you continue in your self-change project?

Anticipating Obstacles

7. Why should you expect mistakes? Why should you not blame them on your personality?
8. What does it mean to take a skills development attitude?
9. What are eight tactics you can use to deal with temptation?
10. What are self-efficacy beliefs?
11. What steps can you take to increase your self-efficacy beliefs regarding the behaviors you want to change?
12. Explain the advantages of optimism. What can you do to decrease pessimism?

Choosing Goals

13. Explain how a person might be ambivalent about changing. How can listing the advantages and disadvantages of changing be helpful? How do you make such a list?
14. Explain how many problems in self-change are due to conflicts between long- and short-term goals. What can you do about this kind of conflict?
15. Explain the five stages of change that many people pass through.

16. Explain the use of subgoals in working toward a long-term goal.
17. How can you tie your target goals to larger life goals?
18. What is a self-contract?

Tips for Typical Topics

Chapter Summary

Your Own Self-Direction Project: Step 2

You are preparing to depart on a voyage, the journey of behavior change (Marlatt & Gordon, 1985). This is your guidebook; it suggests the best routes, warns of the difficult passages, suggests how to pack. You must prepare yourself for the journey. Forethought now will make your passage easier.

Every challenging journey has pitfalls and obstacles to progress. A careful traveler takes these into account before the trip begins and leaves prepared to deal with difficulties as well as pleasures. Unexplored areas of ancient maps were sometimes inscribed, "Here be dragons," and even the intrepid traveler knew either to avoid those spots or enter with sword drawn. This chapter illuminates the map, reducing the dragons and helping you prepare for travel farther than you have ever gone before.

Will you persist long enough to reach your destination? Throughout this chapter we will explain activities to make it easier to hang in when the going gets tough, and we will pull these together at the end into a full plan.

As you consult the map of the future, the first crucial question arises: Where exactly are you going? To begin, you must clarify your destination. Considering your goal is the first task of this chapter.

Specifying Targets for Change

On a walking tour of England a few years ago one of us luckily found what is known in Yorkshire as a "darts pub," a tavern where darts—the game—is so important that when serious players are playing no one talks; everyone watches. Each pub has a champion and a team, and there are contests to see who is the best darts player and the best darts pub in Yorkshire. We talked to a young man there, and although we could barely understand his heavy Yorkshire accent, we learned what he was saying. "I wanted to play championship darts. So I focused on practicing. For months every day I came in for three hours, had a pint, and practiced darts. I never thought about whether I was winning or losing any of those games. I just focused on executing perfect form. After each throw I didn't ask myself, 'Where did the dart land?' but instead, 'Did I throw it correctly? Did I hold my fingers, hand and arm correctly? Did I focus?' Sometimes I won; sometimes I lost. That didn't matter. What mattered was the practice. Then one day I realized I'd just beaten the club champion."

The Yorkshire man's target for practice and improvement was the way he threw the darts, not where they landed. *He didn't think about his goal, to be a champion player; he thought about what he was doing to reach the goal.* Think about the list of goals for change you made at the end of Chapter 1. What is your target for practice? What should you do to reach your goal? If your goal is "more friends," for example, what exactly should you practice?

Specifying Behaviors-in-Situations

Here are several tactics that will help you specify your targets for practice.

Tactic 1: Make a list of concrete examples. Suppose you're dissatisfied with yourself. You think, "I'm too self-centered." This self-statement doesn't tell you what to change, because it is too vague, too general. Give a concrete example of the problem: "I talk about myself too much when I'm with my friends." This specifies both the behavior and the situation in which the behavior occurs.

"I eat too much" is also too vague. Do you eat too many carrots? Do you eat too much at every meal? A better statement might be, "I eat reasonably enough at breakfast and lunch, but tend to overeat at supper," or "Whenever I go on a picnic or eat buffet style, I eat too much."

Sometimes thinking of examples of the problem in question will make you more aware of the kinds of situations in which the behavior occurs. Sally started with the statement, "I'm not assertive enough." But when she gave specific examples, she turned a vague idea into a clear statement about her behavior and the specific kinds of situations in which her problem occurred. "It's not that I am always unassertive. I can deal with people who try to push ahead in line or with friends who ask too much of me. But when men my age ask me to do things related to dating, going out, or being together, then I am not as assertive as I want to be." Now she has labeled the kind of situation in which her problem occurs and can begin to change the way she reacts in those situations.

Tactic 2: List the details of your problem. To solve problems, you must attend to the details (D'Zurilla & Nezu, 1989). Make a list of these details; then select those that seem critical to the solution of the problem. Often our thinking about a problem is unfocused, and listing the details helps us to see precisely what our target goal should be.

A woman originally entered psychotherapy seeking treatment for severe anxiety while taking tests. She had two university degrees, but lately was becoming so nervous during tests that her performance was in jeopardy. The first detail she listed concerning her problem was that she did not have enough time to study. Listing other details revealed that because of her newborn baby, she sometimes had difficulty getting to class and sometimes couldn't even get to exams on time. Instead of treating her test anxiety directly, her therapist suggested she focus on coping with the problems that were interfering with her schoolwork. After learning ways to cope with the details of her problem, she found that her test anxiety was reduced (Mayo & Norton, 1980).

Tactic 3: Observe your behavior; don't speculate about it. Your thoughts about your "problem" will probably remain unfocused until you begin to actually observe your behavior and think about the patterns you see. Sally, who wanted to be more assertive, began observing herself. When a man asked her out on a date and she said yes even though she was too busy, she later asked herself, "Was that an example of my being unassertive?" She decided it was. Later a man who lived in her rooming house barged into her room, but she said nothing to him. Again, she asked herself, "Was that an example of being unassertive?" Eventually she saw that her problem was not that she was generally unassertive, but specifically that she was often not assertive with men her own age.

When You're Not Doing What You Want to Be Doing

Sometimes your goal is to start doing something that at present you're *not* doing. For example, you may think you are flunking college because you're not studying. What can you do? Specify the situation in which you want the behavior to occur:

My goal is _____ when _____.
　　　　　(what you want to do)　　　　　　　(the situation)

Paul wanted to increase his studying. He kept a journal to record situations in which he might study. It had entries like this:

Wednesday. Roommate went out. Room quiet. Got out my history text and turned to the assignment. Remembered a baseball game was on TV and started watching it. Tried to study between innings but gave up. Studied about 5 minutes the whole afternoon.

Thursday. Went to the library to study. Saw Karen. Didn't study.

These notes specify two situations in which studying would have been desirable. The journal also tells Paul what he did instead of studying. He was not simply "not studying." *He was actively performing other behaviors that made studying impossible.* As far as studying was concerned, he was performing the wrong behaviors.

Tactic 4: Specify not only the situation and the fact that the desirable behavior is not occurring, but also the behaviors that occur instead of the ones you want. If Paul filled in the formula above, it would look like this:

My goal is *studying instead of watching TV*
　　　　　(what he wants to do)

when *in the room and it's quiet.*
　　　(the situation)

Or:

My goal is *studying instead talking to someone*
　　　　　(what he wants to do)

when *at the library.*
　　　(the situation)

Getting Rid of Undesirable Behavior

Paul might express his goal in one of two ways:

1. I want to quit goofing off and study more; or
2. I want to increase studying in those situations in which I should study.

The second way is preferable, because it expresses the goal in terms of some behaviors that need to be increased. It tells you where to begin.

Tactic 5: *Your strategy should always be to increase some desirable behavior.* Even if the problem is that you are doing something you want to stop, specify your problem in terms of an alternative behavior. You can't just get rid of a behavior: Something always pops up in its place. There's no such thing as a behavioral vacuum. Therefore, you have to develop an alternative behavior to replace one you want to get rid of.

Suppose you procrastinate too much. You might say, "I have to stop procrastinating." But what do you actually have to do? You need to increase certain behaviors: planning work ahead of time; working out goals, subgoals, and plans for meeting them; taking small steps to get yourself started; keeping records of your progress; assigning priorities to your work and then doing it in priority order; planning to cope with diversions; dealing with the negative elements of the work to be done; and so on (Watson, 2001). Those are the behaviors you want to increase. As you do, you will automatically decrease procrastination.

Laura complained about depression. Many situations seemed to produce depression. A friend's mild criticism, her cat's disappearance, spilling coffee on her new dress—minor occurrences set off hours of deep sadness. When asked to specify a desirable alternative, she replied that feeling good was an alternative. We suggested that she search for events that made her feel good and keep in mind the goal of attempting to increase them. She found, for example, that exercising each day made her feel good, so she set out to increase her exercising, and in the process, decreased her depression.

Denise began by saying that she wanted to be more assertive. But what exactly did that mean? What would she do when she was more assertive? She kept records of instances in which she had not been assertive, and later thought of what she could have done in each situation that would have been properly assertive. This gave her ideas for the kinds of behavior she wanted to increase. Here is a portion of her records:

Situation: 10:00 P.M. Buddy called me for a date.

What I did: I started to lie. "I have to work. I'm so busy. . . ." He wanted me to come over to his apartment. I didn't know what to say. Finally I told him I would see him. (Damn!)

What I should have done: I wish I had said, "No, Buddy, I don't feel comfortable around you. We just don't get along. So no, thanks."

Situation: 3:00 P.M. A guy sat next to me on the bus and put his bag right in my lap. I was in a state of shock.

What I did: I didn't know what to say. I pretended not to notice, looked out the window, but I was thinking, "You s.o.b." He started a conversation, and I irritably gave one-word answers.

What I should have done: I should have said, "Excuse me, can you get your bag off my lap?"

When You Aren't Sure What to Do

Suppose you're not reaching some goal and aren't sure why.

Tactic 6: Specify the chain of events that will lead to the goal. What do you have to do, what has to be overcome, what has to happen, in order for you to reach the goal?

Joanne, for example, wanted to be a poet but complained that she never seemed to get around to writing poetry. We pointed out that writers usually set aside some time during which they sit at a desk to write, whether they feel inspired or not, and suggested that she choose a specific hour, every other day, to do nothing but write poetry. She agreed, but just as she was leaving, she turned back to say, "Actually I tried something like that last week, but I couldn't keep the schedule." She went on to explain that she had worried about how her poem would sound to other people before she had even written it. This fear prevented her from writing.

The things that happen to you are the result of a series of events. There is a chain of behaviors (your own and other people's) that, once set in motion, leads inexorably to a conclusion. The case of Joanne and her poetry illustrates such a chain. She needed to set a schedule for writing, sit down at the assigned times, focus on the poem, and not think how others would react to it. *Your task in designing a plan for self-modification often involves specifying not only the simple, targeted behavior, but the chain of behaviors that will produce it.*

Suppose that your goal is to avoid eating ice cream before you go to bed at night. What chain of events might enable you to reach this goal? One is simple: Don't buy the ice cream. Then it won't be there at bedtime, calling out your name. This tactic is often used by successful weight watchers. Some overeaters break their unwanted chains by shopping only from a list, avoiding the items that would later place them in a tempting situation.

Tactic 7: Observe people who are successful at what you are trying to do, and then try their tactics yourself. Sometimes you just don't know what the chain of events is that would lead to your goal. Ken wanted to "be a nicer person socially, have more friends." What should he do to reach that goal? What chain of events should he try to set in motion? He decided to observe a friend of his, Mary, who was a really nice person. "You know what she does?" he asked us. "She listens to other people when they talk. She is the world's champion listener. When you're talking to her, she concentrates on you fully. She doesn't look around the room or interrupt or talk to other people or anything. She listens. That makes her seem terribly interested, and very nice." Now he knows one event—listening—that will lead to his goal of being better liked, and he can build that into his social behavior.

We can't emphasize enough the value of observing others who do well what you want to learn. Tennis players know this, for example, and carefully watch what champions do. One of our friends said, "After watching the U.S. Open on TV, I realized that a lot of the time the players weren't blowing the opponents away with power or speed. Instead, they were making a lot of sharp, cross-court shots. Even if the opponent got it, he was out of position for the next shot, so it was a really good thing to do. I started doing it in my game and my scores went up right away."

It is better to observe other people performing than to ask for advice. The advice may not tell you specifically what to do. A very slim friend saying to you, "Just quit eating so much," is useless. Instead, observing that slim friend might help very much indeed. One of our overweight students reported watching his slim wife when she ate. "I was amazed. She never takes seconds. Not even at Thanksgiving. Not even when the food is fantastic. Never."

If the crucial behavior does not occur where you can observe, and you have to ask an "expert" about his or her success, try to phrase your questions in terms of specifics: "Jan, you always get As on your term papers. How do you go about researching and writing them?" Press Jan until she can respond specifically: "I schedule two library sessions, consult with the reference librarian about what materials are available, then write a draft and ask the professor to look it over and make comments." That is useful to know, because it describes the chain of events that leads to a good term paper.

Tactic 8: *Think of alternative solutions to the problem and then select one or more to implement.* (D'Zurilla & Nezu, 1989). It's helpful here to use a technique called brainstorming. This technique has four simple rules:

1. Try for quantity; quality will follow.
2. Don't be critical, greeting every idea with a "Yes, but . . ." Criticism can come later; for now, just produce ideas.
3. Be freewheeling. Some ideas may be unrealistic or even weird, but that's OK.
4. Try to improve ideas by combining them. The case described in Box 2-1 illustrates this approach.

When You Think Your Goal Isn't Behavior Change

Tactic 9: *Even if your goal is not a specific behavior, reaching the goal will require changing—subtracting or adding—certain behaviors.* This is equally true if your goal is to write many poems or to have a lovely garden. You need to eliminate old behaviors that contribute to the problem *and* develop new ones that help you reach the goal.

The goal of slimness is not a behavior, but to reach it certain behaviors must be changed. Here's a sample of behaviors engaged in by many overweight people: They keep a ready supply of fattening foods in the house; they eat to avoid waste; they pile too much food on their plates; they eat rapidly and while reading or watching TV; they eat when they are emotionally upset (instead of making some other, nonfattening response); and they eat many times each day (LeBow, 1981; Stuart & Davis, 1972). They rarely weigh themselves and don't exercise enough. They often skip breakfast. They starve themselves and then overeat (Mayer, 1968). In the long run, to lose weight these behaviors will have to be changed. So even if the goal is not behavioral, such as "losing weight," we have to change behaviors to reach that goal.

Begin observing yourself. You will begin to see relationships between what you do (or don't do) and the goal you want to reach. You'll notice patterns. For example, you may observe that each time you get down in the dumps, you respond by overeating. Or you might see things you do in social situations that put others off—such as not listening or interrupting—and discover things that you can do that will make you more attractive. Look for aspects of your behavior that prevent you from reaching your goal and find new behaviors that will help you to reach it.

Find the answers to two questions:

"What acts do I perform, what thoughts do I have, that keep me from reaching my goal?"

"What behaviors do I need to develop in order to reach my goal?"

Box 2-1
The Case of the Worn-Out Student

Ruth is 26, married, working, and going to college. She first majored in elementary education, then added a second major, general science, to increase her chances of getting a good teaching job. Her first attempt to state the problem was vague: "I'm losing my motivation for school. I've become too emotional. I argue with my husband too much. I can't really get into my science projects, even though I love the field." We asked Ruth to list all the details of her problem and search for a specific goal. She wrote:

> I feel that the arguments with my husband are due to my being upset about my schoolwork.
> My generally bad moods are also reactions to school. I haven't been going to classes regularly.
> I feel under a lot of pressure from the buildup of assignments. My study habits are deteriorating.
> Classes just don't seem as important to me as they used to. I am spending more time playing tennis.
> The pressure is strongest in the two graduate courses in education.
> I am having trouble with these two courses. I'm actually getting frightened. The most difficult is History of Education.

Ruth then brainstormed several possible solutions to her problem:

> I could drop out of school.
> I could change my major, go back to elementary education.
> I could drop the education courses and forget about graduate school.
> I could find someone to help me with my studies.
> I could sell my car, so I couldn't get to the tennis courts.
> I could go to a hypnotist.

After thinking about various solutions, Ruth decided to drop the difficult History of Education course, a plan she had not even considered in the beginning. She reasoned that the time she gained would enable her to catch up and do well in her other courses. At the beginning she had difficulty specifying her problem, but by listing details and brainstorming several solutions, she was able to formulate a reasonable plan.

Refocusing Targets as You Learn More

As you learn more about how your own thoughts or actions interfere with the goal you want to reach, you may go through a series of self-discoveries. A night-school student of ours named Michael was often depressed. He began a self-change project with only a vague idea of how to get rid of his depression. His first step was to record the situations that made him feel depressed. From his record, he learned that daily frustrations were a major cause of his depression. Michael then observed his reactions and realized that once he was frustrated, any additional disappointment made him depressed. He continued observing himself, now asking, "Why do frustrations make me feel so bad?" The answer was that he brooded over the frustrations. For example, if his child misbehaved, he'd spend hours thinking that he was a terrible father and that he was responsible for raising a spoiled child. He decided that brooding was self-defeating and unnecessary.

After several weeks of self-observation, recording, and analyzing his records, Michael made a breakthrough. "All along I've suspected that not all frustrations have the same effect on me. My kid isn't really at the root of the problem. It's my own self-esteem. Frustrations that call my self-esteem into question are the ones that I magnify." Michael analyzed what "frustrated self-esteem" meant in terms of behavior and realized that he often compared himself with people at the top. In his sales job, he knew what the top people were achieving, and he felt bad because he couldn't do as well. He concluded that his standards were too high and that always comparing himself to the leaders made him unhappy. "I seem to think that if I'm not the very best, I'm no good at all." So he set out to change his reference group. He would learn to compare himself to people who were at his own level.

Those who are successful at self-change go through a series of successive approximations, often changing the target of their self-change efforts several times. As you learn more about yourself and about the actions that support or hamper your progress, you add new target behaviors. The more you practice the skills you are trying to develop, the better you will understand what your goal actually requires.

Throughout the process of self-change, ask yourself two questions:

"What is the target I should be working on?"
· *"What techniques should I use to reach that target?"*

The answer to these questions comes from your self-observations, and from searching for patterns in your actions.

People seeking permanent weight control, for example, might start off with the goals of reading the nutritional labels on foods, exercising a little, and trying to eat less. As they learn more about their personal eating habits, they set new targets for themselves— for example, eating breakfast, eating more slowly, eating low-fat foods, or not saying, "I'm starving!" to themselves when they are merely a little hungry. Later, the target of not eating when depressed might be added, or substituting fruit for candy snacks, or exercising more vigorously.

If developing more friends is your goal, start observing yourself in situations where you could work on friendliness, and try to specify what behaviors you want to develop. How do you act when you are with other people? What behaviors might you develop? If stress control is your goal, you might observe your stress-related thoughts and behavior. What are you doing or thinking before and during stressful times? What changes can you imagine?

Anticipating Obstacles

You've picked your target, but are not yet totally prepared to begin the voyage of self-change. Smart travelers know that there may be stormy passages ahead, and they set out with a plan to negotiate them. This is the section where you mark "Here be dragons" on your map.

Expect Mistakes: Take a Skills Development Attitude

You should expect to make mistakes. Mistakes are common. One mistake is not a disaster and will not doom your journey to failure. You are learning a new skill, and skill development requires practice to smooth out the mistakes we make. The journey toward perfection is always a path of successes and mistakes.

When old, unwanted behaviors have been automatic for a long time, everyone slips back into them at unguarded moments. After all, you are trying to change habits that you may have followed all of your life. They are strong habits and will not disappear easily. You will fall into mistakes, perhaps many times. Particularly in times of stress, habitual behaviors that helped you get through the difficulty will return.

So the question is not "Will I make mistakes?" because you will. The important question is "How should I respond to my errors?" Mistakes are only a disaster if they cause you to stop trying to change.

Take a *skills development attitude* toward your progress and your mistakes (Pintrich, 2000). This means that each time you try to perform the behaviors you want to perform—push away from the table, not swear when stressed, smile in a friendly fashion at someone, get out to exercise—you ask yourself, "What does my success or mistake show me I have learned so far?"

People often use the verb, "to have," when speaking of willpower and self-control. "I couldn't do that. I don't have enough willpower." Or "She can do it. She has lots of willpower." This defines willpower and self-control as entities that you either have or don't have. It's a dichotomy: You either have it or you don't. The trouble is, modern research does not support this false dichotomy. If you believe it, however, and believe that you "don't have enough willpower," you won't try to change yourself. It would be pointless to try.

Answer these questions (adapted from Dweck, 1999). Do you believe that:

1. willpower is something you can't change very much?
2. you can learn new things but can't change your basic level of self-control?
3. you have a certain amount of willpower and can't really do much about it?

If you believe these (false) ideas, you are dooming yourself before you start. You're thinking of willpower as an entity, but that's not the way it works. We learn willpower, and we have more of it in some situations than in others. It is a skill, not a mental entity. We could say we "have" it, but that's like saying someone "has" tennis because she has learned to play well.

The advantage to thinking about willpower as a skill is that it implies that with practice we can improve it. We can develop the skill.

Think about your target for change. Suppose you could have one or the other pieces of information below about it. Which do you choose? (Adapted from Grant & Dweck, 1999.)

1. Information about where you stand compared to others in your ability to control the behavior.
2. Information about strategies for improving your control over this behavior.

If you said number 2, you are taking a learning skills approach to the problem. That is the attitude that is going to help you.

Skills are developed through practice. When you make mistakes, give in to temptation, or backslide, think of this as caused by a need for more practice. The bad habits you are trying to get rid of were learned long ago and are very easy to do. The new, good habits you want to learn must be developed through deliberate practice, and like any new action, you will sometimes make mistakes when trying to perform. *Mistakes are simply feedback about the need for more practice.*

Do not blame the mistakes on your personality. Don't say things like, "I just don't have enough willpower." When dieters fail to stick to their diet and tell themselves it's because they don't have enough self-control, they are more likely to stop the diet (Jeffery, French, & Schmid, 1990). If you blame problems on lack of enough practice, on the other hand, the implication is that there is something you can do—develop your skill more through practice.

Prepare for Temptations

Temptations to stop your self-change project are almost certainly going to occur. There will be times when studying seems like a dumb idea, or when exercising seems ridiculous, or when a cigarette is calling out to you. Temptations occur because there are aspects to our bad habit that we like. Goofing off can be more fun than studying, overeating can be relaxing, yelling at a friend can feel cathartic, even if these habits are undesirable in the long run. As Edwin Chapin said, "The trouble with resisting temptation is you may not get another chance."

Temptations almost certainly will occur. *If you have a plan for dealing with temptation, you are more likely to be successful in your self-modification project* (Shiffman, 1982; Sobell & Sobell, 1995a). It's best to make these plans long before the temptation occurs, so you will be prepared when the tempting time comes.

Here are some ideas to follow to cope with temptation.

1. *Avoid situations you know will be tempting.* Don't go to the places where you might be tempted. Later, when your newly developed behavior has become more or less automatic—"I'll have a ginger ale, please"—you can go back to parties where beer drinking is heavy. Some people think that the only way to show "real" self-control is by meeting temptation head on and staring it down, as Gandhi did when he slept beside female members of his entourage. But it is wise to pick your own time and place to do battle with your dragons. Begin by choosing situations where you will win.

2. *Ask your friends not to tempt you.* If you're trying to lose weight, and Grandma says, "I baked this especially for you," you will feel the pressure to eat. Other people can put pressure on you to keep you enmeshed in your old habits, or they can undermine your new behaviors, and this will make it much harder to change (Goodall & Halford, 1991).

Try asking for your friends' support. Explain that you're trying to change your habit and would appreciate help in not being tempted. People like Grandma sometimes tempt out of their feeling of hospitality and social obligation. Once you've asked them not to tempt you, you can just smile sweetly and say, "No, thanks." Temporarily avoid the friends who can't seem to resist tempting you.

3. *Make a public commitment that you are going to change* (Meichenbaum & Turk, 1987; Shelton & Levy, 1981). Ron, in Box 2-2, told all his friends that he was going to quit smoking. If you tell people you intend to change, the threat of a public failure may keep you working on your project. Once teaching this course one of us told the entire class he intended to train for a marathon that semester, and the fear of the class's derision helped him keep jogging all term.

Box 2-2
Borrowing Self-Confidence and Dealing with Temptation:
A Well-Planned Attack on Smoking

Suellen Rubin
Cabrillo College

Ron was a 30-year-old student in an introductory psychology class in a California college who decided to do a self-modification project for extra credit. He wanted to give up smoking by using the techniques of self-modification, and he drew up a very careful plan. He had successfully given up drinking too much earlier, and that had built up his confidence that he could now give up smoking.

First, he spent a week keeping a diary of every cigarette he smoked, noting when, where, and how he felt, plus any consequence of smoking. He was smoking one and a half to two packs each day.

Ron decided to cut down by one cigarette per day, so that he would be completely off smoking in 35 days. He hoped that by cutting down only one per day he would minimize the withdrawal symptoms. He decided to set aside the money he saved (which was considerable!) toward buying a motorcycle he had wanted for a long time. He figured that the money he saved by not smoking would pay for the cycle on the installment plan.

Ron knew that if he carried lots of cigarettes he might smoke them, so he coped with that temptation in advance by carrying only the number of cigarettes he was allowed each day. He stopped carrying his pack in his breast pocket and instead carried only a few cigarettes at a time in a plastic baggy. He stored the rest of the daily allotment with his friends or in his car.

Ron committed himself publicly to his plan by talking about it with his instructor and his friends. He discussed it at length in his weekly AA meeting. He talked with his instructor and believed that he would only receive credit for his project if he succeeded. (His instructor wasn't sure about this, but thought not to disabuse Ron at this point.)

Ron also substituted some new behaviors. He found himself hitting his breast pocket with his right hand whenever he would normally go for a cigarette. The empty pocket served as a reminder that he was now "clean" in yet another area of his life, and that made him feel good about not smoking.

Ron was able to buy his motorcycle, and after a year and half he has not gone back to smoking.

Note that Ron felt he could stop smoking—he had high *self-efficacy*—because he had been able to stop drinking. He knew it required a thoughtful plan, however. He set realistic goals and had many subgoals (cutting down each day), so he could see frequent progress. He kept records so he knew he was progressing. He knew there would be many temptations, however, and he planned in advance to cope with them. For example, he didn't carry more cigarettes than he was allowed each day, and he used his friends to help him stay straight. He substituted hitting his breast pocket for pulling out a cigarette, and that reminded him that he was moving toward his final goal. He also arranged to be rewarded for quitting, both by his friends' encouragement and by the instructor's grade in the class.

4. *Minimize the tempting quality of the situation*. For those who want to reduce alcohol consumption or overeating, it is useful to drink water before going out so as not to arrive thirsty or hungry. This reduces the tempting quality of the food and drinks that are offered. A woman who drank a glass of skim milk whenever she started feeling hungry minimized the temptation to overeat. A man who found many women attractive but wanted to remain faithful to his new wife told us, "Whenever I meet someone who is very attractive, I immediately find something about her I don't like, and think about that a little bit, so I won't be tempted to flirt or think she might be as desirable."

5. *When you are in the tempting situation, distract yourself*. Research on various ways of coping with temptation shows this is one of the most effective (Gollwitzer, Fujita, & Oettingen, 2004). Faced with a luscious but fattening sundae, think about the person sitting across from you at the dinner table, the chair you're sitting on, the topic of conversation—anything but the sundae. Get up, go for a short walk, or go to the restroom. A man who lost a lot of weight told us, "I realized that I would eat my meal and then sit looking at the rest of the food on the table. Just staring at it. And, sooner or later, I'd start eating it. So I consciously tell myself, 'Don't look at it. Look away.' If I still look at it, I get up and move around the room to distract myself."

6. *When you are tempted, remind yourself of your goal* (Graziano, 1975; Lazarus, 1971). Making statements about your long-term goals can help you resist temptations. Grace took up jogging to lose weight and be healthier. But she realized that she jogged along thinking, "This is so boring—I'm going to quit." These thoughts were self-defeating, so instead she reminded herself, "I really want to look better and be healthier, and the best way is to jog. It's worth it. I won't quit."

Prepare a written list of self-reminders you can use when temptation strikes. Include in your self-reminders all the advantages of reaching your goal: "I'll feel so great when I have caught up with my homework—free as a bird!" "I'm going to look terrific when I've lost 10 pounds—slim and sexy!" "I'm going to enjoy having new friends, so it's worth overcoming my shyness and going to the party."

Remind yourself also of the delayed punishments for unwanted behaviors. "Yeah, I want to smoke a cigarette right now, but in the long term it could kill me." "Telling him off would feel good right now, but in the long run he'd stop being my friend, and I don't want to lose any friends." "Not studying might feel neat right now, but in the long run I'd really pay for it."

Sometimes you will be tempted to think, "Well, just this one time . . ." But life can become a string of just-this-one-times, and before you know it years have gone by without your being a step closer to your goal. Prepare a special reminder for the just-this-one-time situation: "I'm always telling myself, 'Just this one time.' But I really do want to (reach that goal)."

7. *Ask other people to remind you*. You can increase your chances of success if you prearrange with another person to remind you when you are faced with temptation (Passman, 1977). Darrell has been trying to cut down on his drinking. Tonight he and his wife, Tina, are going to a party. Darrell says to Tina, "Do me a favor. I'm going to be tempted to drink too much tonight, and you know I want to stop that. So if you see me taking a second drink, would you please remind me that I really want to cut down?" Groups such as Weight Watchers and Alcoholics Anonymous use this technique (Stuart, 1977).

Box 2-3
Eight Tactics to Cope with Temptation

1. Avoid tempting situations.
2. Ask your friends not to tempt you.
3. Make a public commitment to change.
4. Minimize the tempting qualities.
5. When tempted, distract yourself.
6. When tempted, remind yourself of your goal.
7. Ask other people to remind you of your goal.
8. Prepare "if . . . then" plans.

You are *not* asking the other person to punish you. Darrell doesn't want Tina to tell him he's a lush and a bum because he has taken a second drink. He wants her to remind him of his own resolve not to drink too much. If the others misinterpret the task and begin to inflict punishment on you, remind them that you're asking for a reminder of your own goal, not punishment.

At the same time, you need to be aware of the tendency to punish the person who does the reminding: "I know it's my third drink! I'm not stupid!" Sometimes people work out a code in order to avoid an embarrassing interaction. One of our students reported that she and her husband had agreed that he tended to put her down in conversations with others, and he agreed to stop. He still occasionally did it out of bad habit, though, and both agreed she should remind him when she felt he was doing it. But they soon discovered she couldn't say, "You're putting me down," in front of others, as everyone involved found that embarrassing. Now when she feels he's putting her down, she touches the corner of her mouth. He gets the message, but others do not.

8. *Prepare "if . . . then" plans.* Normally we set a goal and then cope with obstacles to the goal as they arise. That usually works, but it is a mistake if the obstacle to our reaching the goal is our own faltering motivation. Temptation means there's a part of us that wants to slip, that wants to give in, and that's hard to cope with as you are experiencing it.

In the heat of the moment when you are sorely tempted it helps to have a fallback plan that you immediately put into use. This is your "if . . . then" plan (Gollwitzer, Fujita, & Oettingen, 2004). If a certain situation occurs, *then* this is what you are going to do. You don't just form an intention to reach the goal, you form an "if . . . then" intention. "If situation A occurs, then I will do anti-A."

"When I get to the party, if I look around and don't see anyone I know, then I will go over to the drinks, get one, and start talking to whoever is there about the party." "If I'm tempted to smoke, then I will immediately get up and go for a walk." "If I want to overeat, then I will take out my list of the advantages of weight loss and read it. If I still want to overeat, I will call Beth." Such plans make it easier to deal with temptations.

To work well, "if . . . then" plans need to be very specific. You don't plan, "If I'm tempted, I'll cope." You plan, "If I'm tempted, I will do the following two specific actions. . . ."

The advantage of an "if . . . then" plan is that you don't have to rely on making a good decision while you are under stress. You have already made the decision about what you are going to do, and now you just carry it out automatically. An "if . . . then" plan shows your intention to resist temptation. "If . . . then" plans lead to trying longer to reach your goals, and increases the chances that you will succeed (Gollwitzer et al., 2004).

Your task, therefore, is to think of temptations in advance and make "if . . . then" plans to deal with them. This means, in turn, that you will be looking for cues that some temptation is going to come up. A student who has been fleeing social encounters for fear of rejection thinks, "Okay, I'm going into this party. It's possible I won't know anyone there. In the past I would have left immediately. But now I'll put my "if . . . then" plan into operation. If I don't know anyone, I will go over to the drinks and start talking to someone there about the party."

If you do give in to temptation—and many of us do on the way to greater self-regulation—then try not to let it happen a second (or third or fourth) time. Dick reported:

> I think I spent about a year trying to control my overeating, but each time giving in to temptation when I was confronted by a buffet. Then I realized, I'm trying to cope with this like Gandhi and his maidens. Teeth gritted, facing down that tempting buffet. Staring at the pasta and desserts but not eating them. Thing is, I'm not Gandhi. Finally I realized if I'm ever going to cope with those tempting buffets, I need an "if . . . then" plan. "If I encounter a buffet, then here is what I will do to avoid overeating." So, after a clueless year, I made the plan, and it worked.

Self-Efficacy Beliefs

Think about your goal for change: Do you believe you can get there? If you think, "Maybe I can get there," we need to minimize that "maybe." You may need to work directly on your own beliefs about success and failure, for the more confident you are, the better your chances.

For several years, the Russian heavyweight weight lifter, Leonid Taranenko, a huge, immensely strong man, held the world record for free-lifting 499½ pounds. He had tried on several occasions to lift 500 pounds above his head but had failed. In his third Olympics he was once again at the top of the class in lifting, and many hoped he would break his own record. His trainer knew that Taranenko did not believe he could lift 500 pounds. At the end of the trials, when all the other strong men had been eliminated, Taranenko was allowed one more lift. "No point in failing now," he told his trainer, "I've already won. Put on 499½ pounds. I can tie my record."

"Sure," said the trainer. But he put on 500½ pounds. Taranenko looked fierce, turned red, strained—and lifted the weight above his head. It was a new world record, one not soon to be broken, and it was achieved primarily because Taranenko thought he was lifting 499½ pounds—a weight he believed he could lift.

A self-efficacy belief is your own estimation of your skill in handling some task (Bandura, 1997). It's not a general belief about yourself, but a specific belief that is tied to a particular task. It's not abstract (such as the question, "Can I stick to my diet?") but very specific, such as, "Can I resist eating while watching TV?" It is not a yes-no belief, but a yes-maybe-no continuum.

What we believe about our ability to change affects how hard we try to change, and that in turn affects our success. To achieve, you have to believe. Taranenko believed he could lift 499½ if he tried hard enough, so he tried very hard. He didn't believe he could lift 500 pounds, so he avoided that situation.

When your self-efficacy belief regarding a task is high, you try harder, use better problem solving, are less distracted, persist longer, and are less likely to give up in the face of failure (Brown, 1991). When you don't believe you can do something, you either avoid it, become emotional when trying to deal with it, or make up excuses in advance for why you are going to fail (Maddux, 1991; Thompson, 1991).

A large number of research studies have shown that if people believe they can change difficult target behaviors, they are more likely to be successful (Bandura & Locke, 2003; Cervone & Scott, 1995, Maddux, 2002). For example, people who believe they can cope with a tension headache are more likely to reduce the headache, children who believe they can do difficult math problems are more likely to do them, women who believe they can deal with a threat of violence are better able to cope with a real threat, people who think they can tolerate pain are better able to tolerate it, and athletes who think they can get the job done show greater endurance and strength and are therefore more successful (Bandura, 1992, 1997).

A self-efficacy belief can influence whether you start a plan for change or not, and whether you continue it or not (Cervone, 2000). For example, whether you take up an exercise plan is affected by your self-efficacy belief that you can do the needed scheduling of your time and whether you believe you can cope with the inevitable obstacles that will come up (Maddux & Gosselin, 2003; Rodgers & Sullivan, 2001).

It is possible to increase one's self-efficacy beliefs. In one study, people who were extremely afraid of snakes learned to calmly handle a 6-foot Burmese python. The subjects were given a detailed series of training experiences—they watched a person who was not afraid of the snake approach and handle it, and used the same kinds of skill-building techniques we will teach you in this book. They were gradually taught first to approach and finally to fondle the snake (Bandura, Reese, & Adams, 1982). Their self-efficacy beliefs about performing the various steps increased and so did their actual ability to perform the steps leading to touching the python.

If people practice the behaviors necessary to reach some goal, their belief that they can do the things necessary to reach the goal increases. Julie, one of our recently in-shape students, confided, "When I started Weight Watchers they told me my ideal weight was about 140. At that time I weighed 180. I thought, 'That's ridiculous. There is no way I can reach 140.' But after I lost twenty pounds and was down to 160, I thought, 'Oh, yeah, I can do that. I'll just keep on doing what I was doing.' Now and then along the way I fell off the diet, but each time I remembered, 'Yeah, I know what to do, and I can do that,' and I'd get back on the program." She believed she could do what was necessary, and therefore did it, and that lead to her success. Most important, she did not ask herself, "Can I weigh 140?" Instead, she asked herself, "Can I do what I have been doing to lose weight?" *She focused on doing the process, not the final goal* (Schunk, 2000).

The belief that you can cope does not, of course, eliminate all difficulties. But self-confidence in your ability to execute the process leads to greater effort in attempting to overcome difficulties and allows you to tackle problems with less emotionality. The self-confidence also allows you to think of the specific skills you need to develop, and encourages you to put out more effort when the going gets tough.

Box 2-4
Never Give Up: Invincible Self-Efficacy

Abraham Lincoln (1809–1865), 16th president of the United States, must have felt great self-efficacy about his ability to be elected to high office, for he kept on trying in the face of many failures. The next time you're thinking of giving up, remember Lincoln's record:

    1832 defeated for the Illinois legislature
    1834 elected to the legislature
    1838 defeated for Speaker of the legislature
    1840 defeated for Elector of the legislature
    1843 defeated for Congress
    1846 elected to Congress
    1848 defeated for Congress
    1855 defeated for U.S. Senate
    1856 defeated for Vice President
    1858 defeated for U.S. Senate
    1860 elected President of the United States

      Many people who become famous fail many times before succeeding. For example, Gertrude Stein, a famous modernist writer, wrote poems for 20 years before an editor accepted one. Vincent Van Gogh sold only one painting in his lifetime but continued painting right up to the day he died. Claude Monet, now one of the most popular painters of all time, was rejected for many years by the main art shows in Paris. Edison tried 250 times before inventing the light bulb. And even the Beatles were rejected by the first two recording companies they approached (Bandura, 1994). As Christopher Morley, the modern editor of *Bartlett's Quotations* said, "Big shots are only little shots who keep on shooting."

Do you believe you can do the things you have to do in order to change your target? Notice we are *not* asking, "Can you reach the goal?" We're asking, "Can you do the process you need to do?" Answer these questions:

1. Will you read carefully to the end of the book? This means thinking about what you read and applying the ideas to yourself, figuring out how to use the ideas so you can change.

    Yes ☑   Maybe ☐   No ☐

2. In order to change, you will have to try out the ideas in this book. Will you be able to try the ideas in the book before you evaluate them?

    Yes ☑   Maybe ☐   No ☐

3. Will you to carry out the exercise at the end of each chapter, in which you apply the ideas from that chapter to your own self-modification project?

    Yes ☑   Maybe ☐   No ☐

4. Sometimes people are willing to change if it isn't going to be hard, or require much effort. But are you willing to try to change even though it will require effort?

    Yes ☑   Maybe ☐   No ☐

How to Increase Your Self-Efficacy Beliefs

There are steps you should take to increase your confidence that you can make the changes you need to make (Schunk & Ertmer, 2000).

1. *Pick a project for which you can say "yes" or a strong "maybe" to the questions above.* Do not start with something you don't believe you will do. Success in your first project will increase your belief that you can succeed in more challenging areas. Julie, who eventually went from 180 to 140, told us, "I started just trying to get myself to keep a record of my food intake. That worked well, so I began changing some of the things I ate. Less fat. To my surprise, that worked well, too, so then I thought, 'Well, I'll try exercising, see if I can get myself active.'" She wisely began where she believed she could succeed, and that increased her belief that she could do the more challenging parts.

2. *Focus on the process of change, not on the final goal* (Zimmerman & Kitsantas, 1996, 1997). Don't ask, "Can I lose weight?" but, "Can I keep a record of the foods I eat? Can I substitute fruit for candy at snack time?" Don't ask, "Can I make more and better friends?" Ask, "Can I smile at people and be interested in them and what they're doing?" Don't ask, "Can I make better grades?" Ask, "Can I do the steps in a time management project?"

Remember the idea of holding a skills development attitude. Keep your focus on carrying out the process of change. Don't focus on the final goal. This will increase your self-efficacy one small step at a time (Schunk, 2000). Think of the next step in the process of change and remind yourself, "I can do this."

Practice the steps in the process. Each practice session will increase your self-efficacy slightly, and the more you practice, the more you will believe that you can execute the process necessary to reach your goal.

If you know others who are dealing with the same kinds of problems, talk with them about what they do. "How do you get yourself to exercise?" "How do you get yourself to study?" That will give you ideas on what to practice.

3. *Discriminate between your past performance and your present project* (Goldfried & Robins, 1982). You may have learned from past failures that you cannot do certain things. But past failures are not necessarily a portent of future failure. You can gradually develop skills you never had before. All the people who successfully learned to handle the Burmese python had previously been extremely afraid of snakes. The researchers used techniques such as gradual approximations to a goal or learning by observing a good example. These techniques will be taught in detail in Chapter 6. You will be able to do things you haven't done before.

Sometimes people fear they cannot do certain things because they think they have personality characteristics—such as "weak willpower"—that keep them from performing adequately. These negative judgments are often wrong, however, and are not strongly rooted in reality (Cervone, 2004). Suspend negative judgments until you have tried the techniques. Try it, then evaluate it.

4. *While focusing on the process, not the final goal, keep records of your progress, as we suggest in Chapter 3.* They will show you small improvements, which will increase your belief that you can make changes. For Julie, for example, it was a big deal when she realized she'd gone just one week without eating any M and M's, which had been her nemesis food. "I was still overweight, but wow, I could resist M and M's."

Pay attention to your successes, no matter how small they are. "Victory over M and M's!" A person who sticks to a study schedule for 4 days and then fails to do so on the fifth should not think, "It's no use. I can't do it." Attend to the 4 days of success: Build on that. Next time try for five.

Some people have a tendency to remember their failures but not their successes. If you expect failure, you are likely to look for signs of failure. If you force yourself to look for signs of success, it affects your beliefs and your behavior. George, who wanted to improve his social relations with women, said,

> I think I always expected not to make a nice impression, so I was looking for that. If there was a pause in the conversation, I'd think, "Oh, she's bored," or "I'm not making a good impression." I taught myself to look for positive signs instead. Now if there's a pause in the conversation, I think, "She feels relaxed—good."

5. *Realize that just being emotional in a challenging situation does not mean you cannot perform adequately* (Maddux, 1991). Emotions can lower your self-efficacy beliefs irrationally (Cervone & Scott, 1995). Emotions frequently reflect troubles from times past and may not be appropriate for a current situation. Being emotional does not necessarily mean you are straining at the limits of your ability. This is a tremendously freeing notion: You can do it even when you are tense. Being tense just means you are tense; it does not mean you can't do it.

Manly Arthur Watson, a father, used to say, "Being brave doesn't mean you aren't afraid. Being brave means you do it anyway." Many times in life we have used this saying to talk ourselves though challenging situations. Sure, I'm tense, but I can still do it.

In your normal emotional state, you may be confident of a certain ability, but when depressed, self-doubts are stronger. You can overcome these negative effects. "I'm just doubting myself because I am depressed (or anxious). In a calmer time, I knew I could succeed. That is the judgment that I should believe."

6. Make a list of the specific situations in which you expect to have the greatest difficulty. Rosa, who wanted to become more assertive, made a list of "situations in which I have a hard time doing what I need to do."

> Easiest: dealing with strangers (for example, clerks)
> Fairly easy: students at school
> Moderate: my two brothers, my mom
> Getting difficult: my boss
> The most difficult: my dad

Once she had made this list, her strategy was clear: Begin with the easier tasks and tackle the harder ones after she experienced success and built some skill with the easier ones.

Rank-ordering the situations in which you anticipate difficulty allows you to put off dealing with the harder ones until you are better prepared and helps you avoid discouraging failures early in your self-change plan. It also allows you to discount mistakes you make early in the plan. If Rosa finds herself in a situation in which she fails to be assertive with her father, she can say to herself, "Well, I knew I was going to have a lot of trouble being assertive with my dad." Then she can remind herself of successes in other, easier situations. This way she is less likely to abandon a potentially successful plan.

Many projects require several separate subprojects. To lose weight, for example, you have to increase exercise, cut out fatty foods, eat slowly, and so on. Improving your study habits might require subprojects on time management, changing how you study, and changing your attitude toward studying. Begin with the easier subprojects.

Use a scale like the one Rosa used to evaluate the different kinds of situations you will face in terms of how difficult they will be for you:

	Situation
Easiest	EATING MORE DURING DAY
Fairly easy	MAKE FOOD BEFORE HAND
Moderate	EAT ENOUGH DURING DAY TO NOT BE HUNGRY
Getting difficult	NOT BINGE EATING OTHER FOODS AT NIGHT
Most difficult	NOT BINGE EATING FRUIT AT NIGHT

For example, Andrew intends to give up smoking. Here's how he filled out this scale:

	Situation
Easiest	midafternoon smokes
Fairly easy	late-night smokes
Moderate	smoking alone
Getting difficult	with coffee or alcohol
Most difficult	after meals

This kind of analysis brings realization that you have greater control in some situations than in others, and suggests that you should begin with the situations in which you have greatest control (see Box 2-5 on pp. 52–53).

Summary: Six Steps to Greater Self-Efficacy

1. Pick a target you feel there is some chance of reaching.
2. Focus on the process of change, not on the final goal. Hold a skills development attitude, practice the steps, and note how others do them.
3. Distinguish between past performance and the present situation.
4. Keep records of your progress in the process. Pay close attention even to small improvements that you make.
5. Don't let emotions hold you back. Realize you can do it even though it makes you emotional.
6. Rank situations according to their difficulty for you and start with the easier ones.

Whenever you falter, whenever you begin to believe that you cannot make the changes you would like to make, come back and read this section again. These ideas really work.

Applying Self-Efficacy and Self-Direction to Test Taking and Study Skills

You can apply the concepts of self-efficacy to improve your study skills. Preparing yourself by better self-direction in studying will significantly improve your academic performance. Even so, examinations themselves must be taken, and test taking is a skill that you can also improve. As seen in Box 2-6 (pp. 54–55), an easily mastered system—PIRATES—can help develop the specific skills needed for mastering multiple-choice tests.

Becoming Optimistic

How we think about a problem affects how we react to it. Our beliefs create self-fulfilling prophesies in which what we expect affects our behavior, and that in turn affects our outcome. Students who have unrealistically optimistic views of their own ability as students—they really aren't that much superior—nevertheless show more improvement in their grades than pessimists or realists (Wright, 2000). You get what you expect.

Optimists actually fare better in life than pessimists do (Seligman, 1991). The advice "Be optimistic" seems too simpleminded to be useful, but it turns out that people who are optimistic are not just mindlessly hopeful. Optimists, for example, cope with stress better than pessimists do (Scheier & Carver, 1993). "Optimists are more likely than pessimists to take direct action to solve their problems, are more planful in dealing with adversity they confront, and are more focused in their coping efforts" (pp. 27–28). As a result, they are actually less stressed by the problem than pessimists.

Pessimists, on the other hand, are more likely to try to avoid dealing with problems, use more wishful thinking, and are more likely to quit when they encounter problems (Carver & Scheier, 2002). Optimists expect a better future, but they also do things to make the future better (cf. McCullough & Snyder, 2000).

Thinking, "I really can deal with my target problems if I work hard at it," is *realistic optimism*—optimism grounded in the reality that change will take work, but at the same time asserting that change is possible. If that's not your current attitude about your target problem, don't be pessimistic. Optimism can be learned in two steps: (1) *Write*

Box 2-5
How's Your Self-Efficacy About Your Study Skills?

Professors Margaret Gredler and Linda Schwartz Garavalia (1997) developed a questionnaire to measure students' self-efficacy beliefs concerning a variety of their study skills. The questionnaire measures beliefs about one's ability to carry out different study behaviors in a variety of situations. Answering this questionnaire will allow you to see the areas in which your study skills are well under your control, and to see those in which you would benefit from a self-change project.

Even if study skills is not your target for change, it's a good idea to read this to develop your understanding of the nature of self-efficacy, and, who knows, perhaps improve your own study skills.

Directions: There are no right or wrong answers to the questions. Rate your response to the first twelve questions using the following scale:

1	2	3	4	5
not well at all				very well

How well can you ...	not well at all				very well
1. finish assignments by deadlines?	1	2	3	4	5
2. prepare for courses when there are other interesting things to do?	1	2	3	4	5
3. concentrate on school subjects?	1	2	3	4	5
4. take notes in class?	1	2	3	4	5
5. use appropriate resources to get information for class assignments?	1	2	3	4	5
6. plan your class work?	1	2	3	4	5
7. organize your class work?	1	2	3	4	5
8. remember information presented in class?	1	2	3	4	5
9. remember information presented in textbooks?	1	2	3	4	5
10. arrange a place to study without distractions?	1	2	3	4	5
11. motivate yourself to do your assignments?	1	2	3	4	5
12. set and honor priorities?	1	2	3	4	5

Further directions: Rate your responses to the next set of statements by circling the option that represents how often you do the activity.

1	2	3	4	5
not very often				very often

	not very often				very often
13. I turn off the TV/radio so I can concentrate on what I am doing.	1	2	3	4	5
14. I fail to write down things that I want to remember.	1	2	3	4	5
15. Before beginning a project, I get as much information as possible about the project.	1	2	3	4	5
16. When preparing for a test, I reread my textbook.	1	2	3	4	5
17. I plan what I am going to do before I begin a class project.	1	2	3	4	5
18. If I have problems with an assignment, I ask a teacher for help.	1	2	3	4	5
19. I paraphrase written information when I am studying.	1	2	3	4	5
20. When preparing for a class meeting, I reread class notes.	1	2	3	4	5
21. I usually wait until a day or two before a big project is due to start working on it.	1	2	3	4	5
22. When preparing for a test, I reread my class notes.	1	2	3	4	5
23. I check over my work to be sure I did it right.	1	2	3	4	5
24. I isolate myself from anything that disturbs me when I am studying.	1	2	3	4	5
25. I don't remember facts and ideas presented in class.	1	2	3	4	5
26. Each week I begin class with an idea of what I want to accomplish that week.	1	2	3	4	5
27. I take notes during class lectures.	1	2	3	4	5
28. Each day I make a list of things I plan to do.	1	2	3	4	5
29. I study for my courses in a quiet room or area.	1	2	3	4	5
30. I *don't* plan my day before I start it.	1	2	3	4	5
31. If I have problems with an assignment, I ask a friend for help.	1	2	3	4	5

SOURCE: Reproduced with permission of authors and publisher from Table 1, "Factorial Structure of the Self-efficacy for Self-regulated Learning Scale," by M. E. Gredler and L. S. Schwartz, 1997, *Psychological Reports, 81,* pp. 51–57. Copyright © 1997 *Psychological Reports.*

Box 2-6
Taking Tests Like a Pirate

What would you rather do, take a test or have an injection? When we asked one large class that question, 84 percent said they would rather have an injection. One shouted, "Give me the shot!"

There are, fortunately, strategies you can use to perform well on tests that will enable you to do better. Here is a proven test-taking strategy for multiple choice tests.

Hughes and Schumaker (1991) developed a system they called PIRATES. Each letter stands for a step you take as you work through a multiple-choice test.

P—Prepare to succeed. This takes less than three minutes. When you begin the test, write down PIRATES to remind yourself what to do. Take a minute to relax. Think a positive thought such as, "I'm well prepared. I ought to do well." (Make sure this isn't a lie by actually preparing well. The best technique for avoiding test anxiety is to be well prepared for the test.) If there is more than one section to the test, do the easiest one first.

I—Inspect the instructions. Many students misread instructions on tests and get lower grades as a result. Read instructions twice. You'll often notice things you overlooked at first.

R—Read, Remember, and Remove. *Read* the question. Before you make any choices, *remember* what you know about the material in the stem of the item. Try to complete the item from what you know before reading the choices. This activates your memory. *Remove*—eliminate—any obviously wrong answers. Scratch a mark through them so you won't think about them anymore.

For example, here's an item from Ben's psychology test:

The famous Skinner box was used to
   a. study animals.
   b. confine B. F. Skinner.
   c. study operant conditioning.
   d. all of the above.

Ben first recalls that Skinner used a box to study learning in pigeons. He realizes *b* is a silly answer, so he scratches it out. Answer *d* includes *b*, so it's out, too. Already he's cut his chances of selecting the wrong answer in half.

---

down reasons why you will be successful. Even if you believe failure might happen, write out all the reasons you can think of to be optimistic. (2) *Write out a chain of events that can lead to success* (McLeod, 1994). This will affect your future behavior, increasing the chances of a good outcome. The Weight Watchers program encourages participants to write up a series of events similar to the plan for a movie, showing how each scene leads to the next. Keep your notes, and look at them later.

A—Answer or Abandon. If you know the correct *answer*, mark the answer sheet. If you don't know, *abandon* the item. Mark it with a check. You'll come back to it.

The **R** and **A** steps are repeated over and over for each item. For each item, you Read/Remember/Remove and then Answer or Abandon.

T—Turn back to answer. Once you've gone through the test, go back and deal with any items you didn't answer the first time. Sometimes reading other questions will jog your memory about the answer to some you abandoned earlier.

E—Estimate (guess). Guess at an answer if you don't know the correct choice. If you leave it blank, it's definitely wrong. Some folks use rules like "never or always" are always wrong (notice the contradiction), or "the longest answer is usually right," or choose "c" or "all of the above," but truth to tell none is these is reliable. Here are two more reliable paths to follow in guessing:

1. Before guessing, try to eliminate as many choices as possible. The odds are better if you're choosing between two instead of four choices.
2. Look for something in the question that gives away the answer. Read the stem very carefully. If the test has been professionally created, like the SAT, it won't give away answers, but most tests you take are made less carefully. For example, here's a test question from a literature course (Scruggs & Mastropierri, 1992). See if you can guess the correct answer.

The hungry coyote in Tippecanoe county was observed
   a. sleeping in a ditch.
   b. stalking prey.
   c. looking for shelter.
   d. near the park.

Can you figure it out? Think about the item: What do "hungry" animals do? Look for shelter? Sleep? No, they look for food. So *b* is the correct answer. This shows the benefits of reading the stems of items very carefully. If you just skimmed over the stem, you might not have noticed the word "hungry," but if you are reading slowly and carefully, you think, "Wait a minute...."

S—Survey. The last step. Check for clerical errors. Also, an amazing number of students miss points on a test because they don't answer all the questions. Make sure you did.

Here are four examples:

When I do my final write-up for this course I'm going to want to be able to say I was successful, so I will work hard at changing, and that will help me change. I can imagine sometime thinking, "I won't try," but then I will remember that I have to do the final report, and I will keep trying.

Sometimes I will be stiff, but I'm going to start feeling so good from exercising that I will want to keep it up. I'll think, "I'm stiff, but it's worth it, because I feel so much better." I'll ignore the stiffness, or work through it, or stretch it out.

My grades will start to improve, and I will know it's due to my new study habits, so I'll continue with them. I might be tempted to quit, but I will remember that I really want to get better grades, so I will keep on working. My grades will gradually go up as I get more studying done.

I'm going to learn techniques that will help me relax and cope with the stress better than I have before. I will feel more relaxed, and that will encourage me to continue.

Notice in these examples that the person actually specifies a chain of events. This is more than just saying, "I'll reach my goal." These students have envisioned how they can reach it.

Monitor your thinking for negative thoughts. If you notice that you're thinking, "This is impossible," or "I can't do it," or "This is too hard," substitute thoughts like, "I can get there one small step at a time. I'm developing new skills, and I will get there." Then think of counter-pessimism thoughts and add them to your notes.

Notice it's not the emotional feeling of pessimism you are trying to avoid; it's the inaction when faced with a problem. You might be feeling negative, but if you take positive action you are acting like an optimist, and that's what you want, because it increases your chances of success in self-regulation.

Choosing Goals

Ambivalence About Goals: The Pros and Cons of Changing

Teruko initially said she was bothered by her poor performance at college. She had been valedictorian of her high school class and was considered brilliant by everyone, but now she was earning mostly Cs. She started a self-change plan to increase her studying, but after a few days it fizzled. "You know," she said, "it's really comfortable this way. I don't have to work at all to make Cs. And I don't have to find out what my upper limits are, something my dad is always urging me to do. I can just coast. For now, that's all I want." Teruko found her present behavior rewarding and really didn't want to change.

Changing can lead to new situations that we are not prepared to deal with. Faith had been about 50 pounds overweight, and in the previous year she had lost almost 40 pounds. She explained:

I didn't lose it equally all over, though, and I was, to be candid, pretty busty. Men liked this, but I didn't like it at all. I hated all the attention they paid to my body. So I just let myself go and regained 30 pounds. Now I'm fat and unbothered once more.

Any behavior that you have continued for a long time offers some advantages. People who bite their nails find comfort in their habit. People who don't exercise enjoy the pleasure of inactivity. People who accomplish little may enjoy the freedom of not working

Box 2-7
Conflicts Between Short-Term and Long-Term Goals

	Short–Term	*Long–Term*
Behavior excesses (undesired acts that bring some pleasure)	wanted	unwanted
Behavior deficits (desired acts that may bring some displeasure)	unwanted	wanted

SOURCE: Rakos (1992), personal communication.

on a schedule. Problem drinking, for example, may arise because people like to drink (Baumeister, Heatherton, & Tice, 1994). They like relieving the tension, overcoming boredom, or being the life of the party. So they may have something to lose by giving up drinking.

Many problems in self-control are a conflict between your short-term goals and your long-term goals (Malott, 1989; Rachlin, 2000). Sometimes "having self-control" means giving up what you want right now for what you want in the longer run (Logue, 1995, 1998). You give up lazing around now, a nice short-term goal, in exchange for a college degree that gets you a much better job in the future, a long-term goal. Someone who wants to quit smoking has the long-term goal of being healthier, but when the addiction calls she has the short-term goal of gratifying the urge to smoke. A person who wants to lose weight faces the same kind of conflict: In the long run, she wants to be slimmer, but in the short run she may strongly want to eat.

Procrastination is often a conflict between a short-term goal of leisure and a long-term goal of accomplishment. In the short run leisure is appealing, but in the long run that defeats your goal of getting through college. In this case, too, you need to cope with the conflict between your short-term desire to goof off and your long-term desire to get through college. When you are tempted to give up, remind yourself of your long-term goals (Lydon & Zanna, 1990; Schwartz & Inbar-Saban, 1988). Box 2-7 outlines these kinds of situations.

Sometimes we will choose the short-term goal, even though in the long run we want to stop that behavior. This can seem inexplicable to us: Why do I keep on doing the thing I want to stop doing? *You should expect this to happen, particularly if you benefit from the behavior you are trying to change.* Drinking, for example, is often used to relieve tension and to become a "fun" party person. That makes it harder to give up drinking, because some of the time the drinker will choose the short-term goal—tension relief, laughs—over the long-term goal of not being a drunk. Eating can be used to calm oneself—hence the idea of "comfort food"—and that makes it harder to give up because sometimes we want comforting. Again, the trick is to develop other ways of getting comfort.

Box 2-8
Advantages and Disadvantages of My Self-Change Project

Instructions: Consider the short-term and long-term advantages and disadvantages of changing. Take into consideration the effects on you and others, both tangible and intangible. Consider how you will feel about yourself and how others will feel.

Short-term advantages of changing:

- NOT STARVE DURING DAY
- REGULARIZE METABOLISM + DIGESTION
- MORE ENERGY + LESS CRANKY DURING DAY

Long-term advantages of changing:

- POSSIBLE LOSE WEIGHT AND KEEP IT OFF
- FEEL BETTER ABOUT MYSELF
- BODY WILL BE OVERALL HEALTHIER

Short-term disadvantages of changing (advantages of staying the same):

- FEELING HUNGRY + ANXIOUS AT NIGHT
- HAVE TO DEAL W/ ISSUES INSTEAD OF EAT THEM AWAY
- LOSE A SENSE OF COMFORT

Long-term disadvantages of changing:

- LOSE A LONG-TIME, STABLE CORRECTION OR OTHER HABIT
- POSSIBILITY OF DEPRESSION AGAIN IF DOESNT WORK
  OF THINKING OF HURT FEELINGS

Don't be deceived when this happens. It doesn't mean you don't want the long-term goal, it just means that at the moment you need the short-term one more. Your focus has narrowed, and you temporarily forget the vague, longer-term goal (Rachlin, 2000). You can think of other ways of getting the short-term goal. For example, the drinker should develop other ways to achieve the pleasurable goals so that drinking alcohol isn't the only way to reach them, learning other ways to relax and be fun at parties.

Ask yourself, "What will I lose by changing?" There are long- and short-term advantages and disadvantages to any self-change plan. It is entirely normal to feel ambivalent about changing. You are more likely to succeed if you examine your ambivalence at the beginning of your self-modification project.

Make a list of the long- and short-term pros and cons of changing your behavior. Use Box 2-8 as a guide and Box 2-9 as an example. List your hopes and your fears about changing. For example, you might hope to look good and feel like you're in control if you

Box 2-9
The Pros and Cons of Stopping Drinking

Here is a detailed example of the considerations a heavy drinker might think about in making the decision to drink less (Curry & Marlatt, 1987):

1. Why should I moderate my drinking?

Short-term considerations

Pros	*Cons*
Feeling that my drinking is under my control.	It's work to break old habits.
Avoiding illness from overdrinking.	Social pressure from heavy drinkers.
Reducing tension.	Initial awkwardness with new habit.
Saving money.	
Social approval from light drinkers.	

Long-term considerations

Pros	*Cons*
Increased self-control and self-confidence.	Loss of friendship with heavy drinkers.
Improved health.	Loss of the joy of being blasted.
No hangovers.	
Weight loss.	
New friends and hobbies.	

2. Why should I continue or resume heavy drinking?

Short-term considerations

Pros	*Cons*
Immediate gratification.	Illness from overdrinking.
Consistency with past self-image.	Financial loss.
Approval from heavy drinkers.	Social embarrassment.
Excuse for irresponsibility.	Disapproval from light drinkers.
Faster sleep onset.	Impaired coordination.
Perception of increased personal power.	Possibility of personal injury.

Long-term considerations

Pros	*Cons*
Consistency with old self-image.	Decreased self-esteem.
Friendships with heavy drinkers.	Financial loss.
	Added health problems.
	Interpersonal conflicts.
	Occupational disruptions.
	Physical dependency on alcohol.

lose weight—advantages—but also fear that you will be hungry all the time or suddenly start binge eating—disadvantages (Fanning, 1990). Or you might believe you would have more energy and feel good about yourself if you took up vigorous exercise, but also think that you might be uncomfortable exercising in public or in bad weather (Marcus, Rakowski, & Rossi, 1992). Face the real advantages of *not* changing, and think about them. People who make this kind of list are more likely to be successful in their plans for change (Janis, 1982; Kirschenbaum & Flanery, 1984).

Once you've made this list, keep it. Take it out now and then to remind yourself of the reasons why you want to change. Once your project is under way, you will forget some of the reasons, or they may no longer seem as important as they did when you were really suffering with your problem. If you falter in carrying out your project, rereading your list can help you see the reasons to keep going (Curry & Marlatt, 1987).

Why does making this kind of list help? First, it helps you anticipate obstacles to changing, so you can take steps to overcome them. For example, if you know the new you will make your spouse uncomfortable, you can make the changes gradually or try to build protection into your plan. Michelle, for example, had lost 150 pounds, and had changed from a very fat wife to a very attractive one. There was a beautiful woman hiding under all the weight. This had several effects on her husband, not all positive. He was jealous of the interest men showed in her for the first time ever.

Second, it encourages you to be realistic—to face what you want and don't want, and what you are willing to do to get what you want. If you know you hate to sweat but think you ought to exercise more, realizing this now may enable you to work out a plan to deal with this obstacle. Try swimming, for example. Swimmers don't get hot.

Third, it allows you to plan ahead. You can be more realistic in your plans and goals, which makes it more likely you will succeed. If you know you are going to resent the time you spend studying, you can think ahead to deal with that problem.

Lani, a 19-year-old sophomore living off campus, wrote: "It helped a lot when I listed the pros and cons of changing and then did something to minimize the disadvantages. My goal was to increase my studying. I modeled myself on Linda, who did all her studying at school while I seemed to spend a lot of time socializing during the day. I thought I'd be more efficient if I did my work during the day, too. But when I listed the disadvantages of changing, I realized I was going to lose all that time with my friends at school. Linda wasn't a good model for me. She is married, and when she goes home at night she's with her husband all evening. I live by myself, so my socializing comes during the day, and I really wouldn't have wanted to give it up. I revised my plan to increase my studying but during the evening. That worked great!"

Suppose you have made your list and right now it seems like you really don't want to change. *Before abandoning the project, ask yourself one more question: If you do not change, where will you be in 5 years?*

A young man had consulted some psychologists about decreasing his rather heavy drinking (Sobell & Sobell, 1995a). The psychologists asked him to list the pros and cons of cutting down on his drinking, and he concluded he didn't want to cut down. "I'm a barfly. I hang out in bars, drink, and socialize a lot. I have a great time in bars. So I don't think I want to cut down on the booze." The psychologists asked him to clearly describe what he would be like in 5 years if he continued at his present level of drinking. He said, "In some doctor's office." Thinking about that convinced the young man to work out a plan to cut down the drinking but continue socializing in bars.

Stages in Your Thoughts About Changing

The balance between the pros and cons you thought about above tells you how ready you are to change. While not everyone agrees (Littell & Girven, 2002), theorists have suggested that people pass through the a five-step process when they think about changing a problem behavior (DiClemente & Proschaska, 1998; Prochaska & DiClemente, 1992):

1. A period of precontemplation, in which people are not thinking about changing;
2. A period of contemplation, in which people think about and perhaps experiment with changing "sometime in the next 6 months";
3. A period of preparation, in which people get ready to change during the next month;
4. An action period, in which the change occurs;
5. A maintenance period involving continuing change after the first goals have been reached.

People may be stuck at one of the early stages for years or even for life. A man might drink so much that he loses interest in all of life's other pleasurable activities, but never see a problem, remaining in the precontemplation stage until he dies (Prochaska, DiClemente, & Norcross, 1992). Many smokers stay in the contemplation stage— "I may quit in the next 6 months"—for 2 years or more (Prochaska & DiClemente, 1984). One of our friends spent 3 years saying to herself, "I need to start exercising within the next month or two."

The process of thinking about change usually does not move in a straight line. See Figure 2-1. Progress is more of a spiral, from pre-contemplation to contemplation to

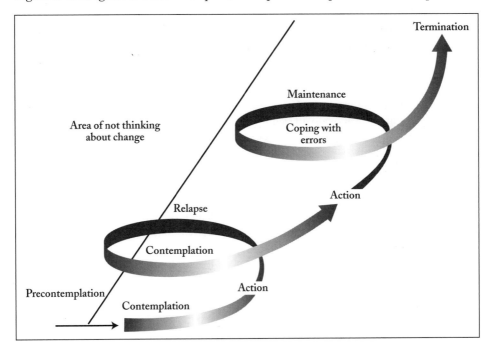

Figure 2-1 The spiral process of change
SOURCE: Based on Prochaska, DiClemente, & Norcross, 1992.

preparation to action, followed by relapse or a series of mistakes, after which people may feel bad about their failure and go back to not thinking about change for a while (Prochaska, DiClemente, & Norcross, 1992). Many people relapse along the way to final change, and almost everyone has to learn to deal with errors that occur or cope with unexpected situations that threaten progress. Chapters 8 and 9 are full of details on how to cope with these problems.

When the disadvantages of changing outweigh the advantages, people tend to be in the precontemplation stage: They don't think about changing. If the balance between the advantages and disadvantages of change is altered, however, a person may begin to contemplate changing. A smoker, for example, might spend years not thinking about quitting, but after a visit to a doctor for a persistent cough might begin to think more of the advantages of quitting.

What tips the balance and puts people into the preparation and action stages is feeling that the advantages of change definitely outweigh the disadvantages. When people actually get off the couch and take up exercise, for example, it is because they have come to think that the advantages of exercise outweigh the disadvantages (Marcus, Rakowski, & Rossi, 1992). It does take some time, and you can get tired, but those inconveniences are outweighed by the fact that you have more energy, feel better, are less stressed, look better, and so on.

This suggests that to move yourself into the preparation and action stages, you should think about two things:

1. why the advantages of change really are strong for you, and
2. why the disadvantages are not as strong as you thought.

If you have been focusing on the costs of exercise, for example, try to focus on the benefits, instead, and think of ways in which the costs may not be too high after all.

Go back and look at your list of pros and cons of changing again. Can you think of reasons why the pros really are stronger than they might first appear? Can you think of reasons why the cons are actually weaker than they first appear? Try to think of personal reasons, ones important to you (Curry, Wagner, & Grothaus, 1990). For example, quitting smoking because you will feel like you are in control of your life is a stronger, more personal reason than quitting because others will no longer be upset with you. If you can think of reasons why the advantages of change are actually stronger than you first thought, and the disadvantages weaker, you increase your chances of doing the work that is necessary for you to change.

This does not mean that you should be unrealistic about the prospects for change (Polivy & Herman, 2000, 2002). Some change is hard to make and only effort will allow you to reach the goal.

Set Goals and Make Plans to Reach Them

You need to set goals in your self-modification plan. If you don't set goals, you won't get started, for there is no destination. As Yogi Berra said, "If you don't know where you are going, you'll end up somewhere else." Without both long- and short-term goals, you won't keep trying. Short-term goals provide the start, and the long-term goals keep you on the journey (Locke & Latham, 1990, 1994, 2002).

Make a specific statement of your final goal, and then break it into subgoals you can work on one at a time. For example, Patricia's long-term goal was to place her relationship with her spouse, Rick, on a more egalitarian basis. This would include issues such as who did chores, who made decisions, who would be responsible for child care, and so on. She started with one subgoal, being more assertive in one issue relating to their daily life. She gave herself instructions about how to act in a particular situation: "When Rick touches my body when I'm not expecting it, I'll say to him, 'Rick, please don't do that when I don't know it's coming. It just startles me, and I don't enjoy it.'"

The advantage to subgoals is that they are reachable, while the long-range goal may not yet be attainable (Stock & Cervone, 1990). You know you can reach certain sub-goals, and so you have a feeling of self-efficacy, and it seems worth the effort to try. Patricia knew it was going to take a long time to place her marriage with Rick on a to-tally equitable basis, but on the other hand, it wasn't going to be too hard just to work on the one subgoal of asking him to stop startling her.

People who only have high-level, long-range goals open themselves up to frustra-tion. One of our colleagues who weighs about 240 pounds was told by his doctor, "You need to get down to 180." That was so far from where he was that he didn't even start trying. The goal was just too far away. He should have started by trying to lose 5 pounds. A young woman whose career goal was to be "a famous writer" observed that she never sat down to write. The problem was, she had set no immediate subgoals, such as getting one story finished, and the big goal seemed so far away that while it was alluring, it was often not worth the effort. People who procrastinate suffer from this problem: no short-term goals that they can reach right away, and so no reason to get started. If your only goal is to make all As and you are currently making lots of Cs, the long-range goal may seem so far away that it's not worth moving toward.

Therefore, set subgoals. A woman who wanted to learn to control her temper began with the short-term goal of leaving the room and not saying anything when she felt she was getting too angry at her husband. A student who wanted to develop more friendships began with the short-term goal of learning to be a better listener. The student who wanted to make As began with the subgoal of making an A in one course, and then divided that into the subgoal of making an A on the next test.

Specific goals and subgoals—"I'm going to study at least 15 hours per week"—*are better than general goals*—"I'm going to study more" (Cervone, Jiwani, & Wood, 1991; Kirschenbaum, 1985). When managers in business urge their employees to "do your best," they think they are motivating them. But the research shows that setting very specific goals—"Try to turn out five percent more next month"—is actually more effective, because it is specific (Locke & Latham, 2002). "Do your best" is vague, so we aren't sure whether we are or not, but "five percent" is totally clear, and we will know if we're doing it or not. Similarly, "I want to lose weight," is vague, but "I want to lose one pound this week," is not.

Be specific, but leave room for flexibility. Do not tie your goal to a particular time or place. It's the final result that matters, not precisely where or when you do the work. It is better to say, "I'm going to study 15 hours per week," than to say, "I'm going to study Friday night from 6:30 to 8:20." If that particular goal is not met, you might assume that you are not capable of self-control and stop trying. If your goal is to study a set number of hours per week, on the other hand, then if circumstances prevent it on Friday night, there's always Saturday afternoon for catching up (Baumeister, Heatherton, & Tice, 1994).

Don't make your subgoals too easy (Locke & Latham, 1990, 2002). They should be at least slightly challenging. Otherwise, they're not motivating. "I'm going to study 15 minutes this week" isn't challenging enough to motivate you to study at all. Each of us, of course, has to decide what is challenging, because what is easy for one can be hard for another. "I'm going to skip supper so I can lose a pound," may be easy for one person but nearly impossible for another.

In summary, goals should be specific, attainable but challenging, and flexible.

Stop. Before going on, take out a pencil and paper and write down your final goal. Then work out a series of subgoals that will allow you to reach it. An older man whose long-range goal was to "get myself not to be so angry with people" said, "My plan was to evaluate a variety of situations in which I might get mad, then rank them according to how easy I think it will be to control my anger in them. I will start off with the easy ones, then work up the scale until I can deal with any type."

Relating Your Target Goals to Life Goals

Sometimes it's easy to change because we become aware that what we are doing violates our own values. Miller and Rollnick (1991) give the example of a man frantically wanting a cigarette who was walking his two little children home. He saw a store across the street that was open, and left his two kids standing in the rain while he dashed across and bought a pack. Later he was horrified that he'd left them out in the wet, and immediately gave up cigarettes. His behavior appalled him because he had violated his own strongly held value of protecting his children.

You can tilt the odds for your success in our favor by tying your target goal to the larger goals in your life. We are more likely to work for goals when they fit with our general life goals (Karoly et al., 2005). A friend told us, "I'd always wanted to lose weight, because I knew I'd look better, but I never got around to it even though I reached 60 years old. Then I realized this: There are no fat old men. I thought I'm going to die sooner than I need to if I don't get the weight off." Once he tied his value of living longer to weight loss, it was easier for him to proceed.

After reviewing a large number of studies, Martin Ford (1992) suggested that there are four major categories of goals that most of us strive for in life:

1. experiencing positive emotions such as happiness or relaxation;
2. maintaining positive self-evaluations;
3. feeling connected to others, caring for and feeling accepted by others;
4. being physically active and energetic.

Think about your self-change project. How will achieving your goal further you in terms of these four major goals of life? Write a memo to yourself about this.

A student who wanted to develop more and closer friends realized he was focused on one of these major life goals, number three above, but that also he would reap benefits in other areas. He wrote:

With more friends . . .

1. I will be happier.
2. I will like myself better because I will have become a more likable person.

3. I will definitely feel more connected to others.
4. Maybe I will even get a girlfriend.
5. I will probably be more energetic because I will have friends to do things with instead of just watching TV.

See "Self-Directed Happiness" in Chapter 10, as well. How will achieving our goal further your happiness?

Do You Intend to Do the Work of Changing?

After completing the answers and lists in this chapter, you should consider the issue in its fullest. Is this a journey you want? Is the self-change goal one that you will work for? After this reading and thinking, do you intend to change in this way (Ajzen, 1991; Ajzen & Fishbein, 1980; Ford, 1989)?

Check your response to this statement:

I intend to do the work necessary to reach my goal.

Yes ☐   Maybe ☐   No ☐

If you can't say "Yes," there are still several alternatives:

Read the relevant sections of this chapter again, and do the work required at each step. For example, if you don't believe you can reach your goal, work on your self-efficacy beliefs. If you aren't sure you want to change, try to resolve your ambivalence about goals.

Pick a target goal you are willing to do the work for. If you don't want to do the whole thing, consider working on part of the larger goal. One student, for example, said he was willing to increase his exercise but wasn't yet sure about eating a low-fat diet.

The Self-Contract

When you have selected a self-change goal you intend to work toward, put it in writing. Write out each element of your plan as a self-contract. Write your goal and intentions as clearly as possible. You will add more details at the end of Chapters 3 through 8. The first paragraph of the contract is a statement of your intention. Write, "I am willing to change my behaviors as necessary to reach the goal I have chosen and will carry out the steps suggested in the text. I am willing to do the work suggested in Step 2 at the end this chapter even though it will take an hour to do." Then—if you are willing to do the work—sign your name.

Does this really help? Yes. In different experiments, a segment of people who attempted a self-change project were asked to write a self-contract, while others were not, and in all cases the people who signed the contract increased their chances of success (Griffin & Watson, 1978; Putnam, Finney, Barkley, & Bonner, 1994). By itself, a self-contract won't keep you from all temptation, but it is one more effective technique to use in the passage to self-regulation.

Also consider posting your contract publicly. A wide variety of self-directed projects have benefited: increased studying, reduced eating, more assertive self-expression. Varsity college football linebackers, when posting their goals in the locker room, improved their positioning and tackling (Ward & Carnes, 2002).

Tips for Typical Topics

Most chapters of this book end with a section called "Tips for Typical Topics," in which we point out how you can apply the ideas discussed in the chapter to the most common types of self-modification projects. Specific pieces of information that are helpful for each kind of project are included in the Tips sections. Here is a list of topics that are commonly addressed in our classes in self-directed behavior:

- Anxieties and stress
- Assertion and assertive behavior
- Depression and low self-esteem
- Exercise and athletics
- Relationships with others: social anxieties, social skills, and dating
- Smoking, drinking, and using drugs
- Studying and time management
- Weight loss and overeating

For each topic, the Tips section suggests specific ideas, but these cannot be substituted for reading and thinking about the principles offered in the whole chapter.

At the end of the book is a Subject Index, which lists all discussions of each topic throughout the book. For example, everything said about "depression" is listed together for ready reference. You can check the Subject Index and read all the information about your particular topic for self-modification now, if you like.

Chapter Summary

Specifying Targets for Change

You need well-defined objectives that are specified in terms of particular behaviors in particular situations. The aim is to be able to complete this sentence:

My goal is to change _____ when _____.
                 (thought, action, feeling)   (situation)

To specify behaviors-in-situations, try these tactics:

1. Make a list of concrete examples.
2. List the details of your problem.
3. Become an observer of yourself.

Even if your goal is to eliminate some unwanted action,

4. Always try to increase some desirable behavior.

If you aren't sure what to do,

5. Specify the chain of events that will lead to your goal.
6. Observe other people who do well what you are trying to learn to do.
7. Think of alternative solutions.

And even if your goal is not some behavior,

8. Reaching it will require changing certain behaviors.

With complex problems, you are likely to move through a series of approximations to your goal as your self-understanding deepens.

Anticipating Obstacles

You should expect to make mistakes, and should not blame them on your personality.

Eight tactics for dealing with temptation:

1. Avoid tempting situations.
2. Ask your friends not to tempt you.
3. Make a public commitment to change.
4. Minimize the tempting quality.
5. If in the situation, distract yourself.
6. When tempted, remind yourself of your goal.
7. Ask other people to remind you of your goal.
8. Develop "if . . . then" plans to be prepared for temptation.

Several steps were suggested to increase your self-efficacy beliefs:

1. Pick a target you feel there is some chance of reaching.
2. Focus on the process of change, not on the final goal.
3. Distinguish between past performance and the present situation.
4. Pay close attention even to small successes.
5. Don't let archaic emotions hold you back.
6. Being depressed can lower your self-efficacy, but knowing this can help you overcome the negative effects.
7. Rank situations according to their difficulty for you and begin with the easiest.

There are practical advantages to being optimistic. To counter pessimism, make a list of the reasons why you can succeed at your task.

Choosing Goals

People are sometimes ambivalent about changing, as there may be losses as well as gains. Make a list of the advantages and disadvantages of changing, so you can with a clear head evaluate if you really want to change.

Many problems in self-control can be seen as a conflict between your short-term goals and your long-term goals. Your "undesired" acts may be desired in the short run, even if unwanted in the long run, and your desired acts may be wanted in the long run, but not so appealing in the short term.

Many people pass through a set of stages in the process of change:

Pre-contemplation, in which they aren't thinking of change;
contemplation, in which they think of change in the next 6 months;
preparation, in which they plan change within the month;
action; and
maintenance, in which they cope with errors in order to maintain their change.

To move yourself into the preparation and action stages, think of reasons why the advantages of change are stronger than you first thought, and the disadvantages weaker.

Work out goals and divide them into subgoals. Plan how to reach them. Work out specific subgoals that are attainable, but somewhat challenging, and flexible enough to be met more than one way. Tie your target goals to larger life goals.

The crucial question is, "Are you willing to do the work, the thinking and planning, necessary to change?"

Write a self-contract detailing the work you have to do in order to achieve self-change, and sign it if you intend to do the work.

Your Own Self-Direction Project: Step 2

Before going on to Chapter 3, do the exercises suggested here for specifying the problem, anticipating problems, and setting goals. A few students have moaned to us about this "big assignment." But a bit of thinking is needed to overcome the bad habits of the past. If you've been doing some of the thinking as you went along, your task is already partially done.

Part One: Specifying the Goal

Specify your goal as some behavior-in-a-situation that you wish to either decrease or increase. Even if you want to decrease some undesirable behavior, you should be able to state as your goal an increase of some other behavior that is incompatible with the un-desired one. If at this point you cannot state your problem as a behavior-in-a-situation, go through each of the procedures in this chapter, step by step, for your chosen goal.

Part Two: Anticipating Obstacles

Make plans for what to do when you make mistakes. Make plans for dealing with tempting situations. Make a list of reminders to give yourself when you are tempted. What are the delayed punishments for your unwanted behavior? Make a list of the people you are going to ask to remind you. Develop your "if . . . then" plans for tempting situations.

Answer the questions on page 48 about your self-efficacy beliefs. Make plans to increase your self-efficacy beliefs by taking the suggested steps. For example, make a list of the situations in which you expect to have difficulty performing the desired actions, and rank the situations according to their degree of difficulty. Write out counter-pessimism statements.

Make a list of the pros and cons of changing. What will you gain? What will you lose? What are the short-range and the long-range pros and cons of changing? Work on reasons why the pros of change are stronger than the cons.

Part Three: Setting Goals

Establish subgoals leading to your final goal, and make plans for reaching them. List the reasons why accomplishing your target goals will further your life goals.

Now write a self-contract. First specify your goal, and then include this statement: "I am willing to change my behaviors as necessary to reach the goal I have chosen and will carry out the steps suggested in the text." Sign the contract. The point of this self-promise is that you start with a goal that is important enough for you to actually perform the steps in self-modification.

Chapter 3

Self-Knowledge: Observation and Recording

Outline and Learning Objectives

Why Observe Ourselves?

1. What are the two reasons for careful self-observation?

Structured Diaries

2. What do you record in a structured diary?
   a. What can you record under Antecedents?
   b. What can you record under Behaviors?
   c. What can you record under Consequences?
3. What is the point of a structured diary?

Recording Frequency and Duration

4. Give an example of recording the amount of time you spend doing something or the number of times you do it.
5. Why is it important to record successes as well as failures?

Rating the Intensity of Emotions

6. Give an example of a rating scale. What are the advantages of making a rating of some target emotion or feeling?
7. How can you combine various systems for keeping records?

Practicalities of Record Keeping

8. What are the reasons for recording your target behavior as soon as it occurs?
9. What can you do to make recording easier?
10. How does one use written storage records?
11. What are the four rules of self-observation?
12. What does it mean to say that self-observation is reactive?
13. How can you use this reactivity to your advantage?

14. What is negative practice, and in what kind of situation is it most useful?
15. How do you record behaviors you perform absent-mindedly?
16. How do you record behaviors that occur while many other things are going on?
17. Suppose you don't want to make the records or forget to do so. What should your first plan for change be?

Planning for Change
18. What is the baseline period?
19. For how long should you record in the baseline period?
20. What is reliability? What can you do to increase it?

Tips for Typical Topics

Chapter Summary

Your Own Self-Direction Project: Step 3

Why Observe Ourselves?

"Know thyself."

—Socrates
Greek philosopher (469–399 B.C.)

"You can observe a lot by watching."

—Yogi Berra
American baseball player

Self-knowledge is the key to successful self-change. Most of us assume that we understand ourselves, and we place considerable faith in our memories of our own behaviors. We rarely feel that we need to employ any systematic self-observation techniques. "Common sense" tells us we can trust our memories, but "common sense" is not always right. Real surprises and genuine discoveries are in store for the person who begins careful self-observation.

Socrates was right, it is good to know yourself, but he didn't add that knowing yourself is not automatic. We can't call up a video of our lives to see what we were really doing, and just thinking about ourselves can be misleading. We humans do not necessarily remember our own past accurately (Ross & Conway, 1986; Wilson & Dunn, 2004). Sometimes we don't remember because we were not paying close attention in the first place (Robins & John, 1997). Sometimes our memories are affected by the mood we are in at the time (Eich, 1995; Martin & Tesser, 1996) or by what we expect to remember (Libby, Eibach, & Gilovich, 2005). We sometimes develop false memories yet come to believe they are true (Loftus, 2004).

Thus our casual self-assessments are often inaccurate (Nisbett & Ross, 1980). Fairly often we arrive at the wrong conclusions about our own behavior (Gilovich, 1991; Wilson & LaFleur, 1995). It's amusing to note that we are most likely to overestimate our skill level at something we are particularly bad at (Dunning, Johnson, Ehrlinger, & Kruger, 2003). We underestimate the extent of certain health risks we engage in, overestimate our educational attainment, and overestimate our level of competence at work (Dunning, Heath, & Suls, 2004). Is this because we want to believe these errors? That is only part of the story. A primary reason for our misestimation is not gathering proper information. We don't self-observe accurately.

Sometimes, of course, we don't want to remember accurately. In one study a group of people who wanted to lose weight were asked by the researcher how much they ate. Many said, "I really don't eat very much. I just have a slow metabolism." They were asked to remember and write down everything they had eaten in the preceding 2 days. Their lists were checked, and it appeared that the people really were not overeating. But were their memories accurate? The researcher then put them all on a diet consisting of all the foods they had reported eating. Every one of them began to lose weight (Stunkard, 1958).

What we believe and what is so are not always the same. This can even be for our benefit, as we forget the bad parts of life and get on with the good (Brown, 1991). But when we want to change ourselves, we need to know reality, the good, the bad, and the ugly. "Reality testing" is a central part of all plans for change, (Wiser, Goldfried, Raue, & Vakoch, 1995). We won't necessarily see all of ourselves accurately (Wilson & Dunn, 2004), but we must strive to see the parts we want to change accurately, else we will fail to change. "The most serious obstacle to self-control is faulty perception of one's own behavior" (Rachlin, 2000, p. 145).

Self-observation provides information—feedback—that allows us to gradually improve. Ongoing assessment of progress is absolutely essential in the development of skill (Ericsson, Krampe, & Tesch-Romer, 1993), and ongoing assessment is a central feature of successful plans for change (Kazdin, 1993). Knowing the truth allows us to correctly adjust a newly developing skill (Forsterling & Morgenstern, 2002). If you were hitting practice golf balls and they all veered off to the left, you'd want to know that so you could make corrections.

When we are changing, improvement is not often sudden and dramatic, but slow, a bit at a time. Without careful records, we will not notice small advances nor consistent errors. In one experiment, for example, a group of college sprinters were divided into two groups. One group was told their time for each sprint, but the second group was not. Both groups ran 10 sprints over the course of the afternoon. After 10 trials, the sprinters without knowledge of their times—no feedback—were running no faster than they had at the beginning of the trials. But the group who were given feedback all ran faster in the later trials. They used the knowledge they had to improve (Patrick, 1992).

In order to change yourself, you must know what you're doing. This chapter presents a set of techniques for gaining knowledge about your behaviors, thoughts, and feelings and about their relationships to specific situations. In order to select and design the best possible plan for change, you need careful records of your behavior and the specific situations in which it occurs. In Chapters 5, 6, 7, and 8, you will learn to use this information to design a plan for self-directed change.

Structured Diaries

A *structured diary* is a record you keep of your target for change and also of its antecedents and consequences. Journalism students learn that to write a clear story they must answer five questions: Who? What? Where? When? Why? In order to keep a good structured diary, you must answer these same questions. Keeping this record will allow you to see what kinds of situations have an effect on your target.

If your goal is to stop some unwanted behavior, it is important to discover when the behavior occurs, that is, find the A-B-C patterns. Finding the antecedents that lead to the unwanted behavior or the consequences that encourage it are essential in devising a successful plan for change. This reveals the high-risk situations in which you are likely to perform the behaviors you want to stop (Sobell & Sobell, 1995a), and it allows you to work out new ways of dealing with tempting situations, so you don't give in to your bad habit (Gollwitzer, Fujita, & Oettingen, 2004).

Start with the target. Under Behavior (B), list the action, thought, or feeling that is your target for change. Then enter the antecedents that precede it and the consequences that follow.

Antecedents (A)	*Behaviors—actions, thoughts, or emotions (B)*	*Consequences (C)*
When did it happen? Whom were you with? What were you doing? Where were you? What were you saying to yourself? What thoughts were you having? What feelings were you having?	What were you saying to yourself? What thoughts did you have? What feelings were you having? What actions were you performing?	What happened as a result? Pleasant or unpleasant?

As an example, here's Les, whose goal was to eliminate nail biting. Les kept a record of the antecedents and consequences of biting his nails. Here are some entries from his diary:

Antecedents (A)	*Behavior (B)*	*Consequences (C)*
Waiting for the bus	Nail biting	Embarrassed that others might see
Sitting in class listening	Nail biting	Same
Lying in bed thinking	Nail biting	Just wish I would quit
Reading	Nail biting	Same
Stressed	Nail biting	Gives me something to do

Les wrote, "I knew I bit my nails when I was stressed, but I was surprised to find that I did it in other situations, too. It happens when my mind is occupied but my fingers are not." Knowing this, Les is in a position to make a plan to eliminate nail biting in those situations.

Here is a selection from the structured diary of Mike, a father whose goal was to stop spanking his children and start using nonphysical punishment. After he disciplined the children, he made an entry in his diary:

Antecedents (A)	Behaviors (B)	Consequences (C)
April 3. Sat. morning at breakfast. Kids bickered a lot.	I spanked both of them.	Made them even more cross.
April 6. Came home from work feeling tired. My boy talked back to me.	Started to spank him but stopped. Grounded him for an hour instead.	Felt pretty good about that. Was glad I didn't hit him. He calmed down while he was grounded.
April 10. Had an argument with Dora [his wife]. Then in the car the kids started quarreling.	Spanked them—actually, slapped them.	It spoiled our whole outing. I felt guilty. They felt rotten.

Mike sees from his diary that he feels better when he doesn't spank. See Figure 3-1. He also notes that it's not simply the behavior of the children that determines whether he spanks them or not. An argument with his wife or feeling "down" after a hard day at work influences his behavior, too. By noting both his feelings and his behaviors, Mike can see what leads to the spanking that he wants to stop. Note that Mike made a note not only of the times he spanked his children, but—just as important—of the times he used a nonviolent discipline technique.

Evelyn, a young college student, felt that she needed to be more assertive, but she wasn't sure when and in what situations. She recorded in her diary the times when she thought she could have been assertive but was not, and the times when she was assertive.

Several days of observations revealed a pattern: When other people asked Evelyn to go places with them, and she had nothing else specifically scheduled, she usually went, even if she didn't want to. If they asked but she had something specifically scheduled, she didn't. "But," she wrote, "why should I have to have something scheduled before I feel I can say no? Isn't the need to go to sleep enough? I need to be able to refuse even when I have no specific activity planned but just don't want to do it."

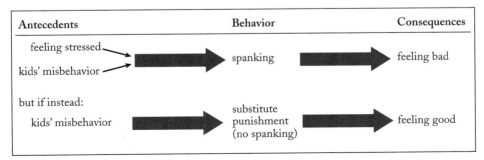

Figure 3-1 Relations between antecedents, behaviors, and consequences: The case of Mike's disciplining of his children.

Antecedents (A)	Behaviors (B)	Consequences (C)
11:30 P.M. I am about to fall asleep. Ed telephones. He starts to ramble.	I'm angry, it's late, and he is boring, but I don't say anything.	He talks about 20 minutes.
Noon the next day. Walking to work, I see Ed, try to avoid talking to him. He calls me. I keep on going. He grabs my arm. He asks me to lunch.	I look away, say "I don't know . . . (pause) okay."	We have lunch. He asks me out again.
Polly wants me to see a movie I swore I would not see. She complains that I haven't been to a movie with her in a long time.	I say, "I really shouldn't. I need to get some rest." But I give in and go.	The movie was gross.
1:00 P.M. Went to meet Jill. We were supposed to go jogging, but she wants to do it later in the day.	I tell her I can't go later. I have to work.	
6 P.M. My sister comes over to ask me to baby-sit.	I tell her I can't. I have other plans. A bunch of us are going out.	

Once pointed out, Evelyn's goal seems obvious, but it was not apparent to her until she began keeping a structured diary.

The Mechanics of Diary Making

As soon as you realize that you have performed some undesired target behavior or failed to perform some desired one, make an entry in your structured diary. Describe the physical setting, the social situation, your thoughts, and the behavior of other people.

Be sure to make the diary entries as soon as the target problem occurs. Don't wait. It's easy to overlook important details when you're reconstructing a past event. For example, if Mike had waited until the next day to record the events just before spanking his children, he might never have realized that coming home tired from work or having an argument with his wife was affecting how he disciplined his kids.

Recording Actions, Thoughts, and Feelings

Thoughts, feelings, and your own actions can be the antecedents to your problem or the target problem itself. Therefore, they are listed under both columns A and B in the chart. Thoughts can lead to behaviors, behaviors can lead to thoughts, feelings can lead to both, and both can lead to feelings—there are no one-way signs in the streets of the mind. Causation can go either way—see Figure 3-2. All three may be considered both as antecedents and as the target problem itself. You can record all three: feelings, thoughts, and actions.

Here is an example of the relationships among thoughts, feelings, and actions. Martina was an older woman who returned to college to finish her degree. Although doing quite well, she was bothered by feelings of insecurity, which she called "my stupid

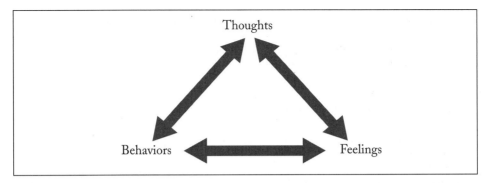

Figure 3-2 No one-way streets: Thoughts, behaviors, and feelings can be the target problem, its antecedent, or its consequences.

lack of self-esteem." Sometimes this problem appeared as a bad feeling, sometimes as an unwanted behavior. The records in her diary looked like this:

A	*B*	*C*
Classmate made a very good comment in a class discussion.	I thought, "He's so smart. I can't express myself like that."	So I said nothing, even though I had a comment. I felt stupid.
Woke up thinking, "There is so much work to do! How will I ever be able to keep up this pace?"	Then thought, "And this is only undergraduate school. I'll never be able to cope with graduate school." Had a fantasy of being exhausted in graduate school.	Felt depressed. Thought about changing my plans, not going to graduate school.
Typing my notes into the computer. I had to type something I had studied last semester, but couldn't remember correctly.	Thought, "God, there's too much to learn. I'll never be able to remember all of it." Had a fantasy of being in an important test in graduate school and not being able to remember all I needed to know.	Felt discouraged.
In class. The instructor was rattling off information like a computer.	Thought, "I'll never be able to remember things like that. I can't even remember things I learned last semester. I'll never be able to be a Ph.D." Actually went to my advisor to talk about changing my plans for graduate school.	Was depressed; felt really bad for several hours.

After a week and a half of this pattern, Martina realized that her overgeneralized self-criticisms and unflattering comparisons of herself to others were discouraging her. "I saw three kinds of negative thoughts I was having, which sometimes lead me to feel bad, and sometimes lead to self-defeating behavior, such as not asking a question in class or thinking about dropping my plans." Now she could begin a plan to rid herself of these negative thoughts. Notice that sometimes her thoughts led to bad feelings she wanted to be rid of and sometimes to behaviors she wanted to change.

Thoughts can be visual as well as verbal. Sometimes Martina's thoughts came in the form of things she said to herself—"He's so smart. I can't express myself like that"—and sometimes in the form of fantasies, like little film clips she ran in her mind, as when she fantasized being exhausted in graduate school.

Record your thoughts or fantasies as soon as they occur. If you delay making entries in your structured diary, it is difficult to remember all the important details—and you will need to see those details in order to see what effect the thoughts and fantasies have on your actions and feelings.

What the Diary Tells You

People working on indulgent behaviors—such as overeating, drinking, or smoking—find that situations they think are unrelated to the problem can be closely connected to it. For example, a man who had been dieting successfully for several weeks kept a diary of the times he indulged in binge eating. He found that the only two times he had binged—such as eating most of a box of Girl Scout cookies—came in the evening of days when the stress at work had been severe. This surprised him, as he had been unaware of any connection between the day's stresses and his overeating problem.

A smoker who kept a structured diary centered around the question, "Why do I light a cigarette?" found that all of the following situations stimulated smoking: any social gathering; a cup of coffee; being bored, angry, depressed, or excited; certain times of day; and after every meal. If you don't believe that a situation can control your behavior, watch people who are trying to stop smoking when they are in certain settings—for example, during a morning coffee break when others are smoking. Smokers feel impelled to light up when in certain situations.

The point of keeping a structured diary is to find out which situations affect your behavior. Discovering the pattern of your behavior may take time and patience, and you may need to make many entries. We suggest that overeaters keep track of all the food they eat over a period of several weeks. Often they find that they eat in response to particular situations rather than in response to an internal feeling of hunger. Excerpts from the eating records of our student, Tracy, are shown at the top of page 77.

Over several days Tracy saw that when she made impulsive decisions about what to eat, she tended to eat high-fat junk food. When she planned ahead, she did much better. She also saw that she uses food to pep herself up. Later she substituted exercise to energize herself.

The process of diary keeping is most helpful in showing you what it is that you need to change. The analysis may shift your focus of interest from the original behavior of concern to some feature that seems to influence it. For example, Tracy realizes that she needs to focus on planning her eating.

A	B	C
Easter dinner. I knew it would be a feast, so I tried not to overeat.	Just took one helping of most things.	Worked out well; didn't overeat.
Watching TV, felt sluggish.	Went to kitchen to get potato chips to eat.	I felt pepped up.
About 4:30 P.M., felt hungry.	Ate a large ice cream cone.	Less hungry, but, boy, that's a high fat snack!
Too busy to make lunch to take to school.	Bought chips and a baloney sandwich and a Coke.	It was a lunch. But yuck.

Here is another example of this process. An elementary school teacher, Jill, observed her patterns of depressed feelings. She wrote:

> I was in my yard gardening, which usually makes me feel very happy. But I began to feel uncomfortable and stopped to think why. It felt like depression, but there was nothing to be depressed about. So I wondered about what I had been thinking just before I felt depressed. And then I remembered that, a minute before, I had imagined this scene: I'm in my classroom, at the beginning of next year, and I'm teaching fifth grade (just as I will be) instead of my usual third. The class is a shambles. The kids aren't understanding anything, they are misbehaving, and I can hear the principal coming down the hallway. She comes in the door, stands, and glowers at me. . . . I imagine things like this often. I even have a name for them—my incompetence fantasies. And I believe they depress me. So I'm going to record instances of fantasies about incompetence, find out what sets them off, and try to get rid of them.

She moved "incompetence fantasies" to the center column of her diary and recorded antecedents and consequences of her fantasies.

Notice events that lead to your unwanted actions, feelings, or thoughts. Tell yourself, "Notice what happens just before my target appears." Jill started noticing what she was thinking just before feeling depressed.

A man who wanted to lose weight was trying to hold himself to 1800 calories each day. He realized that every day he went over the limit. So he told himself to notice what he was doing, feeling, or thinking when he made the decision to go over the limit for the day. In this way, he noticed a pattern of thinking, "Well, just this once, a couple of hundred extra calories won't matter." But of course it did because he did it nearly every day. Keeping records enabled him to discover the pattern.

Keeping records encourages you to think about why you are doing certain things. Martina, the woman who overgeneralized her weaknesses and too often compared herself unfavorably to others, said,

> I felt I was being realistic in my self-evaluations, but I wasn't. I'm still an undergraduate, but I was comparing myself to graduate students and my professors. It's because I'm their age that I made the comparison, but it isn't realistic, because they have had lots more training. Someday, maybe, I'll be as good as they are.

You learn to make this kind of differentiation by keeping records of your thoughts and behaviors and analyzing the patterns that emerge.

Stop. The changes you are undertaking require thought. Before reading on, take a few moments to reflect on how you can use the ideas just presented. Make a few notes to yourself. How could you change your behavior by changing the situation, the antecedents, or consequences?

An example: "Let's see, I want to stop pulling my hairs out. How could I use these ideas? Well, I could keep a diary to see what the antecedents of the hair pulling are, or what the consequences are. Okay, each time I pull my hair, I'll make a diary entry like that. I wonder what I'll find?"

Peter, whose target was to reduce what he considered an "unhealthy" amount of time viewing pornography on the Internet, noted at this point, "Okay, Ill keep a record of what happens before I flip to the porn channels—what I'm thinking, the physical setting, stuff like that—and what happens after."

Recording Frequency and Duration

Sometimes you don't want to know the As and Cs of your target as much as you want to know how much or for how long you do it.

Simple Counting—Frequency or Duration

The easiest kind of record is a simple count of how often you do something, called the frequency. Hal wanted to get more exercise by walking up the three flights of stairs to his office instead of taking the elevator. He put up a piece of paper just inside his office door, and for each day, he made a check if he climbed the stairs.

Climbing Stairs	
Monday	✓ ✓ ✓
Tuesday	✓ ✓ ✓ ✓
Wednesday	✓ ✓ ✓
Thursday	✓ ✓ ✓ ✓
Friday	✓ ✓

Ray wanted to keep his total number of drinks to no more than 12 per week, so he made a mark on a sheet he kept at his desk each day:

Sunday	✓
Monday	✓ ✓
Tuesday	
Wednesday	✓ ✓
Thursday	
Friday	✓ ✓ ✓
Saturday	✓ ✓ ✓

Debbie wanted to increase her vocabulary. When she encountered a word she didn't know, she wrote it down in her notebook. Later she looked up its meaning in the dictionary. Inside the dictionary she kept a chart like this:

Number of words looked up		
Monday ✓	Monday ✓	Monday ✓✓
Tuesday ✓✓	Tuesday	Tuesday ✓
Wednesday ✓	Wednesday	Wednesday
Thursday ✓✓✓	Thursday ✓✓	Thursday ✓
Friday ✓	Friday ✓	Friday ✓✓✓

Maureen decided to record the number of minutes she actually spent studying and the number of minutes she was "ready to study." The latter category included long sessions deciding which course she should study for, as well as sitting at her desk talking to her roommate, thinking about other things, or reading a novel that was not assigned. Her chart looked like this:

Maureen's time studying					
	Monday	Tuesday	Wednesday	Thursday	Friday
Ready to study	45	30	35	50	0
Actually studying	15	10	20	30	0

Maintaining a strict count like this helps one see the difference between engaging in the actual, desired target behavior and engaging in other, related behaviors. By keeping a strict count of the amount of time you actually engage in the target behavior, you can learn what you are doing *instead of* the desired behavior and how that interferes with meeting your goals. You may come to realize, as in Maureen's example, that you spend a large amount of time doing things that are not your target behavior. Being "ready to study" is not studying. Many productive writers keep a "strict count" of the time they spend writing and don't allow themselves to count the time they spend on the phone, making coffee, and so on.

Maureen recorded the *duration* of her behavior. This is desirable whenever length of time is an issue. Some students find that they spend too much time on their easy courses and not enough on their hard ones, so they keep records of how long they spend studying their easy versus hard courses (Richards, 1985). When studying for a test, many students spend more time studying the material they already know than the material they don't yet know, which clearly defeats them on the test (Lan, 1980). It's reassuring to study material you already know, but may not be the best strategy when getting ready for the test. Once you know this, you can take steps to avoid it.

People who eat too rapidly can keep track of how long they take to eat each meal (Britt & Singh, 1985) because slowing down helps control overeating. An elderly couple who had been advised by their doctor to exercise at least 45 minutes several times a week made a record on a sheet they kept above their desk:

Monday:	Walked 50 minutes
Tuesday:	
Wednesday:	Walked 20 minutes
Thursday:	Walked 50 minutes
Friday:	
Saturday:	Walked 60 minutes

People undertaking self-change projects have counted many different behaviors. For example:

- A woman sets daily goals for herself and counts how many she reaches each day.
- A man who wants to improve his relations with co-workers counts how many times per week he is nice to one of them.
- A college student records the number of "chews" of smokeless tobacco he takes each day.
- A volleyball player who wants to improve counts the number of times he successfully spikes the ball per game or practice hour.
- An exerciser keeps track of the number of times per week she uses her exercise machine.
- A man records on a chart on the wall of his home office if he has paid his bills each month.
- A student records each day if he goes to class or not. Later he records how often he speaks in class.
- A young man records what he spends his money on, particularly concentrating on impulse buying.
- An office worker records the number of self-critical thoughts she has when dealing with rejection by others.
- A young woman who feels she is "way too pessimistic about myself" counts the number of times she thinks something positive about herself.
- A father records how much time he spends with his children.
- A writer makes a note of the exact time she begins her daily writing, carefully notes each time she takes a break, and at the end of her scheduled writing period marks down the total time spent writing.
- A jogger keeps track of how many miles he runs each week.
- Another dieter keeps track of junk food eaten, between-meal snacks, and bed-time snacks.
- A student keeps track of the number of times per week that he says something nice to his parents.

Sometimes counting frequency or duration will also provide ideas about the antecedents or consequences of the target behavior. Trent wanted to know how often he was jogging. "I had been going out several times a week, but since Thanksgiving a funny thing happened, and I've hardly gone out at all." He kept a sheet on his bathroom wall on which he made a mark each day he went jogging. The sheet looked like this:

	Jogging			
	Week 1	Week 2	Week 3	Week 4
Sunday		✓		✓
Monday				
Tuesday	✓	✓	✓	✓
Wednesday				
Thursday			✓	✓
Friday				
Saturday	✓	✓	✓	✓

Trent could see how many times a week he jogged and ask himself whether it was enough. But the chart yields even more pieces of information. Just by glancing at it, Trent noticed that he never seemed to go out on Mondays, Wednesdays, or Fridays. Tuesdays and Saturdays, on the other hand, seemed made for jogging. This observation led him to ask, "Why don't I jog on those three days?" and "What makes it easy on those other two?" He could determine what it was that interfered with his exercising on certain days, but made it easy on others.

Positive and Negative Self-Recording

Positive self-recording means keeping track of your successes, no matter how small, while negative self-recording means keeping track of your failures (Kirschenbaum, 1994).

Tracy, our student who was trying to control her weight, had difficulty avoiding the high-fat muffins when the snack wagon came around at work. Day after day she marked in her eating diary, "10:00 A.M. bran muffin." This was increasingly discouraging: "I felt like I couldn't resist the damned things. As soon as I saw one, I took it." On day six, however, she said to herself, "This is ridiculous!" and she selected a banana from the wagon instead of a muffin. Proudly she recorded the banana in her eating diary—at last a success! In the next few days she lapsed back into eating muffins again, but she said, "I knew now I could control those muffins, and it was just a question of time until I began selecting fruit every day instead." A week later she noted that she had eaten a banana or apple every day and no muffins.

Recording only your failures is discouraging. A lengthy record of all the times you are depressed or have negative thoughts about yourself can lead you to think even more negatively about yourself. It can be so discouraging that you give up your attempts to change. On the other hand, keeping records of your successes, even if they are small compared to your eventual goal, will increase your confidence that you are making progress and will enhance your feelings of self-efficacy—the belief that you are capable of reaching your goal.

Record positive behaviors as well as negative ones (Johnston-O'Connor & Kirschenbaum, 1986). This allows you to see progress as well as problems. Smokers should keep records of the times they *avoid* the temptation to light up, as well as the

Box 3-1
The Art of Virtue: Early American Self-Modification

© Bettmann/CORBIS

Benjamin Franklin—statesman, scientist, inventor, and author—knew the value of record keeping in changing one's behavior. He had in mind writing a book called *The Art of Virtue* on how to achieve goals such as not overeating or overdrinking ("temperance," to use his word), letting others talk, keeping things in order, meeting goals, avoiding waste, being clean, staying calm, and being industrious (Knapp & Shodahl, 1974). *The Art of Virtue* never did get written, but Franklin left records in his personal journal of his attempts at self-modification, using techniques of self-observation much like those in this book.

times they give in to temptation. A mother should record the times she avoids spanking her kids and thinks of some more positive response, as well as the times she hits them. If you stick to your diet for 6 days and then overeat, you should feel good about the 6 days even if you regret the 7th. Too often, dieters notice only the times when they fail to stick to their diet (Ferguson, 1975) and become unnecessarily discouraged. Depressed people suffer a similar distortion of perception, failing to notice the pleasant events of life. As a result, they see their whole lives as disappointing (Rehm, 1982). One of the current treatments for low self-esteem and depression is to teach clients to notice the good things that happen to them and not to focus only on the bad (Layden, 1982).

In fact, those who record only a series of failures are likely to stop self-observation altogether (Kirschenbaum & Tomarken, 1982), and that will lead to the collapse of your self-modification plan. The woman who wanted to decrease her "pessimistic" thoughts about herself was careful to keep records of the positive thoughts she had about herself, so she wouldn't become discouraged and stop her plan to change.

Your successes may be small at first, but this is all the more reason to record them. "Well, it's true that I only studied for the scheduled amount of time one day last week, but I *did do well* on Tuesday. Now I've got to build on that. I'll make better grades if I do."

Franklin first made a list of the target behaviors, which he called virtues. He then kept records of his successes and failures for each of the targets. Here is a sample of one of his record sheets:

	Sun	*Mon*	*Tues*	*Wed*	*Thurs*	*Fri*	*Sat*
Temperance							
Letting others talk	X	X		X		X	
Keeping things in order	XX	X	X		X	X	X
Meeting goals			X			X	
Avoiding waste		X			X		
Being clean							
Staying calm							
Being industrious							

He worked on one set of behaviors at a time, writing an X each time he didn't meet his personal goals. (Note: This was a mistake. He hadn't read our section on positive and negative recording. He should have checked off when he met his goals, not when he didn't.)

He says he was successful, however. "I was surprised to find myself so much fuller of faults than I had imagined, but I had the satisfaction of seeing them diminish." He learned something about himself from his self-observations, and used that to improve.

Stop. Before reading on, take a few moments to think of a way you can record how often you perform your target behavior or for how long. Be sure that you think of ways to record your successes instead of just focusing on your failures. This will make your work easier when you come to Step 3 at the end of the chapter.

Steven wants to reduce the number of "senseless arguments" he has with his girlfriend. He decides he can count the number per week. He then thinks, "But I should also count the number of nice interactions we have, too, so I won't just be focusing on the negative. Then I guess I'll try to increase the number of nice times while reducing the stupid arguments."

Rating the Intensity of Emotions

Sometimes your target for change is an emotional reaction, such as anxiety or depression. You wouldn't want to record simply whether you felt the emotion or not, because you will want to see if it grows more or less intense by your efforts at change. You'll want to discover what leads to intense reactions—positive or negative—so you can know what to do to improve things.

A rating scale is useful to measure intensity of emotion. You assign each event a number according to a prearranged scale. For example, a psychologist asked a client to rate how distressed she felt as she tried to cope with frightening thoughts that she had (Kirk, 1989). The client rated how distressed she felt using this scale:

0	1	2	3	4	5	6	7	8	9	10

not at all   moderately   extremely distressed;
distressed   distressed   as bad as I could
                                                 possibly feel

Susan Baird and Rosemary Nelson-Gray (1999) suggest rating either anxiety or depression on a scale that uses the familiar 0 to 100% idea:

Nervous:

    0%   20%   40%   60%   80%   100%
  calm   panic

Depressed:

    0%   20%   40%   60%   80%   100%
not at all   very

Jon Carlson (1995) conducts courses in stress management and asks his students to rate their stress from 0 to 10. Students rate their stress before and after their attempts to reduce the stress. This allows them to see if their strategies are having any effect, even if it's only a small one at first. They can also ask, "What do I need to do to have a larger effect?" Here is a sample of one student's records:

	Before Stress Management	*After Stress Management*
Monday	7	3
Tuesday	9	6
Wednesday	3	2
Thursday	6	3
Friday	3	2
Saturday	9	7
Sunday	3	2

The student concluded that when her stress level was very high—9—she needed to do all the stress management tricks, and do them more than once, so that she could reduce not just from 9 to 6 or 7, but even lower. (Whether you use 0 to 10 or 0 to 100 makes no difference.)

Interesting facts about yourself can be learned by ratings. For example, people who rate their energy or tension levels may discover that some undesirable behaviors, such as overeating or smoking, are actually efforts to increase their energy or reduce their tension

(Thayer, 1989; Thayer, Peters, Takahasi, & Birkhead-Flight, 1993). This knowledge allows them to begin substituting other behaviors that have the same good effects—energy increase, tension reduction—without the bad side effects.

When your goal is to change some emotional state, you won't go immediately from discomfort to total comfort. By rating your comfort, you will be able to see that you are making progress, as the next case demonstrates.

Stuart's goal was to increase his feelings of happiness and make his depression less intense. He used a 9-point rating scale (Tharp et al., 1974) in which the points had these meanings:

+4   superhappy
+3   happy
+2   good feeling
+1   some positive feeling
 0   neutral
−1   some negative feeling
−2   bad feeling
−3   sad
−4   superdepressed

(Note: Stuart might have better chosen a 10-point rating scale. When in doubt, use a 10-point or a 100-point rating scale.)

Stuart rated his feelings four times a day—at each meal and at bedtime. He also made notes about antecedents that led to feelings of depression. His records for two days looked like this:

Time	Rating	Comments
Breakfast	+1	Feel okay.
Lunch	−2	Sinking. Reason is that I ran into John and he made a couple of "funny" remarks about my not making the basketball team.
Supper	−1	
Bedtime	−3	Had an argument with Beverly [his girlfriend].
Breakfast	0	
Lunch	−1	Had to take a test. Worried because my grades have been dropping.
Supper	−3	Beverly says I'm getting "paranoid and irrational" because I worry too much.
Bedtime	−3	Just want to get this day over.

After several days Stuart reported, "I rely on external sources for approval and positive reinforcement—friends, co-workers, Beverly. Disagreements, confrontations, and disputes create tension and frustration. My mistake is that I dwell on them too long and end up either thoroughly angry or very depressed." By rating his reactions, he discovered what sorts of events made him feel bad and began taking steps to change his reactions to them. On another day his records were:

Time	Rating	Comments
Breakfast	+1	
Lunch	−1	At least it's an improvement, because I had another argument with Beverly. I'm staying calmer, didn't freak out over it.
Supper	−1	My grade on the test wasn't good, but I've started on a plan to increase studying.
Bedtime	+1	Randy said I seemed to be feeling better. It shows!

If you are rating your depression over the course of a day, you should record four times per day or more. If you are rating your anxiety, you can rate it each time you confront the situation that makes you anxious. For example, if you are dealing with anxiety about interacting with the opposite sex, you might make two ratings in the morning because you have two opportunities to talk to others, then not make any ratings for several hours while you are at work, then later make several ratings when you are off work, socializing in the dorm.

Whenever you discover the antecedents that lead to changes in your emotions, be sure to note them immediately. That gives you important information you can use to change yourself. If one person makes you a lot more nervous than another, you'll want to know that, to see if you can figure out what it is about the one that is less anxiety producing. Rodrigo reported, for example, that he felt calm when talking with "average" female students, but got nervous when talking to "sophisticated" ones.

You may change your scale as you learn more about your own behavior to allow for distinctions that are important to your particular goal. For example, a man whose goal was to overcome nervousness about speaking in front of a group started with a scale that ranged from 1, "perfectly calm," to 5, "panic." After rating a few experiences, he noticed that he often wanted to assign a number in between two of the numbers on his original scale, so he expanded it to a 10-point scale. "In class giving a speech" was about 9; "having a speech assigned" was around 3; "preparing the speech" was 5; "waiting to give it" was 8.

Combining Types of Record Keeping

In the example above, Stuart not only rated his emotions, but also kept a structured diary of the antecedents that led to various emotions. Adele, whose case was presented at the end of Chapter 1, rated her level of stress in dealing with her girls' basketball team and also counted the number of times she yelled during practice or a game. Box 3-2 provides examples of combined ratings and other forms of self-recording.

One of our students was trying to avoid depression by fighting her tendency to dwell on thoughts that people didn't like her. To achieve this goal, she decided to replace

Box 3-2
Brain-Power Bowling and a Headache Diary:
Examples of Combined Record-Keeping Forms

Here are two record-keeping forms that combine aspects of structured diaries, counting, and ratings of emotion, just to give you more ideas you might use in your own recording. Note that each form reminds the person keeping the records what to do and gives a chance to rate how well it was done.

I. **Headache Diary**. Adolescents who are receiving psychological help—with the same kinds of techniques you are learning here—use this for migraine headaches (Lascelles, Cunningham, McGrath, & Sullivan, 1989). The teenagers learn to record their negative and positive coping reactions to stress, and rate how they feel as a result:

Stressful situation: _____

Negative thoughts: _____

Tension level rated   1   2   3   4   5   6   7   8   9   10

Coping strategies: _____

Praising self for coping: _____

Resulting tension level   1   2   3   4   5   6   7   8   9   10

II. **Brain-Power Bowling**. A record-keeping form on which the person records seven different aspects of his or her bowling stance, and rates how well each was carried out (Kirschenbaum, 1984).

$$0 = \text{didn't do it well}$$
$$1 = \text{good}$$
$$2 = \text{very good}$$
$$3 = \text{excellent}$$

_____ *Foot position:* same starting point each time.

_____ *Stance:* shoulders squared, elbow tucked into hip, knees relaxed.

_____ *Grip:* same grip for every shot, thumb and palm position correct.

_____ *Spot:* pick a spot and watch your ball roll into it.

_____ *Approach:* take 2–3 second delay, walk in a straight line.

_____ *Push away:* elbow tight and locked, straight pendulum-type swing near body.

_____ *Finish position:* lead foot pointed toward spot, body balanced, square at the line.

Box 3-3
Mitch's Records of Antecedents
and Feelings

Antecedent	Crossing street in front of cars.
Thought	Thought everyone would be looking at me; felt my posture was bad and I was too stiff.
Feeling	
Behavior	Became really self-conscious and ended up fulfilling my prophecy by not walking naturally.
Consequence	Felt dumb.
Antecedent	Saw a fantastic girl walking my way.
Thought	
Feeling	
Behavior	Wanted to smile but ended up looking at the ground as she passed.
Consequence	Felt stupid because I know girls like confident guys.
Antecedent	Morning class, wanted to clarify a word on the board.
Thought	Pictured myself raising my hand, speaking, and mumbling—Mitch the klutz.
Feeling	My heart began to pound very rapidly. Rated -1. [He was using a rating scale of $+2$, $+1$, 0, -1, -2.]
Behavior	Told myself to relax, and raised my hand.
Consequence	Very nervous at first, but glad I had asked the question.
Antecedent	Sitting down, saw a girl from last semester's geology class whom I never got to know. She looked right at me.

her negative thoughts with memories of situations in which people had clearly liked her. She used a rating scale to keep track of her feelings but also counted "the number of times each day that I successfully switch from thoughts that people don't like me to memories of times when people did like me." Thus, she combined rating her feeling with counting how often she was able to change her feeling.

Mitch combined keeping a structured diary and rating his emotional reactions. He wrote: "I tend to be very self-conscious, especially when I feel I am drawing attention to myself or being evaluated by someone whose opinion I value, which is just about everybody. I tend to think too much about the consequences of my behavior before I act and to focus on the negative outcomes that are possible. This makes me uptight, and it also makes me lose the timing of my actions, so they seem awkward."

Mitch decided to keep track of the Antecedents to being too self-conscious; the physical setting, his Thoughts, Feelings, and Behaviors in the various situationsand the Consequences of his actions. Box 3-3 has his records of the more outstanding examples.

Thought	
Feeling	
Behavior	I didn't smile (I don't like my smile). I thought she would look again, but she didn't.
Consequence	Felt bad, but . . .

Behavior	I got up purposely, caught her on the way out, and started to talk to her.
Consequence	Felt nervous, rated −1. But I was glad I made the effort.

Antecedent	In the library, came to a table with a girl sitting on one side.
Thought	
Feeling	
Behavior	I was hesitant to sit down right away, so went to the restroom to make sure I looked okay. Came back, sat down, looked at my ring binder.

Thought	Began to think about my bad points; thought I'd make a bad impression if I spoke to her.
Feeling	−2
Behavior	Didn't say anything.
Consequence	Left later feeling disappointed.

Antecedent	In class, teacher said he was going to go around the room asking for comments.
Thought	
Feeling	My heart started to pound. Panicked. Rated −2.
Behavior	Started to rehearse what I would say.
Consequence	Ended up okay, but mad at my nervousness.

Note that Mitch kept track of his successes as well as his failures. Note also that by recording his emotions, he saw that he could perform even when he felt uptight. This, he told us later, increased his self-confidence and actually lowered his nervousness. It's one of the most encouraging findings we've seen over the years: People can often do something that they think they cannot do because they are too nervous, and finding this out decreases their nervousness.

Stop. Are there parts of your target problem for which you should make a rating? Any part for which *intensity* is an issue—such as an emotion—should be rated for its intensity. Pause now and think how you will make that rating. This will help you do the planning exercise at the end of the chapter. For instance, Kanoa wants to reduce the level of stress he experiences in his job, which involves a lot of throughway driving. He begins by rating his stress level on a 10-point scale four times a day, then searches for ways to reduce the stress level.

Practicalities of Record Keeping

Record your target behavior as soon as it occurs. Don't wait until the end of the day and then try to remember how many times or for how long you engaged in the target behavior. Your count will not be accurate. As soon as the target behavior occurs, stop and record it (Epstein, Miller, & Webster, 1976; Epstein, Webster, & Miller, 1975). Don't wait until the end of the day to record your depression or anxiety level for the entire day, either—many people make too pessimistic a rating when they do.

You may find yourself thinking that you don't need to write something down. You're sure you will remember how much time you spent doing the target behavior or what the situation was or how you felt emotionally. *Wrong.* If you don't keep fairly strict written records, you'll find that your records are useless.

When we teach self-modification, a few students are adamant: They do not need to keep records. They're sure they know what they're doing. If you are one of these, please try this little test (Brown, 1987). Jot down your estimated frequencies of the target behavior—cigarettes smoked, food eaten, or whatever—for several days. Then really keep records for an equal number of days and compare for accuracy. If you try this, we bet you'll end up agreeing that your estimates were inaccurate. Besides that, you won't have the information on antecedents and consequences that record keeping provides. Try it.

What to Record

Notice in Box 3-2, on brain-power bowling, that the bowler does *not* record the number of pins knocked down. Instead, she records the behaviors performed while bowling. Where did she place her feet; where were her hands? This makes an important point: You may want to keep track of your progress toward some goal, but the important thing to pay attention to *via* recording is the *process* you are going through (Zimmerman & Kitsantas, 1996). You don't record your number of strikes and pins knocked down; you record adherence to good bowling posture.

Similarly, someone wanting to lose weight may weigh once a week or so to note progress toward the goal, but the important thing to record is amount and kind of food eaten and exercise. If you record food eaten and exercise taken you are much more likely to reach your goal of weight loss.

A student wanting to improve his grades, as another example, would of course pay attention to grades on tests and papers, but the critical thing for him to record are the behaviors he has to perform in order to get good grades: time management, good study procedures, adequate test preparation, and so on.

Pay attention to the *process* so you can improve the process, and the goal will happen. In one study a group of high school girls were taught how to be competition-level darts throwers (Zimmerman & Kitsantas, 1996). Half the girls focused on the question, "Where is the dart hitting the dartboard?" The goal, of course, was to hit the center. But the second set of girls were taught to focus on questions like, "Did I hold my elbow close to my body? Did I finger the dart lightly? Did I notice how my arm worked?" In short, they focused on the process to reach the goal, and they focused on improving the process. This group of girls ended up much better dart throwers than the first group. *Focus on the process. Keep records of the process, and try to improve it.*

Making Recording Easy

The recording device has to be portable and readily accessible. A smoker can keep a note card inside the cigarette pack. Many people use a 3" × 5" card or some other piece of paper that will fit conveniently in a pocket, bag, or notebook. If you have a portable, handheld computer, you can use it to punch in your records. This has the advantage that it may total your daily or weekly output, too.

Fit record keeping into the pattern of your usual habits. Devise your system so that it will remind you of itself. For example:

- Time management—a sheet inside your day timer
- Spending money impulsively—a card inside your wallet
- Too much TV watching—a chart beside the chair where you sit to watch
- Going to bed too late—a chart beside the bed
- Not studying—a record inside your notebook or at the place where you study
- Eating too much—a card beside your place at the table
- Between-meal snacks—a record sheet on the pantry or refrigerator door
- Exercising—a chart by the closet where you keep your exercise gear
- Socializing—a 3" × 5" card that is always in your bag or pocket, or an entry in your PDA

Verna had a hard time dealing with one of her co-workers. She made a list of four things she wanted to remember to do when she was with him: listen to him without interrupting, ignore his slightly rude remarks, pause before replying to him, and stop trying to figure out his motives, which just made her frustrated. She kept this list in her desk. When she was about to talk with the man, she would take out the list, glance over it, and then hold it while talking to him. As soon as she finished talking, she would check off each item she had successfully performed.

In some cases, you can use a wrist counter (which is worn like a watch) or a golf counter. This helps when the target is something you do very often, such as some nervous or verbal habit. For example, Ed wanted to stop swearing and found that it happened about 200 times a day. Taking out a 3" × 5" card and marking it so often would have been tedious, so he used a golf counter. Use whatever sort of counter you find convenient. The easier it is to keep records, the more likely you are to keep them.

If you anticipate recording problems, you are more likely to deal with them. One of our students wanted to keep track of certain thoughts he had while talking with other people. To make notes on a card while talking would have looked silly. On the other hand, he was afraid he would forget if he waited until the conversation ended. His solution was to move a penny from his left to his right pocket each time he had the thought he wanted to record. After he left the person, he would count the pennies in his right pocket to see how many times the thought had occurred in the course of the conversation. Then he recorded the information on a note card.

A woman who wanted to increase the number of times she performed a particular behavior carried toothpicks in her purse and moved one into a special pocket of the purse after each occurrence. A cigarette smoker started out each day with thirty cigarettes and counted how many he had left when he got home in the evening.

If you perform the behavior but discover that your counting device—a 3" × 5" card or whatever—is not there, improvise. For example, a knuckle cracker found a big leaf at the beach and tore a small hole in it each time he cracked his knuckles. Later he transferred this record to his regular chart. A smoker who left his scoring card at home kept the matches he used to light his cigarettes as a record of how many cigarettes he had smoked.

Written Storage Records

When using 3" × 5" cards or other devices for keeping records, you need to transfer the information to a more permanent storage record. A woman with the nervous habit of pulling off the skin on her feet and legs kept a count like the following one:

	Pulling Off Skin													
Day	1	2	3	4	5	6	7	8	9	10	11	12	13	14
Number of times per day	7	9	11	8	4	8	12	7	10	7	9	2	9	2

For her storage record, she made a graph that she posted on the wall of her room.

A woman who wanted to be a professional writer kept a record of the number of hours she wrote each day and the number of pages she wrote. At the end of each week, she added up the daily totals and transferred this information to a permanent chart she kept posted on the wall next to her writing desk.

	Total Hours Writing per Week	*Number of Pages Written per Week*
Week 1	14	5
Week 2	17½	20
Week 3	17½	19
Week 4	15	22
Week 5	9½	9

Some people keep their storage records in terms of percentages. For example, you could keep a record of the percentage of occasions for assertion on which you actually were assertive or the percentage of "study time" that you actually spent studying. For many students who are inefficient in their study time, keeping a record of the amount of time one is "on target," that is, truly studying, is helpful, and sets the goal of increasing the percentage. This can have the delightful effect of reducing the total amount of time required, for as the percentage of time on target goes up, the total time required to get the job done goes down (Watson, 2001).

Sometimes you can combine your daily observations with the permanent record. For example, Allan kept his chart with his musical instrument. This way, the chart was always there when he needed it and could serve as both a daily record and a storage record.

Record keeping and record storing must be adapted to each person's own behaviors and situations. If the various systems described here don't suit you, improvise one that does.

Summing Up

There are four rules for self-observation:

1. Do the recording when the behavior occurs, not later.
2. Be accurate and strict in your counting. Try to include all instances of the target.
3. Keep written records.
4. Keep the recording system simple. Fit it into your usual routine.

Stop, again. Before going on, sketch out a plan for your own recording—you'll be asked to do it more formally at the end of this chapter. Does your tentative plan fit the four rules above?

The Reactive Effects of Self-Observation

When a behavior is being observed, it often changes. Think what it's like to have someone closely observe your behavior. When your track coach or dance teacher or lab instructor says, "I'm going to watch you very carefully now," don't you perform in a different way than you do when no one is observing you? You feel self-conscious; you take greater care.

Perhaps the behavior will become less smooth or automatic, as Mitch's did when he became self-conscious about the way he walked across the street. Or it may improve, just as an actor's performance can be enhanced by the presence of an audience. These effects are also produced when you are your own observer. Behavior "reacts" to the observation, and the effect is known in psychology as *reactivity* (Baird & Nelson-Gray, 1999; Mace & Kratochwill, 1985). The size of this effect depends on a number of factors (cf. Critchfield & Vargas, 1991; Kirby, Fowler, & Baer, 1991), but reactivity is so common that some effect can be anticipated.

Occasionally students will complain that they are unable to work out a plan. When asked why, they explain that their problem has gone away. "I started recording my observations regularly, but then I just quit the undesirable behavior I was observing." This, of course, is the happiest form of reactivity. Undesirable behaviors tend to diminish, and desired behaviors tend to increase, because you are observing and recording them. An older man reported, "I developed this irritating habit of plucking out the hairs on my goatee while I was reading. I just started making a note each time I did it, and pretty soon, I stopped."

If you care about a behavior, self-recording often changes the behavior in the direction of your values (Fixen, Phillips, & Wolf, 1972; Lipinski, Black, Nelson, & Ciminero, 1975). This effect is so reliable that clients in psychotherapy may be assigned to observe themselves as part of their therapy, a first step in changing problem behavior (Bornstein, Hamilton, & Bornstein, 1985; Gross & Drabman, 1982). In one study college students who complained of frequent unwanted thoughts of suicide kept track of the thoughts. Self-recording led to fewer unwanted thoughts and less depression (Clum & Curtin, 1993).

The effect works only as long as you record, of course. If self-recording is the only thing you have done in your effort to change, stopping the recording may stop the improvement (Holman & Baer, 1979; Maletzky, 1974). Pablo reported, "I keep records of my daily and weekly exercise. As long as I keep the records, I find I keep exercising regularly. If I quit the records, in a few days I quit the exercise. It's like that little record on the closet door causes me to exercise."

The reactive effects of self-recording can be turned to your advantage. A student reported:

> For some time I felt guilty for not sharing kitchen chores with my wife. But I always seemed to have something else to do, and cooking and doing dishes were not exactly appealing, so I just continued to do nothing. Then I put a chart in the kitchen. Each time my wife cooked or cleaned up, she made an entry, and each time I cooked or cleaned up, I made an entry. It took only a week to get me moving. Now I check the chart each weekend to make sure I'm doing my share.

Another student wrote:

> I enjoy reading, and for a long time I wished I did more of it. But I'd come home from work tired and mindlessly switch on the TV. Then I bought a little notebook and began to keep a list of all the books or articles I read. I got very interested in my growing list. I enjoyed finishing reading something and making an entry in my notebook. I'd get the list out and skim it to see how I was progressing. I'm sure I read more now than I did before, because keeping track of my reading is meaningful to me. It makes me feel good.

You may be able to increase reactivity by changing the timing of recording (Rozensky, 1974). This works particularly well for behaviors we want to stop. For example, people who are dieting can record food intake either before or after they eat. Does it make a difference? In an experiment, some subjects first ate and then recorded the calories, while others reversed the order. Those who recorded *before* eating ate less (Bellack, Rozensky, & Schwartz, 1974).

Absent-Minded or Too Busy to Make a Record?

Some target behaviors are difficult to record accurately because you don't pay close attention to them. For example, you might absent-mindedly pick at your face while watching TV or reading. Other behaviors such as talking too loudly or overeating may be so well practiced that you don't notice them anymore. But if you do not get accurate records, it is difficult to work out a plan for change.

How can you make yourself pay attention? The first step is to deliberately practice performing the problem behavior while consciously attending to it. This paradoxical prescription is actually very sensible: It amounts to practicing paying attention. Once you have learned to pay attention to the habitual target behavior, you can begin a plan to eliminate it.

Garrett, who habitually cracked his knuckles, spent 5 minutes each morning and 5 minutes each evening deliberately cracking his knuckles while paying close attention to every aspect of the behavior. He learned to pay attention when he cracked.

A sophomore had developed the habit of scratching her arms while sleeping. The practice had become so bad that some mornings she woke up to find her arms bleeding. How could she pay attention while she slept? Each night when she went to bed, she deliberately scratched her arms for several minutes while paying close attention to what she was doing. Being awake, she was not in danger of scratching until she bled. But the situation was similar to actually being asleep—she was sleepy and in bed. The woman worked out a plan to replace scratching—first she rubbed her arms, then she patted them, and finally she just touched them. After a few nights' practice, she was not scratching in her sleep anymore (Watson, Tharp, & Krisberg, 1972). The case was followed up after 18 months and then again after 7 years. In the first 18 months, the woman had two relapses and used self-modification both times to correct the problem. During the next 7 years she had no more relapses and remained free of nighttime scratching.

Another way to deal with unconsciously performed behaviors is to ask your friends to point out instances of the target behavior. "If you see me picking my face, will you say something to me? I want to stop." Be sure the reminder is not punishing. If it is, you will focus on the punishment, not on correcting your problem behavior. When Ed's wife said "Ed! You're overeating!" he was embarrassed and irritated. So she changed her reminder to, "Ed, dear, aren't you . . . ?" after which she dropped the subject.

Some people habitually pay little attention to themselves (Buss, 1980). If you are one of these, you may want to take steps to increase your self-awareness, at least so that you can get good records of your own behavior. There are at least three things you can do to increase your self-awareness: (1) listen to your voice on a tape recorder, (2) make a videotape of yourself, and (3) act in front of a mirror (Wegner & Guiliano, 1983).

Solana, for example, had come to realize that she had trouble keeping friends because she often interrupted them and talked while they were talking. She had done this all her life and often did so without paying much attention to her talking—or the other person! "I seem to just say whatever is in my head." Her first task was to learn to notice when she was talking, so she talked in front of her bathroom mirror while paying close attention. She wanted her attention to switch on when she was talking. Later she worked on practicing listening to her friends instead of talking.

Sometimes you are too busy doing something to record a problem behavior right when it occurs. Or perhaps other people are present, and you would be embarrassed to pull out your notebook and make an entry. A widowed man who was looking for a new relationship found that he put off potential partners by rushing too quickly into discussion of marriage. He wanted to learn to go more slowly, allowing the relationship to develop. His rushing behavior occurred while he was socializing with a woman, and of course he didn't want to take out his notepad and record the event while it was occurring. Yet he wanted to be sure to remember to record it afterward, so he could think of better ways of dealing with the situation. He carried a few dried peas in his pocket, and when his conversation drifted too close to marriage he unobtrusively moved a pea into his "target pocket" and said to himself, "Remember this and record it later." These self-instructions to remember helped him recall the specifics later, and that allowed him to develop a plan to better deal with such situations.

A young woman who was lonely at college concluded that her negative opinions of people when she first met them were one of the main causes of her loneliness. "I judge them and find them wanting before I ever get to know them. It's a terrible habit, but I pounce on every little thing the person says and think things like 'What a nerd.'" To keep a record of these thoughts, she moved her pen from one part of her purse to another, to remind herself of the event later. Then, as soon as she could, she would make an entry about the event in her structured diary.

Don't save all your reminders up until the end of the day. If you must use a temporary reminder, make a full record of the incident as soon as possible.

Devising a Plan for Record Keeping

Suppose that the very act of making observations is upsetting to you. You don't keep records because you can't stand the news—smokers hate to learn how much they smoke; overweight people don't like facing up to how much they eat each day; socially unskilled folks will not enjoy seeing how rude they sometimes are. This is *not* an unusual situation, and if you're in it, you will be tempted to stop keeping records. That's when your focus should be most clearly on keeping good records however. The records force you to recognize the conflict you are in: You'd like to quit smoking, but you do enjoy your cigarettes. Too often the solution is simply not to record the unwanted acts, but that ensures that you will continue the unwanted behavior.

You can use self-direction strategies to develop record keeping. Self-recording is itself a behavior, and it follows the same principles as other behaviors. If you are failing in this first step at self-change, then self-recording itself is the most appropriate first target in self-improvement. Make accurate record keeping your first target behavior. Here are four techniques that you can use to deal with problems in keeping records.

First, when keeping records seems too hard, try adding just one item at a time (Hayes & Nelson, 1986). Start with a simple plan, get used to it, and make it more complicated later. Remember Verna, who had difficulty getting along with one of her co-workers. She needed to keep track of four different aspects of her relationship with him, but this seemed too complex. So she required herself to record only one aspect—ignoring his unfriendly remarks. After she practiced this for a few days, she added a second aspect—listening carefully to him. After several more days, she was able to record both. She then added the third, and then the fourth.

Second, provide a cue that reminds you to make records (Heins, Lloyd, & Hallahan, 1986). Powell wanted to keep records of his studying each night, but he often forgot to do so. He simply set the beeper on his wristwatch to go off at 11:30 to remind himself to make an entry on his record sheet.

Another cue to keep records are your own reminders to yourself. As Janice passes through the lunch line, she murmurs to herself, "Remember to write down what I eat." As Emanuella decides to stop studying for a while, she says to herself, "Be sure to write down what time I started and stopped, so I'll know how much I studied." Hal, who wanted to lose weight, posted his food-eaten record right on the refrigerator to remind himself to make entries if he snacked in the evening. As you will see in Chapter 5, self-instructions are a powerful way to control your own behavior.

Third, ask someone else to check whether you are keeping records. You don't have to show the actual records to the other person; just indicate that you are keeping them. For example, a young man who wanted to cut down on his drinking was upset when his records showed that he drank an average of nine beers a day. His first reaction was to stop keeping records. But he wanted to cut down, so he asked a friend to inquire each morning if he had kept records for the previous day.

Fourth, reward yourself for keeping records (Stuart & Davis, 1972). A woman who had been overweight for several years realized that she needed to keep records of what food she ate if she was going to lose weight. At first this seemed a burden, so she rewarded herself with $5 a week to spend on her hobby if she kept records of her food intake. Once this became a habit, she switched to rewarding herself for exercising.

Last Stop. One of the main reasons self-modification projects fail is lack of good records. If you suspect that record keeping will be difficult for you, use one or more of the ideas above to your developing plan.

Jules wanted to lose weight, but knew that he also loved overeating, and suspected that he would not want to record what he ate every day. "I want the joy of pigging out." Sure enough, when he began a self-change plan he often failed to keep records. After a few weeks he realized he'd never lose weight if he didn't know how much he was eating, and in what situations he was overeating. He decided to keep his eating record in a little 3" × 5" notebook that he always carried, to remind himself, "Keep the records. I have to get control of my eating!" and to ask his wife to inquire each evening meal if he was keeping records. These steps helped him gain control.

Planning for Change

You are now in a phase known technically as the baseline period. This is a time when you make self-observations but don't engage in other efforts to change. Your records constitute a baseline against which future changes can be evaluated.

Sometimes your baseline is just the beginning point, and you use it to evaluate your progress. Jules decided he needed to exercise to lose weight, so he joined a gym and went there to lift weights. On his first visit he did two 10-rep sets of bicep curls, two sets of presses, and two sets of thigh exercises. Six weeks later he was doing three sets of seven different exercises, so he could see that he was making progress in the process of exercise.

If a target behavior never occurs—such as if Jules never went to the gym—there is no point in trying to record it. If you never study and your target is to develop studying, you already have a baseline count—zero. Yet even in this situation, there is value in self-observing: to pinpoint the cause of your not studying. A period of self-observation in which you ask, "What are my opportunities to study?" or "What am I doing instead of studying?" or "What thoughts do I have that keep me from studying?" is valuable in formulating a plan for change.

Juan reported, "I don't think I realized, but after keeping this kind of record I saw a pattern in my nonstudying: I sit down to study, then ask myself, 'What's on TV?' switch it on, just to check, and end up watching TV and never studying. Or I think, 'Wonder what Sal is doing,' call him, and don't study."

In general, it is best to make self-observations before trying to change. The advantages gained with more self-understanding outweigh the disadvantage of a short delay.

How Long Should You Gather Baseline Data?
The baseline period should be continued until it shows a clear pattern. You might want to know the average number of times per day or week you perform some action. For example, you could find the average number of minutes per week that you study, or the average number of cigarettes you smoke each day, or the average amount of exercise that you get each week. There is often daily fluctuation, and an average is needed to get the big picture.

Once you know the average, you can see if you are gradually improving as you begin your plan for change. Important changes usually occur gradually, not instantly. You

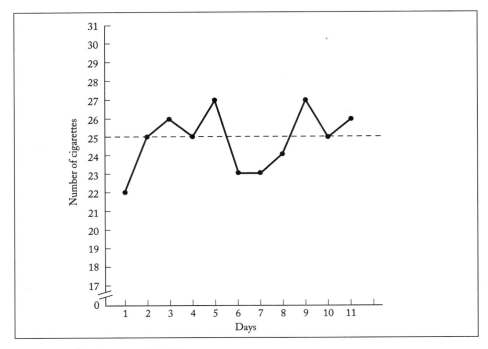

Figure 3-3 Cigarettes smoked daily

don't go from a little exercise to a lot of exercise in a couple of weeks. Knowing your average allows you to see that you are making progress toward your goal.

A graph is useful for this purpose. (Chapter 8 includes detailed instructions for constructing graphs.) Figure 3-3 gives an example of a fairly stable baseline. From the graph, you can see that this cigarette smoker shows some variation in the number of cigarettes smoked each day. For the first few days, the pattern is not clear. By the end of the 11th day, however, it is apparent that his daily average is about 25. He also needs to discover the antecedents that lead to smoking, but he does know his average and can begin a plan for changing.

Figure 3-4 shows the number of hours a college student studied each night. At the end of the first week, she has only the roughest idea of her weekly study time because within that week her schedule varied so much. She needs to continue her baseline period for at least another week. During this time she can discover when opportunities for studying occur.

You probably won't get a stable baseline in less than a week. Daily activities vary from day to day, and even for behaviors that occur quite frequently, it will take several days for a consistent pattern to emerge. Some behaviors never show a stable baseline. Complaining, for example, or outbursts of anger may be quite variable because they depend at least partly on how provoking other people's behavior happens to be.

You need to ask yourself, "Is the period of days or weeks during which I have been gathering baseline data representative of my usual life?" If, for example, you are counting the number of hours spent studying and midterms were last week, then that week wouldn't be considered a typical week and shouldn't be used to make an estimate. If you smoke more at parties and in the last 3 days you went to three parties, you shouldn't use that

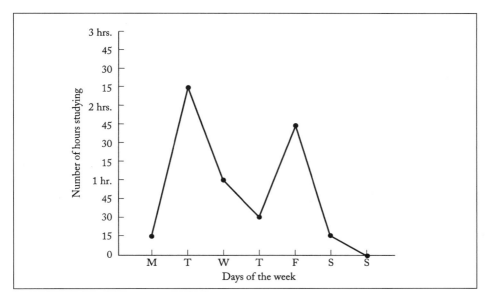

Figure 3-4 Number of hours studied daily

period as a base for estimating how much you smoke on the average. The record does have value in suggesting an antecedent that you could avoid later: Don't go to parties when you're trying to stop.

Reliability

You need to be concerned with the accuracy or reliability of your self-observations. In the self-recording of behavior, ask yourself, "Am I really recording each occurrence? Am I recording the same events in the same way each time they occur?" People are often a bit inaccurate or unreliable in their self-recording (Nelson, 1977), but if you are very unreliable, you won't learn enough about yourself to be able to work out a good plan for change. Particularly, if you try to make estimates of how often you do something instead of actually counting it as it occurs, you will not get a reliable measure (Farmer & Nelson-Gray, 1990; Nelson-Gray et al., 1990). Remember, you are trying to develop new skills, and that requires knowledge of results so you can improve (Patrick, 1992).

You must have relatively accurate records and self-observations in order to know how to begin to change or whether or not you are changing. If you think that you tend to snack too much whenever you're at home, but in fact the problem behavior occurs only when you're watching TV or are lonely, your plan for self-change is not likely to be successful. You've got to discover the A-B-Cs of your problem behavior. If you are unsure how many hours per week you really do study, then you may not notice a small but definite improvement in your study time and may abandon a self-change plan that in the long run would have worked.

There are several tactics for increasing the reliability of your observations:

1. Make direct observations at the time the behaviors occur.
2. Have careful definitions of the target behavior, so you are sure whether it occurs or not.

3. Pay careful attention and, if necessary, practice paying attention.
4. Have a simple recording device, not one too complicated to use.
5. Use cues to remind you to record, such as keeping the recording device where the target behavior occurs, or instructing yourself to remember to keep records.
6. If necessary, ask others to remind you to record.
7. Work out a self-reward plan to encourage recording.

In some cases, you won't be sure of everything you should observe until you have read Chapters 5, 6, and 7 as you learn more about antecedents, behaviors, and consequences of your target problem.

Tips for Typical Topics

These "Tips for Typical Topics" at the end of some chapters provide general ideas that researchers and clinicians have found useful in organizing for change. In the material below, you will also find some contraindications for certain topics—goals that should not be attempted through these methods. If your situation matches these contraindications, we recommend that you choose some other topic for learning the skills of self-direction.

Anxieties and Stress

What are the situations—antecedents—that make you anxious? Is it a specific kind of situation such as taking a test or being in a social situation? Record the situation, and then rate your feelings in it (Deffenbacher, 1981). Use a rating scale from 0 to 10, for example, where 0 is no tension and 10 is maximum tension. Keeping track of your rated anxiety may lower it (Hiebert & Fox, 1981).

In studying the situation, note your own thoughts and reactions, as they may cue the anxiety. For example, people who get anxious on tests tend to think less about the test than about their anxiety or the consequences of failure (Wine, 1980). They attend to the threat and not to the task at hand. People who become fearful in social situations do the same thing, attending too much to their worries about making a bad impression and too little to the other people (Watson & Friend, 1969).

If you feel stressed, keep a daily log of confrontations with problem situations. Record your thoughts, feelings, physical reactions, such as sweaty palms or rapid heartbeat, and your relevant behaviors (Meichenbaum, 1985). Also record anything you do during the day to relax, as you'll want to increase this later.

People who are anxious typically notice events that touch on their anxiety more than they notice other events (Sarason, Pierce, & Sarason, 1996). This means that if you are anxious, you have to be careful to record events that make you feel good, instead of just focusing on what makes you feel anxious, for you will tend to overnotice what makes you anxious.

Do not use this self-observation period to focus more on possibly failing. You may already do that too much (Spurr & Stopa, 2002; Woody & Rodriguez, 2000). What you need to discover is what sets off too much anxious self-focus, so you can reduce it.

Contraindications. Do not attempt this topic if you are suffering from panic attacks or other disabling, severe intrusions of anxiety that are mysterious and frightening to you. Determining the antecedents of panic attacks is difficult and may require professional assistance. If you are unsure about the issue, consult with your instructor or counselor.

Assertion

The assertive person is one who (1) behaves appropriately in social situations, (2) is honest, and (3) is able to express thoughts and feelings straight forwardly while taking into account the feelings and welfare of others (Rimm & Masters, 1979). Assertion is not the same thing as aggression. It is quite possible to be appropriate, honest, and expressive while staying courteous. Some people spend a lifetime full of resentment and disappointment because they are unable to assert their own self-interests and consequently feel used, bullied, or exploited. Yet many (especially women) are ambivalent about becoming too assertive, for fear that they will be disliked or shunned for being too "aggressive."

To develop a more effective assertive repertoire, first record instances in which you feel you were assertive. Second, note specific kinds of situations in which you could have been assertive but were not. Also record what you did and its consequences. Later, make a note of what you might have done instead.

Why weren't you assertive? Two classes of targets have been suggested for increasing assertiveness (Mizes, Morgan, & Buder, 1987). First, you may not know how to perform the appropriately assertive behaviors. You're not sure what to do, or you fear you would do the wrong thing. What did you do instead of being assertive? Second, your thoughts about assertiveness may interfere. What did you fear would happen?

Keeping a structured diary will help you discover the reasons why you are currently not assertive enough. Look for some or all of the following obstacles: not knowing how to be assertive, anxiety, thoughts about disasters that might happen, and actual reactions from others.

Being assertive is a social skill. You'll benefit from reading the section on social skills below.

Depression and Low Self-Esteem

This topic includes feelings of low self-worth, discouragement, negative moods, and mild depression. In Chapter 1 we reported a case of self-modification of depression, and your general strategy should parallel that one.

How you think about yourself is affected by your mood. Mood affects memory and colors your view of life. Lowered mood affects what you notice in your daily life (Kohn, Lafreniere, & Gurevich, 1991; Strauman, 1992). You tend to notice the negative. Mood also affects what you remember about the day's events (Eich, Rachman, & Lopatka, 1990; Rohde, Lewinsohn, & Seeley, 1990). Again you tend to remember the negative. Some people have a tendency to notice negative events in their lives and to remember them better (Swann, Wenzlazff, & Tafarodi, 1992) and to cast everything, including their view of themselves, in a negative light (Jorgensen & Richards, 1989; Malle & Horowitz, 1995). Their mood darkens their view. They may even feel that this negative view is realistic (Ackerman & DeRubeis, 1991; Epstein, 1992) and gives them true insight into themselves (Lyubomirsky & Nolen-Hoeksema, 1993). If you are depressed, your self-view will probably be unrealistically pessimistic (Brown, 1991) even though it may seem realistic to you.

Being depressed—or being anxious—can also cause you to focus too much on your inner states, your moods, or dark thoughts (Wood, Saltzberg, & Goldsamt, 1990; Wood,

Saltzberg, Neale, Stone, & Rachmiel, 1990). The need for self-observation is *not* an invitation to this kind of unpleasant rumination.

Definitely do *not* focus on your own perceived inadequacies or negative characteristics (Kuiper & Olinger, 1986). You probably do that too much already, and doing so will only decrease your self-esteem further. Do record *positive* self-evaluations (Gauthier, Pellerin, & Renaud, 1983; Layden, 1982) and note *positive* events in your daily life (Rehm, 1982).

Rate your mood at least four times each day. Work out a scale for this. You will probably find more fluctuation in mood than you thought, including pleasant moments. Only rarely is a day all bad (Rehm, 1982), but when we are depressed we sometimes remember only the bad parts. Keeping a record of the better parts will correct this "mis-memory."

You may be depressed because of specific problems that are worrying you. For example, are you not getting along with important others (Biglan & Campbell, 1981)? Do continuous thoughts about these problems lead to lowered mood? Counting such thoughts, and later taking steps to reduce them, may be the best strategy.

There are several different causes of depression (Heiby, 1987). Some people need to develop specific skills—for example, the ability to get along well with others—while others may need to eliminate negative thoughts about themselves (Heiby, 1986). If you can target your plan for change to specific problems, you'll increase your chances of success (McKnight, Nelson, Hayes, & Jarrett, 1984).

The thoughts that bother depressed people often involve excessively high standards for personal behavior, self-criticism or mental self-punishment for transgressions, and over generalization of a single failure to the whole self-concept (Carver & Ganellen, 1983). People with low self-esteem probably suffer these same problems. Each can be recorded and targeted for change.

Contraindications. Do not attempt this topic if you are having ideas of self-harm or suicide, or if your depression is severe enough that you are disabled from performing your daily routines. The procedures in this text are those that would be suggested by a counselor or psychotherapist, but severe depressions require some professional guidance.

Exercise and Athletics

What are the antecedents that you need to do your exercise? What currently keeps you from exercising? For example, how does it fit into your schedule? What excuses do you make to yourself? You need to discover the answers to these questions.

For many years one of us kept daily records of exercise using a coded system:

VB	Time each day playing volleyball
Ten	Time playing tennis
R	Number of miles jogged
su	Number of sit-ups
pu	Number of push-ups
G	Number of grip exercises
Sw	Number of yards swum

The codes are entered for each day. A typical day might look like this: R 2.5, su 30, pu 10. Another day might be: Sw 300, G 60. This allows one to keep records in a compact form. They can be displayed on a paper, perhaps taped to the closet door, so that you can inspect them daily to check on progress. We've found that for us just keeping the record is enough to keep us exercising; it's reactive.

Over the years the type of exercise may change. As it does, new codes are invented. Our new system is Wts. For time spent lifting weights, B for miles biked or time spent biking, W for miles walked or time spent walking, and Sw for swimming. Making the record easy is important.

Relations with Others: Social Anxieties, Social Skills, and Dating

A variety of problems fall in this category—inability to get along with others, shyness, need for better communication—but all involve monitoring the effect that others have on you and increasing your skills to deal with social situations. Plan to record the details—the A-B-Cs—of your social interactions.

Probably you will do the recording later, not while you're with people. When you are actually interacting with others, do not make the mistake of paying too much attention to your own behavior and too little to them (Gambrill & Richey, 1985). One of the best ways to make a nice impression is to pay attention to—show interest in—the other person. Don't focus much on what the other person thinks about you; many shy people worry too much about that (Hope, Rapee, Heimberg, & Dombeck, 1990).

Discovering antecedents is vital in understanding shyness because shy people often avoid social situations. What are the antecedents that lead to avoidance—physical situations, social situations, your own thoughts? For example, do you tell yourself you can't make a good impression? Or do you suspect the other person is thinking negative things about you?

Try writing down what you did in a social situation, and then write down what you might have done instead. This will help you see what behaviors you want to develop. Be sure to record positive instances of good social behavior as well as negative.

Problems with other people often involve communication—not listening, not saying what one feels, being abusive, not communicating at all—and the way problems are solved—no solutions or poor solutions. Watch for these as you record the details of your target behavior.

Smoking, Drinking, and Drugs

Don't hesitate to choose problem drinking as a goal for self-change. Research indicates that behavioral self-control strategies are more effective than other approaches (Walters, 2000). Keep track of the situation you are in, and make a rating of your emotional state when you indulge (Marlatt, 1982). Record the antecedents and consequences of your indulgence. When do you smoke or drink too much? What are you saying to yourself just before you indulge? What do you get out of it?

You are trying to find out *why* you indulge as well as *how often*. Certain situations or moods may lead to indulging. When you have coffee, for example, you smoke. When you are nervous, you drink. Later, you will be able to use that information to formulate a good plan for change (O'Connor & Stravynski, 1982). For example, if you find that you often indulge as a way of relaxing, you may start a plan to learn to relax in other ways. Or you might discover what situations are most tempting and begin to avoid them (Marlatt & Gordon, 1985).

Be sure to record urges to indulge that you resist. If you want to have a cigarette but resist the urge, record that (O'Banion, Armstrong, & Ellis, 1980).

Once you have quit, plan to continue keeping records. It's been shown that it helps you keep abstaining (Kamarck & Lichtenstein, 1988).

Don't avoid trying to quit smoking just because you've tried before and failed. Many people try three to five times before finally stopping (DiClemente, 1994). You may experience, for a period of about 30 days, some increases in anxiety, difficulty concentrating, irritability, and restlessness (Hughes, 1992).

Including nicotine chewing gum or transdermal patches as a part of a self-control strategy increase success rates (Cepeda-Benito, Reynoso, & Erath, 2004; Fortmann & Killen, 1995) and reduces noxious side effects. When you use these you are changing the behavioral habit but not the addiction and will have to gradually wean yourself from the addiction later. So if you can succeed without nicotine replacement, it's probably easier, but if you cannot succeed, then use the replacement long enough to control the habit, and then wean yourself from the addiction.

Some smokers are worried that quitting will cause undue weight gain. There is no reason to avoid launching a plan both for weight loss and smoking cessation; neither will undermine the other (Spring et al., 2004).

Studying and Time Management

Controlling your study time is the single most important thing you can do to do well in college, more important even than your SAT score (Watson, 2001). Students who develop good time management tend to do much better in college than those who do not, so it is worth the effort to develop the skill.

Before establishing a full time-management schedule, you'll need to know how you currently use your time. Prepare a daily log, and mark the beginning and ending time for each change of activity. Buy a small daily appointment book for this purpose or make your own daily sheets. Mark when an activity begins and when it ends. For example:

7:00 A.M. Woke up and got ready to go to school.
7:42 A.M. Watched television while I ate breakfast.
8:15 A.M. Left the house.

For studying, record how much time you were in a position to study and how much time you actually spent studying. This will allow you to find the percentage of time you're on target. Many students find to their surprise that they are on target only a small percentage of the time that they're in position. For times when you did *not* study, record what you did instead and the consequences. For example, did you mean to study but end up watching TV or talking with friends?

Record your actual studying behaviors. The quality of your studying is as important as the quantity. Do you read and underline? Do you make notes? The kinds of study techniques outlined in Box 1-1 in Chapter 1 significantly improve learning. Also, see Box 2-6 on taking tests in Chapter 2. Focus on the process of studying—that's what you want to improve—and don't worry about the grades. Improve your skill and they will come.

Weight Loss and Overeating

"Most experts on the treatment of obesity agree on at least one thing: Self-monitoring is the single most important element of effective weight control" (Kirschenbaum, 1994, p. 100). See Box 3-4 on "The Mindful Diet." Many overweight people seriously underestimate how much they eat every day, and heavier people are

Box 3-4
The Mindful Diet

One of us (DLW) was overweight as a child and has fought it most of his life. Through most of adult life I was able to keep my weight under control through some degree of self-control and a lot of exercise. But as I neared the magical age of 70, and retirement, my exercise decreased, I slowed down a little, and I went up to 40 pounds overweight.

Permanent weight loss means changing bad habits. The research is very clear: Those who lose weight and keep it off for long periods of time make at least three changes (Fletcher, 2003; Wing & Klem, 2002). They exercise, they eat less-fattening foods, and they keep track of their weight and take action before they regain what they have lost. How was I going to achieve this? *By becoming much more aware of my eating behavior.*

The idea was to gradually increase my self-control over eating by keeping a constant record of what I eat, a self-therapy based in self-observation (cf. Karoly, 2005). The first key to weight loss is self-monitoring; without it, self-control over eating doesn't occur (Baker & Kirschenbaum, 1998; Latner & Wilson, 2002).

I began keeping a complete daily eating record, on a thick 5" × 8" notebook kept on the shelf between the kitchen and dining room (or on a pocket notebook when away). The rules were simple: Watson, write down everything you eat! And second, if I ate too much, write down the probable reason: "lost in TV watching, and ate the whole sandwich" or "wanted to feel full" or "we were all in a party mood, and I had a drink." Those were the situations—or antecedents—that set the occasion for overeating.

What was I learning by writing this? First, I was learning that certain situations, antecedents, led to unwanted eating, but others did not. I rarely overate at breakfast, for example, but often did in the evening. I learned that almost always when I thought, "I'll just have a few," of some tempting food, I would eat too much of it. Using the techniques you will learn in chapters 5, 6, and 7, I worked on gaining control in these situations.

Second, I noticed a conflict between my motive to lose weight and my motive to enjoy eating, and saw that the strength of the two motives changed over time. Neal Miller first observed this in classic research on conflict in the 1940s (cf. Dollard & Miller, 1950). When I was not hungry, when I was not confronting attractive food, my motive to control my eating was stronger, and I would make plans to do so. For example, I would set a rule: "When snacking, don't eat more that 100 calories worth of nuts." But when confronted by the snack food, it seemed my motive to control would switch off, and I would break my rule and eat too many nuts. In theoretical terms, when I was distant from the goal of eating, my motive to control was stronger, but when I was close to the food, my motive to eat was stronger, and the self-control switch was turned off.

By recording all I ate I was seeing this process in my life. If you force yourself to keep records even when you are out of self-control, you force yourself to

(continued)

Box 3-4 *(continued)*

see that you are violating your own standards (cf. Carver, 2003; Silvia & Duval, 2004). Keeping the record lets us see how we are behaving and forces a comparison between how we want to behave and what we actually do.

The important element is persistence. Bad habits change slowly. You must practice through your mistakes. It's like learning to play the piano: You expect to make many mistakes but understand that if you continue practicing then one day you won't make the same mistake any more.

Keep honest records, and then think and write notes to yourself. For example, if your weight is up today and you know you had three beers last night, you have to see the relationship and admit it to yourself. Epictetus (A.D. 55–135) wrote, "Self mastery depends upon self-honesty." Once you have the habit of recording, it is no longer tedious; it is effortless. Try it. It might change your life. It certainly improved mine, by 30 pounds.

---

most prone to this error (Klesges, Eck, & Ray, 1995); many underestimate their daily calorie intake by as much as 2,000 calories (Chedd-Angier, 1994).

People who are successful at weight loss keep self-observations of their food intake and the reasons for it (Foreyt & Goodrick, 1994). In one study overweight people who did *not* keep track of their eating over the (dangerous) Christmas period gained 57 times as much weight as overweight people who did keep records (Baker & Kirschenbaum, 1993). In fact, the best way to be sure you don't gain weight over the dangerous holidays is to keep careful track of your eating (Baker & Kirschenbaum, 1998; Boutelle, Baker, Kirschenbaum, & Mitchell, 1999).

Learn the antecedents to your eating: the time, physical place, and social situation (Campbell, Bender, Bennett, & Donnelly, 1981). What were your feelings, the location? Were you with particular people or alone? What were you saying to yourself just before you overate? Also record the consequences: What did you get out of it? You may eat to relax, to get rid of stress, to celebrate, or to escape boredom or depression. If you do, you want to find out so that later you can consider seeking rewards or relaxation in other ways.

Focus on the process of controlling your eating, not on how much you weigh. Weighing once a week is enough. Weighing too often can be discouraging.

Contraindications. Do not attempt weight loss if you really don't need to lose weight. The majority of females and about one-fourth of men who are objectively normal weight perceive themselves to be overweight (Cash & Hicks, 1990). There is a near epidemic in this country of excessive and unnecessary dieting for purely cosmetic reasons, and you should be very cautious in determining whether you actually need to lose weight before setting out to diet. Cosmetic dieting can produce a mind-set that can lead to anorexia and/or binge eating. We recommend that you carefully consider, in consultation with your friends or physician, whether you really do need to lose weight before selecting dieting as a self-change topic. Instead of dieting, for example, you might better try to increase your exercise, which will change your body shape without endangering your health.

Chapter Summary

Why Observe Ourselves?

Self-observation is the first element of self-direction. In deliberate self-change we observe ourselves because we often do not remember our own past accurately, and because it provides information to detect gradual improvement.

Structured Diaries

The situations that control our behavior can be divided into antecedents and consequences of the behavior. To identify both, keep a structured diary in which you record the behavior, its antecedents, and its consequences:

Antecedents (A)	Behaviors (B)	Consequences (C)
When did it happen? Whom were you with? What were you doing? Where were you? What were you saying to yourself?	Actions, thoughts, feelings	What happened as a result? Pleasant or unpleasant?

Entries should be made as soon as possible after the event. The diary will tell you what situations affect your actions, thoughts, and feelings. Use entries to figure out how to change your behavior by changing the situation.

Recording Frequency and Duration

You can count either the amount of time you spend doing something or the number of times you do it. Record successes as well as failures, even if your successes are at first infrequent.

Make plans for how you will carry out your self-observations. Anticipate what problems may come up, and figure out how you will deal with them.

Rating the Intensity of Emotions

Rating scales allow you to gauge the intensity of an event. They are particularly useful for recording feelings and emotions. A good technique is to combine the use of rating scales with counts of actual behaviors.

Practicalities of Record Keeping

Keep records of the behaviors that will lead to whatever goals you have, not just the goals.

Four rules for self-observation are:

1. Do the counting when the behavior occurs, not later.
2. Be accurate and strict in your counting. Try to include all instances of the behavior.

3. Keep written records.
4. Keep the recording system as simple as possible. Try to fit it into your usual habits.

Sometimes the very act of recording your behavior is enough to produce change if the change is something you want.

If you perform the problem behavior absentmindedly, practice performing it while paying close attention so that your attention is switched on whenever the behavior occurs. Ask others to point out instances of the target behavior. For behaviors that are difficult or impractical to record immediately, find some way to make a mark and instruct yourself to remember and record the incident later.

If you are failing to self-observe, your first plan for change should be to work out a system to increase accurate self-observation. Develop record keeping one step at a time. Give yourself instructions to record at the appropriate time. Reward yourself for keeping records, and have others check on your record keeping.

Planning for Change

Data recorded before beginning a plan can serve as a baseline against which future progress is measured. The baseline record should be continued until the pattern is stable. This usually requires at least a week.

Reliability is increased by specific definitions, careful attention, simple recording procedures and cues to remind you, and practice. A plan for self-change should not begin until after a stable, reliable baseline has been achieved, because only then will you really know the extent of the problem and its exact nature.

Your Own Self-Direction Project: Step 3

You should now begin self-observation for the behavior-in-a-situation you chose in Step 2. For your self-observation, use a structured diary, a frequency count, a rating scale, or a combination of the three.

Make record keeping easy, and build it into your daily schedule. Don't go directly into an attempt to change. First observe the target behavior as it is now occurring. Collect baseline records for at least 1 week. Be as accurate as you can.

While you are gathering data, read the next five chapters, which deal with the principles of behavior and the techniques of change. When you have adequate self-observations, you will be ready to begin your plan for change.

It only takes us a few lines to make these suggestions, but it should take you quite a bit of planning and thinking to work out a good self-observation system and begin it. It's worth it: Almost all successful self-change plans start with adequate self-observation.

Chapter 4

The Principles of Self-Regulation: Theory and Practice

Antecedents
17. What role is played by the cue, or antecedent, in operant behavior?
    a. When does an antecedent become a cue to behavior?
    b. What guides avoidance behavior? To what does the person respond?
    c. What is stimulus control?
    d. Why is avoidance behavior resistant to extinction?

Respondent Behavior and Conditioning
18. What is respondent behavior?
19. Explain respondent conditioning.
    a. What is higher-order conditioning?
    b. How does emotional conditioning occur?
    c. After a reaction has been conditioned, what effect does the stimulus—or antecedent—have?

Modeling
20. Describe learning through modeling.
21. List the principles presented in Box 4-1.
22. What is reward discounting?

Chapter Summary

Your Own Self-Direction Project: Step 4

You have taken several steps toward self-change: selected a goal, identified the behaviors that need to be adjusted, and begun to keep records of your present behaviors. These steps are giant ones. Establishing goals and collecting self-observations are in many instances sufficient to bring about behavior change. This is often astonishing to people who find that they are somehow changing a problem behavior after failing before, and the only apparent difference is that they are keeping records. This phenomenon has also puzzled psychologists. But in the past 25 years, psychologists have begun to solve the mystery. The power of setting goals and keeping records is now well explained by theory.

In this chapter we review the major psychological theories that offer explanations for self-directed behavior. During the past decade, the major energy in the field of self-directed behavior has been in theory development—a necessary process for scientific advancement. But none of the various theories is dominant, and at the present time, none alone is sufficient to guide the practicalities of all self-change. Each theory has particular strengths; each faces continuing challenges. Considered together, they provide understanding and guidance for how to achieve personal goals.

Regulation Theory

Regulation theory is a body of thought in psychology derived initially from cybernetics (Wiener, 1948). Cybernetics, or the science of self-regulation, has had a major impact on contemporary scientific thought, from physics to sociology, and has produced all manner of self-regulating machines, from automatic pilots to the self-tuning radio. Cybernetics has also influenced a number of psychological theories of self-regulation, each with different emphases, but all sharing certain basic cybernetic principles (Carver, 2004; Carver & Scheier, 2001; Kanfer & Stevenson, 1985; Miller, Galanter, & Pribram, 1960; Mithaug, 1993). What are these basic and highly influential principles? What is cybernetic regulation theory?

The thermostat of your home heating system is a simple example of the mechanisms discussed in cybernetic theory. The thermostat has very few parts and functions. It has a *standard* set to the desired indicated temperature. It has a *sensor* (a thermometer) that responds to actual temperature. It has a *comparator*, a device that compares what the temperature is to what it should be. And, finally, it has an *activator:* When the discrepancy between actual and desired temperature is too great, the activator closes the circuit and turns the heater on or opens the circuit and turns it off. Thus, a reasonably good fit between actual and desired temperature is maintained. These few elements are at the core of all self-regulating machines, from self-guiding rockets to home robots.

Most self-regulation of human behavior contains the same elements: We each have *standards* for our behavior; we have *sensors* to see what our behavior actually is; *comparisons* are made between the two, and when we perceive a discrepancy, we *activate* to change. Now you can see why your own first steps toward self-direction—setting standards and collecting observations—may bring about significant change. If you collect those observations and compare them to your standards, you will activate for change. This activation requires an energy source (in machines, perhaps electric current or a battery). In cybernetic control theory, the energy required for human activation is attributed to physical energy provided by food or to *attention*. Simply *attending* to a problem area can activate us for careful observation and comparison. Another source of activation is *emotion*. When you compare your own behavior to a standard, a favorable comparison produces feelings of optimism or happiness; a disappointing comparison evokes negative feelings, such as frustration, discouragement, or depression. This in turn affects further goal setting, particularly raising or lowering standards (Carver, 2004; Mischel & Ayduk, 2004).

This theory is a very powerful tool for the understanding of all human behavior, even behavior that is not going well. For example, we know that much behavior is *not* effectively regulated. The reason—according to cybernetic theories—is that no change would be expected when standards are lacking, when we do not notice our own behavior, when we do not compare it to our standards, or when actions are not available to us that would bring behavior into line with our standards.

Regulation theorists vary in the "purity" with which they use cybernetic formulations. Carver and Scheier (e.g., 2001), the influential social psychologists, center their analyses of self-regulation on cybernetic formulations. Kanfer (e.g., 1975), an influential figure in self-regulation theory, incorporates considerations of reward, punishment, learning, and thinking. Karoly (1993) adds elements of systems theory. Mithaug (1993) adds and emphasizes problem solving to account for the variety of responses that we make between "comparison" and "activation." And there are others, such as radical behaviorists, psychoanalysts, and humanistic psychologists, who do not use cybernetic concepts at all.

What are the challenges facing cybernetic theories? First, psychological and behavioral systems are infinitely more complex than are mechanical systems. A thermostat activates by either opening or closing. But when a person discovers a discrepancy between standards and actuality, he or she must choose among a thousand alternatives, and cybernetic regulation theory does not guide us to understand these choices.

A second challenge is that in complex human behavior the "standard" or goal is adjusted continuously as one moves closer toward the goal and better understands the real conditions that the goal entails. That is, intentions, images, anticipations, and values cause the standard to continuously evolve. Some cybernetic theorists discuss a "feed-forward" mechanism, so that the sensors "feed back" our self-observation data to the standard for comparison, but also "feed forward" the data to the goal, which is also modified (Ford, 1987). Now, in complex machines like self-guiding missiles that "feed-forward" mechanism is hard-wired into the circuits (Karoly, 1995). For these and other reasons, Carver and Scheier (1982) incorporate elements of systems theory into their view of self-regulation.

A third challenge to cybernetic theory is that activation is not always possible: We may never have learned the appropriate action to bring our behavior closer to the standard. Other theories, discussed below, treat ways in which alternative behaviors are learned and kept at ready strength.

Finally, in the actual practice of self-directed change, cybernetics is limited by this fact: *Not all human behavior is self-regulated.* This is particularly obvious in very young children, who are closely regulated by others, but in many instances it is also true for adults. Some behavior is under the regulation of the environment, not the self. Even for the most self-determining person, behavior is intimately connected to the setting in which it occurs.

We have discussed the limitations of cybernetics to illustrate the state of theorizing in this field: Each individual theory faces its own limitations, as will be seen in the presentations below. Cybernetic theory remains a clear, powerful model for understanding much of the structure of situations and actions in which we live. In fact, we exist in a complex ecology of these interlocking systems. Often we have to change one system in order to change our own; much self-regulation is actually learning to control the environment that controls us.

Therefore, the next step in understanding the principles of self-regulation is to examine the relationship between regulation by others and regulation by self. This relationship is a specific focus of *social constructivism,* a developmental theory.

Social Constructivism: Regulation by Others and Regulation by Self

Social constructivism emphasizes that all behavior, as it develops, passes through the following sequence: (1) control by others, (2) control by self, and (3) automatization. Thus, not all behaviors, much less all persons, are self-regulated. Self-regulation is a stage of development that lies between the point where assistance is required from other people and the point where the regulation or assistance is no longer needed—it has become automatic. The automaticity of everyday life is pervasive (Wyer, 1997). Even for the most self-actualized adult, each new learned behavior passes through this same sequence (Tharp & Gallimore, 1988).

Try to recall what learning to drive was like. Your instructor is beside you. The traffic is moderately heavy as you approach an intersection, and you are concentrating on staying in your lane at a safe distance from the car ahead. Twenty yards from the intersection, the traffic light snaps from green to amber. "Stop!" your instructor says. "There won't be enough time to get through." You stop slowly and safely.

Approaching the next intersection, you watch the traffic light more closely. When it changes to amber, it is likely that you'll say to yourself, "Stop!" and do so. You may actually speak to yourself aloud; more likely, it will be a "mental" message—subvocal speech. In either event, this is self-regulation—a self-instruction that helps you come to a smooth, safe stop. Soon you need no regulation. Braking at the sight of the amber light is now so automatic that you need no instructor or self-instruction—you just stop.

Each new behavior that you develop through your self-modification project will go through that same sequence. In most instances, either this text or your instructor or other advisor will provide the needed regulation, assistance, or "control" by others. The second stage of the sequence will be represented by your own acts of self-regulation: refining your standards, inventing observational methods, or using self-instruction. In the last stage, your new behavior will become as automatic as driving your automobile, and you will need to think about it as little as you think about your driving.

This sequence of behavior development is widely discussed in contemporary developmental psychology (Rogoff, 1982; Rogoff & Lave, 1984; Tharp, Estrada, Dalton, & Yamachi, 2000; Tharp & Gallimore, 1988; Vygotsky, 1978). All the details of this theory do not concern us here. The main point is that each new competence added to your repertoire passes from regulation by some outside source to self-regulation. At the point that competence is fully developed, the behavior becomes automatic—consciously regulated neither by others nor by you.

Does automatic, fully developed behavior run free, entirely disentangled from the world around? Not at all. When behavior is fully automatic, it has come under the control of antecedent cues in the environment. But if at any time your automatic behavior does not meet your standards, it is possible at any time to bring it back under your own self-regulation. This is accomplished by directing your attention to your own behavior. The simple acts of attention will break up the automatic sequences of habits. Just as highly skilled desirable behavior can suffer by paying attention to it, automatic undesirable behavior can be "broken up" by attention. This is another reason why the prescriptions in this book for careful and systematic self-observation are so important. Self-observation involves the redirection of attention, and attention breaks up automatic behaviors, which in turn produces the condition for self-change. Of course, once self-regulation has produced the desirable balance between environment and behavior, the behavior will come under the control of new environmental stimuli—that is, it will become automatic again. This recurring cycle is typical of the self-directing, well-adjusted individual (Karoly & Kanfer, 1982).

Learned resourcefulness is the bundle of skills that allows us to retrieve our behaviors from an automatic, "mindless" state. Rosenbaum (1988) has discussed how learned resourcefulness is activated when "mindless" sequences are disrupted. The resourcefulness you will learn will allow you to self-consciously disrupt your unsatisfactory, mindless sequences and bring them under self-regulation.

To understand this recurrent cycle, it is important to understand the basic principles of regulation. Regulation of behavior, whether by others or by the self, takes place through the same basic mechanisms: language regulation, consequences, antecedents, respondent behavior and conditioning, and modeling. Each mechanism operates first by control from the outside and then through control by the self.

Development of Language Regulation

The most common method of controlling behavior is through language. We give orders: "Platoon, halt!" or "Take out your driver's license, please!" We make requests: "Please pass the salt." We give hints: "I suppose it's a good movie, but I'm so tired tonight. . . ." We coach: "Good, good; a little more to the right; that's better. . . ." Hundreds of examples occur in everyone's daily life. Of all forms of antecedents, the language of others (both spoken and written) may well have the strongest and most immediate effect on our behavior. Of course, we do not always comply. We may refuse, ignore, argue, resent, or laugh. But the effects are there. Language is a pervasive, inescapable influence on our reactions. In charting chains of events, you will find that the language of others represents the immediate antecedent of many of your behaviors, both desirable and problematic. The human environment is in many ways a language environment, and the environment controls behavior largely through language.

"Talking to oneself," or self-directed speech, is often considered comical, if not aberrant. It conjures up a picture of an old man muttering to himself on a city street or even of someone in a mental hospital. Actually, self-directed speech is common, useful, often highly adaptive, routine, and normal. For most adults, however, self-directed speech is subvocal. What is the relationship between talking to oneself aloud and talking to oneself subvocally (that is, silently, covertly, or "mentally"—thinking in words)? In fact, the effects of these two forms of self-speech antecedents are virtually identical.

As very young children develop, a first task of their parents is to bring them into the language community. Children learn to heed language and use it. Psychologists Luria (1961) and Vygotsky (1965, 1978) have studied this developmental process in detail and found a regular sequence that is roughly linked to the child's age. Some aspects of this sequence are illustrated in the following example.

"Don't kick over the wastebasket!" the father shouts to the 2- or 3-year-old child. Too late; the trash is on the floor. The father rights the wastebasket and says again, this time more gently, "Don't kick over the wastebasket now." Next day, the child approaches the basket, draws back the foot for a happy kick—and stops midway through. "Don't kick over the basket!" the child says and walks on by. The sight of the wastebasket may for some time cause the child to mutter the instruction aloud. For a while longer, the father may see the child's lips moving in a silent self-instruction. Eventually, all traces of speech disappear, and the child merely walks by, leaving the basket unmolested. No external evidence of self-speech remains. In all likelihood, subvocal speech itself drops out, and the behavior becomes "automatic."

In transferring from control by others to self-control, very young children imitate and incorporate adult speech. First the father says, "Don't kick!" Then the child says the same thing, often imitating emphasis and inflection. Control of the child's behavior passes from parent to child. But notice this: The control by language instruction is maintained. Regardless of who says it, the antecedent "Don't kick!" affects the child's behavior. It is normal for young children to use imitated, spoken-aloud self-instructions for self-control (Tharp, Gallimore, & Calkins, 1984; Vygotsky, 1965, 1978).

At a certain point, around the age of 5, this self-controlling speech "goes underground," in Vygotsky's (1965) apt phrase. That is, the use of self-controlling language becomes subvocal—steadily more silent, rapid, and condensed. Many psychologists would argue that this is when thinking begins, because so much thinking can be seen as subvocal speech. During earlier stages, before language "goes underground," self-instructing aloud helps children perform tasks more efficiently (Luria, 1961).

Even in adulthood, the power of self-directed speech as an antecedent is not lost; it is merely not used as often. Donald Meichenbaum (1977) has demonstrated that verbal self-control can be reinstituted for older children and adults when new skills are being learned, when self-control deficiencies are present, or when a person is in a problematic situation. Self-directed speech (vocal or subvocal) is a powerful controlling antecedent of behavior. It is particularly useful and natural in new or stressful situations. It was useful and natural for you to say, "Stop!" to yourself when you were learning to drive. You probably no longer do so. But the next time you are driving in a strange city, when the amber light stays on a much longer or shorter time than you are accustomed to, you may need to talk to yourself again. When the smooth flow of behaviors is somehow disrupted, conscious self-regulation comes into play (Kanfer & Karoly, 1972). Difficult situations make us more likely to use self-speech. This is one way we "rescue" automatic behavior when it no longer meets our standards.

Thus, you probably talk to yourself in precisely those situations that you find most fearful, most depressing, or most difficult to cope with. This self-speech is likely to be "underground"—probably no more than a mutter, or only a quick "speech in the mind." Regardless of the form it takes, this self-speech antecedent has a powerful influence over your responses to difficulties. Have you ever said to yourself, "This is probably one of those situations in which I'll make a fool of myself," and walked away, lonely and depressed? This kind of self-speech can perpetuate shy responses.

A more general and powerful form of verbal self-regulation is seen in what psychologists call *rule-governed behavior* (Hayes, 1989). People establish rules of conduct for themselves, often by adopting rules taught to them by others, and often distilled from their own experiences. These may be general rules of a high moral abstraction, such as rules to always be kind or loyal. Other rules concern daily schedules such as always rising early, or never having a late assignment. Even children, when doing schoolwork, say rules aloud to themselves to cope with difficult tasks or stress (Berk, 1986). Each rule is actually a verbal statement, self-spoken, that guides interpretations of events and sets standards that people can compare to their actual conduct. These rules are powerful regulators of behavior; indeed, they often insulate our habits from almost any other influence (Catania, Matthews, & Shimoff, 1990). In the self-change procedures presented in this book, self-established rules will play an important role.

In your self-observation, observe yourself carefully as a problem situation unfolds. Try to detect the things you are saying to yourself; they act as instructions.

Principle 1: *From early life to adulthood, regulation by others and the self (particularly through verbal instructions) acts as a powerful guide to behavior.*

Operant Theory: Consequences

A child walks up and kicks a wastebasket. Her mother scolds her and makes her replace the trash. This consequence makes it less likely that the child will upset the basket again. Another child walks by the basket and does not kick it. "Good, Ginny!" her mother says.

"What a good girl!" This rewarding consequence makes it more likely that Ginny will leave the basket unmolested in the future.

Two groups of workers in a furniture company decided to form "quality circles"— discussion groups that management consultants recommend as a way of increasing employee production and morale. One group's supervisor was resentful and accused the group of trying to "go union." The workers dropped the idea. The other supervisor encouraged his subordinates and praised them for their initiative. That group formed its quality circle and put real energy into it.

Different consequences in the form of supervisors' reactions strongly affected each group's behavior. Within the quality circle, when the discussions grew difficult, the workers encouraged themselves with reminders that their supervisor valued their initiative. In this way, they transferred the positive consequences from the supervisor to themselves and moved into the stage of self-regulation.

Operant Behaviors

Behaviors that are affected by their consequences are called operant behaviors. The dictionary defines *to operate* as "to perform an act, to function, to produce an effect." An effect is a consequence. Through operant behaviors, we act, function, and produce effects on ourselves and on our environment. Through the effects—the consequences—the environment acts once again on us. Much of our behavior is operant. Operant behavior includes all the complex things we do as we weave the fabric of our daily lives. Our bad habits are operant behaviors we want to eliminate. The things we don't do but wish we did are operant behaviors we want to develop.

We develop operant behaviors—that is, we learn them—through the consequences of our actions. Operant behaviors are changed—learned or unlearned—as a result of their consequences.

Principle 2: Operant behavior is a function of its consequences. No matter what we are learning to do—type, speak, write, study, eat, kiss, or compose a string quartet—our skills will be strengthened or weakened by the events that follow them. A child learning to speak, for example, will become more verbal if praised rather than scolded for talking. A composer will be more or less likely to write a second quartet depending on the events that follow the first attempt.

Consequences That Strengthen Behavior

The strength of behavior refers to the chances that a particular behavior will be performed. The best practical index for gauging the probability of a behavior is its frequency. We usually infer the strength of a behavior from its frequency. That is, we count how often the behavior occurs. This is why the chapter on self-observation placed so much emphasis on counting occurrences of a behavior.

Reinforcers

If a consequence strengthens a behavior, it is called a reinforcer. How reinforcers strengthen behavior depends on the nature of the consequence.

Principle 3: A positive reinforcer is a consequence that maintains and strengthens behavior by its added presence. Positive reinforcers may be anything—kisses, food, money, praise, or the chance to ride a motorcycle. What is a positive reinforcer for one person is not necessarily a positive reinforcer for another. The list is inexhaustible and highly individualized.

A little boy goes to his father and shows him a picture he has drawn. "That's lovely, son," the father praises him. "I really like it. Hey, what's this part?" he asks, giving the child attention. The father's praise and attention are probably positive reinforcers for the child. They increase the chance that in the future the child will continue to draw and will show his pictures to his father.

A positive reinforcer is anything that, when added to the situation, makes the behavior that preceded it more likely to recur. The composer is more likely to attempt a second quartet if the first act of composing is positively reinforced. This positive reinforcement might consist of one or more consequences: applause from the audience, the pleasure of hearing the work performed, a sense of satisfaction in knowing that the work meets high standards. It is important to note that praise from critics or friends has positive reinforcing effects. Thus, language acts as a reinforcing consequence, as well as an antecedent.

Principle 4: *A negative reinforcer is a consequence that strengthens behavior by being subtracted from the situation.* If you are standing outside and it starts raining hard, you might put up your umbrella to keep the rain from falling on your head. The act of putting up the umbrella is thus negatively reinforced by the removal of the unpleasant consequence of getting wet. The act that took away the unpleasant situation is reinforced—that is, made more likely to happen again.

Picture a person talking to a friend. The friend seems bored. The more the person talks on a particular topic, the more bored the friend seems to be. So the speaker changes to a new topic. Immediately the friend appears less bored. The act of changing topics is negatively reinforced by the fact that the friend is no longer bored. In other words, changing topics removed the unpleasant consequence—the friend's boredom.

Just as with positive reinforcers, what is a negative reinforcer for one person is not necessarily so for another. The saying, "One person's meat is another's poison," expresses this concept.

Contingency

The conditions necessary for a reinforcer to strengthen a behavior are expressed in the concept of *contingency*. For any stimulus to function as a reinforcer, it must occur after, and only after, a certain response. If you gain a reward whether or not you perform some behavior, the "rewarding" stimulus will not actually reinforce the behavior; in fact it probably will not affect it at all. If instead you can gain the reward only by performing the behavior, that behavior will be reinforced and strengthened—that is, it will be more likely to occur again. It is the contingent relationship that is important, not the reinforcer alone. This same principle applies to punishment, as we will discuss later: Both reinforcement and punishment must be contingent in order to function.

Escape and Avoidance

The principle of negative reinforcement explains how we learn to escape or avoid unpleasant consequences. Suppose a mother says, "Come here, please," to a child who is refusing to budge. The child does not come. The mother reaches over and swats the child. The child still does not come. The mother raises her hand again. The child comes. The mother drops her hand. By complying, the child has escaped or avoided a second swat.

Technically, *escape learning* refers to behaviors that terminate an unpleasant consequence. The mother keeps spanking until the child submits and comes along. *Avoidance learning*, on the other hand, refers to behaviors that remove the possibility of an unpleasant consequence. The next time the mother says, "Come here," the child obeys, thus avoiding a spanking like the one he got in the past. In escape learning the unpleasantness is actually delivered, but in avoidance learning it is avoided. (Both escape and avoidance are routes to learning. However, there are side effects—other unintended consequences—to spanking and other forms of punishment that will be discussed below.)

When you analyze your own behavior, you may discover that you do things for which you get no apparent reward. People sometimes think of these behaviors as being "unmotivated," but they are often avoidance behaviors. For example, you may tend to go off by yourself rather than to places frequented by your friends, even though being by yourself is not reinforcing. You might ask, "What am I responding to?" You may have learned an avoidance behavior. An important characteristic of well-learned avoidance behaviors is that often they are performed in an unemotional, even blasé, way. Such behaviors are not motivated by anxiety. Until it is called to your attention, you may be totally unaware that some of your behaviors are based on the avoidance of discomfort.

Reinforcing Consequences

You can see why an analysis of consequences is an important part of a plan for change. You may find that you are not in fact positively reinforced for the behavior you want to perform. You may even find that you are being positively reinforced for some action that makes the desired behavior difficult or impossible. For example, one student wrote in a self-analysis: "I would like to be nicer to my roommate and be able to solve our little difficulties in a friendly way. But I usually fly off the handle and shout at him. The terrible thing is that I get reinforced for that: He gives in!"

By understanding how reinforcing consequences work—positively or negatively— you can form better plans for changing your behavior. In self-change, sometimes you learn new behaviors—for example, an overeater learns to deal with tension in some new way instead of eating—and sometimes you are reinforced for acts you already know how to perform—for example, a nail biter is reinforced for not biting his nails.

Reinforcements are important for both learning and performance of actions. Theoretical psychologists argue whether, strictly speaking, reinforcement is necessary for learning or only for performance. But it is clear that your *performance* of behavior is affected by the reinforcement you get. You do what you are reinforced for doing.

Punishment

Principle 5: *Behavior that is punished will occur less often.* Psychologists distinguish two kinds of punishment. In the first kind, after a behavior is performed, some unpleasant event occurs. For example, a child says a naughty word and is immediately reprimanded by her parents. An adult says something rude and immediately receives disapproval from friends. If these disapprovals are unpleasant enough to reduce future naughtiness and rudeness, the disapprovals are a punisher.

In the second kind of punishment, after a behavior has been performed, something pleasant is taken away. For example, a child who is playing with her parents says a naughty word and is put in her room by herself. A man says something rude, and his friends go away. In both cases, the loss of something pleasant—playing with parents, being with friends—punishes the behavior that preceded it.

What is the difference between punishment and negative reinforcement? In negative reinforcement, an act that allows the person to escape or avoid some event is reinforced by *removing* the unpleasant event. In punishment, behavior probabilities are reduced in one of two ways: (1) an unpleasant event follows a behavior, or (2) a pleasant event is withdrawn following a behavior.

The following summarizes the difference between negative reinforcement and punishment:

	What Your Behavior Leads To	*Effect on Future Behavior*
Negative Reinforcement	Escape or avoidance of a (usually unpleasant) consequence	Behavior is strengthened
Punishment, Type 1	An unpleasant event	Behavior is less likely to recur
Punishment, Type 2	The loss of something pleasant	Behavior is less likely to recur

Note that punishment, like reinforcement, must be delivered contingent on the behavior in order to work; that is, both must occur when and only when the behavior occurs.

The strong effects of punishment on behavior have been demonstrated in animal laboratories for more than a century. Punishment's effects on human behavior remain problematic and continue to be debated (Axelrod & Apsche, 1983). Should punishment be used to regulate human behavior? Punishment has sharp disadvantages: It creates strong emotional reactions, its side effects are volatile and unpredictable, and it creates aggression. Strong punishment can brutalize both the victim and the punisher. "Punishing" others is often only a justification for releasing anger and frustration. On the other hand, mild punishment—keeping off-task students in from an occasional recess until they finish assignments; quick, quiet scolds or objections—is characteristic of all human relationships, and can provide valuable information about social standards and performance feedback.

The effectiveness of punishment for humans has one very serious limitation: Punishment has no effect if the punishing situation can be escaped (Azrin, Hake, Holz, & Hutchinson, 1965), and in a free community, it usually can—often merely by apologizing or lying. This succeeds only in teaching people to apologize and lie.

In self-directed behavior change, punishment can always be avoided. For these and other reasons, explained in detail in Chapter 7, we urge you not to include punishment in your plans for self-change unless you consider it very carefully. The same advances can be made through the use of other learning principles, such as extinction.

Extinction

Suppose you first learn to do some act because you are reinforced for it, but then, on later performances, no reward follows. What was once reinforced no longer is. As a consequence, your act loses some of its strength. This is called *extinction*.

Principle 6: *An act that was reinforced but no longer is will begin to weaken.* Two people have been going together happily for several months. But then a new pattern begins. He calls her, but she's not home. He leaves a message, but she doesn't call back. Or she drops by to see him, and he doesn't seem very interested. Life, alas, changes, and acts that were once reinforced may no longer be. He will be less likely to call in the future. She will be less likely to drop by.

Extinction occurs all around us, continuously. It is the process by which we adjust our behavior to a changing world. If the woman never returned the man's calls, he wouldn't want to keep calling back forever. Nor would the woman want to continue dropping by to see an uninterested man. Behaviors that are no longer productive are gradually dropped.

Extinction and punishment are not the same. In extinction there is *no* contingent consequence to an act. In our example, the calls are simply ignored. If the woman said, "Don't call me anymore. I don't want to talk to you," that would *punish* the act of calling. If she simply didn't return calls—that is, if she did nothing—his behavior of calling would be *extinguished.*

Imagine what would happen if she simply ignored the calls (extinction). Quite probably, there would be an initial frantic *increase* of his calling. That is a common effect of extinction: an initial *bur*st of the previously reinforced behavior, followed by its decline.

Do all acts extinguish equally? No.

Principle 7: *Intermittent reinforcement increases resistance to extinction.* Reinforcement that follows each instance of a behavior is called *continuous reinforcement.* This can be described as a 100% schedule of reinforcement. But most behaviors in the real world are not reinforced at each instance. Sometimes they are reinforced, and sometimes they are not. This is called *intermittent reinforcement.*

As you might expect, continuous reinforcement provides for rapid new learning. But intermittent reinforcement has a most interesting effect: *It makes behaviors more resistant to extinction.* The behaviors weaken more gradually. A behavior that has been reinforced randomly but on an average of every other time (a 50% schedule) will persist longer when reinforcement is withdrawn than if it had been reinforced continuously.

Let's go back to the example of the spurned lover. Suppose the woman has been careless about returning the man's calls, and he has been reinforced about half the time for calling her. Finally, she loses interest in him entirely and no longer responds at all to his telephone messages. (Each call/response sequence during this time is called an *extinction trial.*) The intermittent reinforcement schedule he was on before (when she returned about half his calls) means that it will take *longer* for his calling behavior to be extinguished than if he had been reinforced 100% of the time. If her nonreinforcement continues, of course, extinction will eventually occur. But the number of trials to extinction is affected by the previous reinforcement schedule.

This effect of intermittent reinforcement is significant for self-change because it helps explain the persistence of maladaptive behaviors. Why do you do things you are apparently not reinforced for or things you don't even want to do? You may not notice the rare reinforcement—perhaps 1 in 50 or 100 times—that keeps your behavior going. Or you may have been intermittently reinforced for maladaptive acts in the past, so now they are very resistant to extinction. A casual observer, not realizing the effect of intermittent reinforcement, might label such behavior "stubborn" or "foolish." Many maladjusted behaviors you see in yourself or other people persist because they are reinforced on intermittent schedules.

Paradoxically, changing from reinforcement to extinction often produces an extinction "burst"—an initial increase in the behavior before the gradual decline begins. At first, when the woman does not return the calls, the man calls more often; then his telephoning gradually tapers off and is finally extinguished altogether.

Antecedents

We now turn to a general consideration of *antecedents* and how antecedent control of behavior develops. Regardless of the power of consequences, your behavior can never be stimulated by its consequences alone. Consequences, after all, occur after a behavior is completed. Antecedents, on the other hand, are the setting events for your behavior. As such, they control it, in the sense of calling it up or stimulating it. When an antecedent calls up a behavior that is subsequently reinforced, the behavior and the environment are in good balance. When a behavior is firmly integrated with its antecedents and consequences, we experience a smooth flow. No thought or self-regulation intervenes, and the behavior has become "automatic."

Antecedents and Positive Reinforcement

Throughout our lives, most of our actions are controlled by cues (signals). For example, when the bell rings or the lecturer says "That's all for today," students leave their seats and move toward the door. Each student knows perfectly well how to leave a classroom, but ordinarily no one does so until the cue is given.

Principle 8: Most operant behavior is eventually guided by antecedent stimuli, or cues, the most important of which are often self-directed statements. The interesting question is, "How do we learn the cues?" In any hour of our lives, the environment provides thousands of cues. The world is rich with stimuli—conversations, sounds, sights, events, smells—and our behaviors are orchestrated into this complexity. Cues that evoke a particular action are called *discriminative stimuli*. This useful technical term helps us understand how a cue works. A cue identifies the conditions in which an action will or will not be reinforced or punished. In college you soon learn that when the lecturer says, "That's all," you can leave in good conscience. You also learn that in the absence of that cue, it is wiser to stay in your seat. How do you learn to make this discrimination? By observing: Students who leave before they are dismissed are punished by the instructor (by scolds or frowns), while those who wait for the cue are not punished at all. You can see this by observing what happens to others or by experiencing the contingency yourself. The technical term for these experiences is discrimination learning, that is, learning to discriminate the cues that determine the contingencies for behaviors.

An antecedent, or stimulus, becomes a cue to a behavior when the behavior is reinforced in the presence of that stimulus and not reinforced in the absence of the stimulus. When a stimulus and a behavior occur and the behavior is reinforced only when stimulus and behavior occur together, the stimulus becomes a cue for that behavior.

This process can be studied in the laboratory by reinforcing a hungry mouse with food for pressing a lever when a light is on and by not reinforcing it for pressing the lever when the light is off. The mouse will learn to press the lever only in the presence of the light. In our everyday lives, this process occurs continually. For example, couples that date regularly can "tell" when it is time to leave a party. Each has learned that when one partner gives certain cues—perhaps becoming quieter or acting edgy—the other will be reinforced for preparing to leave. In the absence of that cue, neither is likely to be reinforced for leaving.

Role of Antecedents in Avoidance Behavior and Extinction

To avoid an unpleasant outcome, you have to know that such an outcome is about to occur. This means that your avoidance behavior is guided by the antecedents— the cues—you get from your environment. If your avoidance behavior is successful, the unpleasant event does not occur.

Principle 9: *An antecedent can be a cue or signal that an unpleasant event may be imminent. This is likely to produce avoidance behavior.*

Suppose that when you were in your early teens, you weren't adept at social niceties and often made a poor impression on others. This may have led to unpleasant experiences, and you may have gradually learned to avoid certain social situations. You learned to be shy. Now, several years later, you are much more adept at social behaviors. But you continue avoiding particular kinds of social events—parties, for example, or dancing and other situations that in the past would have been unpleasant. You continue responding to the antecedent as a cue to avoidance, even though the actual unpleasant event doesn't take place anymore. Why?

Avoidance learning is highly resistant to extinction because the antecedent stimulus evokes the avoidance behavior, and the person who has learned the avoidance response has no opportunity to learn that the old, unpleasant outcome is no longer there.

This is how much "neurotic" or maladjusted behavior is learned. Because you were once punished—in childhood, for example—in the presence of a particular stimulus, you continue engaging in old habits of avoidance that to someone else might seem quite "foolish." You may avoid situations that could be pleasant for you, because the signals that control your avoidance behavior continue to operate. One of the techniques of self-modification is to gradually make yourself engage in previously avoided behaviors and situations that now seem desirable. Only then can you know whether you will still be punished for the behavior.

Stimulus Control and Automatic Behaviors

Now we are in a position to return to our discussion of the ways in which behavior evolves. Social constructivism emphasizes the developmental sequence: from regulation by others, through self-regulation, to automatic stimulus control. How can we reduce *maladaptive* automatic behavior and bring it back under self-regulation?

When an antecedent has consistently been associated with a behavior that is reinforced, it gains what is called stimulus control over the behavior. We respond in a seemingly automatic way. As an experienced driver, you no longer slow down at lights while yelling, "Stop!" to yourself, or even while saying it subvocally. You slow down and brake when the amber light appears even though you are singing, listening to the radio, or thinking about last night's movie. Because of its previous association with a variety of reinforcements, the amber light has stimulus control over your stopping the car. Coming to a halt at the amber light has repeatedly allowed you to avoid collisions, escape fear, earn the praise of your driving instructor, and even elicit your own self-congratulation. In the normal processes of performance, language control is dropped because immediate recognition of and response to specific situations is much more efficient. In most situations, excessive self-speech is undesirable, because it can actually interfere with our performance. Like Hamlet, we become "sicklied o'er with the pale cast of thought." It is better that we run on the automatic pilot of stimulus control.

Better, that is, when we are running well. Unfortunately, those undesirable behaviors that you now wish to change are very likely under stimulus control, and that stimulus control must be broken and rebuilt. For some people, the stimulus control is so strong that it seems almost irresistible, in spite of the fact that it evokes an undesired behavior. One of our students wrote:

> I have been losing some weight, but there is one situation I just can't resist. That's when people who work in my office bring in doughnuts from King's Bakery. They are too much. When I get to work, as soon as I see that King's Bakery box, I know I'm in trouble!

Many overweight people have the same problem. The sight of certain foods automatically stimulates them to eat whether they are hungry or not. Their task, therefore, is to reduce the automatic control of certain stimuli.

A most important tactic for rescuing behavior from an undesirable automatic condition is to insert new antecedents at the very time the old antecedents are about to begin their work. Self-speech antecedents are particularly useful when the "automatic" cue is also self-directed language. For example, you might stop saying to yourself, "I can't resist eating this," and say instead, "You can do it. Hang in there!"

Stimulus control can be the goal of a self-modification plan even when no automatic sequence exists. An antecedent can be set up, a desirable behavior arranged to occur in its presence, and reinforcement programmed to follow. In this way, a new automatic sequence can be created. One of our students, for example, wanted to be more efficient. She wrote:

> I always do my planning as soon as I get off the bus that takes me to school. This puts the planning under the control of that antecedent. I go straight from the bus to an empty classroom and spend a few minutes planning the day, then reinforce myself for the planning.

For this student, getting off the bus had gained stimulus control over the act of planning.

Respondent Behavior and Conditioning

Some behaviors are automatically controlled by antecedent stimuli. That is, not all learning is based on reinforcement of operant behavior. These automatic behaviors have built-in, nonlearned triggers. For example, when the knee tendon is struck lightly, leg extension follows automatically. The antecedent stimulus of striking has control over this reaction. A fleck on the eyeball is the controlling stimulus for eye blinking. Milk in the mouth produces salivation automatically from the earliest hours of life. Behaviors for which original, controlling antecedent stimuli exist are sometimes called *reflexes*. Humans have fewer of these automatic behaviors than do organisms with less complicated nervous systems, but we do have reflexes, and they are important.

Here is a small experiment that will illustrate one of your reflexive responses. Have someone agree to surprise you with a sudden loud noise sometime in the next few days. For example, ask a friend to slam a book onto a table when you seem to expect it least. Observe your reactions: You tense, whip around, and blink. This is a reflexive response; the stimulus alone is sufficient to cause it. Only repeated familiarity with the stimulus will allow the behavior to fade. But notice, too, that there is an emotional component to your reaction—a feeling of arousal and emotional fullness, a discomfort that is much like a small fear reaction that reaches its peak a second or two after the stimulus and then gradually subsides.

This experiment illustrates the control that the antecedent stimulus has over emotional reactions. Behaviors of this type have certain properties in common: For example, they are largely controlled by the autonomic nervous system, they involve smooth muscles, and they are highly similar among individuals of the same species. These behaviors are sometimes called *respondent* behaviors because they occur originally in response to the antecedent stimulus.

The most important characteristic of all respondent behaviors is that the antecedent stimuli are adequate to produce the behavior. This kind of antecedent control over reactions is important because, through this basic process, many emotional reactions become associated with particular antecedents so that the antecedent comes to elicit them.

A person who is very shy may experience considerable anxiety when meeting strangers. Some people become very upset if they have to stay in an enclosed place. Others are extremely afraid of heights or airplanes or snakes. How do these stimuli come to gain control of the person's reaction so that an emotion such as anxiety is elicited? *An answer requires an understanding both of operant and respondent behaviors. In life, the two processes intertwine.* We will return to that interaction after fully discussing the way that some antecedent stimuli gain control of a person's reactions through the process of *respondent conditioning.*

Respondent Conditioning

Respondent conditioning involves pairing a stimulus that elicits some response with one that does not, in such a way that the two stimuli occur together. The individual reacts automatically to the original stimulus in the presence of the new, or *conditioned*, stimulus.

After a number of such pairings, the person reacts to the new, conditioned stimulus by itself and in nearly the same way that he or she reacted to the original stimulus. In this way, automatic reactions can be transferred to what was originally a neutral antecedent (that is, an antecedent with no stimulus control over a reaction). What was once a neutral stimulus becomes a conditioned stimulus—a stimulus that has control over a reaction—by being associated with an antecedent that already has stimulus control. A new stimulus control is developed.

In "commonsense psychology" this process is well recognized. Certain places—restaurants, rooms, parks—have the power to produce strong feelings because it was there that we heard some news, received some shock, experienced some strong emotion. Even the feel of the air in a certain season can produce emotions of sadness or delight. These are highly individual reactions, and come from the previous association of emotions (produced by powerful events). Respondent conditioning is the technical term for this process of association.

Schematically, first comes an antecedent—call it A_1 that elicits a response. If A_1 is always accompanied by another antecedent—call it A_2—then, after a few such associations, A2 will develop nearly the same stimulus control over the response that A1 has. If the response is some emotional reaction, through this process of respondent conditioning the new antecedent (A_2) will develop the capacity to elicit the emotional reaction even if A_1 does not occur. A_2 is then a "conditioned stimulus."

This conditioned stimulus (A_2) can then be paired with a new neutral stimulus (A_3), and A_3 will then come to elicit that emotional reaction. This pairing of A_2 with A_3 (and then A_3 with A_4, A_4 with A_5, and so on) is called *higher-order conditioning*.

These processes are far subtler than simple reflexes, and they are *not* often recognized in commonsense psychology. Once the room or the restaurant or the feel of the air themselves (A_2s) are conditioned to produce the emotion, further events that occur there and are paired with those feelings can also then produce the emotion. A new acquaintance, first met at that "sad restaurant," might then produce that feeling of sadness when seen again, even in a new place. We never fully understand the mysterious patterns of our own emotions and reactions, because higher-order conditioning happens subtly and mostly unnoticed.

The following chart summarizes respondent-conditioning processes and explains how we develop emotional reactions to so many antecedent stimuli.

Reflex	$A_1 \longrightarrow$ Response	Automatic, unlearned, triggered response.
Respondent conditioning	$\begin{cases} A_1 \\ A_2 \longrightarrow \text{Response} \end{cases}$	Pairing the "trigger" stimulus with some new neutral stimulus.
Conditioned response	$A_2 \longrightarrow$ Response	In the absence of A_1, A_2 produces the response.
Higher-order conditioning	$\begin{cases} A_2 \\ A_3 \longrightarrow \text{Response} \end{cases}$	A_2 (conditioned stimulus) is now paired with a new neutral stimulus.
Higher-order conditioned response	$A_3 \longrightarrow$ Response	Now A_1, A_2, and A_3 can all elicit the response, frequently an emotion.

An example of A_3 level conditioning can be seen in our running example of the "sad restaurant." *Once the emotion is present, it can become conditioned to concurrent thoughts.* As you sit in the restaurant, melancholy thoughts run through your head of people, events, and old times. Some thoughts you may even try to suppress; you may not want to dwell on thoughts of someone or something that will make you feel even worse. Later, another day, another month, when the same mood of melancholy returns (even if you are not in the "sad restaurant"), those same thoughts will be more likely to return, *even the thoughts that you were trying to suppress* (Wenzlaff, Wegner, & Klein, 1991).

Emotional Conditioning

Emotional conditioning, of course, can be produced directly (A_1–A_2). More than 85 years ago, John Watson and Rosalie Rayner (1920) demonstrated how an emotional reaction could be conditioned so that it comes to be elicited by an antecedent that was previously neutral. From the earliest days of our lives, a sudden loud noise is an adequate stimulus for a fear reaction. To associate that stimulus with one that was neutral, Watson and Rayner followed this procedure: A baby was presented several times with a white rat; the baby showed no signs of fear. Then he was presented with the rat, and a few seconds afterward, a very loud, unexpected noise was made behind him. The baby reacted automatically to the startling noise with fear. After several experiences in which the rat was presented just before the frightening noise (so that fear was experienced while seeing the rat) the rat became a conditioned stimulus. The rat itself became sufficient to elicit the fear, even if the noise did not occur. Thus, what had been a neutral stimulus became a frightening one.

Once a conditioned reaction has been established, a new stimulus may be associated with the conditioned stimulus so that the new antecedent also acquires stimulus control over the emotional response (higher-order conditioning). For example, if the experimenters were to play a certain tune every time the rat were presented, through higher-order conditioning the baby would come to fear the music.

In a similar way, emotional reactions can be transferred to many new stimuli in your life. As you have new experiences, you may undergo new associations between conditioned emotional reactions and new stimuli so that the new stimuli will come to elicit the original emotional reaction.

This process has been described for many decades; it is sometimes called "classical conditioning." More recent studies have raised doubts about whether the unconditioned and the conditioned stimuli must be presented together in time. In this view, conditioning is not a stupid process in which simple co-occurrence produces learning, but rather the learner is seen as an information seeker who discerns relationships between events and responds to those perceptions (Rescorla, 1988). We will return to this topic in Chapter 6, in examining the development and correction of specific fears.

Principle 10: *Through conditioning, antecedents come to elicit automatic reactions that are often emotional.*

In most everyday situations, respondent conditioning and operant learning are intertwined. Most chains of events contain both behavioral and emotional components (DiCara, 1970; Miller, 1969; Staats, 1968). For example, think of a person who, having failed a driver's test once, goes back for a second try. The person is walking into the testing station (the observable behavior) and experiencing feelings of anxiety or tension. Most important environmental circumstances produce both a behavioral and an emotional reaction. That is, antecedents have an effect on both your behavior and your feelings.

Respondent Conditioning and Language

Many, if not most, conditioned stimuli are words. Parents deliberately try to condition emotional reactions to language as they reinforce their children ("Good kids!") for avoiding the street that is "Dangerous!" or the burner that is "Hot! Hurt you!" As explained above, both an operant behavioral and an emotional reaction come to be cued by the same stimulus. The child both withdraws from the dangerous situation and develops an emotional response not only to the stimulus but also to the word for it. For adults, too, emotional reactions are often conditioned to words. If we are told that a spider or snake is "poisonous," we have a different emotional response to it than if we are told that it is "harmless."

This effect is also present when we use language to ourselves. A situation that we tell ourselves is dangerous or depressing can produce fear or depression even before we actually experience it. Some fears are "cognitively learned" (Wolpe, 1981). Therefore, many situations affect us not so much because of their consequences but because of the way we define the situations to ourselves.

Carver (2003) has recently emphasized the negative emotional consequences of failing to meet our standards. Frustration and disappointment typically lead to negative self-statements—for example, "I can't cope with this situation"—that actually produce higher cardiac levels and respiration rates than do positive self-statements (Schuele & Wiesenfeld, 1983). Goldfried (1979) has developed strategies for restructuring self-statements to produce more adaptive emotional reactions as well as more effective problem-coping skills.

Operant and respondent processes continue to be intertwined into adulthood and to the oldest of age. As we will see in Chapters 5 through 7, every effective self-modification plan must consider both behavior and emotions, because that is the way life is.

Modeling

Much human learning occurs by simply observing what others do. This is called learning through *modeling*.

Principle 11: Many behaviors are learned by observing someone else (a model) perform the actions, which are then imitated. Golf, dancing, chess, and bridge; expressions of love and of anger; even fears—all are learned through modeling. By simply observing a model, you learn behaviors. This kind of learning allows you to develop wholly new behaviors and to modify old ones.

You learn both desirable and undesirable acts this way. For example, you may have grown up with hardworking, ambitious parents. Now you realize that you, too, have these characteristics. Your parents may also have been rather irritable and inclined to blow up when frustrated. To your chagrin, you see that this description fits you as well. Of course, in your life hundreds of people have set different kinds of examples for you. Your present behavior is not a carbon copy of any one person. Rather, you have borrowed a bit of this from one, a bit of that from another, and blended them together to make the unique you.

Learning through observation follows the same principles as direct learning. The consequences of your model's behavior will determine whether you will imitate the behavior. Reinforced model behavior is strengthened in you, and punished model behavior is weakened in you. We learn cues and signals from models. We can even gain emotional conditioning from seeing models frightened by stimuli such as snakes or spiders (Ollendick & King, 1991; Rachman, 1977). And there is evidence that we learn to be calm, at least to a certain degree, by watching models behave calmly before stimuli of which we are afraid.

In your own self-change project, you can deliberately use this ability to learn through modeling to develop new behaviors. For example, a young man who wasn't very sure of himself on dates asked a friend if they could double-date; then he could see how his friend behaved. A woman who had an unreasonable fear of birds accompanied a friend who didn't have that problem in order to see how her friend dealt with birds flying around a park.

Box 4-1
The Principles of Self-Regulation

Principle 1:   From early life to adulthood, regulation by others and the self (particularly through verbal instructions) acts as a powerful guide to behavior.

Principle 2:   Operant behavior is a function of its consequences.

Principle 3:   A positive reinforcer is a consequence that maintains and strengthens behavior by its added presence.

Principle 4:   A negative reinforcer is a consequence that strengthens behavior by being subtracted from the situation.

Principle 5:   Behavior that is punished will occur less often.

Principle 6:   An act that was reinforced but no longer is will begin to weaken.

Principle 7:   Intermittent reinforcement increases resistance to extinction.

Principle 8:   Most operant behavior is eventually guided by antecedent stimuli, or cues, the most important of which are often self-directed statements.

Principle 9:   An antecedent can be a cue or signal that an unpleasant event may be imminent. This is likely to produce avoidance behavior.

Principle 10:   Through conditioning, antecedents come to elicit automatic reactions that are often emotional.

Principle 11:   Many behaviors are learned by observing someone else (a model) perform the actions, which are then imitated.

These examples also illustrate that behavior learned through modeling follows the same developmental sequence as all other behavior. In developing their dating behavior and relaxation around birds, both people were first having their new behaviors regulated by *others* (the models). Soon they were able to move to the stage of self-regulation through self-modification programs that included practice and self-reinforcement. And eventually both of them developed automatic competence and relaxation.

This concludes the discussion of the 11 principles of self-regulation, which are listed in Box 4-1. The search for the basic principles of self-regulation continues and will continue so long as human society wants to understand itself. We do not believe that the 11 principles are likely to change, but with each passing year, we understand them in more complex ways, and they become more inclusive. This evolution proceeds by discovery and by debate, sometimes heated. The hot edges of the current debate are described in Box 4-2. We present this controversy as an illustration; for another example of theoretical disputes, the interested reader can follow the references in the section on regulation theory.

Actually, the development of theory has outpaced practical application (Karoly, 1995). Our approach in this chapter has been to present a balanced view among theories, and to concentrate on those principles that have direct application to improving behavior and experience.

Box 4-2
Thinking and Behavior

Science progresses through a series of arguments—always vigorous, sometimes fierce. Today psychology is embroiled in such an argument over the role of *thinking* in determining behavior. What guides our behavior? Thinking? Or external conditions and events?

This tension has been present in philosophy since the dawn of history. During the first half of the 20th century, psychology emulated the physical sciences by concentrating on only what could be objectively observed and measured in the physical world. "Thoughts" were not considered legitimate for scientific inquiry. The very great successes of that program had the temporary effect of subduing its opponents—those psychologists who believed that humans' overt acts should be seen as expressions of the basic controlling power of the human mind.

Now the shoe is on the "cognitive" foot. "Cognition" (the study of thinking and mental operations) is *in,* just as "behaviorism" was the enthusiasm of the preceding period. And even most behaviorists have adopted an intermediate position, called "cognitive behaviorism," that includes thoughts, self-speech, and rules among antecedents, behaviors, and consequences. Cognitive behaviorism is the position described most often in this text.

During recent years behaviorists mounted a major counteroffensive, with more sophisticated and complex views of reinforcement, behavior, and self-control and cognition (e.g., Ainslee, 2001; Logue, 2004; Rachlin, 2000; Timberlake, 1995). Here is one fascinating example. *How can behaviorists, without considering "thinking," explain commitment to long-term goals?*

Here is the basic theoretical problem. Effective self-control requires a willingness to work for larger-later (LL) rewards instead of smaller-sooner (SS) ones. (We have discussed this issue as the necessity for commitment and concentration on long-term goals.) But the new research of the behaviorists demonstrates that *everyone sometimes chooses SSs,* depending on three factors: the length of the delay of the LLs, the sizes of the rewards, and how fast the reward can be used.

For example, college students would prefer $450 per day for a year starting *now,* to $500 a day if they have to wait a month to start the year's use. In terms of straight arithmetic, they would be losing $50 per day for 365 days, or a total of $18,250! In the language of economics, they are *discounting* the maximum available reward by 10%, because having it now makes the money more valuable. When offered the same kind of choice, but with smaller amounts of money, students discounted the LL ($50 per day) even more sharply; they would prefer $39 per day now, to waiting a month for $50 (Raineri & Rachlin, 1993). These "discount rates" that people apply to delayed rewards are very consistent mathematically and can be predicted with some reliability. Discount rates are higher when rewards have to be consumed more quickly. For example,

(continued)

Box 4-2 *(continued)*

$1000 a day that has to be spent by the end of each day is much less valuable than if the money can be put in the bank; it takes work to spend that much that quickly every day. Likewise, a $25 steak may not be worth even $1 to you, if you have to eat it in the next hour; you may have just eaten a whole pizza and are back in your dorm. So Rachlin (1995) argues that discounting is rational, and therefore many SS choices are reasonable; in fact everyone will choose smaller-sooner, if the delay, amount, and time available to use the reward are in balance to favor the SS. Actually, the discounted amount is the "true" (market) value of the reward. Therefore, "commitment" (to a long-term goal of lesser actual value) is not a very convincing explanation for the high achievements of those with good self-control.

But in fact self-controlling people do choose long-term goals, even when the apparent "discount rate" is very high. So how can that be explained? How do people discipline themselves for delayed rewards, even when it appears to "makes no sense"?

Rachlin's answer is that self-control comes about when we move from "act" to "pattern," because acts organized into *valued patterns increase the* size *of the reward enormously.* Consider this list of behaviors:

a. swinging a hammer
b. hammering a nail
c. joining one piece of wood to another
d. building a floor
e. building a house
f. providing shelter for his family
g. supporting his family
h. being a good husband and father
i. being a good person (Rachlin, 1995, p. 115)

Each item is patterned within the next item on the list, all the way to the top. The swinging, the hammering, and the joining are organized into patterns of highest values. The true rewards for high-value patterns are enormous, so large that even if discounted for long delays, a person will hammer and hammer, even through weariness and pain, to achieve the love of his family and his own self-respect. All of us will delay rewards when we are able to organize our lower-level goals into higher-value patterns and keep those patterns in our attention.

Chapter Summary

Regulation Theory

Merely setting goals and collecting observations on behavior can often bring about behavior change. This process is explained by regulation theories, all of which include some principles of cybernetics. Just as a thermostat regulates temperature, setting a standard and comparing real information to that standard can regulate behavior. To some

That enables the very valuable LL rewards to be attached even to the minor acts of hammering and joining. This radically changes the "economics" of the rewards and makes choosing the LLs very sensible indeed.

This inventive "teleological behaviorism" argument was elaborated with rich data and mathematical formulae in a special issue of *Behavioral and Brain Sciences,* along with the comments of 36 distinguished researchers and theorists—a brilliant intellectual free-for-all. Cognitive scientists were in a special uproar over Rachlin's argument that we don't need "thought" or "commitment" to explain self-control. As a true behaviorist, he argues that when we pattern our acts, the absolute values of LLs are increased, so even when they are discounted, they are still more valuable than the SS rewards. So it is possible to calculate the reinforcement to the patterns, and thus to predict self-control delay or short-term taking. It can all be understood by analysis of the "economics" of reinforcement.

This by no means satisfies the cognitivists. Just how, they ask, do you think acts get patterned? And answering their own question, they insist: Through thinking and self-talk, that's how patterning is achieved.

Debaters assembled their opinions again, in a special issue of the *Journal of Behaviour Therapy and Experimental Psychiatry,* about "The Causal Efficacy of Human Thought." One result is clear: Both research logic and philosophical preference play roles in what one thinks about thinking.

This dispute between the objective and the subjective will not likely ever be completely silenced. Which is a good short-term *and* long-term reward for those who enjoy the vigorous intellectual contests of science. In the meantime, thinking of self-control as rationally maximizing more valuable long-term rewards can be helpful in designing self-directed behavior changes. In the following chapters, particularly in our Tips for Typical Topics, you will recognize many tactics as designing plans to make your rational choices more likely. Readers interested in this explanation can find a full discussion in Logue (2004).

SOURCES: Raineri, A., & Rachlin, H. (1993), The effect of temporal constraints on the value of money and other commodities. *Journal of Behavioral Decision Making, 6,* 77–94. Rachlin, H. (1995), Self-control: Beyond commitment, *Behavioral and Brain Sciences, 18,* 109–159. With open peer commentary (many authors), 122–159. See also: Ainslee, G. (1992), *Picoeconomics: The strategic interaction of successive motivational states within the person,* Cambridge University Press. Cognition, behavior and causality: A broad exchange of views stemming from the debate on the causal efficacy of human thought, *Journal of Behaviour Therapy and Experimental Psychiatry, 26,* Special Issue (September 1995).

extent, human beings appear to be "hard-wired" to self-regulate in this way, like the robots we have created in our own image. Other aspects of self-regulation are not as well explained by cybernetics. Human beings make choices that are not anticipated and change their goals in-flight. Sometimes we cannot "automatically" self-regulate because we do not know how to perform the required behavior. Further, not all our behavior is self-regulated; the external environment controls much of it. In particular, much of our behavior is strongly affected by other people.

Social Constructivism: Regulation by Others and Regulation by Self

All behavior, as it develops, passes through this sequence: (1) control by others, (2) control by self, and (3) automatization. Control by others is exercised by parents, instructors, models, books, bosses, spouses, and friends. When a new behavior is being learned, it is regulated by these external sources. As we gradually become more skillful in a behavior, we take over self-regulation—by reminding ourselves, practicing, setting goals, and collecting observations. When a behavior is fully learned, it becomes automatic. In this stage, it is under environmental control. That is, it is a smooth response to situations and does not even require any thought. When this smooth flow is interrupted—by a change in the environment, or through careful self-observation—it is possible to retrieve behavior from this automatic condition and bring it back under self-regulation. The skills we use in retrieving and regulating these automatic behaviors are called learned resourcefulness. Learned resourcefulness includes skills in managing self-observation, language, consequences, antecedents, respondent conditioning, and modeling.

The Development of Language Regulation

The most obvious method of controlling behavior is through language. Children gradually incorporate the speech of their parents and teachers and give themselves the same kinds of instructions they have heard from others. Even as adults, we are controlled by the speech of others. In difficult situations, or when we are retrieving behavior from automaticity, our own self-directed speech powerfully regulates our own behavior. Even when behavior is automatic, it may occur in response to subvocal speech. What we say to ourselves, particularly self-statements that are rules for our conduct, controls what we do.

Operant Theory: Consequences

Operant behaviors are strengthened or weakened by what follows them. Behavior is said to be "stronger" if it is more likely to occur in a particular situation.

A positive reinforcer is a consequence that strengthens behavior by its added presence. A negative reinforcer is an unpleasant consequence that strengthens behavior by being removed from the situation. You learn to escape or avoid unpleasant consequences.

What is a reinforces—positive or negative—for one person is not necessarily so for another and is not necessarily a reinforcer at all times. Some people dislike pastrami; even those who like it would not find a pastrami sandwich reinforcing immediately after a Thanksgiving feast.

Behavior that is punished will occur less often in the future. Punishment means either taking away a positive event following a behavior or adding a negative event following a behavior. Both kinds of punishment decrease the likelihood of the behavior. Both reinforcement and punishment must be contingent on the behavior to affect it; that is, they must occur if and only if the behavior occurs.

An act that is no longer reinforced, either positively or negatively, will weaken. This is called extinction. In this process, the behavior has no reinforcing consequence and therefore weakens. Intermittent reinforcement, however, increases the resistance of a behavior to extinction.

Antecedents

Eventually, antecedents guide most behavior. These guiding antecedents, called discriminative stimuli or cues, come to control behavior that has been reinforced only when the cues were present. Many cues signal that danger is imminent. Escaping from those cues is reinforced by a reduction in anxiety, and we learn to avoid them. Avoidance behavior is highly resistant to extinction. Thus, many problem behaviors continue even after real danger has disappeared because the cue causes us to act as though something we used to fear is still a threat. (This is a description of many "neurotic" behaviors.)

It is normal for behavior to develop to the point that it is automatically controlled by antecedent stimuli. When these sequences are undesirable, automatic behavior can be retrieved and brought back under self-regulation. Tactics that can be used include inserting new antecedents, narrowing the behaviors that follow an antecedent, and constructing entirely new sequences of Antecedents-Behavior-Consequences.

Respondent Behavior and Conditioning

Respondent behavior refers to those behaviors that are originally controlled by antecedent stimuli. In respondent conditioning, a neutral antecedent is associated with a stimulus that can elicit an automatic reaction; after a series of associations, the once-neutral stimulus becomes capable of eliciting the same reaction. In higher-order conditioning, another neutral event is paired with this antecedent, and it, too, acquires the capacity to produce the reaction.

This process is important because many emotional reactions may be conditioned to particular antecedents in this way. Various emotional reactions, such as joy or depression, may come under the control of antecedent stimuli so that just encountering the antecedent elicits that reaction. Normally, both operant learning and respondent conditioning are going on at the same time.

Conditioned stimuli are frequently words. Thus, language—even language we address to ourselves—produces emotional reactions. Because operant and respondent processes are both present when language is antecedent to behavior, what we say to ourselves affects both behaviors and emotions. Many self-change programs require a change in our self-speech.

Modeling

Many behaviors are learned simply by observing a model. Learning through observation follows the same principles as direct learning. The consequences of the behavior for the model will determine the strength of the behavior in the observer. Even emotional conditioning can be learned by watching models that are frightened or calm.

Your Own Self-Direction Project: Step 4

This chapter has presented background material you need in order to embark on a successful self-modification project. It's important, therefore, that you have a good grasp of the principles that govern your behavior. To make sure that you do, answer the learning objectives questions at the beginning of this chapter.

If you can answer these questions, you can feel confident that you understand the principles that explain your behavior and that you are ready to apply these principles toward self-understanding. If you cannot, reread the chapter. Find the answers, and write them down. Then answer the questions again.

Now think about your behaviors that you have been observing, get out your observation notes, and answer the following questions about your own target behaviors.

First, consider the antecedents of your behavior:

1. What stimuli seem to control the behavior? In what situations does the behavior occur?
2. Do you react automatically to some cue with undesirable behavior?
3. Do you react to some cue with an unwanted emotion? What is the conditioned stimulus for it?
4. What are you saying to yourself before the behavior?

Second, look at the behavior itself:

5. Is it strong and quite frequent, or is it weak and not very frequent? What does this tell you about what you can do to change it?
6. Is any element of your problem due to something you are avoiding, perhaps unnecessarily?
7. Are you aware of models in your past whose behavior (or, perhaps, some aspects of it) you may have copied?
8. Does any part of your goal involve changing behaviors that are resistant to extinction, either because they are intermittently reinforced or because they are avoidance behaviors?

Third, examine the consequences of the behavior:

9. Are your desired behaviors positively reinforced?
10. What actions make the desired behavior difficult? Are they reinforced?
11. Is it possible that the desired behavior is being punished?
12. Is your own self-speech rewarding or punishing your behavior?
13. Are the consequences for some behaviors difficult to identify, perhaps because of intermittent reinforcement?

Answer these questions carefully. In the next four chapters, we discuss various ways to move toward self-change by using techniques that solve different problems. Some techniques are designed for the person who is not being reinforced for a desired act. Others are for the person who needs to develop stimulus control for a desired act. Still others are for the person who already has inappropriate stimulus control over undesired acts. Also, some techniques are for those who are showing conditioned emotional responses. Your answers to the preceding questions will tell you which kinds of techniques you should use in your own plan for self-change.

Chapter 5

Antecedents

Outline and Learning Objectives

Identifying Antecedents

1. How do you identify antecedents? What are three possible points of difficulty in identifying them?
2. What two kinds of self-statements can be antecedents?
   a. Explain self-instructions.
   b. How do beliefs and interpretations serve as antecedents, and how can you identify them?
   c. What are two common maladaptive beliefs?

Modifying Old Antecedents

3. In the first steps of a self-change plan, how can you avoid the antecedents of problem behavior?
4. What are some of the situations in which indulging in consummatory behaviors is most likely?
5. Explain the strategy of narrowing antecedent control.
6. Explain reperceiving antecedents. What are "hot" and "cool" cognitions? How does distraction work?
7. Explain the strategy of changing chains.
   a. What is the advantage of building in pauses?
   b. Explain pausing to make a record.
   c. How do you unlink a chain of events?
   d. At what part of the chain is it best to try breaking the chain?

Arranging New Antecedents

8. How can you use self-instructions to promote new, desired behavior?
   a. Which are best, precise or general self-instructions? Why?
   b. How can you use self-instructions to remind yourself of beliefs or long-range goals?
   c. When you use self-instructions, which is more effective—saying them to yourself or thinking about them?

9. What are negative self-instructions? How can they be eliminated?
10. Instead of trying to suppress or stop an unwanted thought, what should you do?
11. Explain how you can build stimulus control to cue a desired new behavior, such as concentrating while studying.
12. What is stimulus generalization? What can you do to develop it for a new, desired behavior?
13. Explain the precommitment strategy. How can you use other people's help in precommitment?

Tips for Typical Topics

Chapter Summary

Your Own Self-Direction Project: Step 5

At this point, you have a clear understanding of the principles that govern your behavior, and you should have gathered data about your behaviors, the situations in which they occur, and their consequences. Each of the next three chapters discusses one of the A-B-C components. The present chapter discusses A issues—ways of arranging antecedents so that desired behaviors become more likely. Chapter 6 treats the B issues— how behaviors themselves can be changed, replaced, and originated. Chapter 7 is devoted to the C issues—ways of rearranging the consequences of behavior to gain better self-direction. Finally, Chapter 8 discusses ways of organizing and incorporating all these ideas into an effective plan.

The separation of these topics is unfortunate, but unavoidable. It is not possible to present them simultaneously on the same printed page. But remember: *You cannot design a full self-direction plan until you have read all the material in these four chapters.* A, B, and C units are all required for full analysis and planning, although each person may emphasize one or another somewhat differently. A good self-change plan is based on all three. Continue working at your self-direction project as you read these chapters. The material is organized so that each chapter allows some planning and analysis, but a full plan will require all elements.

Identifying Antecedents

In Chapter 4 we explained how antecedents control behavior, thoughts, and feelings. Self-regulation principles 8, 9, and 10 summarized the way in which any antecedent, when it occurs in regular patterns before or with behaviors, thoughts, or feelings, can stimulate those behaviors, thoughts, and feelings. Because of previous conditions of learning, even logically unrelated antecedents can become discriminative stimuli or conditioned stimuli. In everyday language, these controlling stimuli act as cues, and we will use the terms *cues* and *antecedents* as synonyms in this chapter. An effective plan for self-improvement depends on accurate discovery of your current system of cues. Discovering antecedents is the first task in designing an effective plan.

A married couple had been quarreling. In the past, they tried constructive arguments to solve their differences. Lately, however, the man found himself flying off the handle in the middle of an argument, calling his wife names, and swearing. We suggested he keep a record of what happened just before he lost his temper. He thought about what happened in the past and made current observations for several days. As a result, he discovered a consistent antecedent of his anger: "It's a particular expression on her face. I think of it as her holier-than-thou expression, and it makes me angry."

In this case the unwanted behavior was cued by a single stimulus. For other behaviors, there may be several antecedents that have stimulus control. When any one of them occurs, so does the problem behavior. "Hurt feelings" was the concern of one young woman, who discovered all these antecedents:

(a) Her mother or brother questioning specific decisions or behaviors, (b) her roommate asking her not to be around for a while, (c) her ex-husband questioning her dating or implying that the separation was her fault, and (d) her boyfriend failing to meet her as planned or flaunting the fact that he dated her acquaintances. (Zimmerman, 1975, p. 8)

Do you understand the antecedents of your own problem behavior? Our student Lui-Ling examined her self-observations and wrote:

Here are the events and situations that lead to *not exercising*: (1) hot and humid weather, (2) when exercise becomes monotonous and boring, (3) when there's an exam or important assignment approaching, (4) when I don't have a set exercise schedule beforehand, and (5) when I allow myself to list "all the good reasons why I deserve a rest from exercise today." I knew that to achieve my goal, I would have to figure out ways to counter these hindering factors. So, I did.

If you are not as successful, consider three possible points of difficulty in discovering antecedents. First, have you been recording fully and accurately? *Not keeping complete, accurate records is the most common (and most self-defeating) error.* Many fine students have told us, "You can't seriously mean that I'm supposed to write all that stuff down. I know what the problem is, and I do notice the situations. Writing them down is just a made-up exercise for a course." But we are very serious. Written records force you to keep your attention on problem situations, those that have become automatic, and those you don't like to notice and remember.

A second difficulty in recognizing antecedents is not beginning early enough in your chain-of-events analysis. If you begin recording at the moment your problem is clear and overt, you can be nearly certain that you have not begun early enough in the chain. This point is illustrated by one student who was alarmed by his increasing amount of beer drinking. "It happens at night," he reported. "I stay home, cook a little something, turn on the TV. I'm bored, get depressed, start popping the beer cans. The antecedent seems to be that I feel lonely." Recognizing his feelings of loneliness was a giant step forward, but those feelings were clearly not the first link in the chain. We suggested he work further backward: What chain of events produced the loneliness? He wrote:

I've had three disastrous love affairs in the past year: self-confidence—zero. Every time I meet a woman, I tell myself not to bother. I've been staying home. Even telephone invitations become occasions for feeling worse. Twice last week I could have gone out, once to an auto show and once on a blind date. I declined. The next time a chance like that comes up, I'll try to notice what I'm saying to myself. It's probably some self-putdown.

Not every antecedent is so far removed from the behavior as this self-putdown made a week before. But this student saw the long chain that linked his refusal of a date last week to his lonely drunkenness this week. Discovering this distant antecedent allowed him to design a self-modification plan for a more stimulating social life. The student's discovery of the role his own feelings played in this chain of events was critically important. Emotion frequently triggers our automatized habitual problem behavior. Feelings should always be examined to see if they are cues for problem behavior. Overeating, for example, is often triggered by feelings of restlessness, tension, irritability, anger, depression, or frustration. Many people feel unable to control their eating under such conditions (Glynn & Ruderman, 1986). Identify those feelings and record them.

The third most likely difficulty with discovering antecedents involves not recognizing self-statements; this will require a lengthier discussion.

Discovering Self-Statements

Self-directed messages and thoughts are among the most powerful influences on subsequent behavior. There are three types: (1) self-instructions, (2) beliefs, and (3) interpretations.

Self-instructions. Self-instructions can be obvious: "Get out of here!" "I've got to study tonight!" "Go three blocks and turn left." "Be calm; be relaxed." However, self-instructions are sometimes difficult to identify because they occur in a "still, small voice," so swiftly that only careful attention reveals them. The task is to amplify the words until they are loud and clear. It's like bringing self-directions back from the underground so they can be consciously controlled. Once this principle is understood, most self-instructions can be detected by turning up the amplifier of your still, small voice. Hear yourself thinking. Then record your thought as an antecedent.

Beliefs. Beliefs may be more difficult to discover. Belief statements may occur so rarely that they are not often observable. You must infer them by logically analyzing your self-observations. By beliefs, we mean the underlying assumptions on which your self-speech and other behaviors rest.

Recall the example of the young woman with "hurt feelings." All the instances in which she felt hurt, whether by mother, brother, roommate, ex-husband, or boyfriend, presented a common theme. If she had discussed her records with us, we would have asked her, "What is common to all these situations? What do these events mean to you? What belief can you see operating here?" She might have answered:

> I guess I'm telling myself that no one loves me. It seems as though I want approval from everyone all the time. I suppose I believe that I must be loved by everyone and that each disapproval means I'm not loveable.

The conversation might have continued as follows:

> "Do you really believe that?"
> "I suppose so; it's the way I behave."
> "Is it logical?"
> "Not really. People can disapprove of some things their loved ones do."

"Must everyone love you, constantly?"

"No. That's absurd."

"What would be a preferable belief?"

"That it is acceptable to be disapproved of sometimes, even by those one loves."

People torment themselves with an infinite number of self-destructive belief statements. Many of these statements are so habitual that they become abbreviated and no longer even fully stated: "I'm just . . . !" and the sentence remains an unfinished self-insult. These are some of the reasons why belief statements are often difficult to discover. But however great the variety, these statements tend to fall into certain predictable groups.

For example, Albert Ellis classifies specific irrational and destructive beliefs into three major groups: "I must!" "Others must!" and "Conditions must!"

1. *I must . . . :* "I must be thoroughly competent, adequate, achieving, and lovable at all times, or else I am an incompetent worthless person." Ellis hypothesized that this belief leads to feelings of anxiety, panic, depression, despair, and worthlessness.

2. *Others must . . . :* "Others must treat me kindly and fairly at all times, or else I can't stand it and they are bad, rotten, and evil persons who should be severely blamed, damned, and vindictively punished for their horrible treatment of me." This hypothetically leads to feelings of anger, rage, fury, and vindictiveness and to actions like verbal and physical aggression.

3. *Conditions must . . . :* "Conditions must absolutely be the way I want them to be and must never be too difficult or frustrating. Otherwise, life is awful, terrible, horrible, catastrophic, and unbearable." This, Ellis believes, leads to low frustration-tolerance, self-pity, anger, depression, and to behaviors such as procrastination, avoidance, and inaction (Kendall et al., 1995, p. 172).

Changing such beliefs often leads to widespread benefits, emotionally and behaviorally. For instance, a group of unassertive people believed that standing up for themselves would be followed by disapproval and embarrassment. They came to see that they let themselves be mistreated by waiters, cashiers, and even friends because of these illogical, imagined outcomes. Once they began to anticipate different outcomes—such as greater respect and comfort—their assertiveness increased (Goldfried, 1977).

In examining your self-observations for relevant antecedents, don't overlook the possibility that a maladaptive belief may be contributing to the problem. Be systematic in searching out these beliefs. A useful way to uncover them is to ask yourself, "If my fears come true, if I fail, what does it mean?" (Samoilov & Goldfried, 2000). That is, what about yourself does failure imply? A most common destructive belief is that every negative social outcome means unfavorable personal characteristics (Wilson & Rapee, 2005). This belief is not logical; social interactions are too complex for such a simple explanation. But that belief maintains high levels of social anxiety.

Another form of belief is your expectations—what you expect will make the arrival of that emotion more likely (Catanzaro, Wasch, Kirsch, & Mearns, 2000).

Consider each instance of your problem. Look for some common theme, some assumption that underlies all these instances. Write out that theme as precisely as possible and examine it. Is it rational? Is it adaptive? Do you really believe it, now that it is explicit? After bringing maladaptive beliefs to light, many people find that they can readily accept a quite different belief. One doesn't have to be always perfect. One can do very well with some disapproval. Occasional errors don't mean some underlying personal flaw. By accepting a more reasonable belief, you can change a controlling antecedent and begin a new pattern of self-direction (Thorpe, Amatu, Blakey, & Burns, 1976).

A mother who screamed at her children, particularly in the early morning stress of getting the family off to work and school, was growing depressed because of it. She learned that after these screaming incidents, she always said to herself, "I'm a terrible mother—even worse than my own mother." But she was able to refocus her attention to a broader range of evidence and reformulate her self-speech to reminders that she is an attentive and dedicated mother—she plays football with the kids, works with them in geometry, and listens to them sympathetically. She learned to say, "I'm fine with the kids in the afternoon and terrible in the morning. . . ." And that made it possible for her to substitute positive statements to her children, instead of the impatient screaming.

The "Best Friend technique" developed by Richard Rakos (1991) suggests that when you are critical of yourself, immediately think of the same situation as if it were not you, but your best friend. What would you say to him or her? You might have just said to yourself, "You are a rotten idiot!" But to your best friend, wouldn't you be more likely to say, "Sure you might have done better, but no one is perfect. Don't be so hard on yourself." Be a friend to yourself; speak to yourself with the same courtesy and good intentions that you use with a best friend.

Undergraduate students at a Dutch university were instructed to develop a list of their positive characteristics, put them on small cards, and read them to themselves twice daily for three weeks. As compared to control subjects these students developed more feelings of adequacy, self-esteem, and confidence (Lange, Richard, Gest, de Vries, & Lodder, 1998).

Interpretations. One of this book's authors reports:

> When I had to start wearing an eye patch, I hated it. Children stare, and that particularly upset me. But my daughter said, "Dad they're just kids. They're curious. Maybe they think you're a pirate." So I tried out that interpretation. Now whenever a kid stares at me, I say, "Have you ever seen a pirate before?" I've had so many charming conversations from that. One little girl said she wanted to join my ship right away. Now this eye patch isn't half bad. (DW)

The way we interpret events contains self-instructions. For example, the person with a problematic bad temper will interpret a situation as an affront, a putdown, an insult, or a loss of face. Each of these interpretations can be discovered by listening to the self-statements that result: "I won't let that SOB get away with that!" or "Nobody puts me down like that!" One of the key elements in bringing anger under control is changing the self-statements that trigger angry reactions (Masters, Burrish, Hollon, & Rimm, 1987).

The first task of self-modification is to use the power of antecedents to reach goals. The strategies you can employ to accomplish this task fall under two main headings: (1) modifying old antecedents (including avoiding antecedents, narrowing antecedents, reperceiving antecedents, and changing chains); and (2) arranging new antecedents.

Modifying Old Antecedents

Avoiding Antecedents

If all you have in front of you are two pieces of celery and a bowl of soup, you have already avoided some antecedents of overeating—the sight of an open box of chocolates, for example. Chronic alcoholics who successfully control drunkenness often do so by never confronting the crucial antecedent of overdrinking—the first drink. Most people who stay off cigarettes also follow a policy of not having the first one. If you are a habitual overeater, smoker, or drug user, sometimes almost nothing is as reinforcing as your "habit." For such behaviors, perhaps the most promising type of self-modification plan is one in which you avoid the antecedents that set the time and place for your *consummatory behavior*—behavior that is *consummated*, or climaxed, by its own ends, such as eating, drinking, or sexual activity. The smoker avoids cigarettes, the drinker avoids drinks, and the overeater avoids fattening foods. Exposed to those stimuli, they will very likely perform the undesired behavior again.

A middle-aged, overweight man wanted to diet but reported that his progress was always followed by disaster. So he began recording the antecedents of his eating binges and realized that, although he normally stayed on his diet quite regularly, in one situation he always ate too much: when he and his wife were invited to someone else's house for dinner. Their friends were good cooks! He solved his problem by setting a simple rule, to which his wife agreed. Until he lost 20 pounds, they wouldn't accept any dinner invitations. He would explain to his would-be host or hostess that he had to lose weight and that he couldn't possibly resist such fine food, so he must regretfully decline.

Self-control becomes most difficult when you are around others who are indulging. Marlatt and Parks (1982) have conducted extensive research on people trying to resist addictions to alcohol, heroin, marijuana, or tobacco. Relapse is very likely when in the presence of other users. For example, among women who gave up smoking during pregnancy, 56% returned to smoking within a month postpartum; living with, or socializing with, other smokers seems to be the major condition of relapse (McBride & Pirie, 1990).

A person may need to avoid social cues for a variety of behavioral goals. For example, Heffernan and Richards (1981) studied students who initiated attempts to improve their poor study behaviors. Those who succeeded were more likely to use the simple procedure of studying in an environment where they would *not* have to interact or talk with other people.

In other circumstances, a private environment can be the cue for problem behavior. A young man was concerned about masturbation, in which he indulged three times a day. The reinforcer was fairly obvious—the sexual pleasure itself—although by masturbating he also gained some temporary relief from social anxieties. The young man avoided the antecedent—the place in which masturbation usually occurred. He began using a less private campus restroom.

Avoiding antecedents for drinking, drugs, smoking, or overeating is particularly important when you are emotionally upset. Feelings of anger, fear, depression, or disappointment are certain to make indulgence more tempting, and thus more likely. Even the excitement of unusual happiness tends to make abstainers more likely to violate their resolutions, particularly when combined with social encouragement—such as the "celebrating party" (Cannon, Leeka, Patterson, & Baker, 1990). But negative emotions are the most dangerous conditions for relapsing into indulgence (Marlatt & Parks, 1982; Shiffman, 1982). Therefore, avoiding your problem antecedents is especially wise during periods of emotional arousal.

This strategy of avoidance is one you can begin immediately. Later you will learn how to develop new behaviors for situations in which you cannot avoid the antecedent. After all, you can't avoid parties all your life. But avoiding the antecedents to unwanted, indulgent behaviors will allow your self-controlling responses to be strengthened before they are again tested in tempting situations. By the time you return to parties, you will know when you must say "no" and how to do it.

Narrowing Antecedent Control

Undesired behavior can be deliberately linked to a gradually narrower range of antecedents. The idea is to narrow the range of situations that control the behaviors down to a fine point, or to narrow the behaviors that occur in a situation. For example, Goldiamond (1965) helped control sulking behavior in a client by a program that allowed the client to sulk, but only on a particular "sulking stool." Nolan (1968) reports a case of restricting smoking to a certain uncomfortably located chair. Even unpleasant thoughts can be restricted to a certain "worry chair" and to a specific half-hour per day (Borkovec, Wilkinson, Folensbee, & Lerman, 1983).

This technique has been studied best in the control of insomnia. The insomniac wants the situation of being in bed to produce sleep, but instead it stimulates tossing, turning, thinking, reading, turning the radio on and off, and everything but sleep. Bootzin and Nicassio (1979) recommend narrowing the stimulus control of the bed. Except for sex, nothing else should be done there—no reading, television watching, conversation, or worrying. If the insomniac is still awake after 10 minutes, he or she should leave the bed and not return until sleepy. This system of narrowing appears to be the best self-modification technique for insomnia, even in severe cases (Lacks, Bertelson, Gans, & Kunkel, 1983; Turner, 1986).

A similar strategy for making studying more automatic is for the person to leave the study desk when he or she is daydreaming, eating, or chatting (Spurr & Stevens, 1980).

Reperceiving Antecedents

Some antecedents cannot be avoided or narrowed. For this situation, a useful strategy is to change the nature of the situation by changing the way you think about it.

Kent wanted to extend the amount of time he could stay under during scuba diving by an additional 30 minutes; he was tired of being the first one out among his diving group. He wrote:

> Most of the time I think negative thoughts like the water is too cold or that there are no fish there anyway. That's what led to the short diving time. So I told myself to think positive things like, "Maybe there are a lot of fish here," or "The water is not that cold," or think how nice a day it is for diving, or imagine all the fish I would catch.

An Olympic fencer often hurried her warm-up because officials frequently delayed her from getting to the fencing strip on time. Her self-defeating reaction was to think,

"I'm holding everyone up; they're mad at me; I shouldn't take any more time." Without a decent warm-up, she would also think, "I'm not really ready to fence. . . . I haven't even warmed up, I can't possibly perform well. . . . oh, well, let's get it over with." With help from her coach, she reperceived this situation and changed her thoughts: "I have a right to warm up. They kept me waiting, so now they can wait a little for me. If I'm taking up too much time, it's the judge's obligation to tell me and not my responsibility" (Suinn, 1989).

Another way to reperceive is by attending to some specific parts of the situation and not to others. For example, it is possible to attend to either the "hot" or the "cool" aspects of any situation. In Chapter 2 we told of the work of Walter Mischel and his associates on the ways that children learn to resist temptation (Cantor, Mischel, & Schwartz, 1982; Mischel, 1981). By the sixth grade, children are aware that attending to the "cool" rather than the "hot" qualities of tempting things will help them resist unwise choices. A "hot" perception of marshmallows is, "They taste yummy and are chewy." A "cool" marshmallow perception is, "They are puffy like clouds" (Mischel, 1981). A "yummy" marshmallow is more likely to be snatched and eaten than is a "cloudlike" marshmallow. Adults as well as 12-year-old children know this technique, but *in indulgent responses we often err by letting hot perceptions dominate our attention.* Instead, "delicious pork roast" can be thought of as "dead pig"; "salty and crunchy" pretzels as "little brown twigs" (Mischel & Ayduk, 2004). Transforming an antecedent condition by concentrating on its cool qualities will reduce arousal, frustration, and, ultimately, the likelihood of succumbing to temptation.

As another example, faithful lovers and mates are more likely to focus on the least desirable features of other attractive people; perceiving alternate partners as desirable increases the strength of the temptation (Johnson & Rusbult, 1989). And in resisting tempting situations for alcohol or drugs, successful people are more likely to focus on the unattractive features of those who are drunk or stoned (Brown, Stetson, & Beatty, 1989). "Cooling" may also be achieved by redirecting attention—for example, from "Is he rejecting me?" to "What exact words is he saying?" Cooler thoughts mean less destructive action (Ayduk et al., 2000).

Changing Chains

Another strategy that can be used to control antecedents is to change the chain of events that produces the undesired behavior. Many behaviors are the result of a fairly long chain of events. An antecedent produces some behavior that leads to a particular consequence, which is itself the antecedent of yet another behavior, and so on. Thus, the end behavior, which may be an undesired act, is the result of a long series of antecedent–behavior–new antecedent–new behavior. By the time you reach the end of the chain of events, the impulse to perform the final, undesirable behavior is very difficult to restrain.

Such chains are always present in any form of substance abuse—in the problem drinker who transfers buses just in front of the liquor store, the ex-smoker who buys cigarettes to keep around the house for his friends, or the reformed drug user who decides to go to the party just to be cordial to his druggie friends. These mini-decisions are formed into chains that lead to violations (Cummings, Gordon, & Marlatt, 1980). A good strategy is to interrupt the chain of events early (Ferster, Nurnberger, & Levitt, 1962). An interruption at an early, weak link in the chain can prevent the occurrence of the final behavior.

Building in pauses. When a chain is well established, you may find yourself responding without thinking, whether the antecedent is a rude statement or a plateful of food. A helpful technique for dealing with this automatic quality of chained antecedents is to pause before responding.

The pause technique is particularly useful for indulgent behaviors. For smoking, gradually increasing pauses between the urge and lighting up, or between puffs, is an effective technique for reducing the number of cigarettes smoked (Newman & Bloom, 1981a, 1981b). For excessive drinking, a pause between feeling the urge for another and allowing oneself that next drink is highly recommended. A 2-minute pause in the middle of each meal is one of the most effective techniques dieters can use (Sandifer & Buchanan, 1983). Whether smoking, drinking, or eating is the problem, a 2-minute pause is often enough for the urge to pass. During that pause, you can read your body more accurately. Do you really need that cigarette? Are you getting drunk? Are you really hungry? Merely asking these questions during the pause will break up the automatic sequence of consume, consume, consume.

The pause technique is useful for a variety of problems and combines well with other tactics. A young father was upset because he often spanked his children:

> I know that I hit them when they disobey me—particularly when they bicker with each other and I tell them to stop and they don't. So I tried just pausing for a second before spanking them. Sometimes that worked, but sometimes it didn't. I just waited a second and then hit the child anyway. So I started saying to myself, "Now, think. Don't just stand here being angry and then hit. Think. What should I do right now to get the children to behave?"

This man gave himself instructions during his pause.

Pausing to make a record. Recording an unwanted behavior before you do it may reduce its frequency. If you require yourself to make a record early in the chain of events, you gain greater control over later events than if you wait until the last links in the chain to record the behavior (Kazdin, 1974b). For example, as you feel the first signs of panic coming over you, stop and rate the degree of panic you feel. That gives you time to realize that your reaction is (probably) out of proportion to the actual event and that there are ways you can cope.

In general, the earlier in the chain of events you make the interruption, the more effective your plan will be. A couple who had developed a destructive pattern of arguing learned to recognize the first signs of such a pattern and arranged to stop immediately to make entries in their structured diaries. Usually this pause was sufficient to break the chain of their destructive arguing.

Unlinking the chain of events. A young woman had a problem with excessively frequent urination. She reported that she went to the bathroom an average of 13 times a day, an unsettling and embarrassing situation. She had seen a physician, who assured her that there was no medical problem.

In gathering the baseline data, she realized that two separate antecedents led to urination. First, she almost never went into a bathroom (for example, to wash her face or comb her hair) without using the toilet. Second, she went to the toilet at the first hint of bladder pressure. To break up the control of the first antecedent (entering a bathroom), she used this simple plan. She would go into a bathroom, perform some behavior that didn't involve using the toilet, and walk out. For example, she would enter, wash her hands, and leave. Or she might comb her hair or put on lipstick and then leave. In this way, she broke up the inevitable relationship between going into a bathroom (the antecedent) and using the toilet (the behavior).

To break up the control of the second antecedent (the initial hint of bladder pressure), she used the pause technique. Upon feeling the first hint of pressure, she required herself to pause for 5 minutes before urinating. This technique was sufficient because 5 minutes later she was usually busy doing something else.

This strategy of unlinking a chain is necessary whenever problem antecedents cannot be avoided. The old antecedent must lead to a new, desired behavior instead of the old, undesired act. The next case illustrates an unusual use of this strategy.

A depressed young woman discovered through her A-B-C analysis that her "down" feelings were preceded by interactions with other people that made her feel uninteresting, ignored, and even rejected. These feelings quickly turned into almost obsessive thoughts about her worthlessness, and a deep depression would set in. The chain looked like this:

Step 1		*Step 2*		*Step 3*
Disappointing interactions with others	$\longrightarrow$	Thoughts of personal worthlessness	$\longrightarrow$	Feelings of depression

She reasoned that not every interaction with others could turn out perfectly for her. Her plan called for changing the second link of the chain. Whenever she felt disappointed by an interaction, as soon as she got home she inserted a new, pleasant event— sewing. This was an entirely new activity for her, and she began with no previous interest in or skill at dressmaking. She said, "I never thought of sewing as something good, but I've discovered that those simple things can have a lot of meaning. And now I'm much less dependent on other people." At the end of her program, she felt much more mature, and her depressions were no longer a problem (Tharp, Watson, & Kaya, 1974).

Long chains can be altered most effectively by intervening at both ends. Frankel (1975), who also reported the case study in Box 5-1, has presented the research and theory supporting this position. As you read this case, notice three features in particular. First, the antecedents were changed both at the beginning and at the end of the chain. Second, the father had to learn a new behavior to be inserted in the chain. Third, the outcome of the new chain had to be reinforced. This illustrates how a well-developed plan will often require a combination of strategies.

Arranging New Antecedents

So far we have spoken of avoiding, narrowing, or rearranging antecedents, but a critical factor is often creating new antecedents that will cue desirable outcomes. New antecedents can be inserted at the beginning of a chain or at any point within it. In this section, we will discuss verbal antecedents (self-instructions) and other forms of stimulus control.

Box 5-1
A Family's Chain

Chains of events are often composed of the behaviors of several people. This case illustrates a chain of family behaviors that produced unhappiness for all three members.

The Chain

1. Mother asks Bobby to do something at home. (When Father asks him, there is usually immediate compliance.)
2. Bobby refuses.
3. Mother gets very irritated and screams at Bobby, or hits him, or both.
4. Bobby screams back and rarely complies.
5. When Bobby does not comply, either Mother goes and gets Father or Father hears the incident occurring and barges in. (Or Father is told of the incident on returning home.)
6. Father and Bobby yell at each other. Usually Father hits Bobby or physically forces him to get moving on task. In any case, Bobby eventually complies.

This chain of events lasted from a few minutes to several hours, ending when the father, on coming home, learned of the incident and forced Bobby to comply. The incidents didn't always go all the way through the chain. When Bobby complied with his mother's demands or when she didn't tell her husband about an incident, the incident ended at those points.

Eliminating Negative Self-Statements

When you perform some self-defeating behavior, you may actually be instructing yourself to do it. Your self-observations can show this pattern. For example, a young woman who seemed unable to relax when she was with men reported that as soon as a man started talking with her, she said to herself things like, "He's not going to like me," or "I'm going to be shy," or "I'm not going to make a good impression." These "self-instructions" made her tense and made her act in a less attractive manner.

A man whose job was less than perfect said that while at work, he said things to himself such as, "This is so boring. How depressing! This is awful!" which made him like his job even less. A socially anxious student, whenever someone was short with her or even frowned, thought, "I'm such a social klutz."

In these kinds of situations, *replace the self-defeating thoughts with incompatible ones, including thoughts that contain positive self-instructions.* For example, when the shy young woman realized that she was thinking, "He's not going to like me; I'm going to be shy," she said instead, "No, not this time. Now remember: smile, make eye contact, stay calm, listen carefully to what he is saying." She substituted "self-coaching" for the unwanted self-defeating thoughts.

The Plan

It seemed that Bobby had learned to use one of his parents to get to the other one. A simple analysis of the problem behavior might have stopped after step 3, when Mother screams at Bobby, or hits him, or both. The time lag between steps 3 and 6 was sometimes hours, and the whole behavior chain didn't always occur because sometimes the incident ended without Father's intervention.

To achieve modification of this sequence, Mother was instructed to extinguish her behavior in response to Bobby's noncompliance (step 3). She agreed to either remain calm or leave the room until she could respond to Bobby calmly. In no case was she to call Father or was he to come in. Father also agreed to spend 3 hours a week with Bobby doing something of Bobby's choosing. At the 3-month follow-up, the parents reported that Bobby's incidents of aggression and noncompliance in the home had been reduced to a level not considered a problem. They rated Bobby's aggression at a raw score of 65 (compared to 80 initially). At the 1-year follow-up, the parents reported that Bobby's behavior at home continued not to be a problem.

In the old chain, Bobby received a strong reward for his misbehaviors—interaction with Father, even though it was an aggressive kind of interaction. It turned out that Father had never learned to play with his little boy. In the new chain, the 3 hours a week of play with Dad were strongly rewarding to both Bobby and his father.

SOURCE: Adapted from "Beyond the Simple Functional Analysis—The Chain: A Conceptual Framework for Assessment with a Case Study Example," by A. J. Frankel, 1975, *Behavior Therapy*, 6, pp. 254–260. Copyright © 1975 by Academic Press, Inc. Reprinted by permission of the author and Academic Press.

The "social klutz" corrected herself by saying, "No, I am not. I will analyze this and see what's really going on." The man who didn't like his job substituted thoughts like, "It's not so bad. I need the money, and it's an easy job." Words guide your actions. They are antecedents you produce for your own behavior. Thus, it is important you notice negative words and change them to desirable self-instructions.

Suppose a newly hired salesperson fails to make a sale to her first customer. If she says to herself, "I was never cut out to be in sales," or "I'll never learn to do this," her future disaster is already clear. If, on the other hand, she says to herself, "I'm going to learn how to do this," then there is the possibility of future success. Those two ways of speaking to the self will produce very different actions—and two very different levels of success (Rehm, 1982).

Initiating Positive Self-Instructions

As you discover the role of self-speech antecedents in your problem situations, it is very likely that one of two conditions is present: (1) Either you are giving yourself instructions and assigning labels that cue undesired reactions; or (2) your problem behavior is "automated," and you can't identify any self-statements.

Box 5-2
Talking Through the Music

Even learning how to improvise can be improved by self-directing talk. Jazz pianist David Sudnow has written a book describing how he learned improvisational jazz piano. Here are his words—the ones he said to himself as he played:

> I did nudgings to myself, taking an inner course of action to help the outer one . . . I perked up with the assistance of saying to myself
>
> Springboard—
> get the beat right—
> keep the hand loose and flexible—
> bounce around on a place—
> breathe deeply—. . .
> relax—. . .
> be careful—. . .
> get those shoulders moving—
> keep that hand from tripping—
> get especially bebopical—
> play beautifully—
> get down on it—

SOURCE: *Ways of the Hand: The Organization of Improvised Conduct* (pp. 146–147) by D. Sudnow, 1978, Cambridge, MA: Harvard University Press.

In either event, the same strategy is called for. *Insert into the chain of events new self-instructions that will guide the desired behavior.* Almost every self-modification plan should include the use of some new self-instructions (Meichenbaum, 1977). They are very effective and can help overcome a variety of problems (Dush, Hirt, & Schroeder, 1983).

Designing a self-instruction plan is very simple. The strategy is merely to substitute new instructions for the self-defeating ones that you now use. Stop telling yourself, "I can't do this!" Say instead, "I can" (and then tell yourself how). Decide what you want to do, and tell yourself to do it. The instructions should be brief and clear (see Box 5-2). As a further example, the following are changed self-instructions for reducing angry outbursts. Instead of saying, "Nobody treats me that way!" substitute a coping statement such as, "This is rough, but I can handle it"; "Chill out, this will soon be over"; or "I'm in control" (Deffenbacher, McNamara, Stark, & Sabadell, 1990).

State your new belief aloud as a reminder before you enter a difficult situation (Kanter & Goldfried, 1979). A young student who had just moved into her own apartment (against her parents' wishes) reminded herself while driving back home on Saturdays, "Remember, I can tolerate their disapproval. They continue to love me. I have made the right decision. I don't need to have approval constantly." Even during a problem situation, statements of belief or judgment can guide your reactions. When the topic of living alone comes up once more, this student can say to herself, "I'm overreacting; I don't need to feel upset," and then add a precise self-instruction: "Breathe deeply and slowly. Try to change the subject."

Making absurd statements is of little use. One study of women who attempted to cope with depression discovered that both the successful and the unsuccessful women used encouraging self-instructions. But the successful ones believed the positive things they told themselves (Doerfler & Richards, 1981). Telling yourself, "I am the most brilliant woman in the state of Illinois!" will not affect your behavior much—unless, of course, you believe it's true. Prepare a list of true positive statements about yourself. Use those statements regularly, at moments of quiet as well as moments of stress.

Self-instructions can also remind you of your long-range goals. Before approaching a woman, the shy man described earlier said to himself, "Remember, this is important to me. I've got to learn how to talk to women or I'll die a hermit." This kind of self-statement brings your long-range goal forward in your mind and increases your incentive to perform the next new behavior.

Couldn't you get all these benefits by just "remembering" what to do without actually saying the words? Perhaps, but unless you say the words, your "remembering" may be too vague to be useful. Actually saying the words—in your mind, in your imagination, or even aloud—brings up self-speech from the underground and allows it to exercise full power.

Thought Substitutions

Intrusive or unpleasant thoughts, in their extreme forms, are called obsessions. In their milder forms, self-degrading and self-defeating thoughts—such as, "I'm no good" or "I'm a loser"—are unfortunately common. They may be visual as well as verbal and may take the form of some unpleasant image that, like a persistent tune, you can't seem to get out of your mind.

Attempts to actively suppress unwanted thoughts may make matters worse (Clark, Ball, & Paper, 1991; Davies & Clark, 1998; Warda & Bryant, 1998; Wegner, Schneider, Knutson, & McMahon, 1991). Substituting a distracting thought seems to be more effective (Wegner & Schneider, 1989). As soon as some unwanted thought occurs, immediately substitute a different one—if possible, the opposite of the unwanted thought (Cautela, 1983; Turner, Holzman, & Jacob, 1983). If you think, "I'm going to screw this up," substitute, "I will succeed!" Then give yourself instructions on how to perform adequately.

Amy, one of our students, reported:

> Whenever I was late, I would increase my nervousness by thinking, "I'm always late. Someone will be mad at me. I'm letting them down." During the project, I attempted to stop those thoughts and replace them with others, especially when I was hopelessly late! I would tell myself, "They probably won't even notice. They'll forgive you. Try harder next time. Getting stressed about the situation won't help. You can change." Many times I was on the bus or walking to class, so these statements, just a few of them, would be sufficient to stop the negative thoughts.

Building New Stimulus Control: The Physical and Social Environments

You can also arrange new physical antecedents, or cues, to stimulate desired behavior. The simplest instance of this procedure can be illustrated by expanding our discussion of narrowing antecedents of intellectual work—studying or writing. A good way to develop the habit of increased studying or writing is to increase the environmental stimulus control over concentrated writing. You can arrange a special "writing" environment so that whenever you are in that situation (1) you are concentrating, and (2) you are not doing anything else. Thus, you begin by learning to concentrate while writing at a certain place in which you never do anything else but write.

If you don't have a place you can reserve for this one behavior, you can set up a particular arrangement of cues. For example, a man had in his room only one table, which he had to use for a variety of activities, such as writing letters, paying bills, watching TV, and eating. But when he wanted to do concentrated studying or writing, he always pulled his table away from the wall and sat on the other side of it. In that way, sitting on the other side of his table became the cue associated only with concentrated intellectual work.

Suppose that no matter how diligent you are in removing yourself from your desk when not concentrating, the concentrated work still does not come? Using other people as supporting stimuli can provide the necessary first step. Brigham (1982) suggests that the first environment you choose for studying should be one in which studying is a high probability response, such as the library. He suggests:

A change in behavior could be accomplished by identifying a friend who regularly studies in the library and asking to study with that person. . . [You should] reinforce the friend for being a study partner. Such reinforcement will . . . increase the likelihood that the friend will reinforce your studying behavior. (p. 55)

One of the most powerful cues to behavior is seeing that same behavior performed by other people in the same environment. This effect can be used to positive advantage when you have difficulty "priming" that first behavior step.

A student of ours struggled to begin exercising. She wrote:

About March I dropped the excuses and went to the Y with Derek. And it was so fun! Because I used to be a member, I knew how to use almost all the equipment, the treadmills, the stair-climbers, and Derek even taught me how to squat. And Sheri, my best friend, was there, too . . . so the next two weeks I was really proud of myself. I ran three times at the park with my friend. I didn't run long but at least I wasn't in front of the brain-rot tube, and we had a good conversation during the run, too. Two more weeks of good exercise! I ran once, and snorkeled at Hanauma Bay with Junior. Then I went kayaking, that will make you sweat and use calories! You have to pull your own weight in a two-man kayak, especially when your partner is a guy egging you on and calling you a wus. I want to build up to exercising alone. Would an iPod help? Maybe, but I think I need a friend. If someone will work out with me, I'm there in a second. . . .

It's important to ask yourself if changing some of your social interactions could help you change. Friends, family, and acquaintances interact with us in habitual ways, and these interactions can build cues that are not always desirable. Frequently, the responses are emotional. People who are depressed often find themselves unable to "break out" of frustrating and unrewarding patterns with their associates. Doerfler and Richards (1981) studied a group of women who initiated efforts to control their mild depression. Of those who were successful, 67% made dramatic changes in their social environments, whereas few unsuccessful subjects had done so (14%). For adolescent smokers, time spent with friends who smoke makes quitting less likely (Jones, Schroeder, & Moolchan, 2004).

Box 5-3
Self-Instructions for Studying: A Self-Experiment

A college student's instructors reported the following case:

> Betty was 19 years of age, enrolled as an undergraduate student at a large urban university, and currently sharing an apartment with two students. Although Betty always studied (read) at home, she described the process as a "hassle" in that she frequently talked on the telephone, snacked on "junk foods," conversed with her roommates, and/or listened to music while reading. Because she was enrolled in a class that required a great deal of reading, she wanted to decrease these behaviors.

Behavior Observations

Betty made observations of her studying once every 5 minutes for approximately 1 hour per evening, 5 evenings per week. She noted whether or not she had been studying in the previous 5. Because the length of time spent studying varied, the number of observed time samples ranged from 6 to 15, with the majority equaling 12 per session. Studying was defined as "sitting in a chair, reading a textbook, underlining important facts, and/or taking notes on a separate sheet of paper." All data were transcribed onto an 8 ½" × 11" paper that was divided into squares, each square representing a 5-minute time sample.

Experimental Phases

Baseline. During this 10-day phase, Betty continued studying in the living room. Although most studying occurred during the early evening hours, on two occasions Betty read during the afternoon. Other than recording data according to the described procedures, Betty was asked not to attempt to alter her studying behaviors.

Experimental demands. Betty wrote a series of instructions on an index card:

> It's important to study to get good grades. I need to study to understand new material. I'm not going to talk to my roommates, because it's important that I learn this material. It's important that I learn this material; therefore, I will not talk on the phone. I will remain studying even though I feel the urge to eat or drink something. Because listening to music distracts me and it is important that I learn this material, I will not play the stereo.

Betty read the card once immediately prior to reading. She did this for 13 days.

Self-instructions. Then Betty constructed a second card, listing an additional series of instructions:

> OK. I've got my books out, and I'm turning to the right page. This is what I am supposed to be doing, because it will help me to be a better student and earn good grades. Studying also helps me understand new material, which is important in getting good grades. Because I need to learn this material,

(continued)

Box 5-3 *(continued)*

I will not talk to my roommates or talk on the phone. Even though I feel the urge to get up and get something to eat or drink, I will not, because it is important for me to learn this material. Therefore, I will keep reading the textbook and take good notes.

During the next 6 days, Betty read the second card once every 15 minutes throughout the studying hour. She continued reading the first card prior to studying. All other procedures were similar to the initial baseline phase.

Withdrawal. During the next 10 days, Betty's experimenting instructor asked her not to read either card. This was done to test whether the instructions were still needed.

Self-instructions 2. This 6-day phase was similar to the previous self-instruction phase; she read both cards to herself again.

Results

Figure 5-1 represents graphically the percentage of time Betty studied. Studying percentages were computed by dividing the number of times Betty recorded herself as reading by the total number of observations taken during that session. Baseline rates for studying averaged about 59%. Under the demand-phase condition, studying increased to about 73%. After the self-instruction phase was implemented, studying increased to approximately 96%. During the withdrawal phase, the percentage fluctuated widely, but leveled out again at about 96% after the treatment was reinstated.

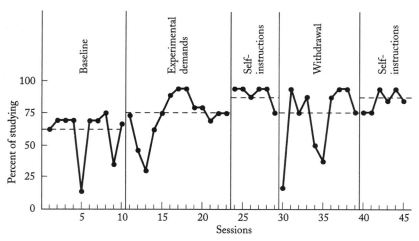

Figure 5-1 A record of Betty's studying across experimental conditions.
SOURCE: Reprinted with permission of authors and publisher from Figure 2, "Application of a Simple, Self-Instruction Procedure on Adults' Exercise and Studying: Two Case Reports," by R. Cohen, P. De James, B. Nocera, and M. Ramberger, 1980, *Psychological Reports, 46,* pp. 443–451. Copyright © 1980 Psychological Reports.

In beginning a difficult self-improvement program, such as giving up tobacco, alcohol, or drugs, it is important that you experience early success in order to increase your feelings of self-efficacy. For this reason, it is often wise to choose one situation or cue condition in which you feel confident that you can resist temptation. Begin by not smoking or drinking in that situation, and when you have experienced that feeling of self-efficacy, expand to more difficult situations (Nicki, Remington, & MacDonald, 1984). Self-efficacy's effects are so powerful that Bandura argues that it provides a more powerful explanation of self-regulation than cybernetic approaches (Bandura & Locke, 2003). But both are examples of deliberately establishing antecedent stimulus control so that you can perform a desired behavior reliably in at least one situation.

For goals of increasing positive behavior, however, you will probably want to perform the behavior in many situations. For example, most busy students are better off if they can study in many situations, so that each opportunity can be seized. For such goals, the range of effective antecedents can be broadened by practicing in a variety of situations, followed by some form of self-reward (see Chapter 7).

Stimulus Generalization

Many behaviors, such as studying, writing, abstaining from drugs, improving social skills, and refraining from overeating, will have to be performed eventually in a variety of environments. *Stimulus generalization* is the process by which a behavior that has been learned in the presence of one antecedent is performed in the presence of other, similar antecedents.

The more similar the new situation is to the original situation, the easier it is to generalize your newly learned behavior. Therefore, you will want to think about the similarity between other situations and the one in which you can already perform the desired behavior. You should begin generalization by performing the target behavior in the situation that is most similar to the original one.

A middle-aged woman suffered from a very strong fear of speaking in front of groups. Through self-modification, she developed the ability to speak to a group of three or four friends. Having accomplished that, she wanted to generalize the newly acquired ability to new groups. She thought it would be easier if the new group contained at least a couple of friends from the old one because the new situation would then be very similar to the one in which she first practiced. She arranged things so that such an opportunity occurred. When it did, she performed the target behavior and then reinforced it.

Once you have developed a behavior that you can perform in certain situations, gradually move into other, similar situations. Use self-instructions. A great strength of self-instructions is that they can be used in many situations, thus creating a bridge from familiar to unfamiliar circumstances. Self-instructions are portable cues. They can be taken with you from party to party, from home to library. Thus, self-instructions enhance the development of a broad skill base, just as stimulus generalization does.

Precommitment and Programming of the Social Environment

Precommitment means arranging in advance for helpful antecedents to occur. This arrangement can be made when some problem situation is anticipated, especially for those moments of maximum difficulty.

A smoker had been off cigarettes for about 2 months. He had stopped several times in the past, but each time he had gone back to smoking. He had been successful this time because he had identified those situations in which he had relapsed in the past and had taken steps to deal with them. One of the problem situations was being at a party. The drinks, the party atmosphere, and the feeling of relaxation represented an irresistible temptation to "smoke just a few," although in the past this usually led to a return to regular smoking. One night, as the man and his wife were getting ready to go out to a party, he said, "You know, I am really going to be tempted to smoke there. Will you do me a favor? If you see me bumming a cigarette from someone, remind me of how much the kids want me to stay off cigarettes."

This man arranged in advance to be reminded, and he made this precommitment at a time when he was not strongly tempted—before going to the party. You can encourage family and friends to help you achieve your goals by asking them to provide cues and reinforcers for the behaviors you want to develop and by asking them not to support undesired behavior (Stuart, 1967).

Family or friends can help, or they may create antecedents to problem behaviors. The dieter whose roommate presents her with a box of chocolates or whose mother bakes her a pie is placed in a situation in which overeating becomes more likely. Loved ones cannot always know exactly what you need; be specific in telling them what kind of helpful antecedents to provide.

Precommitment, in the form of reminders, can also be arranged without the help of others. Setting an alarm clock is one obvious way. Preparing a daily or weekly schedule of obligations is another. A daily plan for social and achievement-related activities increases psychological adjustment for anyone—and these good effects increase with sticking to the plan (Nezlek, 2001).

"My whole life is one stress-out," Suellen wrote. "A job, 18 credits, a tiny social life—there is no time for anything. I freak out and freeze and everything is falling apart. I'm going to make a daily schedule, with everything realistic in it, a week at a time, and see if it helps my psychological adjustment." It did.

Ainslee (1992) points out that *precomittment* can refer to any of the ways that we arrange in advance to alter conditions so that we will choose to act in our long-range best interests. This includes rule setting, distractions from attention, altering perceptions, and avoiding emotions that make us more likely to err.

Tips for Typical Topics

Anxiety and Stress

Find the situations that cue anxiety. What are the antecedents to which you react? Many situations induce anxiety, depending on how you interpret them to yourself.

Thoughts, feelings, or interpretations that a personal threat is present most often precede feelings of anxiety (Beck & Emery, 1985; Sewitch & Kirsch, 1984). Note the worrisome things you tell yourself. Are they true? For example, "I'm failing this test. This is a catastrophe!" First, are you actually failing? Second, is it a catastrophe? Compared to an earthquake? Statements that suggest extreme personal threat—catastrophizing statements, such as, "Oh, God, I can't stand it!"—lead to less-adequate coping (Steenman, 1986). Particularly watch for thoughts in which you tell yourself that the anxiety-provoking situation is uncontrollable (Barlow, 1988). Almost certainly the situation is controllable—by those who have learned how. You are more likely to learn how if you tell yourself, "It is possible."

Box 5-4
Krista Is Crying in Prague: A Continuing Case

Krista came to Prague for a university course in psychology taught by a visiting Fulbright scholar. Krista had two learning goals: to learn psychology and to improve her English. Here is her delightful personal journal, a record of her errors in psychology (and in English), her struggles with her project, and her ultimate improvement.

Krista writes:

For my project I have chosen my crying episodes. Always when I was in a painful situation and I didn't know how to solve it I started crying. By "painful situation" I mean first of all disagreements with other people. Mainly with authority e.g. parents. When I couldn't make any more arguments I felt naked and I started crying. Everybody thought: she is just a little girl and she can't behave like an adult. So when I was small I cried very often. It was my weapon. It always succeeded. I got what I wanted.

I'm trying to change this behavior, because crying isn't suitable for a twenty years old girl. I want to stop and gain the respect of the others and a good feeling for myself.

Goals & Definitions: My goal is to stop crying in all situations (apart from situations when it is tolerated, and when it is natural for a twenty year old girl). Instead of this, I want to be able to tell my opinion and insist on my decision. Not to be cheeky, but self-confident.

Observation & record keeping: For recording my behavior I use a small notepad and I write what happened. I use this structured diary all the time, because I have to note a lot of ideas and feelings. Every crying accident has three parts—antecedents, behavior, and consequences. It is very useful to write down all three parts, because after a few accidents you will see connections and you will be able to modify your plan to work better.

Here is part of my diary:

26th of March—*Antecedents*—I was in a pub in Prague with my friends. I had some beers and I was on the way home. Because I don't know Prague at all, I was lost and I didn't know how to get home. I was only with my dog and she didn't know it neither.
Behavior—I started to cry and it didn't solve my situation. I cell-phoned my boyfriend, he of course helped me, but he wasn't keen that I was crying.
Consequences—I was crying all the way home, but I didn't mind it because people who saw me didn't know me. I came home and felt really happy and I forgot the accident.

(continued)

Box 5-4 *(continued)*

5th April—*Antecedents*—I was in my house in a village. Because I'm allergic to pollen and it was spring, I didn't feel so good. I was in bed. My boyfriend came home and asked me to go with him to the village pub. Of course I didn't want to, but he wanted to go. I wished he would stay with me at home.

Behavior—I didn't tell him anything. I started crying. I was so ashamed of crying that I pretended that I was feeling so bad from allergies that I had to cry.

Consequences—Finally I went to the pub, and it was good.

12th April—*Antecedents*—I was at home, I didn't go with my friend out, because my boyfriend promised to be at home. At the end he finally came home. He had a delay of two hours. I was really mad, I wanted to tell him what I feel.

Behavior—Instead of that I started crying and didn't speak at all.

Consequence—It was in the evening. I was so tired I asleeped.

(I have not changed my recording system, because my crying episodes are infrequent now and it is not a problem for me to write things down. I hope that someday I will not need my notepad at all.)

Components of my behavior change plan: At first my behavior change plan was just stop crying. I thought it would be easy. I tried just to don't cry when I was feeling like crying. Early on I found that plan didn't work. Then I noticed that my problem is more with communication with others than just crying episodes. I noticed it thanks to my structured diary and especially the antecedents. So I made a new plan. I try to prepare (imagine) possible troublous situations. I use information from the past. I remember my past crying episodes and I try to learn what I did wrong and how to improve my reactions.

At this point in the semester, Krista has made progress in understanding the antecedent of her behavior—frustration over not speaking out about her opinions in a firm way. This is a good use of a full and honest note pad. Because of this, we are optimistic for her, but the question is whether she will be able to develop those new behaviors of "self-confident but not cheeky" speaking out. She should be helped by Chapter 6; we will return to this case, to see if Krista is still crying in Prague.

SOURCE: Taught by Karen Budd, to whom we are grateful for providing this case. Reprinted with permission.

Include in your self-contract a very specific self-statement analysis. For example, Altmaier, Ross, Leary, and Thornbookrough (1982) suggest the following items for your contract:

- In order to cope more successfully, I will pause when I notice my stress signals of
  _____ .
- I will examine my feelings, images, and self-statements, such as _____ .
- If I am using negative self-talk, I will switch to telling myself _____ .

Assertion

The assertive person is one who (1) behaves appropriately in social situations, (2) is honest, and (3) is able to express thoughts and feelings straightforwardly while taking into account the feelings and welfare of others (Rimm & Masters, 1979). The difference between assertion and aggression is that one is appropriate, the other is not. Many nonassertive people become very angry before they finally speak up, so when they do act, they are more likely to be verbally aggressive than if they had asserted themselves earlier (Linehan, 1979). Therefore, it is desirable to act assertively early in the chain of events. Increasing assertive behavior has been shown to reduce feelings of anger (Moon & Eisler, 1983).

Early intervention in the chain can be approached through beliefs or self-instructions or both. Goldfried (1979) and his associates have shown that timid people often believe that others will reject or punish them for the slightest bit of standing up for themselves, but objectively this is rarely true. Search out such beliefs. Change them to positive self-instructions. Self-instructions are particularly useful in coaching yourself through unfamiliar behavior: "Remember, be firm. That's right, you needn't be unpleasant. Just state your position firmly. Good."

Depression and Low Self-Esteem

The single most effective antidote to depression is probably a new environment— one that has more pleasant activities available and offers more opportunities for rewarding social interactions. Changing environments is often a sufficient plan for lifting mood and self-esteem (Doerfler & Richards, 1983).

Another major tactic for antecedent control of depression is the scheduling of pleasant activities (Hollon & Beck, 1979). Depressed people do not often use this powerful antecedent of good mood (Fuchs & Rehm, 1977). The type of activity—entertainment, socializing, exercise, fantasizing, or handicrafts—is not crucial so long as it is pleasant for you. Schedule these activities regularly and frequently, and stick to the schedule.

Depression and low self-esteem are closely tied together (Kendall, Stark, & Adam, 1990); students who believe they are poor at problem solving are more likely to become depressed (Dixon, Heppner, Burnett, Anderson, & Wood, 1993). After equivalent events, depressed persons will be more down on themselves for not meeting their own too-high standards (Rehm, 1988). Look for such distorted self-statements as too many "shoulds" ("I should visit my family more"), comparisons ("Compared with _____ I am really flawed"), and perfectionisms ("I must do everything perfectly; otherwise I will be criticized and be a failure"). Perfectionistic students are more depressed after doing poorly on a test than less perfectionistic students (Brown, Hammen, Craske, & Wickens, 1995; Freeman & Zaken-Greenburg, 1989).

These excessive standards suggest two strategies. First, you can reexamine your goals and standards and try to make them more realistic. Second, you can closely examine your self-statements, thoughts, and judgments of your own performance.

When you notice a change in your mood, try to discover what thoughts led to it. Thoughts such as, "I'm a loser," or "I never do anything right," will certainly depress your mood and should be replaced by more positive self-statements (Rehm, 1982). Prepare positive self-statements in advance, even rehearse them, so that you can use them immediately as replacements. Depressed people tend to distract themselves from negative thoughts with other negative thoughts (Wenzlaff, Wegner, & Roper, 1988). When you are depressed, you may even criticize yourself for criticizing yourself: "I just thought that I'm a loser. What a stupid thing to think" (Hollon & Beck, 1979).

When you self-criticize, have a dispute ready: "I'm not a loser. Actually I'm a loyal and sensitive friend." Or remember to speak to yourself as a best friend: "We win some, we lose some. You're actually a great guy."

Be especially vigilant about negative self-statements after some disappointment. Prepare positive self-statements, and expect to use them immediately after disappointments.

Exercise and Athletics

In beginning a lifestyle-change program, such as adopting a schedule of regular exercise, one of the first hurdles to overcome is the pain. Stiff muscles, aches, and weariness in the early stages of running or aerobics can punish the new behavior out of existence. However, self-instructions during exercise-induced discomfort can be very helpful. It is better to use self-instructions that distract from pain rather than those that urge you on in spite of the pain. Tell yourself to "smell the flowers" or "watch the clouds." This is more effective for beginning exercisers than such instructions as, "You can do better!" or "You can make it!" (Martin et al., 1984).

If you are a more experienced athlete who is attempting to increase performance, altogether different strategies may be appropriate (Suinn, 1987). Serious runners, such as marathoners, improve performance by careful monitoring and self-instructions about their form and fatigue levels, even their levels of pain. No smelling the flowers for them! However, if events occur that produce anxiety—such as seeing other runners gaining, or feeling fear of the hill to come—then distracting self-instructions may help even seasoned athletes, who might tell themselves to count the clouds or find the biggest tree.

Relations with Others: Social Anxieties, Social Skills, and Dating

Antecedents for social anxiety often include meeting new people, carrying on a conversation with people you don't know well, being the center of attention, speaking in front of a class, or being evaluated by others. All these conditions have one thing in common: You want to manage your self-presentation to others and be perceived in positive terms. It is completely normal to experience some tension in these situations. But those who suffer from high social anxiety engage in very different kinds of self-talk when they prepare for social interactions. They are more likely to tell themselves that the situation is threatening and that they will be seen as incompetent and unattractive (Carver & Scheier, 1986). Even neutral distracting thoughts are better in reducing anxiety (Heinrichsen & Clark, 2003).

Discover your own self-talk in approaching social interactions. Make sure you are not using catastrophizing statements. Plan for more adaptive, skill-related, and confident self-instructions.

Self-instructions are also very useful as antecedent control in strained relationships. If relationships are severely distressed, you may wish to use avoidance for a time, limiting interaction to certain situations.

In what specific situations do you have problems? Consult the list in Chapter 3. Many students, for example, feel they don't know how to ask for a date, or they fear rejection so much that they never ask. Do certain situations cue you to avoid social interactions? What negative self-instructions do you give yourself, such as, "He'd probably just laugh if I asked him out?" Can you discover any self-defeating beliefs, such as, "If I ask her out and she refuses, it's a disaster," or "If there's a lull in the conversation, it means we are bored, and that's terrible," or "I really need to impress him, so I'd better show off"?

Use self-instructions to coax yourself through particular situations, such as making conversation. "Remember, talk about what she wants to talk about. Ask her what she is interested in, then talk about that. Express interest in her." You may feel you don't know what to do in certain social situations, or you become fearful in them. These problems can be dealt with after you read the next chapter.

Smoking, Drinking, and Drugs

Early success is important in controlling the use of harmful substances. Select one situation in which you are confident that you can resist smoking or drinking. Begin with that situation so that you can have the experience of success and self-efficacy (Nicki, Remington, & MacDonald, 1984).

If your problem occurs frequently at home, change the antecedents by changing the geography of your area—rearrange the furniture, move the television set or the bed where your indulgence occurs. For public locations, as an immediate first step, avoid the antecedent situations that are the cues for your indulgence, particularly those where others will be indulging—for example, a smoker's cigarette cravings are stronger and more frequent around other smokers (Rickard-Figueroa & Zeichner, 1985). Avoiding such situations is particularly important when you are emotionally upset; intense unpleasant moods increase destructive risk-taking (Leith & Baumeister, 1996; Marlatt & Parks, 1982). If you fail to avoid a situation, then escape from it (Shiffman, 1984). If you cannot escape, distract yourself with other thoughts or activities. If you cannot be distracted, concentrate on the abstract, cool qualities of indulging. As a rule, keeping company with nonsmokers can serve as a form of positive antecedent control for people trying to stop smoking (Carey, Snel, Carey, & Richards, 1989).

Drug abstinence has been increased by programs including thought substitution (Azrin, Donohue, Besalel, Kogan, & Acierno, 1994). When feeling the rising desire, as soon as you approach the point of action, say, "Stop!" Follow this immediately with statements describing the negative consequences of using the drug, relax for 5 seconds (see Chapter 6), and then immediately begin some activity that is incompatible with drug use (also see Chapter 6).

Analyze the chains that lead to the problem behavior. The chains often lead as far back as shopping. Not buying the marijuana in the first place is the most effective point at which to break the chain. Don't order a pitcher of beer or wine; order only a single glass (George & Marlatt, 1986).

However, a complete plan should address both ends of the chain. For instance, interfere early in the chain by reducing or eliminating the supply of cigarettes—rationing them if you are cutting down, not buying or carrying them if you are stopping. Interfere late in the chain, right at the moment of the strongest urge, by asking goal questions, such as, "Why do I want to smoke this cigarette (or joint), when I have started a program to quit smoking (or using pot)?"

For alcohol, drugs, and tobacco, taking a 2-minute pause between the urge and the indulgence is an effective technique for reducing violations. Substance cravings have a particular form, like a wave: They rise in intensity, crest, and subside. George and Marlatt (1986) suggest that you "surf" those urges. Ride them out—feel them rise, then feel them fall. Experts suggest a 20-minute pause between deciding to drink and drinking; during this time, reevaluate the decision by asking yourself questions like those above (Sobell & Sobell, 1995a).

Set a definite quit date. You need not quit yet, during the collection of baseline data, but using a definite quit date is associated with successful programs (Hill et al., 1994). Both nicotine gum and the nicotine patch have been shown to increase the success of not smoking for self-helpers (Fortmann & Killen, 1995; Killen, Fortmann, Davis, & Varady, 1997).

Studying and Time Management

Four specific forms of antecedent control have proven effective (Watson, 2001):

1. *Scheduling*. Schedule regular study periods with clear starting and stopping times. Schedule by the week. Write the schedule. Keep accurate records of your performance.
2. *Reminding* of goals and values. Ask several times a day, "Is this the best use of my time right now? If it's not, what would be?"
3. *Organize* all activities: Study time will be more effectively used if your non-studying activities are also well organized. Each day, make a "to-do" list of all the things you need to fit into your scheduled time blocks. If necessary, arrange the items by priority, and select your activities accordingly.
4. *Self-instructing*. Substitute more adaptive self-speech while studying. Do not tell yourself that studying is boring. Do not remind yourself of things you'd rather do. Clarify your goals for the study period, and tell yourself to reach them.

Self-instructing has been studied as a strategy for improving your writing. Specifically instruct yourself to: (1) direct your attention to the important aspects of the task, (2) interrupt an impulsive response in favor of stopping to think, (3) generate alternatives, (4) focus your thinking, (5) perform the sequence of steps required to finish the assignment, (6) achieve calmness, and (7) stipulate your criteria for success (Harris & Graham, 1996).

Weight Loss and Overeating

Weight-reduction efforts commonly reported by adolescent females make things worse, not better. Tactics such as (self-labeled) "dieting," using appetite suppressants/laxatives, incidental exercise, and vomiting for weight-control purposes, all predict an increase in relative weight and an earlier onset of obesity (Stice, Cameron, Killen, Hayward, & Taylor, 1999).

All behavioral programs for weight loss contain features that concentrate on antecedents of eating. Your own self-directed program should include all three of the following:

1. Self-monitoring of eating behavior and activity levels
2. Instructions to control environmental influences on eating
3. Attention to thoughts and self-speech that interfere with the necessary behavior changes (Agras, 1987, p. 31)

Learning to eat properly requires careful observation of all antecedents— emotional, social, and physical (Leon, 1979; Stuart & Davis, 1972). You will almost certainly find that your overeating is dominated by external cues (Herman & Polivy, 2004). The following are four proven tactics for narrowing stimulus control, which, along with exercise and social support, is a most dependable strategy (Kirschenbaum, 1994):

1. *Decrease eating situations,* so that you allow yourself to eat only in kitchens, dining rooms, and restaurants.
2. *Place food only in food areas,* not in candy dishes, glove compartments, or bedside tables.
3. *In food areas, only eat*—discontinue working, sewing, talking, or watching TV in the kitchen or at the dining table.
4. *Make eating a pure experience* by engaging in no other activity while eating: no reading, television watching, or homework. Concentrate instead on the tastes, textures, smells, and pleasures of the food itself.

Analyze the chains that lead to the problem behavior. You can interrupt the overeating chain at several early points—for example, by shopping when you are not hungry (to prevent overbuying), by taking a list of fattening foods not to buy, by avoiding the cookie-and-cracker aisle, by not allowing yourself to become so hungry that you will gorge, and by inserting a full minute's pause in the middle of the meal.

A social support system that can help you plan to avoid or to better handle high-risk situations is a crucial strategy. Your significant others can help make poor food choices less accessible and provide cues and encouragement during times when your environment is tempting or unpredictable (Fitzgibbon & Kirschenbaum, 1992). Involving friends, as fellow dieters or as cheerleaders, increases diet discipline and weight-loss maintenance (Wing & Jeffrey, 1999). Try to eat with others who eat moderately (Herman, Roth, & Polivy, 2003).

If your problem is infrequent but excessive "binge eating," take two additional steps. First, note your self-destructive beliefs, particularly those of the "perfect love from everyone" and "perfect performance from me" types. Binge eaters appear to be especially burdened with these extremely high standards for pleasing others. When they (naturally) cannot always live up to those standards, they react with "self-damnation" statements, and then with eating splurges. Second, replace those beliefs with more reasonable ones; replace your negative self-evaluations with positive ones. This may be just as important as a direct attack on daily eating habits (Heatherton & Baumeister, 1991).

Finally, a tip to the reader who is very serious about weight loss, not only for the time you are reading this book, but thereafter. Acquire a copy of Kelly Brownell's

The LEARN® Program for Weight Management 2000 (Brownell, 2000). This excellent manual organizes all the strategies recommended here, in great detail, specifically for weight management.

Chapter Summary

Identifying Antecedents

Identifying current antecedents requires careful record keeping. Be sure to trace the chain of antecedents to its logical beginning. Discovering self-instructional antecedents involves carefully observing and amplifying the quiet thoughts that instruct you. You can discover self-defeating beliefs by writing down all instances of your problem behavior and identifying their common theme.

Modifying Old Antecedents

The first strategy for achieving antecedent control is to avoid the antecedent for the problem behavior. This is particularly appropriate for consummatory behaviors, such as overindulgence in food, drugs, or sex, because they automatically strengthen themselves on each performance by producing their own reinforcements. Particularly avoid situations where other people are engaging in your indulgent habit. This is especially important when you are in a highly emotional state.

You can sometimes avoid antecedents by narrowing the problem behavior down to a very restricted antecedent. Thus, you should leave the special desk if you are not studying or leave the bed if you cannot sleep. Antecedents can also be changed by reperceiving them—by attending to their "cool," abstract qualities rather than their "hot," pleasurable features. You can also lessen temptation by distracting yourself with thoughts of something else.

Chains of behavior develop as one act becomes the cue for the next, which in turn becomes the cue for the next, and so forth, with the entire chain being reinforced by the final reinforcement. Although it is the final act that is likely to be seen as the problem, the entire chain is implicated. Changing the chain can interrupt the automatic, "uncontrollable" nature of the problem. A chain can be scrambled, interrupted by pauses or record keeping, or changed by substituting one or more links. For long chains, it is advisable to change elements both at the beginning and at the end of the chain.

Arranging New Antecedents

A most effective way to arrange new antecedents is through self-instructions. Before an occasion for a desired behavior takes place, instruct yourself clearly and incisively. These instructions can pertain to actions or to beliefs; that is, you can instruct yourself about the details of the action you plan to take, or you can instruct yourself about your own good qualities and competence.

Self-defeating or unpleasant self-statements can be replaced with more positive ones. A key to success in suppressing negative thoughts is to substitute new, adaptive self-statements. You should actually say self-instructions aloud or subvocally, as clearly as possible and as close as possible to the moment of the actual behavior.

The physical environment can be rearranged to increase stimulus control over desired behavior. The technique is to restrict the desired behavior to a particular environment. You can arrange the social environment to stimulate desired behavior by being in the presence of others who are performing the behavior you desire.

Most behaviors that you want to acquire will be useful in several situations, so that techniques of stimulus generalization are recommended. Desirable behaviors should gradually be extended to similar situations, thus broadening the range of controlling antecedents. If you use self-instructions to bridge between situations, then the self-instructions will become portable, reliable cues, thus allowing self-regulated behavior in many situations.

Precommitment—arranging in advance for helpful antecedents to occur—is especially useful when moments of maximum difficulty are anticipated. When you know that cues to your undesired behavior will be present in a situation, precommit to having cues present that will assist your new performance reminders from others, the ring of an alarm clock, or self-reminders of your goals.

Your Own Self-Direction Project: Step 5

By examining your structured diary or your self-recording or both, identify the antecedents of any problem behavior relevant to your goals. Devise a plan for either increasing or decreasing antecedent stimulus control. As one procedure, use new self-instructions, but use at least one other technique as well.

Write this plan out, just as you have done for those in the previous steps. Don't implement your new plan yet; Chapters 6 and 7 are likely to contain ideas that you'll want to incorporate in your final plan.

Chapter 6

Behaviors: Actions, Thoughts, and Feelings

Outline and Learning Objectives

Substituting New Thoughts and Behaviors
1. What is the best approach to ridding yourself of an unwanted behavior?
2. What is an *incompatible response?*

Substitutions for Anxiety and Stress Reactions
3. What are some activities that are incompatible with anxiety? How would you use them in a self-change program?
4. How do you meditate?
5. What is rumination? Explain how to use distraction to overcome rumination.
6. Explain how to use reappraisal and rational restructuring to turn hot thoughts into cool ones.

Relaxation
7. What are the different types of "relaxation"?
8. Describe the tension-release method of relaxation.
   a. Where do you practice relaxation?
   b. When should you practice?
   c. How is relaxation used as an incompatible response?
   d. How is it combined with self-instructions?
9. What are common problems in mastering relaxation?

Developing New Behaviors
10. What is the fundamental way to master a behavior?
11. Explain *imagined rehearsal.*
12. How are imagined rehearsal and relaxation combined?
13. How does one use models in developing new behaviors?
14. Explain *imagined modeling.* What are the recommended procedures?
15. What is the value of practice in the real world?

Shaping: The Method of Successive Approximations

16. Explain the general procedure for *shaping*.
17. What are the rules for shaping?
18. How can relaxation be combined with shaping?
19. What are some common problems in shaping?

Tips for Typical Topics

Chapter Summary

Your Own Self-Direction Project: Step 6

Any plan for self-modification involves developing some new behavior. The principles for developing new behaviors in self-modification programs are the same as those that govern learning in all settings. Self-modification techniques have been devised and refined by psychologists to assist in the self-conscious use of these principles.

This chapter is organized into five main units. The first section discusses procedures for *substituting a* more desirable behavior for a less desirable one. Bringing a new behavior into position—in place of an undesired one—can be a ready solution to some problems. The second section discusses substitutions for anxiety and tension. The third section concentrates on a particular new behavior—relaxation—because it is such a useful response to substitute for anxiety and worry. Many readers can already relax effectively but will need to bring this "new" behavior into the chains that now produce worry and anxiety. The fourth section is devoted to techniques for developing new behaviors in general, particularly when the behavior is genuinely new or unknown to you. The principal techniques are *modeling* and *rehearsal*. Finally, we will discuss a fundamental strategy for acquiring new behaviors and bringing them into self-modification programs: *shaping*, or the method of successive approximations.

Substituting New Thoughts and Behaviors

Substituting positive self-statements for negative ones, substituting new self-instructions, and substituting new elements into chains are all examples of a general principle of self-modification. *The task is always* to *develop new behavior, not merely to suppress old behavior.* Simply eliminating some undesired habit has been likened to creating a behavioral "vacuum." If something is not inserted in its place, the old behavior will quickly rush back in to fill the void (Davidson, Denney, & Elliott, 1980; Tinling, 1972). Eventually, some new behavioral development is necessary. Beginning immediately with the tactic of substitution is economical because the effort of developing the new thought or behavior may automatically suppress the undesired one.

Andrea, a young woman who was bothered by frequent arguments with her father, observed her own behavior. She discovered the following chain of events: Her father would comment on some aspect of her behavior that seemed to bother him (for example, he disapproved of her career goals). Usually Andrea responded with a frown and the comment that he should mind his own business. This enraged him, and they would have another bitter argument. Andrea knew that her father basically loved her and that he was simply having a difficult time adjusting to the fact that she was now an adult. She reasoned that if she substituted kind remarks and a smile when he opened up some topic about her behavior, they might be able to discuss it in a friendlier fashion. Instead of setting out to decrease frowning and unkind comments, she set out to *increase* smiling and kind comments.

Thereafter, when her father remarked about her behavior or goals, Andrea smiled at him and strove to disagree as pleasantly as possible. (Of course, she kept a record of her responses and also used other techniques to maintain them.) Increasing the desirable behavior had the effect of calming her father, and they progressed through a series of amicable conversations to a new understanding.

Ron, a college junior, used the same tactic of substituting new behaviors for undesirable ones. Ron's girlfriend had told him very clearly that his long daily telephone calls were becoming oppressive. Ron wanted to keep the relationship, and he genuinely wanted to please his girlfriend. He set out to reduce his telephone calls to no more than one every other day. For the first few days, he suppressed the urge to call, but he found himself brooding and telling himself that her attitude proved that he was a distasteful person.

Ron then adopted a plan that used two substitute behaviors. First, he substituted more favorable (and more realistic) self-statements. At 9:00 on nights he did not call, he said to himself, "I am able to be thoughtful and generous in adopting her preferences." Second, Ron systematically substituted another behavior for that time block. Because he was an able student, he substituted an hour of studying for the phone call. Note that merely suppressing the phone calls not only left a vacuum but also allowed feelings of worthlessness and anger to slip in. The substitution strategy allowed him a more realistic self-appraisal, increased his study time, and made him a more desirable friend.

Distracting Behaviors

Another strategy is to distract yourself from the temptation to violate your resolutions. This is not a suggestion to avoid problem solving about the general issue. But when temptation, discomfort, or pain is present and inescapable, think about something else; it will make giving in less likely. Beginning joggers who included distracting thoughts while running were much more likely to be following their running program 3 months later (Dubbert, Martin, Raczynski, & Smith, 1982). For more experienced and able runners, this was not true. For experts, careful attention to actual performance was correlated with success (Okwumabua, Meyers, Schleser, & Cooke, 1983). But in early stages of mastery, distracting yourself from the temptations to smoke, eat, drink, take drugs, ruminate, or stop running is a good device.

The early Buddhists taught self-control of unwanted thoughts by this tactic of self-distracting—by recalling some doctrinal passage; by concentrating on a concrete object, such as a cloud or tree; or by concentrating on a physical activity, such as darning a sock (de Silva, 1985). In using distracters for thoughts, select a single distracter as a replacement, and always use it instead of using several different distracters (Wegner & Schneider, 1989).

Using a distracter is superior to merely trying to suppress an unwanted thought. Attempts to suppress thoughts can make them more frequent (Wegner, 1989).

Controlling emotion through distraction. How we think about our own emotions affects those emotions. Focusing on negative feelings, going over and over their causes and consequences, leads to more negative feeling, not less (Mor & Winquist, 2002; Nolen-Hoeksema, 2000). Likewise, venting emotion by giving hot expression to it does not reduce emotion, it actually intensifies and extends the emotion (Larsen & Prizmic, 2004). Distraction is a far superior means of emotion control.

Incompatible Behaviors

Whenever possible, select a substitute behavior that is *incompatible* with the undesired one. *An incompatible response is a behavior that prevents the occurrence of some other behavior.* Sitting is incompatible with running. Going swimming is incompatible with staying in your room. Being courteous is incompatible with being rude. For many undesired behaviors, several incompatible ones may be available.

Smiling is incompatible with frowning. And there is research evidence that adopting facial expressions has surprising but consistent effects on felt emotions: Smile and you will be happier; frown and sadness is more likely; scowl and feelings of anger increase (Kleinke, Peterson, & Rutledge, 1998).

The use of incompatible behaviors in controlling unwanted thoughts has a long history in religious instruction. The following is paraphrased from Buddhist advice of the fifth century:

> If an unwanted cognition is associated with lust, one should think of something lustless; if it is associated with hatred, think of something promoting loving kindness. If you are confused, think of something of great clarity. Substitute these thoughts like a carpenter driving in a new peg. (de Silva, 1985, p. 439)

A student active in campus politics was elected to the council of the Associated Students. In the meetings, he found he talked too much and lost his effectiveness because he irritated the other members. He felt the impulse to talk, he said, with "the force of a compulsion." He first tried simply being silent. He had some success, but after considering the use of incompatible responses, he reasoned that he could do better by choosing a more active and positive alternative behavior. He chose "listening." This was a genuinely new act, not merely the suppression of an old one. It resulted in less talking, which he wanted, and also in greater listening, which he came to value more and more.

Habit reversal for annoying or self-destructive habits and tics involves substituting an incompatible behavior. After you have focused your attention on the habit (perhaps through negative practice; see Chapter 2), the basic technique is to substitute a similar but harmless response. For example, substitute grooming of the nails and cuticles for biting them (Davidson, Denny, & Elliott, 1980). This proves more effective than any technique aimed only at reducing biting.

It is useful to choose an incompatible behavior even though it is of no particular value in itself. A man who wanted to stop cracking his knuckles all the time decided that whenever he felt like cracking his knuckles, he would *instead* make a fist. A young woman who sometimes scratched her skin until it bled substituted patting for scratching. (For an illustration of some incompatible responses for replacing nervous habits, see Figure 6-1.) The research evidence for the effectiveness of these techniques is excellent—so much so that habit-reversal has been extended to problems far removed from tics or grimaces (Miltenberger, Fuqua, & Woods, 1998).

Perhaps the most important element in almost all contemporary treatments for depression is the substitution of positive self-statements for negative ones. Negative

NERVOUS HABIT OR TIC			COMPETING EXERCISE
Shoulder-Jerking			Shoulders Depressed
Shoulder-Jerking Elbow-Flapping			Shoulders and Hands Pressure
Head-Jerking			Tensing Neck
Head-Shaking			Tensing Neck
Eyelash-Plucking			Grasping Objects
Fingernail-Biting			Grasping Objects
Thumb-Sucking			Clenching Fists

Figure 6-1 A pictorial representation of the various types of nervous tics or habits. The left-hand column illustrates the different tics or habits. The adjacent illustration in the right-hand column illustrates the type of competing exercise used for that nervous tic or habit. The arrows in each of the Competing Exercise illustrations show the direction of isometric muscle contraction being exerted by the client.
SOURCE: "Habit Reversal: A Method of Eliminating Nervous Habits and Tics," by N. H. Azrin and R. G. Nunn, 1973, *Behavior Research and Therapy, 11*, pp. 619–628. Copyright © 1973 by Pergamon Press, Ltd. Reprinted with permission.

Box 6-1
Relieving Depression with Incompatible Thoughts

"My problem is that I get depressed, and then I think about death and suicide, and this frightens me. Sometimes I just don't care what happens." This young woman tried a plan of listening to music or talking to friends when depression began, thinking that they would produce feelings incompatible with depression. Although she kept to this plan for 48 days, no real improvement occurred.

"Then I thought why not fight fire with fire—use good-feeling thoughts to combat depression thoughts. This would be an incompatible behavior (in the mind)."

She selected a fantasy, which she called "my good dream." Whenever a depressed thought or feeling began, she immediately substituted her "good dream" and held the dream in her mind until her feelings moved "back up at least to neutral." Here is a typical entry from her journal, which she kept along with her frequency counts and mood ratings:

> The bus driver was in a foul mood and, just as I was going out the front door, shouted, "Go to the back!" This made me feel like a fool and really started my depression. Ten minutes had gone by when I reached my job, and by then I was really starting to sink. So I took 15 minutes to try and counter my depression with my good dream. I went in 15 minutes late, but it worked.

It worked remarkably well. The graph of her declining depression shows that her depressions dropped from 3 hours a day to virtually zero (see Figure 6-2). After day 67, she stopped using any self-modification plan. We never found out what her "good dream" was.

A full habit-reversal program, of course, involves several methods: record keeping, incompatible responses, relaxation, and self-reinforcement.

(continued)

---

self-evaluations are always a part of being depressed. The following are typical depressed self-statements (Rehm, 1982):

1. After a minor quarrel with a friend: "I'm just that way. I can't get along with anyone."
2. After being praised by the boss: "He's just doing that to make me feel better because he criticized me last week."
3. After making an A on an exam: "It was an easy test. I'll fail a hard exam."

For each negative statement, try to think of substitute statements that emphasize the positive aspects of the events. You should then make these statements in place of the self-critical ones (see Box 6-1 for an example).

It's a good idea to select an incompatible behavior as soon as possible and begin to count it, even if you are still doing a baseline count on the unwanted target behavior. Keeping a record of the incompatible behavior will encourage you to perform it (Kazdin, 1974b).

Box 6-1 *(continued)*

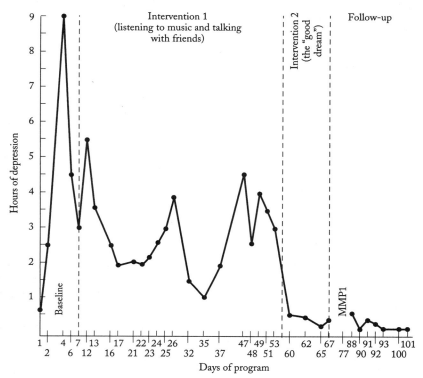

Figure 6-2 Hours of depression per day
SOURCE: "Self-Modification of Depression," by R. G. Tharp, D. L. Watson, and J. Kaya, 1974, *Journal of Consulting and Clinical Psychology, 42,* p. 624. Copyright © 1974 by the American Psychological Association. Reprinted by permission. (Condensed from the Extended Report, University of Hawaii, 1974.)

Substitutions for Anxiety and Stress Reactions

A student complained to us:

> I don't see how this system of substituting incompatible responses will work for me. I really don't need to learn anything new. I just need to get rid of my fears. When my husband wants to make love, I want to make love, too, very much, but when the crucial moment comes, I get so nervous that I can't carry on.

In fact, substituting an incompatible response is probably the best strategy for her. A goal common to many plans for self-modification is to achieve mastery over fears, anxiety, nervousness, tension, or other stress reactions. In this section, we will discuss a variety of responses that are incompatible with anxiety, and we will discuss how to arrange their substitution.

Phobias, Fears, and Avoidance Behavior

There are people who are so afraid of dogs that they will not enter a house until they are certain no dogs are there. Others fear open places so much they will not leave their own homes. An unreasonable fear of heights may prevent a person from using an elevator. Others, like the young woman above, fear sex so that they are unable to respond with any pleasure. These phobias—strong, irrational fears that interfere with normal life—produce avoidance behaviors, and the avoidance is reinforced by reducing the anxiety that would come from dogs, open spaces, heights, or sex.

Many milder, common stresses also cause people to avoid the cues that produce them. Some students feel anxious during tests. The anxiety can grow strong enough to produce extreme avoidance, even to the extent of dropping out of school.

Coping with an unreasonable fear by substituting an incompatible response is the best way to deal with the feared situation (Goldfried, 1977). The basic form of this plan is to develop a new behavior that is incompatible with anxiety and then substitute it for the anxiety as you gradually approach the feared situation.

From Sex to Kung Fu: Substitutions for Anxiety

Many behaviors are incompatible with anxiety. Simple attention to a different aspect of the situation can interfere with anxiety. For example, Frederick Kanfer (1975) has suggested that an extremely withdrawn person go to a coffee shop for a cup of coffee and specifically record for 15 minutes the number and types of interactions among people sitting at the counter. A shy, insecure woman might feel less anxious at parties if she made a point of making notes about the occupational background of a certain number of guests. In other words, if you are attending to the task of recording and interviewing, you will be less influenced by the anxiety-provoking aspects of the situation. This also allows the natural reinforcement of social gatherings to take effect.

Concentrating the attention has been used to reduce test anxiety. Focusing on the test itself (not on the fears, the grade, the consequences, other people, or the instructor) can reduce anxiety in an examination (Sarason, 1980).

Sexual arousal, too, can be used to combat anxiety because the two are incompatible. There are limits to the use of this substitute, but, when feasible, it can be helpful. Gary Brown (1978) reported a case in which a client suffered extreme anxiety whenever he had to drive past a cemetery at night. Usually he avoided driving at night, but if he did have to drive past a cemetery, he had "an overwhelming compulsion to stop the car, turn the inside light on, and look at the back seat." The client was instructed to practice driving past a cemetery near his home while imagining scenes of sexual activity with his wife. He began the imagined scenes when he was far enough from the cemetery that anxiety would not interfere and arranged to be maximally aroused just as the tombstones appeared. He did this 30 minutes each day for several days. His anxiety at the cemetery dropped to zero, and after a few days he was able to drive past without sexual arousal and without fear.

Exercise is a behavior incompatible with many forms of anxiety (Johnsgard, 1989). Marlatt and Parks (1982) recommend exercise as a substitute behavior for drinking, drug use, or smoking. As tension begins, you could substitute a session of vigorous running, aerobics, or racquetball. This can effectively replace the tension that cues indulgence in drugs. One of our students used jogging to replace the stress he experienced during marital difficulties. He found that the reduced anxiety allowed him to do better thinking and problem solving. Another student used exercising at the gym whenever she began to ruminate and get depressed over the boyfriend who broke up with her; she not only recovered from him, but also gained in self-efficacy and physical well-being.

Gershman and Stedman (1971) have reported cases in which Oriental defense exercises were used as behaviors incompatible with anxiety. Their "Mr. P." feared closed places, such as elevators, locked rooms, and trains, and had started feeling anxiety when wearing tight clothes and even his wedding ring. Their plan had Mr. P. going into a large closet and, as soon as the door closed, engaging in kung fu exercises (at which he was already adept). His anxiety disappeared after no more than 20 seconds. After several such trials, he was able to stay in the closet for up to an hour without doing his exercises or feeling any anxiety. He then practiced this in elevators, and it took him only two sessions to feel comfortable there, too. All his anxieties disappeared, and a 6-month follow-up showed no signs of recurrence. These same investigators reported similar results for Mr. R., who used karate exercises to inhibit his anxieties.

Headphones and your favorite music may also help in a feared situation. Highly valued music has demonstrated effects on reducing the anxiety associated with high-stress situations, such as being near feared animals (Eifert, Craill, Carey, & O'Conner, 1988). One of our students, Nicki, uses her own ukulele playing to relax and control her mood. "I played a song I've been working on for about 25 minutes. The melody and harmony that I created put my mind and body at peace and back in control of myself."

Rational Restructuring

Self-defeating statements and irrational beliefs often define conditions in ways that cause stress. When stress reactions, particularly anxiety or anger, begin, it is likely that these self-statements are playing a role. Actually, replacing them with effective coping statements is a form of substitution that will work like other incompatible responses (Goldfried, 1988).

This kind of reappraisal of a situation has been called *rational restructuring*. Here is an example:

> I'm standing here at a party where I know relatively few people. Everybody seems to be talking in small groups, and I'm not feeling part of things. I'm starting to become tense. On a scale of 0 to 100% tension, I'm about at a level of 40. OK, what is it that I'm thinking that may be creating this anxiety? I think I'm worried that I won't do so well in this situation. What do I mean by that? That I might not know what to say or might not come across well. And that would bother me because . . . I would look foolish to these people . . . and that would bother me because . . . they would think badly about me. And why does that upset me? That would upset me because . . . because that would mean that there is something wrong with me. Wait a minute. First of all, what are the chances that they think that of me? I don't know that they would actually think that I was inadequate or anything. At worst, they might think that I was a quiet person. Second of all, even if they did think badly of me, that doesn't necessarily mean that that's the way I am. I just don't show the best side of me in groups. I would still be me. Now that I think this way, I don't feel quite as anxious as I did, perhaps more at an anxiety level of about 20. (Goldfried, 1988, p. 62)

Notice that this reappraisal of the situation refocused on "cooler" rather than "hot" thoughts. This strategy ties back to issues of *antecedents*: the cool, restructured thoughts become cues to calm you.

Meditation as a Substitution for Anxiety

Meditation produces physical and mental conditions that are incompatible with anxiety. When a person practices meditation just before contact with a feared situation, it can produce relaxation. Boudreau (1972) reported the case of a college student who "expressed fears of enclosed places, elevators, being alone, and examinations. His avoidance behavior to these situations was extreme, having started when he was 13. The physiological sensations he experienced gave him the additional fear of mental illness" (pp. 97–98). The man was instructed to practice meditation for half an hour every day after imagining some fear-inducing scenes and *also at the actual appearance of fear-evoking situations*. Boudreau states:

> Marked improvement followed. . . . Within one month, the avoidance behavior to enclosed places, being alone, and elevators had all disappeared. Once his tension level had decreased, he did not experience abnormal physiological sensations, and this reassured him as to his physical and mental state. (p. 62)

In general, the continued practice of meditation and its use in many situations is associated with a better capacity to cope with a variety of stresses (Shapiro & Walsh, 1980). Marlatt and Marques (1977) found that meditation led to less alcohol drinking, and Throll (1981) found that it produced improvement on a variety of psychological tests measuring general stress.

Meditation is as effective as any other way of producing relaxation as a response incompatible with anxiety, according to available research (Delmonte, 1985; Woolfolk, Lehrer, McCann, & Rooney, 1982). In the next section of this chapter, we will present specific training instructions for learning another way to relax, called the tension-release method, or *progressive relaxation*. Select the method that is most pleasant for you.

How to meditate. There are several ways to meditate; every world culture has developed one or more techniques. J. C. Smith's *Relaxation, Meditation, & Mindfulness* (2005) is a useful compendium of new and traditional approaches to self-relaxation. Here is one method that has proven useful to our students.

Sit in a comfortable chair in a quiet room away from noise and interruptions. Pay no attention to the world outside your body. It is easiest to do this if you have something to focus on in your mind. For example, concentrate on your breathing or use a mantra word you say softly over and over to yourself. Here are three different mantras: *making, shiam,* and *wen* (meaningless sounds that apparently help empty the mind). Choose one. Don't say the mantra aloud, but think it, silently and gently.

When you first sit down and begin to relax, you will notice thoughts coming into your mind. After a minute or two, begin to say the mantra in your mind. Do this slowly, in a passive way. As you say the mantra to yourself, other thoughts will come. As a matter of fact, after a while you may realize that you've been so busy with these thoughts that you haven't said your mantra in several minutes. When you become aware of this, just return gently to the mantra. Don't fight to keep thoughts out of your mind; instead, let them drift through. This is not a time for working out solutions to problems or thinking things over. Try to keep your mind open so that as thoughts other than the mantra drift in, they drift out again, smoothly as the flowing of a river. The mantra will return, and you will relax with it.

It is important to make this a gentle process, a relaxing time. Don't fight to keep thoughts out of your mind. Don't get upset if you are distracted. Merely let the mantra return.

It is best to meditate in preparation for activity—for example, before you go to work—rather than after you are already tense. If used as soon as you begin to feel tense, it is a good coping reaction. People often nod off to sleep while meditating. If you do go to sleep, usually you will find that 5 minutes of meditation afterwards will make you wide awake. Some people notice that meditating makes them feel very awake—so much so that if they meditate before bedtime, they can't get to sleep.

Relaxation

Relaxation is a behavior that can be used to cope with a wide variety of problem situations. According to the dictionary, relaxation is "the casting off of nervous tension and anxiety." It is both a mental and a physical response—a feeling of calmness and serenity, and a state of muscular release and passivity.

One of the simplest methods of self-relaxation is called *integrative breathing* (Smith, 1985). It involves a quiet contemplation of your own breathing:

> Think about your breathing. Notice the passage of air through your nose, into your lungs, the swelling of your chest. Forget all else; consider only the air and the quiet. As you breathe out, feel the air flow gently over your lips; imagine it moving a feather softly and gently. You are your breathing; forget all else. Concentrate on the breath moving easily in and out. You have nothing to do but breathe, and feel the air refreshing you.

Relaxation is easily learned, if one is willing to practice it. The method used is not important—but the amount of practice is (Barrios & Shigetomi, 1979, 1980; Lewis, Biglan, & Steinbock, 1978; Miller & Bornstein, 1977; Throll, 1981). Therefore choose a method of relaxation that is pleasant for you, so that you will actually practice it. If you are already adept at some technique for inducing relaxation, there is no reason for not using your own. Any form of relaxation will do as long as you can produce it quickly, thoroughly, and at your own instructions. But don't use alcohol, drugs, tobacco, or any other substance to achieve relaxation. If you do, you won't learn the independent self-direction of relaxation you need to overcome real-life anxieties.

One reliable method for learning to relax is to use deep muscular relaxation. As you read this sentence, try relaxing your hand and arm or your jaw muscles. If you can do so, you will realize how much energy you tie up in excess muscular tension. You can also experience subtle mental changes as your muscles cast off their tensions.

Once you have learned relaxation, you will use it to replace anxiety responses in situations in which you are now uncomfortable or that you now avoid. The basic idea is to learn to produce relaxation at the first sign of tension. That is the reason for the tension-release method, which calls for tensing muscles and then releasing them. As you tense your muscles, you will learn to recognize the signs of tension so that when you feel them later in real-life situations (for example, before taking tests or talking to strangers), you can quickly produce the release that is relaxation. In this way, you can use the first signs of tension as the cue to relax and interrupt the tension process early in its sequence.

Can you recognize tension in your own body? Pause now, and do a tension inventory. Do you feel tension in your shoulders? Your neck? Scalp? Around the eyes? Anywhere?

The tension-release sequence is an excellent training and practice technique that helps us learn to recognize tension, and thus is the preferred way to learn the skill. Later, the muscle tensing can be eliminated. (Lucic, Steffen, Harrigan, & Stuebing, 1991). This method of recognizing tension and producing relaxation is a very effective strategy for coping with any form of anxiety (Goldfried, 1971, 1977; Goldfried & Trier, 1974; Snyder & Deffenbacher, 1977).

The mastery and use of relaxation will be discussed in three steps: (1) how to use the instructions, (2) where to practice, and (3) using relaxation as an incompatible response.

How to Use the Relaxation Instructions: Step 1

The tension-release instructions (Box 6-2) are like a set of exercises, one for each group of muscles. The final goal is to relax all groups simultaneously to achieve total body relaxation. Each muscle group can be relaxed separately. Relaxation cannot be achieved all at once, so you should follow a gradual procedure in learning it. First you learn to relax your arms; then your facial area, neck, shoulders, and upper back; then your chest, stomach, and lower back; then your hips, thighs, and calves; and finally your whole body.

The general idea is to first tense a set of muscles and then relax them so that they will relax more deeply than before they were tensed. You should focus your attention on each muscle system as you work through the various muscle groups. This will give you a good sense of what each set feels like when it is tense and when it is well relaxed. The exercises may take 20 to 30 minutes at first. As you learn, you will need less and less time.

Choose a private place, quiet and free of interruptions and distracting stimuli. Sit comfortably, well supported by the chair, so that you don't have to use your muscles to support yourself. You may want to close your eyes. Some people prefer to lie down while practicing. You may find it especially pleasant to practice before going to sleep.

The basic procedure for each muscle group is the same: *Tense* the muscle, *release* the muscle, and *feel* the relaxation. You may want to memorize the specific muscle groups and the exercises for each. For example, the hands are exercised by making a fist; the forehead, by raising the eyebrows. You will want to know the instructions by heart so you can relax quickly, at any time or place, according to your own self-instructions. This is the reason for the final exercise saying "relax" slowly and softly as you breathe out while totally relaxed. You can then transfer this self-instruction into your natural environment and produce relaxation instead of anxiety (Cautela, 1966).

Where to Practice Relaxation: Step 2

As soon as you have practiced enough that you can tense and relax some muscle groups, it's time to begin doing the exercises in other situations. You can practice tension release of some muscle groups while driving, riding the bus, attending lectures or concerts, sunbathing at the beach, sitting at your desk, or washing dishes. Relax whatever muscles are not needed for the activity you are engaged in at the moment. Choose a wide

Box 6-2
Relaxation Instructions

Muscle Groups	Tension Exercises
1. The dominant hand	Make a tight fist.
2. The other hand	Make a tight fist.
3. The dominant arm	Curl your arm up; tighten the bicep.
4. The other arm	Curl your arm up; tighten the bicep.
5. Upper face and scalp	Raise eyebrows as high as possible.
6. Center face	Squint eyes and wrinkle nose.
7. Lower face	Smile in a false, exaggerated way; clench teeth.
8. Neck	a. Pull head slightly forward, then relax.
	b. Pull head slightly back, then relax.
9. Chest and shoulders	a. Pull shoulders back until the blades almost touch, then relax.
	b. Pull shoulders forward all the way, then relax.
10. Abdomen	Make abdomen tight and hard.
11. Buttocks	Tighten together.
12. Upper right leg	Stretch leg out from you, tensing both upper and lower muscles.
13. Upper left leg	Stretch leg out from you, tensing both upper and lower muscles.
14. Lower right leg	Pull toes up toward you.
15. Lower left leg	Pull toes up toward you.
16. Right foot	Curl toes down and away from you.
17. Left foot	Curl toes down and away from you.

variety of situations. It is best not to begin with a situation that represents a particular problem for you.

It's not necessary to use all muscle groups during this practice. Exercise those groups that you've learned to control in your private sessions. If you detect tension in one group—your face or your throat, for example—practice relaxing those muscles.

This phase of practice has three purposes. First, you learn to detect specific tensions. You will discover that you are prone to tension in particular muscle groups. For some people, it's the shoulders and neck that tense up most often; for others, the arms or the face. Relaxing these specific groups will decrease your overall tension.

Second, you learn to regulate the *depth* of relaxation. Although it is crucial to learn total, deep muscle relaxation—even to the point of physical limpness—it is not necessary or desirable to use this full response to combat all tensions. Relaxation is a physical skill, just as weight lifting is. The strong man does not use his full strength to carry eggs, although he has it available for moving pianos. As we will discuss shortly, you can use *deep* relaxation as a response incompatible with anxiety in specific situations that you find

First, for each muscle group:

Tense the muscles and hold for 5 seconds.

Feel the tension. Notice it carefully.

Now release. Let the tension slide away, all away.

Feel the difference:

Notice the pleasant warmth of relaxation.

Now repeat the sequence with the same group.

Repeat again. Do the sequence three times for each group of muscles.

Tense. Release. Learn the difference. Feel the warmth of relaxation.

Then for the whole body:

Now tense all the muscles together and hold for 5 seconds.

Feel the tension, notice it carefully, then release. Let all tension slide away.
Notice any remaining tension. Release it.

Take a deep breath. Say "relax" softly to yourself as you breathe out slowly.
Remain totally relaxed.

Repeat breathing in and out slowly, saying "relax," staying perfectly relaxed.
Do this three times.

The exercise has ended. Enjoy the relaxation.

In your daily life, in many situations:

Notice your body's tension.

Identify the tense muscle groups.

Say "relax" softly to yourself. Relax the tense group.

Feel the relaxation and enjoy it.

SOURCE: Adapted from *Insight vs. Desensitization in Psychotherapy*, by G. L. Paul, 1966, Palo Alto, CA: Stanford University Press. Copyright © 1966 by Stanford University Press. Reprinted with permission.

---

difficult. But graduated relaxation of muscle groups is a highly valuable skill, and you can begin to learn it by practicing both shallow and deep relaxation. You will be fully skilled when you can totally relax without using the tension technique. Tensing the muscles before relaxing them is only a training method, and it should be dropped as soon as you can relax without it. Then, just saying "relax" to yourself or simply deciding to relax will produce the relaxation at the depth you want.

Practicing relaxation in many situations will prepare you to use it as a general skill for self-direction.

As the next step, it is particularly important to *practice while you are experiencing some tension*. Use tension as a cue for your practice sessions. When you feel the signs of anxiety—whether as mental discomfort or as muscular tension—immediately substitute a relaxation practice session.

If anxiety-producing occasions do not occur during the time you are practicing, you can imagine scenes that have caused tension in the past. While imagining them, go through your complete relaxation practice (Suinn, 1977).

If it is simply not possible to discover the specific moments of heightened anxiety, you can use one of two strategies: (1) practice relaxation before and during a situation that you deem difficult; (2) if you cannot detect increased tensions from moment to moment, practice relaxation at several predetermined times of day no matter what the situation.

The third purpose of practicing relaxation in other settings is to learn to relax in as many situations as possible. Even if you set out to combat a specific anxiety in a specific situation, the odds are high that you will find additional situations in which relaxation is useful (Goldfried, 1971; Goldfried & Goldfried, 1977; Zemore, 1975).

Sherman and Plummer (1973) trained 21 students in relaxation as a general self-direction skill. All but one reported at least one way in which they had benefited from the training; the average was 2.1 ways per person. The most common situations in which the students used relaxation were social situations, sleep problems, test anxiety, handling of interviews, and efforts to increase energy and alertness. Sherman (1975) reported that 2 years after training, the students still used the strategy. Deffenbacher and Michaels (1981) found that students who learned to use relaxation as a coping skill for test anxiety stayed less anxious in tests even after 15 months. Further, they demonstrated a reduction in their overall experience of anxiety. A review of 18 controlled-outcome studies shows that applied relaxation succeeds, that improvements are maintained, and that further improvements are often obtained (Öst, 1987).

Relaxation, then, should be considered a general coping skill. It can be used both as a counter to specific stressors and as a general strategy to prevent maladaptive reactions to stress. A dramatic example of relaxation as a general strategy is demonstrated in a recent study of the symptoms of genital herpes. As many as 20 million Americans suffer from this incurable, sexually transmitted disease, the painful symptoms of which recur unpredictably, but apparently in response to general life stress. Progressive relaxation, practiced regularly at home, sharply decreased the recurrence of these symptoms for 60% of treated patients (Burnette, Koehn, Kenyon-Jump, Hutton, & Stark, 1991).

Using Relaxation as an Incompatible Response: Step 3

Susan, an 18-year-old freshman, was extremely nervous while taking tests. She studied long and effectively but made only Ds and Fs on examinations, even though she could answer the questions after the exam was over. She came from a small rural high school, where the teachers overlooked her poor exam performances because she was one of their brightest students and excelled in projects and reports. In the large university, she lost this personal understanding and support.

Susan's counselor first gave her some brief paper-and-pencil tests to measure her anxiety and also three subtests of a well-known IQ measure. She then attended four training sessions, one per week, to learn how to relax. The method Susan followed was the same one you are learning in this book. She first practiced at home and then extended her practice into real-life situations in which she was reasonably comfortable. After her fifth session, she had to take a number of course examinations. Using her cue word "calm" (like our "relax"), she relaxed during the examinations and performed remarkably well. Before her relaxation training, her average test score was 1.0 (on a 4-point system). After Susan underwent the training, her scores averaged 3.5. She completed the term with a 2.88 grade point average.

Susan then repeated the anxiety and IQ tests she had taken before her relaxation training. When compared with her first scores, the test results indicated that her test anxiety was reduced and that her general level of tension was also lower. She even improved on two of the IQ measures. Obviously, relaxation cannot improve "intelligence," but replacing anxiety with relaxation allowed Susan to perform closer to her real potential (Russell & Sipich, 1974).

Susan's case is a good example of the use of relaxation as a response incompatible with test anxiety. Susan followed exactly the same procedures we have suggested for you, except that she had some assistance from her counselors in the initial stages of her relaxation training. But basically her counselors gave her the advice we are giving you. Susan's success is by no means unique. Research has indicated that "cue-controlled relaxation" is particularly helpful to test-anxious students (Denney, 1980; McGlynn, Kinjo, & Doherty, 1978; Russell & Lent, 1982; Russell, Miller, & June, 1975; Russell, Wise, & Stratoudakis, 1976). It has also been used to correct many other specific anxieties, such as fears of the dental chair (Beck, Kaul, & Russell, 1978).

The usefulness of relaxation as a substituted response is not limited to anxieties. Other problems that have been alleviated by relaxation include insomnia (Gustafson, 1992; Turner, 1986), tension headache, and pain (Levendusky & Pankratz, 1975). Ernst (1973) reports a case in which relaxation was used to stop "self-mutilation" by a woman who repeatedly bit the insides of her lips and mouth, causing tissue damage and pain. She learned deep muscle relaxation during a baseline period in which she recorded with a golf counter the frequency of her self-biting. Then she started relaxing, using the golf counter click as the cue. She paid particular attention to relaxing the muscles of the jaw and lower face. As Figure 6-3 indicates, she almost totally stopped her self-mutilating behavior. That happy outcome continued through months of follow-up.

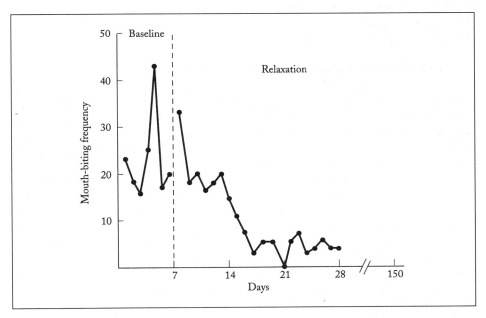

Figure 6-3 Daily self-recorded mouth-biting frequencies
SOURCE: "Self-Recording and Counterconditioning of a Self-Mutilative Compulsion," by F. A. Ernst, 1973, *Behavior Therapy, 4,* pp. 144–146. Copyright © 1973 by Academic Press, Inc. Reprinted with permission.

One of our students reported:

I want to reduce spacing out in class; that is, I want to increase the number of times my attention is on what the lecturer is saying. My mind wanders to all sorts of things, such as feelings I've been having about people or escape fantasies—you know, like backpacking or getting 20 acres of land and living on it with my friends. Another way I have of not being there is one I learned in grammar school, where I felt the teachers were powering me around. I'd find something ridiculous in what they said and laugh to myself about it or tell the person next to me. My plan is to use deep muscle relaxation to feel easy, instead of using my old tricks. That way my mind will wander less. I'll come into the lecture hall 5 minutes early, relax, and then try to listen to what's going on.

This student's plan was very successful; he reduced the frequency of mind-wandering by 50%. You may notice that both the spaced-out student and the mouth-biting woman used two forms of behavior incompatible with their problem behavior—self-recording and relaxation. This may account for their success.

As a rule, *you should use relaxation just before the time you expect your anxiety to begin*—just before the plane takes off, while you are waiting to walk to the front of the room to give your talk, during the earliest stages of sexual foreplay, immediately before you go in for an interview or an exam, or while you sit in the dentist's waiting room.

You may be thinking, "But I can't always predict exactly when tension will begin." Right! This is why you must learn the tension phase of the relaxation program. You will then be able to recognize the beginning stages of tension and use that information as the cue to relax. Typical cues that tension and anxiety are beginning include neck and shoulder tightening, upset stomach, clenched fists or jaws, and teeth grinding (Deffenbacher & Suinn, 1982).

Combining Relaxation with New Self-Instructions

New self-instructions should be combined with relaxation. In an experiment, students using relaxation during examinations were compared with students who combined relaxation with a series of encouraging self-instructions. The combined group performed better on geology multiple-choice and fill-in-the-blank tests (Collins, Dansereau, Garland, Holley, & McDonald, 1981).

Suellen, who we met in Chapter 5 using a daily/weekly planner to reduce her stress, made adjustments to her self-modification plan as she considered adding new behaviors. "When I did get stressed out, I used self-coaching based on past successes. I would say to myself, 'Relax. You've done well before.' I remembered all the times that I felt I would fail an assignment and ended up doing really well." Suellen also used reappraisal and a more rational restructuring of her thinking to produce more adaptive self-instructions. "I also changed my plan to limit it to school and work-related stress. That was the source of my most overwhelming reactions, also I began to see that some stress from regular life happened for a good reason, and there was no reason to change my reaction. For example, when my car was stolen I was really (and still am) stressed out, but that was a completely natural and rational reaction, and actually that didn't distract me from my responsibilities. So I focused my recording and coaching on school- and work-related stress, which is where my problems really are."

Box 6-3
Krista Is Crying in Prague: A Continuing Case

When we last met Krista (Box 5-4, pages 155–156) she had made progress in understanding the social and emotional antecedents of her crying "accidents." She changed her plan to focus more on her response to frustration—to speak up about her opinions and wishes. And then she would have no need to cry. Thus, she had turned her attention to working on *alternate behaviors*.

Krista writes:

> What I do to solve the problem is to replace crying by speaking wisely. Not cheeky, but self-confident. I get ideas for speaking wisely by reading my notepad to learn what I did wrong and how to improve my reactions.
>
> I eliminate high-risk situations. I can feel in advance if some problem will happen—when I don't feel well and when I'm a bit nervous and I get frustrated, that is when I am more feeling like crying. So at those times I prepare, do some relaxation, go somewhere to be alone, have a rest, rehearse in my mind what I want to do, and then go back with a cool head. So I try to wait to solve the problem with the others until I feel better. Then I try to imagine what will come up and I practice what I will want to say.

Krista continues to make some progress. She continues to write insightful statements about herself in her notebook. She is wise to rehearse speaking out on topics that she can anticipate being problematic. However, she should be more systematic in practicing relaxation; if she had this skill fully developed, she would have to withdraw or delay conversations less often. She might also enlist a supportive friend to help her practice speaking even when challenged.

In the next chapter, we will learn how she incorporates consequences into her plan, and whether Krista is still crying in Prague.

SOURCE: Reprinted with permission.

The most effective procedure involves combining relaxation with correcting of self-defeating thoughts (Deffenbacher & Hahnloser, 1981).

Problems in Relaxation

The most frequent problem encountered in developing a relaxation program is simply not practicing it. This is particularly true in the early stages of developing the skills and habits of relaxation—whether the chosen method is meditation, breath concentration, stretching, or progressive relaxation of tension-release. In general, we recommend practicing about 30 minutes a day for the first 2 weeks, then including relaxation at frequent times during the regular course of life, both at home and in the larger world. If you are not giving that 30 minutes, examine these possibilities. Are you telling yourself something? Do the following excuses sound familiar?

I don't have a place to relax. You do need quiet and privacy. Plan ahead. Negotiate for the time and space. Make relaxation practice a priority because of its wide-ranging benefits.

The whole thing is too boring. Relaxation is, in fact, not boring in the least. But your own level of agitation or anxiety may be so great that you can't get to the relaxation pleasure. Try listening to some quiet music you value in order to induce a slower pace of thoughts and a pleasant mood. Listen at low volume as you begin to relax. Use the mood-enhancing effects of music as a bridge to the pleasures of relaxation itself (Eifert, Craill, Carey, & O'Connor, 1988).

There is not enough time in the day. There is never enough time for everything; it is an issue of priorities. Remind yourself of the benefits relaxation can bring to your health, your social life, and your success in school and work. Reassert your goals. Try rational restructuring to talk yourself through the self-defeating prioritizing of less important activities.

And remember the power of self-observation. Set up a record sheet that will not only prompt you to do the exercises but will establish a record of your improvement.

Date & Hour of Practice	Duration of Practice	Body Areas Easily Relaxed	Body Areas with Tension	Tension Level 0–100	
				Before	After
___	___	___	___	___	___
___	___	___	___	___	___
___	___	___	___	___	___

0–100 scale: 0 = No tension; 100 = Maximum tension

SOURCE: Adapted from *Anxiety Management Training: A Behavior Therapy* (p. 331), by R. M. Suinn, 1990, New York: Plenum Press.

Developing New Behaviors

The fundamental way of mastering a new behavior is simply to rehearse it over and over in the situations in which you want it to occur. All the other methods this book teaches are merely ways of making that rehearsal more likely to take place. Practice does make perfect. Actually performing the desired behaviors—that is, rehearsing them—is the final technique for attaining your goal. In a recent examination of expert performance (international level experts in a variety of fields from art to athletics to science), the researchers conclude that highest levels of performance are not attributable so much to "inborn talents" as to "deliberate practice sustained at high levels for many years" (Ericsson & Charness, 1994).

Often, however, it is difficult to arrange actual rehearsals. You can't always rehearse relaxation in the presence of some feared object, such as snakes, because (fortunately!)

snakes are not always around. You may not be able to rehearse enough for relaxing in examinations because no exams may be scheduled for several weeks. And many avoidance behaviors are so strong that approaching them for rehearsal is more than your current anxiety level will allow. Imagined rehearsal may solve these problems.

Imagined Rehearsal

Rehearsing behavior in one's imagination is called *imagined rehearsal.* There is convincing evidence that imagined rehearsal can improve physical skills for competitors in almost every sport (Suinn, 1983). The same principles apply to high achievement in the workplace, for salespeople, and in all fields of endeavor (Seligman, 1991), even to the regulation of emotional states (Taylor & Pham, 1996).

Research evidence points to the fact that in reaching your goals, actual events and behaviors are much more effective than imagined ones. Therefore, actual practice and performance are the final strategies. However, because imagined events and behaviors can influence actual behavior, using imagined events has many advantages. Imagined events and behaviors can be practiced quickly and easily. Most important, they can be controlled: Imagined snakes are less likely to move suddenly toward you than real ones.

Imagined rehearsal can be used to provide *preliminary* rehearsals, to provide *extra* rehearsals, and to provide rehearsals that *emphasize* certain features of a behavior or situation. Thus, imagined rehearsal can often speed up your journey toward your goal. It is a form of visual self-instruction. For example, in 1976 the U.S. Olympic ski team, before making difficult downhill runs, rehearsed the entire run in their imaginations, thinking of each bump and turn and how they would cope with it. They turned in better runs than they had before, and the United States won some surprising medals (Suinn, 1976). These techniques were then used to train athletes for the Summer and Winter Games of 1980 and 1984 (Suinn, 1985). Imagined rehearsal has been used to correct "loss of confidence"; for example, that of a wide receiver who, having missed an easy pass once, developed a fear of dropping the football. Imagined rehearsal of successfully eluding the defensive back, gathering in the ball, and scoring a touchdown restored his confidence in actual games (Cautela & Samdperil, 1989).

To use imaginary practice, try to imagine the situation and your behavior in complete, minute detail. For example, if you imagine an introduction to a stranger, you should visualize how the imaginary person looks, the expression on his or her face, what the person says, how you react, and all the other details of the physical situation. You may have to imagine the situation in its component parts in order to concentrate separately on imagined sounds, smells, and textures. The most effective imagery takes place in a relaxed state. Relax, and imagine vividly.

Imagined rehearsal is particularly appropriate when you are preparing to cope with high-risk situations. Earlier, we mentioned that the dangers of relapse into substance abuse are highest when other people around you are drinking, smoking, or taking drugs. At the first stage of self-modification, these situations should be avoided. But eventually, you will encounter a high-risk situation, and you will want to have coping skills ready. Imagining these high-risk situations—for example, a restaurant, bar, party, or banquet—and rehearsing in your imagination your coping responses to them can be useful in building skills to prevent relapse (Marlatt & Parks, 1982).

In imagined rehearsal, use the coping skills you intend to use in real life, whatever these skills might be. Religious individuals, for example, have profited more from imagined rehearsal of coping skills when they used religious imagery that was important to them. Nonreligious imagery of coping, such as saying, "I see myself coping with that difficult situation," was less effective for Christians than imagining, "I can see Christ going with me into that difficult situation" (Propst, 1980).

Actively imagining yourself in a coping situation is probably the key element in this kind of rehearsal. One technique for getting a good image of yourself coping is to remember a time when you coped well and then to transfer it to the imagined problem situation. Test-anxious students who used this tactic actually raised their grade point averages. The students remembered a previous situation in which their coping skills were high (running a radio broadcast, tending a busy bar, playing in a recital). They then transposed that competent self-image into an imagined test situation (Harris & Johnson, 1980).

Do not drift into imagining failure or focus on factors that could impair performance. This will diminish subsequent actual performance and confidence, whereas positive rehearsal and focusing will improve both (Cervone, 1989; Seligman, 1990).

In summary, imagined rehearsals or mental simulations enhance the likelihood of a real performance; they contain an implicit plan; and they contain specific emotions that enhance both practical planning and effective motivations (Taylor & Pham, 1996).

Imagined Rehearsal and Relaxation

One of the best uses of imagined rehearsal is in the practice of relaxation. In this technique, a form of *desensitization,* you imagine yourself remaining calm and relaxed in different situations, and you carry out the imagined rehearsal while actually being in a state of deep muscle relaxation. You may find it necessary to approach feared situations gradually, maintaining your state of calm relaxation. It is important that you succeed in the early trials at relaxation because success breeds success.

Suppose that you become tense when you take tests. You know, of course, that there are different kinds of tests, some worse than others, ranging from unimportant, simple quizzes to make-you-or-break-you final exams, and some make you more anxious than others. You might write down situations in hierarchical order from easiest to most difficult, as in the following example:

> Taking a test that doesn't count for very much
> Taking a test when I am not prepared
> Taking a surprise test
> Taking a test when the professor watches me all the time
> Taking a midterm exam
> Taking a final exam that determines my grade in the course

These situations are not likely to come along in exactly that order. In imagination, though, you can rehearse them in any order and as many times as you wish.

Liza, one of our students, used the preceding list with imagined rehearsal plus relaxation. Because her courses had only midterms and finals, she wanted to prepare in advance for those situations and to proceed gradually. After learning deep muscle relaxation, she lay on her couch with a pillow, just as she had done when practicing relaxation. While deeply relaxed, Liza imagined the first item in the list—taking a minor test while remaining as relaxed as she was at that moment. She held that scene for a minute or two, imagining all sorts of details—feeling the hardness of the desk at which she sat, putting the end of the pencil in her mouth while thinking of an answer, going back over each answer—and all the while remaining perfectly calm. Then she cleared her mind, checked herself for any signs of tension, relaxed again, and went on to the next item on her list. She tried to do one of these sessions each day.

Liza spent about 10 to 15 minutes on each exercise, although the length of time varied with her mood and ability to relax deeply. In general, she went down her list in order—from least to most difficult. But she sometimes changed the sequence, occasionally trying to begin with a difficult situation. If she couldn't visualize it and stay calm, she relaxed again and moved back to an easier level.

About 5 weeks into the semester, Liza had to take an unannounced quiz in her geology class. She was so surprised that she nearly panicked. However, she was able to induce relaxation by going through a rather hasty tension-release exercise. Liza relaxed enough to do well on the quiz, although she barely finished in time.

This incident illustrates the only error Liza made in her plan. During the same weeks in which she was using imagined rehearsal, she should also have been practicing the relaxation response in many outside situations. Then she would have been better prepared to relax in the geology lecture hall.

The pop quiz motivated Liza to continue the imagined rehearsals. By the time midterm exams arrived, she had been able to imagine being relaxed throughout her entire hierarchy and had used relaxation several times in her actual lecture halls. Both steps were probably important. Imagined rehearsal with relaxation gave her some practice in situations before they came up. Actual rehearsal of relaxation in various physical surroundings gave her practice in the situations in which she would later face the tension-producing tests.

Imagining yourself in tension-producing situations while being relaxed is a good way to get ready to cope with the reality. There is only one caution for the use of imagined rehearsal. If you imagine an incompetent performance, it will cause you to perform in an incompetent way. Imagined rehearsal will not help unless you imagine an effective performance. Remember the benefits that Olympic-quality athletes experienced from imagined rehearsal of their skills. These results were achieved because the athletes knew exactly what to do; their imagined rehearsals were of a correct performance. But novice athletes' performance may be made worse by imagined rehearsals because they do not know what to rehearse. One study found that imagined rehearsals of tennis serves improved accuracy for experienced tennis players but made novices less accurate (Noel, 1980; see also Suinn, 1983). Imagined rehearsal is useless or even harmful when the goals are poorly defined. Imagined rehearsals must be precise and correct (Suinn, 1983). Finding and imitating good models is an extremely important part of self-regulation because models help us identify effective behaviors. If you are uncertain about exactly how to perform an activity—whether social skills or tennis backhand—there is one excellent way to identify the right skills: Find a model.

Modeling

Learning through observation of models is one of the basic processes by which learning occurs—for everyone, from adults to infants. The observation of expert models increases self-confidence, perceived self-efficacy, and willingness to begin a self-improvement program (Ozer & Bandura, 1990).

Where can you discover these specific, correct behaviors? You can discover them by observing models—those who already are expert. Whether your goal is better tennis, better social skills, or any other behavior, a fundamental strategy is to identify a model, analyze the model's skills, and use those skills as your standard.

> A significant element of apprenticeship is the imitation of skilled performers and careful study and copying of their work. In the arts the study and imitation of masterpieces has a long history. For example, Benjamin Franklin described in his autobiography how he tried to learn to write in a clear and logical fashion. He would read through a passage in a good book to understand it rather than memorize it and then try to reproduce its structure and content. Then he would compare his reproduction with the original to identify differences. By repeated application of this cycle of study, reproduction, and comparison with a well-structured original, Franklin argued that he acquired his skill in organizing thoughts for speaking and writing. (Ericsson & Charness, 1994, p. 739)

If you find someone who has the very skills you want, don't hesitate to try straight imitation. None of us minds using imitation when we are learning tennis or driving, but you may be embarrassed to think of imitating others' social or personal behaviors. As we counseled the student who watched how his friend dealt with women:

> If you decide to smile when you meet someone, as he does, you will be smiling your own smile, not his. You will be answering with your own comments, not his. You will do everything in your own style. You'll be yourself, but yourself smiling and answering.

One of our students set out to improve his public speaking skills. He wrote:

> I made use of models, observing both their good and bad habits to use or not while speaking in class. I noticed the effects of eye contact and gestures in communicating, and the importance of a loud and clear voice. However, I feel that the most important effect of observing good, relaxed models was the feeling that if they could do it, so could I. Therefore, these vicarious influences boosted my self-efficacy expectations.

If observation doesn't reveal the crucial part of a model's performance, ask your chosen model to explain something. A talented young swimmer asked her heroine, a conference champion, how she managed such sustained and disciplined practice. The answer was clear and provided an excellent model. "*Preschedule* your practice times and your goals for the day," the champion said. "Never make your decisions on the way to the pool! If we did that, no one would ever practice hard."

Our student Dunston was a pleasant person, but his stooped posture lowered his self-esteem. Dunston's plan for self-improvement was to improve his 6'4" posture to a straight, tall, confident bearing. His plan included the memory of a model, a friend from high school who Dunston remembered as having a self-confident bearing. But he thought the main feature of his plan should be exercise and back-strengthening exercises, using precommitted punishment and self-reward. While he made some progress, his plan stalled. Here is his report:

> In an unexpected telephone call from Illinois, I spent about half an hour talking to the model I chose for my project—Mark L. I asked him to go back to our high

school years, and describe how exactly weight lifting helped him to achieve good posture. To my surprise, he told me his strength had little to do with his posture. His main drive to improve his posture was a result of trying to model after a girl he saw around the tenth grade! She had the greatest influence on his posture, and in his opinion, his back strength played a minor role. . . . Mark became even more important of a model to me after I learned that his posture was a result of modeling, and I began to rely on that more than on my faith in the exercises—they were just a myth, but the model was real. They are an essential part of good posture, but I also see that the strength attained by exercise needs to be put into practice, or it won't be used at all.

Dunston then adopted a program that included negative practice (consciously practicing poor posture, so that he would notice it when he slipped into the old patterns).

We saw Dunston often across campus, his head well above the crowd. After 4 years, we had a note from him. "I still have the ability to spontaneously 'sense' when my head is drooping, which is something I could never do before the project. I can still remember (before the negative practice) the frustration of trying to will myself to better posture. But now, I'm a natural at it—I'm really surprised and satisfied with the results of the technique." And he is still using the self-improvement benefits of learning from models, this time by observing expert weight lifters.

Imagined Modeling

In using imagined rehearsal, some people have difficulty imagining themselves doing acts they cannot perform in real life. For instance, imagining that you are sending back your overcooked steak may seem so unrealistic that you lose the scene or end up imagining yourself eating the steak anyway. If this happens, you might use the technique of imagined modeling.

This process is similar to imagined rehearsal, except that you imagine someone else, instead of yourself, performing the behavior, being reinforced for it, and so forth. This technique has been found effective in a variety of applications (Cautela & Kearney, 1986; Kazdin, 1984). Athletes who have problems with losing their tempers have used imagined modeling to visualize staying cool and in command of their skills when being goaded and baited (Cautela & Samdperil, 1989). Students using this technique actually demonstrated improved grades as well as reduced anxiety during tests (Harris & Johnson, 1980).

When you use others as imagined models, you don't have to use real persons who are known to you, although you may do so. Here are some recommended procedures for imagined modeling, based on Alan Kazdin's (1984) summary:

1. Imagine a model that is similar to you in age and of the same gender.
2. Imagine different models in each situation rather than one person only.
3. Imagine a model that begins with the same difficulties you have—one that must cope with the problem rather than one who has already mastered the problem. For example, your model should also be afraid of pigeons, although able to approach them; fattening food also tempts your model; your model also has to muster up courage to send the steak back.
4. Imagine your model being reinforced for successful coping, preferably with desired natural outcomes.

5. Imagine your model self-instructing during the performance. Make those self-instructions the ones you will use in your eventual real-life performance.

Imagined modeling can be used as a first step in preparing yourself for imagined rehearsal. But increase the degree of your imagined performance, not that of someone else. If you imagine only others as models, the technique is not likely to be effective. There is no need to use imagined modeling if you can effectively use rehearsal, either actual or imagined. If you can successfully imagine yourself rehearsing behaviors, it is probably better to use yourself as your own model. And most effective of all is to move from imagined modeling into actual practice. For individuals learning to be more assertive, for example, those who combined imagined modeling with actual practice showed the greatest improvement in social situations requiring assertive behavior (Kazdin, 1982). As you progress in imagination, begin practicing, at the lower end of the scale of difficulty, in the real world.

Mastery in the Real World

We cannot emphasize too much that, no matter how valuable all the imagined techniques are, they are only bridges to performance in the real world. Imagined rehearsal and all its supporting tactics can help you prepare for real-life situations. *But you must rehearse your developing behaviors in the actual situations in which you want them to occur.* Therefore, no plan is complete without tactics for transferring your behavior from imagined rehearsal into real life.

For example, Gershman and Stedman (1971) had one of their clients use karate exercises as the incompatible behavior for anxiety about his flying lessons. The client constructed a hierarchy of items such as "gaining altitude," "passing over treetops too low," "saying to myself, 'How high am I?'" and so on. He went through the various items while vigorously engaged in his karate exercises until he was able to consider the items without anxiety. Then he transferred the plan into real life. He rehearsed before going to the flying field and again in the men's room before reporting to his instructor. He developed confidence and eventually was able to fly without anxiety.

In a long series of studies, Jerry Deffenbacher demonstrated considerable benefit from programs that include relaxation in real anxiety-producing situations. Specific target anxieties reduced have included test anxiety, fear of flying, fear of public speaking, and fear of cats. In addition, a general reduction in anxiety occurs, so the person is less tense and uncomfortable in ordinary daily activities. There are other side benefits as well: People who use relaxation in real-problem situations also become less depressed, less hostile, and more assertive. Relaxation, when well practiced in real situations, becomes a general coping skill (Deffenbacher & Suinn, 1982).

Whether you have used imagined relaxation and rehearsal for dieting, being assertive, test anxiety, fear of birds, or fear of being outdoors, the next step is transferring these behaviors into real life. Often we do need to begin in our imagination, but the real-life situation is a far more effective learning arena than its imagined substitute (Flannery, 1972; Goldstein & Kanfer, 1979; Sherman, 1972). When one learns new responses, even from models, *it is the rehearsal in the actual situation that brings about long-lasting change* (Bandura, Jeffery, & Gajdos, 1975; Blanchard, 1970; Thase & Moss, 1976). When you can expose yourself to the feared situation and stay there, you will have taken the last necessary, effective step (Emmelkamp, 1990).

Box 6-4
Along Came a Spider . . .

Little Miss Muffet sat on a tuffet
Eating her curds and whey
Along came a spider and sat down beside her
And frightened Miss Muffet away.

And so did Miss Muffet get a spider phobia? Psychologists have always been interested in how irrational fears are acquired. Do they all arise from the classical conditioning of fear to an object (see Chapter 4; Watson & Rayner, 1920)? Or can they be also be acquired indirectly, through modeling (observing someone else's unfortunate emotional experience) or through irrational beliefs (misattributing dangers to feared situations)? Since the 1990s, continuing studies on *spider phobia* have appeared in the scientific journals. That may appear to be more than this rare fear deserves, but a systematic study of various features of a single phobia allows us to better understand irrational fears in general. Perhaps Miss Muffet can illuminate your own specific fear.

For some time, psychologists have accepted three different paths to developing phobia: through conditioning, modeling, or informational learning leading to beliefs (Rachman, 1977). Many spider phobia studies have verified these three routes—at least if we trust the retrospective accounts of spider phobics and their parents (Merckelbach, Arntz, Arrindell, & deJong, 1992; Merckelbach & Muris, 1997). However, many nonfearful control subjects in these same studies also reported frightening experiences with spiders, either to themselves or observed in others, and even more of the nonfearful controls had learned incorrect threatening information about spiders—yet they had no irrational fear.

In some ways, the experiences of those who did not develop phobias are equally interesting. Certainly not all traumatic, frightening experiences create irrational fears in all people. Fears of dentists or automobiles are relatively rare, though many people (phobic and not fearful) recall highly unpleasant experiences in dental offices or in traffic collisions. Meanwhile, other irrational fears are disproportionately common, for example, fears of small animals (especially snakes and spiders). Perhaps that is because spiders are disgusting due to their association with dirt and contamination. In fact, spider phobics *are* more sensitive to disgust in general, though they are not more neurotic or introverted. Perhaps because of that specific sensitivity, they also report more reactions of disgust and fright to spiders than do nonfearful subjects (Merckelback, de Jong, Arntz, & Schouten, 1993; Mulkens, deJong, & Merckelbach, 1996; Tolin, Lohr, Sawchuk, & Lee, 1997). Mothers of spider phobics share their daughters' disgust. The association between disgust sensitivity and spider fear is also verified by a drop in spider-disgust among those whose spider-fear has been successfully treated (deJong, Andrea, & Muris, 1997).

(continued)

Box 6-4 *(continued)*

Seligman (1971) proposed that evolutionary selection has prepared humans to associate fear with potentially dangerous objects; so that even today people are more likely to develop fear reactions to snakes and spiders than to more historically recent dangers such as dentists and autos. This group of fears—called *nonassociative*—suggests itself as a fourth route to phobia (Poulton & Menzies, 2002).

However much species or individual sensitivity contributes to phobia, there is certainly a role for *beliefs*. Spider phobics have more elaborated irrational beliefs about spiders and about their own reactions to encounters with spiders. They believe that spiders will attack them, take revenge, are unpredictable, and that if attacked, the phobics expect a heart attack or to die of fear (Arntz, Lavy, van den Berg, & van Rijsoort, 1993). Even in the cold light of day, with not a spider in sight, they still believe their expectations are reasonable (Jones & Menzies, 2000). They also think about spiders more often, and have more trouble suppressing thoughts about spiders, than do nonphobic subjects (Muris, Merckelbach, Horselenberg, Susenaar, & Leeuw, 1997).

Now for the good news. Regardless of how spider phobia is acquired, or why, effective treatment is readily available, brief, and reliable. The basic principles of treatment are those described in this chapter: systematic controlled exposure, substitution for irrational thoughts and self-instructions, and both modeled and directly experienced desensitization. Remarkable alleviation of fears and irrational beliefs are often achieved in a single session (Arntz et al., 1993; deJong, Vorage, & van den Hout, 2000; Johnstone & Page, 2004; Öst, 1989; Thorpe & Salkovskis, 1997), even when the exposure is provided "virtually," by computer (Smith, Kirkby, Montgomery, & Daniels, 1997). Readers suffering from specific fears severe enough to be psychiatrically diagnosable as phobia should not hesitate to seek out this kind of virtually assisted professional assistance. It is effective, interesting, quick and has long-lasting benefits. (We do not yet recommend self-treatment using computer-assisted virtual exposure.)

However, for specific fears that occasionally cause discomfort, you might first try self-modification according to the principles outlined in this chapter, particularly those involving relaxation, shaping, and social assistance, to be described in the following section. (For a book-length discussion, see Antony & McCabe, 2005).

So if Miss Muffet does suffer from lingering irrational spider fears, we hope she will have an opportunity for gradually sitting closer and closer beside a harmless spider, remaining relaxed, and preferably in the company of a calm and well-informed friend.

Shaping: The Method of Successive Approximations

Whatever your goal behavior may be, you should anticipate that you will not master it at the first effort. Even if you have a perfect model, the expert behavior may have to be acquired a piece at a time. Even though you have become competent in relaxation, you may have to approach the feared situation by taking small steps toward it. A general procedure for behavioral improvement is this: Start from the point in your current store of behaviors that most closely approximates your eventual goal. Practice this approximation, and it will become the basis from which the next (improved) step can be taken. Move toward full mastery in a process of steady, successive approximations. This method is known as *shaping*.

A steady experience of success reinforces and strengthens gradually improving performance. The belief in your own competence/self-efficacy is one of the strongest predictors of eventual success (Bandura, 1994). Given two people of equal skill, the one who believes he or she can succeed is more likely to do so. The use of intelligent shaping steps will bring success experiences, thereby increasing belief in self-efficacy, and thus leading to greater success.

Box 6-5 illustrates the shaping steps of a long and successful journey made by a woman who had far to travel before she could become a student at all.

Relaxation and the Method of Approximations

Often relaxation plans require successive approximations. For example, several of our students have been unable to maintain relaxation when going abruptly into a major examination. They have used graduated steps in approaching the dreaded situation, such as going into the examination room 2 or 3 days before a test and practicing in the empty hall.

Some of our students have used detailed schedules of steps along a shaping continuum. Linda, a college senior, wrote:

> I am really very afraid of birds, under almost any conditions. This sometimes makes me look like a fool—for example, I won't go to the zoo because there are so many birds around, loose as well as in cages—and often causes me unnecessary fear and trepidation. My life would be more pleasant with fewer fears!

Here is Linda's exposure hierarchy:

A. When one or two birds are 15 yards away:
   1. Turn and face the birds.
   2. Take one step toward the birds.
   3. Take two steps toward the birds.
   4. Continue until I have walked a total of 5 yards toward the birds.
   5. Begin step B.

B. When more than two birds are 15 yards away:
   1. Turn and face the birds.
   2. Take two steps toward them.
   3. Take four steps toward them.
   4. Continue until I have walked a total of 5 yards toward the birds.

Box 6-5
Shaping Away School Phobia

by Harriet Kathryn Brown

The most complex "project report" turned in by a student in the many classes in self-modification that I've instructed was this. This shaping program was almost entirely self-invented. The student wrote:

> I was 28 years old, separated from my husband, and wanted to return to the university. But I experienced anxiety attacks when just physically present on the campus—rapid heartbeat, cold sweat, shaking, acid stomach, skin rash, and a mindless urge to flee. A long way to go! I started a plan to shape my way back into school.

> *Step 1:* Drive onto campus through the east gate, around the mall circle, and out the west gate. Do this two or three times a week for 3 weeks. This meant 3 to 5 minutes of anxiety, but it was bearable. I was then ready for the next shaping stage.

> *Step 2:* Park on campus, and walk around for 10 minutes. Do this two or three times a week for 3 weeks. I avoided particular buildings where I felt the most uncomfortable, but I made it and upped the shaping step. I gradually improved, and the next steps lasted 1 or 2 weeks each.

> *Step 3:* Walk around 20 to 30 minutes.

> *Step 4:* Walk around, then sit in an empty classroom for 10 minutes while reading a book.

> *Step 5:* Sit in the classroom reading for an hour. By then it was January, and I wanted to sign up for a noncredit writing class. I knew that I wrote reasonably well, and there were no grades involved. This was the least-threatening class I'd ever find—except that the class was scheduled for a building that I still avoided. There were 2 weeks till class began.

> *Step 6:* Sign up for the class. For 3 days in a row, drive on campus, park outside the scary building, and walk around the outside of it.

She then repeated the procedures, beginning at a 10-yard distance, first from a single bird and then from a group of birds. Next, she repeated the procedure beginning at 5 yards. In the last stages, she would begin at 3 yards from the birds and move to within 3 feet of them, then gradually increase the amount of time, in seconds, that she spent close to them.

At first Linda had difficulty, but she reported that by getting her boyfriend to hold her hand, her anxiety was considerably lessened. This worked well until, perhaps out of boredom, the boyfriend gave her a "playful push," and she found herself frighteningly close to the birds, which set her back about 3 weeks. (It also set their romance back a bit.) Remember, and remind your helpers, that relaxation must be maintained at each step of real-life exposure (McGlynn, Moore, Lawyer, & Karg, 1999).

Step 7: Walk through the building once without stopping—3 days in a row.
Step 8: Sit in the actual classroom. Start with 10 minutes, increase each day as much as possible until I can do 1 hour.

Once I was relaxed enough to actually stay in the classroom, the course was really no problem. In fact, I enrolled in another noncredit writing course during the following semester. Now I was ready to attempt my first class for credit. I checked out the room and felt comfortable enough in it. I was on my way!

The text for that course was [this book]. As a result, my next steps used more techniques. Up to this point, I'd been using food to reward myself for each of these shaping achievements. That was doing my weight no good, so I found a variety of better reinforcers. My favorite is to let myself put on rock music, stand in front of the mirror, and lip-synch while pretending to be a star. But there are others, too—like picturing myself wandering in a beautiful garden. I reinforced myself each day for keeping to my study schedule, with a separate reinforcer just for going to class.

Step 9: Go to class each day. Reinforcement daily. Study each day. Reinforcement daily. Use relaxation exercises daily. I enjoyed them; no reward needed. Use relaxation before and during tests. Use positive self-statements before and during tests. Got an A.

I won't write down all the rest of the steps. I took another credit class the following semester, and after that two at once. I no longer needed to check out the classrooms in advance. Gradually I dropped the reinforcement for attending class; I was falling in love with school, and am now a full-time student. Success on exams was high enough that my test anxiety got killed. I continued to use reinforcement for a regular study schedule; in fact, I still do. My attendance record is now 100%, compared to only 75% in that first noncredit course. I've gone from school-phobic to school-fanatic!

Occasionally I like to look back to my records of those early "walking around" stages. It's all in my journal, which I have kept since I was 12 years old.

Using friends, as Linda did, is a good idea (Moss & Arend, 1977). But be sure to tell them not to give you a playful push. Having a friend around when you are coping with nervousness in a social situation is particularly appropriate, but the helper must have a serious desire to be helpful.

The use of friends to gradually shape advancing steps is a general strategy well worth considering, especially if your goal is behavior in a social situation. For goals such as public speaking, successful employment interviews, improved conversation, or asking for dates, the conditions of rehearsal can be shaped. The first step might be to rehearse in your imagination. The second step should be to rehearse in actual behavior, but privately. The third step can then be rehearsal in the presence of someone you trust; the final step, rehearsal in the actual goal situation (Goldstein, Sprafkin, & Gershaw, 1979).

Box 6-6
A Sample Social Anxiety Exposure Hierarchy

An anxiety exposure hierarchy is useful for both imagined and actual rehearsal. Note that in addition to listing feared situations in their order of difficulty, a hierarchy usually includes ratings (using a scale from 0 to 100) that reflect the extent to which the person fears each situation (0 = no fear, and 100 = maximum fear).

Situation	*Fear Rating*
Throw a party at my home and invite everyone from work, and avoid drinking any alcohol.	100
Attend a party with my spouse at a coworker's home, and avoid having any alcohol.	90
Attend the opening of an art show and make casual conversation with other attendees and avoid drinking any alcohol.	90
Invite another couple (Kevin and Katie) over for dinner at our home.	85
Have lunch with a co-worker and a third person whom I don't know well.	80
Arrive at my night class a few minutes late, so all my classmates stare at me when I walk in to take my seat.	70
Invite another couple (Kevin and Katie) for dinner in a restaurant.	70
Make small talk (e.g., about the weather) with strangers on an elevator.	60
Tell my co-workers about my weekend when arriving at work at work on Monday morning.	55
Eat lunch at my desk, with others watching.	50
Fill out a form at the bank with others watching.	35
Ask for directions at a gas station.	30
Drop my keys in a public place where people are likely to notice.	25

SOURCE: *10 Simple Solutions to Shyness: How to Overcome Shyness, Social Anxiety & Fear of Public Speaking* (pp. 56–57), by M. M. Antony, 2001, Oakland, CA: New Harbinger Publications, Inc.

For each of these steps, an exposure hierarchy is a useful tool. Just as Linda constructed a hierarchy of bird anxiety, based on physical distance from them, any anxiety problem can be arranged in the order of fear intensity. Box 6-6 presents a sample exposure hierarchy for someone who experiences anxiety in most social and performance situations.

Problems in Shaping

You can't expect the course of learning to be smooth all the time. The important thing is to keep trying—staying within a shaping program—even if it is the 39th revision of the original schedule.

Encountering plateaus. When you follow a shaping schedule, you are likely to encounter plateaus. You may make excellent progress week after week and then suddenly level off. Moving up all those previous steps seemed so easy; then, all of a sudden, a new step—the same size as all the others—seems very difficult. The easiest way to continue upward when you reach a plateau is to reduce the size of the steps. If that is not possible, continue the plan for a week or so. The plateau experience is so common that you should expect it and "ride it out." This is particularly true for dieting, where physiological changes in your body can lead to less weight loss for a period of time (LeBow, 1981).

Losing "willpower." You now know enough about the principles that govern behavior/environment relationships to know that there are many reasons why you don't perform a given behavior. In our experience, the loss of self-control in the middle of intervention is most often due to some failure in the shaping program.

For example, a student will say:

> To hell with it. I can't do it. I want to get into that library and stay there, but I just can't make it. I haven't got enough willpower. Besides, this whole idea of self-change is ridiculous because the whole problem is really whether I have the willpower to improve myself. I don't, so I quit.

In our terms, this may be a shaping problem. For example, 2 hours in the library may be much too severe an increase over current performance. Instead of 2 hours, this student should have set his first approximation at only 30 minutes. Some students with a near-zero baseline might, as a first approximation, merely walk to the library and go up the steps, then return home to get their reinforcer. But many self-modifiers are simply too embarrassed to perform such elementary steps. Instead, they increase the step to a "respectable" level, which is often outside their performance capacity, and finally quit altogether in a huff of "willpower" failure.

You may experience this failure of self-control in two ways. First, you simply may not start on a self-modification project. You would like to achieve the final goal but somehow cannot get around to starting toward that goal. This is a shaping problem, and you need to start with a very small step. Remember, if it's embarrassingly small—"I jog around my living room three times every day"—then don't tell anyone, but do it.

Second, you may have started but find that you are not making progress. This may also be a shaping problem, and you need to use smaller steps.

The whole point of shaping is to make it as easy as possible to start and to continue. Therefore, you require yourself to do little more than you can presently do so that it is easy to perform the target behavior. Then, after practicing a bit, it is easy to move up one more short step. With each step, self-confidence increases.

Not knowing how to begin. By referring to the baseline, you can determine your capability for certain tasks. For others, however, you may not know how to begin. You may not know exactly which acts come first in a chain-of-events sequence. In this case, you could use someone else as a model to get an idea of a starting point.

A young woman chose as her model another woman who was effective in getting acquainted with new people. The model's first behavior was merely to smile responsively. So our young woman used "smiling responsively" as the first step in her shaping plan. Observing models is especially appropriate when you are uncertain about the exact behaviors you should choose to develop.

Mark Twain knew about shaping, although he didn't use that word. In *Pudd'nhead Wilson's Calendar,* he wrote: "Habit is habit, and not to be flung out of the window by any man, but coaxed downstairs a step at a time." Coax yourself.

Tips for Typical Topics

Anxiety and Stress

Stress almost certainly is related to negative long-term effects on health. For that reason, it is important that you include a sound exercise program in your overall plan. For example, you could integrate walking into your life in several ways: Walk to go shopping, to school, or to work; at the end of the day; when talking with friends; instead of lingering over a big lunch (Johnsgard, 1989). Aerobic exercise also lowers sensitivity to physical reactions that are often misinterpreted as anxiety (Broman-Fulks, Berman, Rabian, & Webster, 2004).

Recent evidence shows that physical fitness buffers the negative health effects of life stress (Brown, 1991), reduces general anxiety, and improves self-efficacy (Long & Haney, 1988).

Stress reactions—whether anxiety, tension, anger, frustration, or general exhaustion and impaired health—all respond to the same general strategy outlined in this chapter. For reducing these reactions, develop a plan that includes practicing an incompatible behavior (usually relaxation) and gradually approaching the feared situation. Incorporate improved self-instructions, first in imagined rehearsal and then in the actual situation. Some evidence shows that the best order of practice is: (1) learn the relaxation process, (2) practice the self-instructions, (3) use imagined rehearsal while relaxing and instructing, and (4) perform the same process in the actual situation (Knowlton & Harris, 1987).

For anxiety about public speaking, it is important that the imagined rehearsal also include the material to be spoken. Being well prepared includes practicing the performance itself as well as the relaxation. Don't focus on yourself (Barlow, 1988). Instead, focus on getting your message across.

For test anxiety, imagined rehearsal that includes images of competence, such as detailed images of successful test taking, should be combined with relaxation (Harris & Johnson, 1983; Wachelka & Katz, 1999). Self-instructions should also be combined with relaxation so that during tests self-defeating thoughts are replaced with active coping self-instructions (Deffenbacher & Hahnloser, 1981). In fact, self-defeating negative thoughts about performance play a larger role in underachievement than does test anxiety itself (Arnkoff & Smith, 1988). Replace those thoughts with statements of competence and calmness, and use your relaxation. Studying enough to be well-prepared helps, too.

Assertion

You need not wait to practice new assertive skills until real opportunities occur. Use imagined rehearsal as a first stage in developing assertive behavior. When imagining the scenes, use relaxation as a prelude. Be sure to imagine the full scene, including a favorable outcome (Kazdin, 1984). The following assertive responses can be useful in imagined rehearsal:

1. Imagine a scene in a restaurant, where smoke from a cigarette at the next table is making you uncomfortable. Imagine yourself saying to the waiter, "Please move me to a nonsmoking table."
2. Imagine being in your dorm room, unable to sleep because of the noise coming from a room down the hall. Imagine going to that room and saying, "Please try to be quieter; it's late, and others need to sleep."

Scenes such as these, drawn from your own daily hassles, should be imagined fully, with the sounds, smells, and feelings of real life. If you cannot imagine yourself giving these assertive responses, begin by imagining someone much like yourself doing so.

Begin your actual rehearsals in the most familiar and comfortable surroundings, at home or with good friends. Tell your friends that you are going to play the role of a more assertive person. "Playing the role" can be a good place to develop the exact statements and skills that you can then transfer to more unfamiliar situations (Higgins, Frisch, & Smith, 1983).

Those who engage in overt practice make consistently greater gains in assertion, and the gains are maintained for longer periods (Kazdin, 1984).

The key behaviors comprising assertiveness include:

- Eye contact. This communicates sincerity.
- Posture. Face the person, stand or sit appropriately close, lean toward him or her, and hold your head erect.
- Gesture appropriately, though not to excess.
- Make your facial expressions appropriate to the message.
- Voice tone, inflection, and volume should be level and well modulated; this will be convincing without being intimidating.
- Timing should be spontaneous. But the occasions in which assertion is used should be appropriate. For example, a private conversation may be better than a public conversation to prevent embarrassment (Kirschenbaum, 1994).

Depression and Low Self-Esteem

Two basic approaches to the self-improvement of depression have been researched, and they are equally effective (Rehm, Kaslow, & Rabin, 1987). These are (1) increasing specific new behaviors, and (2) increasing positive self-statements.

Specific new behaviors. The new behaviors needed to combat depression are those that lead to pleasant activities. Your plan should be aimed at increasing pleasant activities drastically. Do not overlook small pleasures. Fuchs and Rehm (1977) encourage depressed people to set three personally pleasant behavioral activities for each major goal—perhaps calling a friend for a chat or going to the library to get a book. Our students have used an enormous range of activities: engaging in the "good dream," sewing or embroidering, reading travel folders, cactus gardening, or browsing in the gourmet section of the market.

Noticing and recording the good things that happen can have the same effect as adding new ones.

And by all means, *increase your exercise.* Exercise is a reliable, well-demonstrated corrective for mood depression and low energy (McCann & Holmes, 1984; Simons, McGowan, Epstein, Kupfer, & Robertson, 1985; Thayer, 2001). The benefits come from both aerobic exercises, such as running, and nonaerobic activities, such as weight lifting (Doyne et al., 1987). Even walking briskly for 10 to 15 minutes has startling effects on depression and anxiety (Ekkekakis, Hall, VanLanduyt, & Petruzzello, 2000).

If the depressed mood itself is troubling, temporary relief can be gained by concentrated work; deep absorption in a task reduces the emotions of mood (Erber & Tesser, 1992).

Increasing positive self-statements. Make an effort to make clear, specific self-statements that recognize the positive things you do. You need not fear praising and encouraging yourself excessively. If you now suffer from low self-esteem, you almost certainly lean too heavily toward negative self-appraisal and self-criticism.

Combined programs. The best general strategy for changing a bad mood is a combination of relaxation, stress management, revised self-statements, and exercise (Thayer, 2001).

Exercise and Athletics

To achieve the eventual goal of true physical fitness, most experts say, you must expend about 2000 calories per week in vigorous exercise (Stockton, 1987). For various sports, this translates approximately as:

Tennis	1 hour per day	5 days per week
Aerobics classes	40 minutes per day	5 days per week
Running, 10-min miles	3 miles per day	6 days per week
Walking, 12-min miles	5 miles per day	5 days per week
Swimming	30 minutes per day	6 days per week
Cross-country skiing	30 minutes per day	6 days per week

In adopting a new program for a healthier lifestyle, the gradual, shaped increase of exercise is an important element. If your goals for performance are set in reasonable, realistic, and gradual shaping steps, increases in performance and fitness can be expected. Do not set goals for yourself that are punishing; that only leads to dropping out of your program (Selby, DiLorenzo, & Steinkamp, 1987). For some sedentary people, exercise should be increased as slowly as merely parking farther away from their destination. Two sessions per week of vigorous exercise—low-impact aerobics or brisk walking—may well be a wise first (or even second) step (Dubbert, Martin, & Epstein, 1986).

Skilled and novice athletes should use different approaches to increasing skill level even more. Imagined rehearsal, after relaxing, has been shown to help performance levels of experts in many sports—running, skiing, basketball, golf. In this technique, a successful competitive event is used as the imagined scene. But, as mentioned earlier, imagined rehearsal actually makes novices' performances worse! This is because the wrong skills are practiced. Modeling and actual practice are more effective in the earliest stages of skill building (Suinn, 1987).

Relations with Others: Social Anxieties, Social Skills, and Dating

If social anxiety prevents you from making friends, develop a full plan as discussed for specific anxieties. Some form of relaxation is the incompatible behavior to choose.

Some students feel that their problem is not only feeling anxiety with others, but also not knowing what to do. Making friends with others of the same or the opposite sex is much the same. To be pleasant to others, a few general rules are especially helpful in the early stages of getting to know another person. For example, psychologists teach people to improve their social skills by using more appropriate body language. We suggest you use the acronym SOLER to remind yourself of what to do (Egan, 1977):

S   Sit facing the person
O   with an Open posture (no crossed arms, for example),
L   Lean slightly forward,
E   make Eye contact,
R   and Relax.

Conversational skills are also of great importance in making friends, and the skills themselves are surprisingly simple:

1. Focus on the other person. Open a conversation with something that conveys interest in her or him—pay a compliment, ask for an opinion or advice.
2. Remember to keep the conversational ball moving back and forth over the net, with special attention to keeping it in the other person's court.
3. Avoid insincere remarks. Silence is better than slick.
4. Think about the conversation from the other's point of view. Don't ask yourself, "Does he like me?" Instead, ask yourself, "Is he comfortable in this conversation?" (Farber, 1987)

These common social skills are also vital to good intimate relationships—married couples are often ruder to each other than to complete strangers.

If these lists are not sufficient, and you don't know what to do, ask someone who is successful, or watch carefully. Modeling is especially important in improving social skills (Lipton & Nelson, 1980). If your problem is initiating conversations, for example, observe someone who does it better than you do. It is vital to select some effective behaviors, from the preceding lists or from your own models, and rehearse them before you begin to expose yourself to problem situations.

Relaxation in social situations is very helpful, but those who combine new social skills with relaxation improve significantly more (Cappe & Alden, 1986).

Smoking, Drinking, and Drugs

Prepare to engage in alternative behaviors to drinking, smoking, or drugs—such as dancing, playing games, or having soft drinks. Those who resist the temptation of situations highly risky for abusing alcohol and drugs are more likely to use alternative behaviors (Brown, Stetson, & Beatty, 1989).

Choose one or more alternatives, and perform them at high-risk moments or in response to urges to indulge. When you are in the early period of nonsmoking, the experience of craving can be an appropriate time for alternate behavior. Eating a flavorful noncaloric mint is a good substitute; drinking water is probably the best because of its flushing action. Distraction from the urge will result. Distraction and substitute behaviors are among the most effective methods for resisting temptations to smoke (Shiffman, 1984), and are far superior to the attempts merely to suppress thoughts about the craved substance (Wenzlaff & Wegner, 2000).

Relaxation is an extremely valuable alternative behavior. Tension or anxiety often leads to overconsumption of alcohol, tobacco, drugs, and even food. Include relaxation in your plan. Learn to relax, and apply relaxation at the first cue that you are tense and at the first sign of your craving.

Should you stop smoking "cold turkey" or cut down gradually? A fairly rapid cessation is desirable, but delay setting a definite quit date for 2 weeks or so (Flaxman, 1978), until self-directional skills have been organized and practiced, such as self-observation, designing the plan, thinking how you will cope with urges to smoke, and practicing your plan.

Very heavy smokers may need an alternate approach, because heavy smokers are less likely to quit altogether, so a first goal might be to cut back on frequency according to some regular, shaped daily reduction of cigarettes (Cohen et al., 1989). When smoking has been reduced to a moderate level, then adopting a definite quit date is highly recommended.

Regular exercise is a potent antidote to the use of drugs, alcohol, and tobacco, particularly if you substitute exercise for the usual end-of-the-day snack, cocktail, or drug (Marlatt & Parks, 1982; Murphy, Pagano, & Marlatt, 1986). Exercise has an effect on mood similar to that of smoking (Thayer, Peters, Takahashi, & Birkhead-Flight, 1993).

Studying and Time Management

What you do within a scheduled block of study time does make a difference. Three specific new studying behaviors should be developed. Either by stating aloud or in written notes, add these behaviors in response to text you are reading (Watson, 2001):

1. *Focus* your attention. As the first act of studying, concentrate your attention on the learning task. Note when your attention drifts. Restart. Keep records of the length of focused time you achieve.
2. *Explain* the material to yourself. Restate it. Rephrase it—sentence by sentence, if they are difficult, or at the end of each page, or three pages, or section, as often as necessary to maintain understanding.
3. *Elaborate* the material to yourself. Tie it to your own experience. Search your memory for related experience or prior knowledge from other reading. Observe your self-talk; take opportunities for positive self-statements. Procrastinators apparently delay themselves by negative self-speech (Ferrari, 1991).

For test taking, emphasize the following (Watson, 2001):

1. *Prepare.* Predict questions that may be asked. Focus on material you do not know.
2. *Relax.* Use relaxation techniques in rehearsing the test situation, and during it.
3. *Manage time and effort.* Move through the examination in successive waves: First answer all questions you know. Then return to the beginning. Again, answer all you know; move on. Return again to the beginning, and so forth, until all are answered.

Weight Loss and Overeating

If you're going to take weight off and keep it off, you will have to change some of your behaviors and attitudes. Strategies associated with long-term maintenance of weight loss include: planning, monitoring, amount and quality of exercise, social support, and positive self-talk (Head & Brookhart, 1997).

Using a preliminary "practice" period is a good principle to follow with dieting as well. Choose a moderate reduction of calories as your first shaping goal, and for 2 weeks or so practice the general skills of self-control. Then steadily cut the calorie level to your actual shaping-step goals.

A regular program of exercise is vital to weight control. The evidence is overwhelming: Dieting should be combined with exercise (Stalonas & Kirschenbaum, 1985; Thayer, 2001; Wadden, Vogt, Foster, & Anderson, 1998). Exercisers do not compensate by eating more; in fact, exercisers eat less (Dickson-Parnell & Zeichner, 1985). Supervised exercise programs are more likely to continue, and thus weight loss in the long term is more likely to be maintained (Craighead & Blum, 1989).

If you are a binge eater, some means of replacing negative thoughts with positive ones should be a central part of your program, even though these statements may appear not to be directly related to eating issues. When you are about to binge, examine your self-speech very carefully, and note self-criticisms. Use techniques of thought replacement (Heatherton & Baumeister, 1991).

Chapter Summary

Substituting New Thoughts and Behaviors

Substituting a desired behavior for an undesired one is preferable to following a plan that merely suppresses the bad habit. Substitution of overt behaviors, self-statements, and thoughts should be considered; these can often be effectively combined. Selecting an incompatible behavior is generally a good tactic. If the incompatible behavior is itself desirable, so much the better. But even when the substituted behavior has no intrinsic merit, it is better to substitute a neutral response than merely to suppress the old. Keeping records of the substitution will help strengthen the new behavior.

Substitutions for Anxiety and Stress Reactions

You can reduce fears and anxieties by (1) identifying carefully the situations in which you are uncomfortable, (2) choosing a behavior that is incompatible with anxiety, and (3) practicing the behavior in the situation that produces anxiety. Several behaviors that are incompatible with anxiety have been discussed, including distraction of attention, sexual arousal, martial arts, exercise, reappraisal through rational restructuring, and meditation.

Relaxation

Whenever you want to eliminate an undesired behavior, choose an alternative behavior for that same situation. When emotional reactions are the problem, relaxation is a useful incompatible response.

At the beginning, relaxation should be practiced privately, then quickly employed in many real-life situations. As soon as relaxation is a well-developed skill, it should be practiced in those situations that produce anxiety. Ideally, relaxation should be practiced immediately before the time when anxiety usually begins. You may combine relaxation with positive self-instructions.

Developing New Behaviors

Rehearsing a behavior repeatedly in the actual situation is the best way to master that behavior. When rehearsals are difficult to arrange in real life, you can use imagined rehearsal in the initial stages. Imagined rehearsals must be vivid and must include both situation and behavior. When you imagine behaviors in feared situations, use relaxation. But imagined rehearsal is only a prelude, a bridge to actual rehearsal in real-life situations. Your ultimate plan must include actual performance in actual situations. You can identify effective behaviors by observing models that are achieving the goals you want. Identify a model, analyze the model's skills, and use those skills as your standard. Don't hesitate to ask your model's help in explaining or even coaching those skills. If you have difficulty imagining yourself rehearsing your goal behaviors, imagine your models performing. Imagine more than one model in the situations that are difficult for you. Imagine them coping, self-instructing, and succeeding. This should be only the first step, however. Next, imagine rehearsals with yourself as the performer. The third step is the most important: Transfer those behaviors into real life. It is the rehearsal in the actual situation that brings about long-lasting change.

Shaping: The Method of Successive Approximations

Most self-direction plans, particularly those that call for developing some desired behavior, require shaping. Shaping means that instead of requiring yourself to perform the complete new behavior, you require yourself to perform only a part. Then, in a series of successive approximations to the final goal, you gradually increase the size of your steps. The two main rules of shaping are (1) you can never begin too low, and (2) the steps can never be too small. You can shape your behavior along any desired continuum. Common problems in shaping include plateaus—progress stops and you find it hard to go on—and "lack of willpower"—you require yourself to start too high or use steps that are too large. In the next chapter, which discusses self-reinforcement, you will learn methods for rewarding each step along the way.

Your Own Self-Direction Project: Step 6

You should now be able to draw up another version of your plan for self-modification, taking into account the methods for developing new behaviors. Consider your own goals, and write plans for reaching them. At this stage, try to include each of the basic tactics discussed in this chapter:

- Substituting new thoughts and behaviors (especially relaxation)
- Overt and imagined modeling and rehearsal
- Shaping

Later, you can choose the most effective total package. For now, specify ways you might use each of these tactics.

One of our students, Edward, wrote a fine plan incorporating these suggestions. Here is his letter to us:

> Last semester, I took a course in self-modification using your text *Self-Directed Behavior*. Even then I really wanted to do something about my speech anxiety, which had been a problem for me ever since I could remember. But it wasn't until this semester that I actually had to give a speech in a course. Just thinking about it made me nervous, but I remembered the techniques I had learned in the book and set out to use them. I used imaginary rehearsals while in a state of deep relaxation, picturing the room and people with as much detail as possible. Whenever I felt myself getting too nervous, I would stop, do the muscle relaxation exercises until I was calm, and start over again. I also used the principles of shaping by practicing alone, with my sister, and finally with friends. Realistic positive self-statements to "psych" myself up were also useful. When the time came to give my presentation, I told myself to relax and proceeded. I couldn't believe how relaxed I felt! As a result, I could concentrate a lot better on what I was saying and not what I was feeling. I now feel quite confident that I can give an informative speech.

Write your plan now, but remember—it is not yet complete. The next chapter discusses methods of self-modification through control of consequences. Your final plan will include all three elements: antecedent control, new behavior development, and consequence control.

Chapter 7

Consequences

Techniques of Self-Reinforcement

8. How soon after the desired behavior should reinforcement come?
9. Explain how to use token reinforcers. What is their main purpose?
10. How do you use imagined reinforcement?
11. Explain how to use verbal self-reinforcement.
    a. Why do people sometimes not use self-praise?
    b. What is the relationship of self-reinforcement to depression?
12. Should you ever get noncontingent positive events? When?

Self-Punishment and Extinction

13. Can you count on using extinction to change your own behavior? What is a better procedure?
14. Why is self-punishment usually insufficient?
    a. Is losing a positive event punishment enough? Or should you try to arrange to add on some negative event?
    b. Explain precommitted punishment. Is it properly a punishment or a deterrent?

Reinforcement in Plans for Self-Modification

15. How is reinforcement used in conjunction with antecedent control of behavior?
16. How is it combined with developing new behaviors? For example, how is it combined with imagined rehearsal or shaping?
17. What kinds of self-modification plans should include self-reinforcement?

Tips for Typical Topics

Chapter Summary

Your Own Self-Direction Project: Step 7

One of the basic formulas for self-regulation is the arrangement of reinforcement for desired behaviors.

How is positive reinforcement used in self-modification? *The basic principle is that a reinforcing event is made contingent on the desired behavior.* As discussed in Chapter 4, the idea of contingency is very important. A reinforcer is delivered after, and only after, a certain response. If an event occurs whether or not you perform some behavior, that event will not affect the behavior. If, instead, you arrange that the event occurs only by performing the behavior (arrange that it is contingent on the behavior), then the behavior may be strengthened. If so, that event is then a reinforcer of the behavior. That means that the behavior will be strengthened—that is, it will be more likely to occur again. It is the contingent relationship that is important, not the reinforcer alone.

The use of reinforcement was one of the first techniques studied in the field of self-directed behavior. Thirty-three years ago, when we wrote the first edition of this book, reinforcement was the cornerstone of all self-change plans because it was the best understood technique. As psychology's understanding of self-control processes has deepened, many new procedures have emerged, and these often seem more sophisticated than simple reinforcement. Twenty years ago, many writers seemed ready to put reinforcement out to pasture. Now there is a new consensus: Reinforcement is still the most reliable horse in the stable.

Contingent rewards, when delivered by the social environment, may very well strengthen the behaviors they follow, and thus become reinforcers. Very little in psychology is more certain than that.

Bridging Between Immediate Contingencies and Long-Delayed Consequences

A review of Chapter 4 will remind you how and why we should assume that all our problematic behavior was developed through reinforcement and punishment and is maintained by reinforcement or avoidance. Our harmful impulses, habits, and dodges are

Table 7-1 Immediate and Future Outcomes

Behavioral Deficit	Immediate Contingency	Delayed Outcome
Studying	Lack of reinforcement	Good grades
	Response effort	Graduation
	Reinforcement of competing behavior (TV, parties, phone calls)	Job or graduate school
Exercise	Sore muscles	Better health
	Response effort	Weight loss
	Reinforcement of competing behavior (eating, TV, naps)	Better physique
Healthful eating	Decreased reinforcement value	Better health
	Response effort to prepare more healthful food	More energy
	Reinforcement for competing behavior (eating junk food)	Less constipation
Smoking	Immediate reinforcement (alertness, relaxation)	Lung cancer
	Little response effort	Emphysema
	Response effort for alternate behaviors	Heart disease
		Stained teeth
Unprotected sex	Immediate reinforcement	Pregnancy
	Increased reinforcement value	Exposure to HIV, diagnosis of AIDS
	Less reinforcement and more response effort for condom use	Other sexually transmitted diseases
Eating junk food	Immediate reinforcement	Tooth decay
	Increased reinforcement value	Weight gain
	Little response effort	Pimples

SOURCE: *Behavior modification*, 2nd edition (p. 284), by R. G. Miltenberger, 2001, Belmont, CA: Wadsworth.

likely maintained by some immediate reinforcement, whereas our long-term future goals will reward us only later, after the effort of change. The problem of self-control is to use new patterns of reinforcements and behaviors to create a bridge to that better-but-delayed future.

Table 7-1 illustrates the contrasts between immediate and delayed outcomes, for six common goals of self-management.

Given the human tendency to take smaller-sooner rewards over larger-later ones, your self-management plan will require three strategies: first, through envisioning and reminders, to bring delayed goals forward in time; second, through avoiding problematic antecedents, to reduce the frequency of undesired behavior; and third, by using new and powerful immediate reinforcement, to strengthen alternate, desirable behaviors. To achieve these strategies, the first step is to discover and select those new and powerful reinforcers.

Discovering and Selecting Reinforcers

The simple formula for self-modification is to rearrange the contingencies so that reinforcement follows desirable behavior. To do so, you need to know what reinforcers you have available for rearrangement. This section discusses ways of discovering and cataloging reinforcers so that you'll be able to select reinforcers you can use.

Direct Observation of Reinforcing Consequences: Possibilities and Problems

Ramon kept careful baseline records of his studying behavior. He recorded the situations and opportunities for studying (for example, "at library, 42 min."). He also recorded his actual study time ("4 min.," "15 min.," and so on). The baseline rate of actual study time was very low—less than 20% of the time he was in an appropriate study situation. What was the reinforcer for all this inattention while in a study situation? Ramon was able to report it instantly: Instead of reading, he spent his time talking with the friends who sat near his usual table.

This reinforcer, incidentally, was not only clear but also very available for rearrangement. Ramon designed an intervention plan that required him to spend at least 60 minutes studying in his room, a behavior he would then reinforce with a trip to the library, where he could converse with single-minded devotion. He reported that this plan increased both his study time and his socializing.

Ramon discovered the reinforcer for his undesirable behavior while observing himself. The easiest kind of intervention plan is simply to rearrange the reinforcers that you are already getting so that they are used to reinforce some desirable behavior rather than some undesirable behavior.

Of course, situations are not always so simple. In some cases the reinforcers, although evident, cannot be so easily detached from the problem behavior and rearranged in an intervention plan. This is the case with consummatory responses, such as eating or drinking. Problems can also arise when the reinforcing consequences of behavior are not so obvious. Sometimes the most careful observer can't discover what they are. Three conditions that commonly obscure reinforcers are *intermittent reinforcement schedules, delayed reinforcement,* and *avoidance behaviors.*

Intermittent reinforcement schedules and delayed reinforcement. If each instance of your problem behavior were followed by reinforcement, careful observation could reveal the reinforcer in question. But some of your more persistent actions are followed by reinforcement only part of the time. Remember that intermittent reinforcement leads to greater resistance to extinction. Thus, you might expect to find that an intermittent reinforcement schedule is responsible for maintaining especially persistent problem behaviors. But it might take months of observation to discover the pattern. *Delayed reinforcement* can be problematic in a similar way. If reinforcement does not appear to follow your behavior, one possible strategy is to examine your train of thought before or after the behavior occurs. The time between behavior and reinforcement is often bridged by thoughts or anticipations of the maintaining consequence.

Avoidance behaviors. Avoidance behavior creates even worse problems for the person trying to discover reinforcers because the aversive consequence may not occur at all. When you have been punished for a behavior in the presence of a cue, that cue will come to elicit avoidance of the behavior. Thus, you will not be punished again and therefore will not be able to observe the negative reinforcer because it will not occur. Although avoidance learning probably accounts for many problems, you might observe forever and not detect the specific unpleasantness you are avoiding.

Bill, a sophomore, wanted to try out for his dormitory's intramural basketball team. He had not played competitively in high school and had not even played many pickup games since he was about 14, although he enjoyed shooting baskets alone. Bill told us that he really had a baseline; during three semesters of college, in which he had wanted to try out for a team, he just couldn't make himself do it. He wanted to know how he could discover the reinforcer for not trying out. Of course, he couldn't discover such a reinforcer, and neither could a professional. In a case like this, we suspect a pattern of avoidance learning. During high school, some unpleasant consequence may have followed Bill's efforts to participate in organized basketball. But it is not necessary that Bill discover that lost history. Even if Bill could remember some punishment he once received, and satisfy his curiosity, he would still need to employ new positive reinforcers now.

In summary, if you can discover the reinforcers that support some undesirable behavior, you may be able to rearrange them so that they reinforce some desirable behavior. Three conditions can interfere with this process:

1. The behavior may be unalterably attached to the reinforcer.
2. The problem behavior may be on an impossible-to-detect intermittent reinforcement schedule.
3. You may be engaging in avoidance behavior.

Your strategy, then, must be to discover reinforcers that *are* controllable. The reinforcers don't need to be those that are actually maintaining your problem behavior. You can use *any* desired event, as long as it increases the frequency of your desired behavior.

Positive Reinforcers

If you cannot rearrange or even discover the reinforcers for a particular behavior, you can still modify your behavior by selecting some reinforcer and making it contingent upon a desired behavior.

A *positive reinforcer* is anything that will increase the occurrence of the behavior that contingently produces it. Reinforcers can be things, people, or activities. A "thing" reinforcer might be a doughnut, a $5 bill, a new dress, a fancy shirt, a compact disc—anything you want or would like to have. A "people" reinforcer might be praise or approval, going on a date with your girlfriend, talking with your boyfriend on the phone, or spending time with someone you enjoy. An "activity" reinforcer is any event you enjoy—playing a game, going to a movie, or having dinner out. Even "doing nothing"—talking with friends or loafing—can be a reinforcer. Usually these kinds of potential reinforcers are not limited to any one behavior or situation. You may just feel like going out for a beer or a pizza. Any kind of special occasion like that can be used as a reinforcer. *The task is simply to connect contingently the occurrence of the reinforcer with the target behavior;* that is, only to take the reinforcer if and when the target behavior is performed.

The most important reinforcers are those that eventually help you maintain your new behavior once it is solidly in place. You can use those reinforcers to support the steps along your way. For example, one of our students aspired toward membership in the scholarly society Phi Beta Kappa. That meant harder work, with the reward of higher grades. She used the reinforcer of "grades awarded" to increase her studying time, except that she awarded the grades herself on a daily basis. She entered an A for excellent, a B for good, and so forth, beside each day's entry in her study record. If she studied very well, she gave herself an A; if fairly well, a B, and so on. Another student wanted to increase her range of friends. She reinforced making friendly overtures to new people with phone chats with her best friend.

Using logical reinforcers—ones similar to the rewards you are striving toward—is highly desirable. But if you cannot arrange logical reinforcers, any pleasant event can reinforce behavior. The range of reinforcers is potentially as wide as the range of objects in the world—as wide as the range of human activities. To illustrate this variety, here is a partial list of the reinforcers our students have used:

praising oneself	mountain climbing
making love	spending money
going to the beach	listening to the audio book
spending time at a favorite hobby	of Harry Potter
listening to my iPod	dancing
eating favorite foods	playing sports
going out to clubs	pampering oneself
getting to "be the boss" with a boyfriend	taking a "fantasy break"
taking long breaks from work	putting on makeup
window shopping	doing anything I want to do
not going to work	being alone
going to parties	not doing my duty sometimes
doing only what I want to do, all day	watching TV
goofing off	making long-distance calls
gardening	buying a present for someone
playing with the parrot	reading erotica
spending extra time with a friend	karaoke, or lip-synching
reading mystery stories	(pretending to be a rock star
taking bubble baths	in front of a mirror)
going to a movie or a play	

Activities are excellent reinforcers. Actually, *any activity that you are more likely to perform can be used to reinforce any behavior that you are less likely to perform (when you have a free choice).* This is known as the *Premack principle,* after the psychologist who studied the phenomenon most systematically.

The Premack principle tells you that you can use any one of certain behaviors you engage in every day—such as taking a bath, going to work, eating, watching TV, or talking to friends on the phone—to reinforce the goal behavior by connecting its occurrence to the goal behavior. The object of the plan is to require yourself to perform the goal behavior *before* you perform the behavior that occurs frequently.

A Premack-type reinforcer is (or could be) frequent in free-choice conditions. Thus, you might also select an activity that you do not perform as frequently as you would like. For example, one student chose "dreaming about my trip to Europe" as a reinforcer, in spite of the fact that this daydreaming generally occurred less than once a day. She liked to lie quietly and picture the different routes she might take on her trip, the hotels in which she might stay, and the different museums she might visit. She reasoned that this was a good Premack-type reinforcer because, given the opportunity, she would engage in this behavior very frequently.

A good strategy is to use the behavior that you usually perform *instead* of the target behavior as the *reinforcer* for that target behavior. For example, a man who wanted to spend some time in the evening reading serious literature instead spent all his time reading "whodunits." He did this very frequently, and it interfered with his reading the cultural material. So he used the whodunit reading as a Premack-type reinforcer. If he spent a certain amount of time reading serious material, then he would reinforce that behavior by allowing himself the more preferable activity of reading mystery stories.

Examples of Premack-type activities used in published cases of self-directed behavior change include eating, urinating (Johnson, 1971), sitting on a particular chair (Horan & Johnson, 1971), smoking, and making telephone calls (Todd, 1972).

Given the tremendous scope of any list of possible reinforcers for any one individual, how can you decide which are the potentially effective reinforcers for yourself? Answering the following questions may help:

1. What will be the rewards of achieving your goal?
2. What kind of praise do you like to receive from yourself and others?
3. What kinds of things do you like to have?
4. What are your major interests?
5. What are your hobbies?
6. What people do you like to be with?
7. What do you like to do with those people?
8. What do you do for fun?
9. What do you do to relax?
10. What do you do to get away from it all?
11. What makes you feel good?
12. What would be a nice present to receive?
13. What kinds of things are important to you?
14. What would you buy if you had an extra $20? $50? $100?
15. On what do you spend your money each week?

16. What behaviors do you perform every day? (Don't overlook the obvious or the commonplace.)
17. Are there any behaviors that you usually perform instead of the target behavior?
18. What would you hate to lose?
19. Of the things you do every day, which would you hate to give up?
20. What are your favorite daydreams and fantasies?
21. What are the most relaxing scenes you can imagine?

Wherever you are in your own self-direction project, stop at this point and take a few minutes to think about the preceding questions. You should be able to give specific answers to each question. If you can, you will have a good-sized catalog of possible reinforcers. Eventually you will choose one or more reinforcers from this list.

Consider each reinforcer in these terms: *Can I stand withholding it from myself one or more times if I don't earn it?* Putting a reinforcer on contingency means that you may have to withhold it. Don't choose a reinforcer that you simply will not give up. How potent is this reinforcer? Choosing a trivial reward will bring trivial results. The trick is to strike a balance between too important and trivial. The ideal reinforcer should be something you could stand losing (temporarily) if you had to, but you would be very disappointed if you did.

Using Others to Dispense Reinforcers

Using important other people to dispense reinforcement has proven beneficial in a wide variety of problem behaviors, such as reducing delinquent acts (Tharp & Wetzel, 1969), complying with health-care practices (Becker & Green, 1975; Blackwell, 1979; Brownlee, 1978), dieting (Weisz & Bucher, 1980), and smoking cessation (Coppotelli & Orleans, 1985). When your family, friends, or associates become involved in reinforcing your self-change behavior, long-term maintenance of the behavior is much more likely (Hall, 1980; Shelton, Levy, & contributors, 1981; Stokes & Baer, 1977). When other people dispense the contingent consequences to you, they are called *mediators*.

For example, using money to reinforce good eating habits increases weight loss, but when the money is dispensed by the dieter's spouse, the long-range effectiveness of the program is even greater (Israel & Saccone, 1979; Saccone & Israel, 1978). The praise given by the husband in the case in Box 7-1 dramatizes this point. One of the most effective weight-control studies ever reported used spouses as mediators. Spouses modeled good behavior: They paused while eating, did not eat snacks in the partner's presence, avoided buying high-calorie foods, rewarded habit change, and assisted in record keeping (Brownell, Heckerman, Westlake, Hayes, & Monti, 1978). When spouses successfully mediate a program of weight loss, excellent side benefits are likely. Women whose husbands cooperated showed significant improvement in marital happiness and a drop in depression (Weisz & Bucher, 1980).

Evidence from ex-smokers is similar: Social support from friends, companions, partners, and spouses is associated with greater likelihood of quitting smoking (Cohen & Lichtenstein, 1990; Hill et al., 1994).

Box 7-1
Social Reinforcement by the Spouse in Weight Control:
A Case Study

This interesting case was conducted about 30 years ago. Although both spouses considered it very successful and a positive contribution to their relationship, there are elements in this case that we would no longer recommend (Bell & Higa, 1995). What is your analysis? What element in this case is most unwise? (See answer at bottom of box).

The subject, Mrs. L., was a 44-year-old female, 5'6" tall and weighing 174 pounds. She had made numerous unsuccessful attempts to lose weight over the past 10 years employing treatments ranging from "do it yourself remedies" to an assortment of fad diets and then drug therapy administered under a physician's care. Her husband had also tried a treatment of verbal abuse during which he routinely made statements such as, "You are so fat I am ashamed to be seen with you." He also offered to buy Mrs. L. a new wardrobe if she would lose 30 pounds. The most weight [Mrs. L.] ever lost was 12 pounds in 6 weeks with drugs. She remained at the new weight for 12 weeks of treatment, and gained the weight back within 1 month when medication was discontinued. With all treatments the consistent pattern was weight loss for a few weeks followed by a return to old eating habits and weight gain again. Mrs. L. frequently snacked while cooking or shopping, remarking that she did not have the necessary willpower to lose weight.

During an initial phase of self-observation and the arrangement of new antecedents, she lost less than one-half pound per week. Then a plan involving social reinforcement was added. The subject stated that Mr. L.'s verbal abuse of

---

Developing and maintaining important health behaviors (diet, exercise, adherence to physician-prescribed behaviors and routines) are affected strongly by spouse's type of social control and support. Forty-four couples described the strategies they used in attempting to prompt their partner to engage in particular health behaviors. Strategies that were more frequently mentioned as effective included the partner also engaging in the desired health behavior, modeling the health behavior, discussing health issues, and providing emotional support. When ineffective strategies were used, spouses reported feeling lower self-esteem, less positive affect, and more negative affect in response to their partner's use of strategies. Spouses rated their partners' use of ineffective strategies as less motivated by a concern for the spouse's welfare and more motivated by their own desire to exert control within the relationship (Tucker & Meuller, 2000). So it is no surprise that spouses who experienced more negative social control engaged in more health-compromising behaviors, whereas experiencing positive social control was associated with attempts to engage in the desired behavior (Tucker & Anders, 2001).

If your reinforcer is something tangible, such as money, you can give it to another person and explain what you must do to get it back. If the reinforcer is some activity, you

her weight was highly aversive. Therefore, the frequency of these comments was made contingent on weight loss. If Mrs. L. lost 2 pounds a week, Mr. L. was to compliment his wife two or more times each evening for the progress made on her diet. No derogatory comments about her figure were allowed. If the weekly criterion was not reached, Mr. L. was to verbally abuse Mrs. L.'s figure as frequently as desired. A contract was signed by both persons with each spouse serving as a reliability check for the other. Mr. L. was to assure accurate weigh-ins, and Mrs. L. made sure no verbal abuse of her weight was used inappropriately. When the contract was violated, the offended spouse used a verbal reminder such as, "You just called me a fat hog; this violates the contract we made."

Greater weight losses were reported during the social-reinforcement phase (39 pounds). Mrs. L. attributed her success to self-confidence created primarily by praise she received from her husband. She indicated that maintaining weight at or below the goal (135 pounds) during follow-up was due to praise and gradual weight loss resulting in altered eating habits (i.e., eating only at the dining table and consuming smaller portions).

Mr. and Mrs. L. stated that social reinforcement resulted in better social interactions at home. Both were pleased with the weight loss and increased affection shown toward each other. They indicated that this positive behavior would continue in other aspects of their relationship.

SOURCE: "Social Reinforcement by the Spouse in Weight Control: A Case Study," by J. L. Matson, 1977, *Journal of Behavior Therapy and Experimental Psychiatry, 8*, pp. 327–328. Copyright © 1977 by Pergamon Press, Ltd. Reprinted by permission.

Answer: The use of punishment (Mr. L.'s verbal abuse of his wife).

can arrange to get permission from those who are present, stipulating that permission should be granted only if you perform the target behavior. For example, Carmen, a college freshman, wanted to increase her studying time. She arranged with her daily aerobics classmates that they wouldn't let her join in unless she reported at least an hour's studying already that day. Setting up a fund that will be returned to you as reinforcement for meeting goals has been shown to add to the effectiveness of good programs for weight loss and smoking cessation (Jeffery, Hellerstedt, & Schmid, 1990). As an example, our student Kelly wrote:

> I put little notes on my computer, on the door, on the mirror, even in my planner, telling myself encouragements and compliments. . . . Also, my friends and family have agreed to help me out, and when I say something negative about myself they point it out to me, and I have to put a quarter into this jar, which I call the "Cloudy Jar." But then if I say something optimistic my friends will transfer a quarter into another jar, which I call the "Sunny Jar" because it helps my optimism at the end of every week when I spend those sunny quarters on ice cream!

Carmen—who apparently liked the system of using mediators—felt guilty about her infrequent letters and phone calls to her parents, who were thousands of miles away from her campus. She arranged with them that they would send her monthly allowance only after she wrote or called in the last week of the month. Everyone was delighted. Carmen wrote more letters, and her parents raised her allowance by $10.

Mediators can also provide praise. The power of praise coming from those we care about cannot be overestimated. In all likelihood, praise—for increasing studying, losing weight, staying on a good health regimen, or stopping smoking—is much more effective than material reinforcers. And the more important the mediator is to you, the more powerful that praise will be. A good self-modification plan should almost certainly contain this element. Arrange with your important others to praise your reaching each shaping step. Don't hesitate to call attention to your changed behavior by prompting others to respond with encouragement.

An instructor of a course that uses this book as the text organized her students into special self-supporting groups. For example, those students whose goal was weight loss met regularly and worked out mutual-reinforcement plans for improved eating habits. In such groups, reinforcement can be even more powerful if the group earns (or loses) rewards as a group (Jeffery, Gerber, Rosenthal, & Lindquist, 1983).

Such support groups can be extremely helpful, especially when mediators in natural relationships are difficult to find. For long-term benefits, though, whenever possible the reinforcement plans should involve people who will be close to you in your regular and continuing life. This becomes even more important after the novelty and early enthusiasm of your self-modification plan diminish (Fisher, Lowe, Levenkron, & Newman, 1982). Exercisers who stick with their programs long enough to experience real health benefits are more likely to have a regular aerobics partner (Lawson & Rhodes, 1981) or a supportive spouse (Heinzelman & Bagley, 1970).

Whenever you use a mediator, it is important that the person understand exactly what he or she is supposed to do—namely, to reinforce contingently and not to punish you. If you fail to perform the target behavior and the mediator withholds the reinforcer, that is unpleasant enough. You don't need further punishment such as scolding, which may even cause you to discontinue your plan altogether.

If your behavior change will affect others, discuss the issue fully with them, and decide together how they might serve as mediators for you. For example, Ellen's husband and children warmly applauded her decision to finish her college degree. But when she began a program to increase study time, her family punished her by comments that housework was being neglected (Peterson, 1983). An excellent plan here would be for Ellen's husband and children to reinforce her studying by doing some extra housework.

The "good" mediators' tasks are really very simple: They should give you your reinforcement when you are meeting your standard and withhold it when you're not. But you must appreciate that this can change their relationship with you, and it can sometimes be awkward—especially when they have to withhold your reinforcer. So reinforce their good mediating. Simple praise and expressions of thanks, especially at awkward moments, can help to keep their help.

Finally, always remember that this is your plan, your desire, your goal, and your choice. No matter how much assistance you get from others, it must always be in the service of building your self-control, not a means of passing the responsibility to others. In plans where there is assistance from others, success is associated with strategies that build autonomy and self-mastery, rather than dependence on another person (Ginsberg, Hall, & Rosinski, 1991).

Sharing Reinforcers

Sometimes the reinforcers you select are shared with other people or affect them as much as they affect you. Even in such a case, it is your behavior that establishes the contingency. For example, a young woman chose going to the movies with her boyfriend as a reinforcer. She needed his cooperation in her intervention plan because if she failed to perform the target behavior, she would have to miss seeing the movie with him. But if she did miss the movie, *so would he.* The pleasurable experiences we have with other people—being together, doing favorite things, loving—are often very powerful reinforcers and thus are ideal choices for an intervention plan. But if you want to use them, you must have the other person's cooperation.

Many times one person will decide to modify a particular aspect of his or her behavior because a friend or lover is concerned about it. A man might smoke, for example, and his friend might disapprove. It is often possible to use the other person, who is not changing his or her behavior, as a partner in the process of change. This is particularly true when the partner values your goals. The change in your behavior becomes the reinforcer for the partner's behavior of cooperation. Or the partner may simply care enough to be willing to share a reinforcer. We know of a woman who agreed with her student husband not to talk with him until he had spent so many minutes on a paper he was writing.

Using activities with others as reinforcers is effective not only because the reinforcer is a powerful one but also because it brings another force to bear in your intervention plan. The other person, who may stand to lose if you fail to perform the target behavior, will pressure you to perform it. If your determination lags, your friend may say to you, "You better do it! I want to see that movie!"

A special situation arises when a couple undertakes the same plan together. Before deciding on such a course, both partners should make sure they are equally committed to the plan and goals. When two partners both try to lose weight, for example, and one or both subtly sabotage the other's efforts, they may be less successful than if only one were trying to lose weight (Zitter & Fremouw, 1978).

The people who will help you in your self-change plan sometimes need a little help themselves to know just what to do. Box 7-2 contains a letter we've written to them explaining what you need them to do. Copy this or show it to anyone who is going to help you.

Self-Administered Consequences

Reinforcement dispensed by mediators is a powerful technique for increasing behavior strength, frequency, and probability. But if contingent reinforcement is self-administered, will it have the same effect? After all, the idea of contingency is that the consequences are not freely available. They appear only when a standard is met and otherwise are not available.

Box 7-2
Dear Helper

Dear Helper:

_____ will soon be discussing with you a new program of self-improvement that will probably please you. Because it may also affect you, we are writing this note with some tips on how you can be most helpful.

The details will be worked out with you in conversation. It is very important that you understand exactly what you are being asked to do so that you can follow the plan closely. So make sure your conversation is clear and precise. Your role will be to provide three kinds of help: *reminders, rewards,* and *general companionship and support.*

The plans will concentrate on the positive. These plans should increase the pleasant aspects of life for you both. If reminders are called for, be sure to remind—but *don't nag.* If reinforcers are called for, be sure to provide them if they are earned. If they are not earned, no reinforcer—but no scolding either.

To make things really clear, here are some examples of positive behaviors, likely to be reinforcing, that you could perform:

Compliment small successes.
Help the person think of substitutes for an unwanted behavior.
Celebrate successes together.
Help the person calm down when feeling stressed.
Encourage the person to stick with it.
Express confidence that the person can stick with it.
Express pleasure that the person is changing.

The following are examples of things you should avoid doing:

Nag the person.
Criticize the old behavior.
Get involved in every little decision the person makes.
Comment on your friend's lack of willpower.
Mention being bothered by the old, bad habit.
Express doubt about the person's ability to change.

Success in the plan will be strongly affected by a general climate of helpfulness and a positive overall atmosphere of encouragement. With your help, more can be achieved in many ways.

Sincerely yours,

David L. Watson/Roland G. Tharp
Authors, *Self-Directed Behavior*

SOURCE: Adapted from "Partner Behaviors That Support Quitting Smoking," by S. Cohen and E. Lichtenstein, 1990, *Journal of Consulting and Clinical Psychology, 58,* pp. 304–309.

In the self-administration of reinforcers, they are presumably available whether or not the standard is met. If you know that the reinforcer is there for the taking, whether or not you meet your standard, will self-reinforcement actually reinforce the behavior? This is one of the liveliest questions in contemporary psychology. Because it is so important to self-regulation, it is important that you understand something of the issues.

Actually, there are two interrelated issues: (1) Can people actually self-administer rewards contingently? In self-control terms, can people abstain from taking immediate rewards in favor of gaining long-term rewards? (2) If people do administer consequences contingently, do these consequences really reinforce and punish behavior? We will discuss these two issues in turn.

Learning Self-Reward and Self-Control

The answer to the first question is actually quite clear: Yes, people can and do self-administer rewards contingently. People can and do abstain from taking immediate rewards in favor of gaining long-term, more desirable ones. One can learn self-reinforcing by imitating others (Bandura, 1971), by following instructions (Kanfer, 1975), by receiving rewards for self-reinforcing (Speidel & Tharp, 1980), or through classlike lectures (Heiby, Ozaki, & Campos, 1984). Bandura and his associates have taught even pigeons, monkeys, and dogs to "self-reinforce"—that is, to not take freely available food until after they have performed the desired behavior. These animals were taught by an experimenter who removed the food trays if the animals tried to eat before performing. Once learned, self-reinforcing persisted for some time (Bandura & Mahoney, 1974).

Catania (1975) argues that this isn't really self-control, any more than refraining from shoplifting is self-control. If there were no external punishment for shoplifting (or taking the food), everyone would eventually walk out with whatever reinforcers he or she wanted.

Theoreticians who make this kind of argument point out that there has to be some external reason to self-reinforce and to stick to the planned contingencies. Rachlin (1974) correctly points out that a student would not make movie going contingent on studying unless the external reasons for studying—grades and career success—were meaningful.

In self-modification, the external contingencies are provided by your goals. You choose your goals because achieving them will improve your life. When you work for goals that you genuinely value, self-rewarding and self-punishing can certainly be carried out. Competent self-managers do so all the time. Tens of thousands of students who have used this textbook have done so. Not every student does, of course; and some do better than others in holding to accurate, contingent self-reinforcing. But can people self-control and self-reinforce? Of course they can.

Do Self-Administered Consequences Actually Reinforce and Punish?

After 25 years of puzzling over this issue, psychologists are beginning to phrase the questions as two separate issues: (1) When people administer their own consequences, does behavior actually improve? (2) Does this improvement occur according to the conditioning principles of reinforcement and punishment or according to the principles of feedback and cybernetics?

The first question has been addressed by a multitude of studies (see review articles by Ainslee, 1975; Bandura, 1971; Catania, 1975; Rachlin, 1974; Sohn & Lamal, 1982), and the answer here, too, is yes. When people self-administer contingent consequences, their behavior is indeed likely to improve. Successful self-controllers, regardless of the problem area—overeating, studying, dating, or smoking—are three times more likely to use self-reward procedures than are unsuccessful self-controllers (Heffernan & Richards, 1981; Perri & Richards, 1977; Perri, Richards, & Schultheis, 1977). Though not every study reports this result for every behavior, the vast majority of research supports this conclusion for a wide range of specific programs—weight loss, smoking, assertiveness, and many others. Yes, self-administered consequence programs are very likely to improve behavior. But that does not end the debate. Does self-reward operate as *reinforcement?* Do the principles of conditioning described in Chapter 4 explain the positive effects of self-reward?

The logical problem is this: We have already established that self-reinforcement will not occur at all unless the person is motivated to change and unless the external world eventually provides encouragement. Therefore, self-reinforcement can only be found embedded in a context of external reinforcement.

Bandura (1981) argues that self-reinforcing plans create incentives along the way to the eventual goal. Ainslee (1975), Catania (1975), and Rachlin (1974) point out that self-reinforcement is a very complicated process that contains many effective elements: You are teaching yourself to discriminate between correct and incorrect performances. You are reminding yourself of your long-term goals and of your rules for getting there (Nelson, Hayes, Spong, Jarrett, & McKnight, 1983). You are learning *self-awareness.*

Regulation theorists who work within the feedback/cybernetics model point out that when you reinforce your behavior, you are calling your own attention to it and making the behavior more vivid, even more vivid than by self-recording alone. Thus, you are able to give yourself clearer feedback to compare with your standards and goals.

B. F. Skinner himself (1953), the father of the operant-conditioning movement, expressed doubt that operant conditioning alone is the best explanation for the effects of self-administered contingent reward; the undoubted effectiveness must also come from a different route. Brigham (1989) has described that route in detail: Self-direction plans change the environment so that the environment reinforces behavior the individual is motivated to achieve.

Box 7-3 contains a further example of the continuing debate on whether self-reward and punishment operate according to the principles of reinforcement or of feedback.

So although theoreticians continue to argue about the mechanism, there is really no dispute about the following formulation. You can change the way you relate to your environment. You can learn to change it more effectively. You can assist that learning by the use of contingent reinforcement as you go along. In the long run, success in changing will depend on your setting up a new, improved reciprocal relationship with the world and people around you (Brigham, 1989).

Box 7-3
Self-Reward and Punishment:
Reinforcement or Feedback?

Here is an important and amusing example of research strategies and logic in the field of self-directed behavior. Rachlin (1974) has argued that self-rewarding works not by reinforcing, but by clearly marking behavior, making people more attentive, and so increasing accurate self-observation and self-monitoring. To test this hypothesis, Castro and Rachlin (1980) had people who attended a weight-reduction clinic pay the clinic more money if they lost more weight. These dieters lost as much weight as another group that took money as a "reward" for losing weight. Castro and Rachlin concluded that if these contingencies worked as reinforcement and punishment, then those who paid for losing weight should have lost less because they were punished, and those who took money should have lost more because they were reinforced. Therefore, contingencies work as feedback (as in cybernetic theory) and not according to conditioning principles.

Bandura (1981) attacked this study by pointing out that of course consequences are evaluated according to usual social standards. It is not "punishing" to pay a professional for effective services; we happily pay accountants to save us money, dentists who save our teeth, or clinics that help us lose weight. Therefore, no "punishment" had been studied at all.

The debate heated up and moved to Bogota, Colombia, where Castro and his colleagues (Castro, de Perez, de Albanchez, & de Leon, 1983) resolved to "punish" their weight losers in a way that had no correspondence to ordinary professional life. One group of clients that came to their weight-reduction clinic agreed to a bizarre plan. For each pound lost, each person either mailed one dollar (equivalent) to his or her most hated political party or cut the money into tiny pieces in the presence of the clinic staff. This group lost more weight than another one that took the same amount of money per pound lost to spend on a special treat! The Castro group concluded that contingencies do not operate as reinforcement and punishment.

Castro and his colleagues do not argue that self-reward is ineffective; the self-reward group also lost weight. But they do insist that self-reward and self-punishment operate primarily by providing information—thus making people pay more attention to their own behavior.

Bandura replied that if this game with the money were actually punishing, then the weight loss would have stopped; therefore, the "punishment" was not punishing at all (Bandura, 1986). He did not mention it, but surely there was some rewarding effect in playing this bizarre game with the clinic staff. Would you find it "punishing" to be told to cut money up into little pieces, especially if you were led to believe that it would help you lose weight? Doing something outrageous can be a lot of fun.

The Rachlin-Castro-Bandura debate illustrates the complexity involved in self-administered contingencies. All agree on one point: Contingent consequences work. But how?

Techniques of Self-Reinforcement

Prompt Reinforcement

When should you get reinforcement? The ideal situation is one in which the reinforcement occurs immediately after you perform the desired behavior. The longer a reinforcement is delayed, the less effective it is, partly because it must compete with other reinforcement that is occurring immediately.

Whatever your goal, it will be reinforced at some later time, when it is reached. The dieter is reinforced immediately by overeating. Only weeks from now, when a new, thinner image is reflected in the mirror, will this person be reinforced for *not* eating. At 9:00 A.M., shortly after a nice breakfast, a dieter will choose to diet. At noon, walking through the cafeteria line, our same dieter may choose to ignore the diet. By providing yourself with extra immediate reinforcement, you can tip the balance and cause yourself to choose behaviors that contribute to your long-term goal. If the dieter arranges the reinforcement of, say, watching an enjoyable TV program immediately after (or even during) self-restraint, dieting is more likely to be observed than if he or she depends entirely on the long-range rewards of being slim someday. In other words, it is the TV program that competes right now with an extra bowl of spaghetti, not the dim dream of slimness in what, at the moment, may appear as a faraway future (Bandura, 1981).

A student who was wild about women chose exercise as his goal. So he enrolled in an aerobics class that contained almost all women. He reported that just being in that atmosphere provided all the reinforcement he needed to keep to his goal. A year later, he was a strong and enthusiastic aerobicizer. His new feelings of health and attractiveness were reinforcement enough, and he exercised regularly without women present (though he still liked it better when they were around).

Another student had developed the habit of swearing excessively. His baseline average was more than 150 swearwords per 8 hours. He worked out a plan in which he received strong reinforcers from his wife if he reduced his daily average of swearwords by 10% for 1 week. Unfortunately, he never made it to the end of the week. After 1 or 2 days of good language, he reverted to his old habits. We advised him to reduce the delay of reinforcement. His new contract, agreed to by his wife, called for *daily* reinforcement if he reduced his undesired language by 10%.

The general principle is that the reinforcer should be delivered as quickly as is reasonable after the desired behavior is performed. In some cases, *it is vital that the delay be extremely short.* This is especially true when the undesired behavior consists of consummatory or fear responses. For example, a cigarette in the mouth right now is more reinforcing than the thought of cleaner lungs 6 months from now. A bite of pie in the mouth right now feels a lot better than that remote picture of the scales, weeks or even months from now, showing a drop of several pounds. Biting your nails *right now* is more rewarding than the thought of the movie you will go to as a reinforcer Saturday night.

The same kind of problem exists for people who are afraid of some situation, such as talking in front of an audience or going into the water to swim. It feels much better to avoid the feared situation right now than to think about how good it will feel to get a reinforcer at the end of the week. *Whenever the target behavior involves very strong habits or feared objects, provide yourself with positive reinforcement immediately after performing the desired behavior.* For example, a smoker asked his wife to praise him immediately each time he resisted the impulse to light a cigarette.

Tokens

When you cannot arrange to have the reinforcer follow quickly after the behavior, *token reinforcers* are appropriate. A token is a symbolic reinforcer—symbolic because it can be converted into real reinforcement. Money, for example, is our major token reinforcer, for it is the things money can buy that make money attractive and thus represent the real reinforcement. Such devices as poker chips, gold stars, check marks, ticket punches, and dollar bills have all been used as tokens.

Many people choose a *point system* of token reinforcement to modify their behaviors. The performance of a desired behavior earns a specified number of "points" that can be "spent" for reinforcement. The cost of reinforcement—so many points per reinforcer—is specified in the point-system contract.

The main function of tokens and points is to bridge the delay between the time you perform the desired behavior and the time you can receive the reinforcer. For many people, the chosen reinforcer is something they are going to do at the day's end. They may use a particularly nice supper, an opportunity to watch TV, or a talk with friends in the evening as a reinforcer contingent on their having performed the target behavior earlier in the day. For all these delayed reinforcers, tokens can be used during the day to provide immediacy.

A man who wanted to substitute being nice to friends for being rude to friends selected watching TV in the evening as his reinforcer. He couldn't be sure when the opportunity to be nice to his friends would arise during the day and couldn't rush off to watch TV as soon as he had performed his target behavior, so he decided to use a token system. He carried a 3" × 5" card in his pocket and made a check on it when he performed the target behavior. Then, later in the evening, he allowed himself to watch TV if he had earned the number of points his shaping schedule required for that day. He used his tokens cumulatively. The more points he earned during the day, the more TV he could watch at night. His "menu" looked like this:

1 token	30 minutes of TV watching
2 tokens	60 minutes
3 tokens	90 minutes
4 tokens	as much as I want

This is a simple point system. By adding behaviors and potential reinforcers, a point system can be expanded into a complex token "economy." A group of five students who lived together had difficulty arranging their household duties fairly and reliably. The three men and two women devised a group self-modification plan, using the point system that follows. It specified each important household task, along with the points to be awarded for doing each one, and it specified the reinforcers that the household had to offer, along with the number of points that each would cost. Each member was free to choose both tasks and reinforcers.

Tasks	*Points*
Do laundry	200
Weekly shopping	200
Prepare evening meal	150
Prepare extra snacks	80
Prepare sandwiches	80
Plan shopping	60
Record prices (major)	60
Plan meals	40
Clean bathroom	30
Clean kitchen	30
Clean living room	30
Dry dishes (major)	30
Minor shopping	30
Pay milk bill	30
Put refuse out	30
Take in milk	30
Wash up dishes (major)	30
Write diary	25
Write down recipe	25
Dry dishes (minor)	10
Empty fireplace	10
Record prices (minor)	10
Tidy living room	10
Tidy sink	10
Wash up dishes (minor)	10
Put out milk bottle	5
Tie refuse sack	5

Reinforcers	
Drink	50
Evening meal	50
Film	50
Meeting, etc.	50
Lunch	20

SOURCE: "The Use of a Token Economy to Regulate Household Behaviours," by J. F. Masterson and A. C. Vaux, 1982, *Behavioural Psychotherapy, 10,* pp. 65–78. Copyright © 1982 by the British Association of Behavioural Psychotherapy. Reprinted by permission.

The group members kept careful records and were convinced that the point system made their household run more smoothly. More tasks were performed on time, and the members all felt that the work and benefits were distributed fairly. In fact, it was typical that more points were earned than were ever spent. They concluded that their mutual encouragement and verbal reinforcement provided reinforcement in addition to the points (Masterson & Vaux, 1982).

Notice also that the group's list of reinforcers included several items, from food to watching films. This illustrates another advantage of point systems: You can use a variety of reinforcers for the same behaviors; this helps keep reinforcement fresh and desirable. If you can exchange your earned points for watching TV, having a snack, or playing with the dog, you can choose the reinforcer that is most attractive to you at the moment. One of our students included as the last item on his reinforcement menu: "Every Saturday morning, *anything* I want to do!"

A point system can be adjusted to surgical precision. One of our students, who was trying to lose weight, wrote:

This was my first point system:

Eating a light, balanced breakfast	1 point
Eating a light, balanced lunch	1 point
Eating a light, balanced supper	1 point
Eating no more than two light snacks per day	1 point
Daily exercise	1 point

When I got 35 points, I could buy an art poster.

Then I noticed where I was failing most often—too much snacking on weekends. So I added an item:

On Saturday and Sunday, no more than two light snacks	1 point each

My second big insight was that I would earn 3 or 4 points each day, and then pig out on a snack or supper and blow the calorie count for the rest of the day. So I added another item:

Bonus for a perfect day	3 points

That did it!

Box 7-4 presents an excellent self-modification plan that incorporates three of the principles discussed so far in this chapter. To increase exercising, this woman used self-reinforcement (a small amount of money), a husband mediator to dispense larger ones, and a point system to bridge the gap between performance and the delayed larger reinforcement. Good self-modification plans integrate several techniques.

Imagined (Covert) Reinforcement

If things, people, or activities act as reinforcers, imagining them may also be reinforcing (Ascher, 1973; Krop, Calhoon, & Verrier, 1971). *Imagined reinforcers* have been traditionally called *covert* reinforcers by behavior analysts. Imagined reinforcement is used the same way as any other kind of reinforcement: It is arranged to follow a desirable behavior.

Imagined reinforcers are probably not as powerful as their actual counterparts. But imagined reinforcers have the advantage of being completely portable and easily accessible. Although you may be unable to travel or to go skin diving during the winter, you can imagine doing so. Imagining pleasant and relaxing scenes, such as a lazy swim on a hot day, can be used to as self-reinforcement for performing a desired behavior (Cautela & Samdperil, 1989).

Select imagined reinforcers as you would other reinforcers. While Cautela (1983) insists that imagined reinforcers need not always be based in reality, the best imagined reinforcement is an anticipation of rewarding, realistic outcomes. The relaxed imagining

Box 7-4
Self-Modification of Exercise Behavior

While regular exercise itself can be reinforcing to some persons, for [this woman] it was not. In order to establish and maintain an exercise habit, an attempt at self-directed behavior change seemed appropriate.

Method

A prior attempt to establish an exercise routine using the Premack principle (tooth brushing at night contingent upon the completion of a series of calisthenics) had not been successful, for the contingency was ignored. Therefore, the present plan placed control of the reinforcers in the hands of another person. The husband was the logical choice, and the intervention plan was put into a written contract that he and she signed. The plan had the following features:

1. The form of exercise was jogging.
2. Money and social activities of the woman's choice (for example, going to a movie or eating at a restaurant) were the reinforcers. She received 25¢ immediately after jogging. At the end of each week, if she had jogged every day (and earned $1.75), she could select and engage in one of several possible social activities with her husband. Otherwise, none of the social activities was permitted.
3. The husband dispensed the reinforcers and tabulated points.
4. In addition, points were earned for jogging. The long-term goal was set at 40 points per week . . . where 4 points could be earned by jogging 1 mile within 9.59 minutes and . . . more earned by increasing the distance . . . and reducing the time. This was approached through a series of intermediate steps. The plan was to begin with the jogging of 1 mile, with gradual increments of 0.25 miles.

Results

The results of the intervention plan can be seen in Figure 7-1. At the end of the first week of intervention, 20 points were earned, representing a sharp increase in exercise activity from a baseline of zero. After this initial spurt, progress slowed but increased to 23 points in the second week. Jogging had occurred on only 4 days, but, because of the increased distance run, more points were earned. The third week showed a drop in total number of points to 19. Jogging had occurred on 4 days, and again during the fourth week of intervention occurred on only 4 days of the week. Up to this point, the social-activity reinforcer had not been given, because jogging had not occurred daily during any of the 4 weeks. A change in the program was adopted at the start of the fifth week. The activity reinforcer was made available after earning 25 or more points per week (rather than running every day), and the 25 point payment was eliminated. This was followed by an increase in total points to 27 for the fifth week. The twelfth week showed the highest level of activity, with 38½ points earned—only 1½ points short of the long-term goal, even though the activity reinforcer had been eliminated at the beginning of the tenth week.

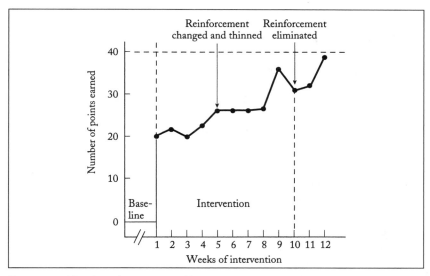

Figure 7-1 Number of points earned by exercising

Formal reinforcement was terminated before the long-term goal (40 points per week) was reached, for two reasons. First, the subject had become satiated with the activity reinforcer. For 2 weeks prior to its elimination, she had earned enough points to gain the reinforcer but had not bothered to "collect" it. Second, the natural positive results of regular physical exercise were being noticed. She felt better and more energetic than when she began the program. She had lost several pounds without any change in eating habits. With these natural reinforcements, the long-term goal was soon reached. As the natural environment had taken over and begun to maintain the desired behavior, the program was judged to have been successful.

The key to the success may have been the placement of control of the program with another person. The mediator, the husband, was firm in his commitment to the plan and the rules agreed upon. The contingency between the behavior and the reinforcers was maintained rigorously.

SOURCE: "Self-Modification of Exercise Behavior," by M. L. Kau and J. Fischer, 1974, *Journal of Behavior Therapy and Experimental Psychiatry, 5*, pp. 213–214. Copyright © 1974 by Pergamon Press, Ltd. Reprinted by permission.

of your ultimate goal condition is a powerful reinforcer. To reinforce dieting, use images of yourself after losing weight—slim, attractive, athletic, fashionably dressed, or whatever image of yourself reflects the wish you want to fulfill (Horan, Baker, Hoffman, & Shute, 1975). This kind of reinforcer has the advantage of being realistic and logical and of representing a bridge to the world of larger-later contingencies. Not only will reinforcement benefits be present, but long-range goals will be brought to mind, and thus commitment will be strengthened again.

Although there are many advantages to using imagined reinforcement, a few words of caution are in order. To be effective, the images must be vivid (Wisocki, 1973). Not everyone can produce vivid, lifelike images; therefore, it is necessary that you practice the imagined reinforcement until you can almost feel the water, almost touch the clothes, or hear the music almost as clearly as if you were at the concert. Use many senses in imagining—smells, sounds, sights, physical feelings (Cautela & Samdperil, 1989). To practice, call up scenes from memory, which may produce more vivid images than purely imagined scenes. If you cannot produce images as vivid as memories, you should not rely on imagined reinforcement.

Imagined reinforcement has been studied most intensely in combination with thought stopping: After saying the word "stop," take a deep breath and relax while exhaling through the nose; then imagine the reinforcing pleasant scene. Cautela refers to this sequence as the "self-control triad" (e.g., Cautela & Baron, 1993).

Verbal Self-Reinforcement

Praise is one of the fundamental methods of control in all human society. Parents, teachers, coaches, politicians, and lovers all encourage behavior by praising. *Verbal reinforcement* is only a technical term for praise and an acknowledgment that praise is a powerful reinforcer. Here we discuss verbal self-reinforcement—that is, self-encouragement following desired behavior. Recall the discussion of the power of bringing self-directions up from the underground. That same technique can be used to increase the reinforcing power of self-speech as well. Every individual experiences pleasure at meeting a goal and at behaving according to his or her own standards. But if that pleasure can be made verbal, brought up from the underground, it takes on stronger reinforcing properties.

The technique is merely to tell yourself, "Good! I did it." Say it either covertly or aloud, but say it clearly. Say it after each instance of your desired behavior (Meichenbaum, 1977; Shelton et al., 1981).

Linda's self-improvement project, to increase her dancing skill, was a rousing success. She wrote:

> After our last ballet class I had a follow-up meeting with the instructor. We agreed that I had improved significantly from the beginning of the semester, especially in my performance level. He commented that my dancing included more of my own personal style of movement, and that my enjoyment during class is more obvious, and he sees more connection between the upper and lower halves of my body. I also noticed that instead of worrying so much about difficult things that were coming up in the combinations, I freed my mind and just let things happen. Instead of worrying about what could go wrong, I pictured myself doing it right and just went for it. If I caught myself making a negative comment like, "Why

can't I do this?" I would stop and take a second to say someth_ know I can do it."

The most helpful thing was my ballet instructor. His ve. effective. He also provided a lot of positive reinforcement by let. things that I was doing well by saying, "Good, Laura," or giving n. signal. I also adopted this form of positive reinforcement and took a m.c. feel happy about the things that I felt I was doing well. The combination of phys-ical cues and mental reminders worked together allowing me to become a much more efficient dancer.

Self-praise is often omitted from self-modification plans for three reasons. First, you may think it sounds silly or absurd. It is not. Don't underestimate the power of language. Second, you may think self-reinforcement is conceited or "bragging." That is also incorrect because bragging is an effort to get reinforcement from others. Verbal self-reinforcement is a way of marking off your successes justly and privately (Rehm, 1982). Third, self-praise may be omitted from self-direction plans because of a long habit of self-criticism and generally low self-esteem. In such cases, the problem is interfering with the solution: Because you are depressed, you are perpetuating depression.

Some individuals reinforce themselves less than others do regardless of their situ-ations or activities. Depressed individuals have a lower frequency of self-reinforcement than do nondepressed people (Heiby, 1981), and depressed people use verbal self-*punishment* frequently (Rehm, 1982). Does low self-reinforcement "cause" depression? Not necessarily, but those who are low self-reinforcers may be at higher risk for depres-sion. When external reinforcement is lost, low self-reinforcers are more likely than others to become depressed (Heiby, 1983a, 1983b).

The loss of external reinforcement and support—a run of bad grades, the loss of a friend or a loved one, the loss of a job—can make anyone depressed. But those who have the skill to reinforce, encourage, and support themselves are less likely to be pitched into a severe depression. Self-reinforcers are better able to ride out periods when external reinforcement is taken away.

Noncontingent Positive Events

Most psychologists recommend that pleasant events be arranged to follow some behavior that will contribute to decreasing depression. Pleasant events can be used to reinforce making new social contacts, to increase assertive responses or better study habits, and the like. But *in addition* to these tactics, are there ever any conditions when positive events should be added to your life freely, richly, and noncontingently? A life that is empty of pleasant events is almost certain to be a depressed life. Psychologists, as well as depressed people, puzzled for years as to whether or not simply increasing pleas-ant events will cause depression to lift. Now the evidence is clear: Increasing pleasant events increases positive aspects of well-being in general. In a study of student diaries, self-reported depressive feelings and negative emotions decrease with increasing general activity and the amount of reward or pleasure that participants obtain through it (Hopko et al., 2003; see also Reich & Zautra, 1981). Peter Lewinsohn's influential the-ory suggests that depression is brought about by the loss of external reinforcement, and his suggested treatment includes increasing pleasant activities (e.g., MacPhillamy & Lewinsohn, 1982).

In fact, a general change in the balance of pleasant to unpleasant events is advisable for people wrestling with a variety of problems. Binge eaters, as an example, are known to lack sufficient "self-nurturance" and to be good to themselves only through eating (Lehman & Rodin, 1989). Marlatt and Parks (1982) discuss this in terms of getting the "wants" in balance with the "shoulds." A life that is too filled with duties that are felt as "shoulds," with little time for enjoying the things that are "wants," is a life set up for problems. Problems are likely to erupt in destructive binges of consumption: food, drink, drugs, or escapism. For such situations, Marlatt and Parks (1982) suggest a change in lifestyle, including time for relaxation each day, time for meditation, time for exercise, or especially "free time"—the opportunity to do whatever is pleasant and available at the moment.

A more general reason for increasing the total quantity of pleasant events is discussed by psychologists under the concept of *response allocation*. The power of a reward to reinforce some (undesirable) behavior is partly due to the total amount of pleasantness present in a person's field. An increase in the total pleasantness available to you reduces the proportionate value of any single reward. This suggests a powerful strategy to weaken the reinforcement of undesirable behavior.

For example, Mishka, a community college student, continued drinking excessively with her old crowd of high school friends. She told us that it wasn't the beer itself, but the parties that she couldn't give up. She then worked hard to increase her social life (noncontingently) through clubs, a sorority, service volunteering, and working on the college newspaper. Gradually her old drinking group—though still pleasant for her—became just one activity among many, and lost its reinforcing value. And her alcohol consumption was no longer at a problem level.

Feeling bad—high negative affect, in psychological terms—is a strong predictor of many maladaptive behaviors, including smoking. That evidence is so strong that current work suggests that a direct intervention on negative affect may be the most logical approach to quitting smoking (Brandon, 1994).

The positive emotions accompanying pleasant events actually facilitate self-control. When feeling depleted of strength for controlling impulses, pleasant emotions produced by enjoyable events actually increase the capacity to resist impulses (Tice, Baumeister, & Zhang, 2004).

Pleasant emotions can be amplified by sharing positive events. When good things happen to you, share the news with others who will be pleased. If you share the news and celebrate it with others, your feelings of well-being will strengthen and persist (Gable, Reis, Impett, & Asher, 2004). As one of our students wrote, "When I manage to act in my desired way I tell my friends and boyfriend and get some praise from them, too!"

The irony is that those people who most need to increase pleasant events are the ones least likely to do so. Mishka did not require it, but for many people, increasing free pleasant events may be the best first goal for self-modification, even if that plan requires reinforcement for increasing pleasant events!

Marsha is a case in point. A 19-year-old student, Marsha was struggling to stay in school. She had registered for morning classes starting at 7:30 because at 2:00 each weekday she reported to the bakery where she was a salesclerk. She worked until 10:00 each night. Then she had papers to write, exams to prepare for, and all the tasks of personal life. She lived with her partially disabled mother, so housework, laundry, and shopping occupied most of her time on the weekends. She dated very rarely, and Sundays she slept, exhausted and dull.

Marsha's first step toward self-modification was to create her catalog of reinforcers. It included such things as new clothes and a new stereo, but it became clear to her that she had no time to wear new dresses and no time to listen to new tapes. Each reinforcer she listed required time for its enjoyment, and what Marsha did not have was time.

Where was it to come from? Where could any pleasant events fit into that life crowded with "shoulds"? On analysis, she realized that the weekend might be rearranged: Saturdays were stuffed with all the duties, Sundays were a dead loss of sluggish sleep and dullness.

There were three things Marsha wanted to do but had never managed to arrange: visit a favorite aunt, practice yoga, and attend a discussion group. How could she motivate herself to rearrange her weekends to allow for these pleasant events? For several weeks, she never "got around" to it. Her final plan involved the use of the Premack principle. Of all her duties, the one she enjoyed most was housekeeping, which she performed vigorously and with pleasure. So she selected one behavior, cleaning the bathroom, and did not allow herself to perform it until after she had done at least one of her desired pleasant activities. The outcome of this plan was an increase in the three desired activities, less sleeping and moping on Sunday—and the bathroom stayed as clean as ever.

This is the point of Marsha's case: Although it is often desirable to make changes in your lifestyle so that free, noncontingent pleasant activities are increased, it may be necessary to use reinforcement plans to bring that about.

Self-Punishment and Extinction

Extinction

Extinction is the weakening of a behavior by withdrawing reinforcement from it. This is a simple strategy when used in the laboratory. If an experimental animal is no longer given food pellets, it will eventually quit pressing the bar. In self-direction, however, extinction is more complicated. When real-life reinforcers are withdrawn, an immediate burst of the undesirable behavior may occur. Following that, even when the behavior is reduced, other behaviors will certainly rush in to fill the vacuum, and if those new behaviors are not planned for, they may be as problematic as the original. When used alone, extinction is very rarely an effective self-directing strategy.

The following case illustrates the point. A student wanted to reduce the frequency of cutting his trigonometry class. His midterm grade was D, and poor attendance was the obvious reason. His A-B-C analysis clearly showed that class cutting was reinforced by shooting pool and playing pinball because he was going to the Billiard Palace instead of the classroom. His plan called for withdrawing this reinforcer: When he cut class, he would go home immediately. But this plan didn't result in less class cutting; instead, he found himself listening to the stereo in his room. The correct procedure here would have been to reinforce class attendance, perhaps by making the Billiard Palace contingent on it. *When you withdraw reinforcement from an undesired behavior, you should simultaneously increase reinforcement for the alternative, desired behavior.*

Why Punishment Alone Is Insufficient

Punishment alone is usually an undesirable strategy. This is true for either kind of punishment—adding an aversive stimulus to a situation or removing a positive event. Most plans that rely solely on punishment don't work. For example, people who used self-punishing statements and thoughts for smoking transgressions were less able to resist the urge to smoke than those who used other kinds of strategy (Shiffman, 1984). In fact, self-punishment can make things worse. One way that behaviors become resistant to punishment is by being first mildly punished and then positively reinforced. You might actually increase the behavior's resistance to punishment by supplying a small punishment followed by the usual reinforcement.

A second reason for avoiding punishment is that punishment alone doesn't teach new behaviors. Punishment suppresses the behavior it follows, but what happens instead is determined by the reinforcement that follows the substituted behavior. Your plan should provide for designating and reinforcing desired alternatives to your problem behaviors. Otherwise, the plan is incomplete.

One of our students had three part-time jobs plus a full load at college. Her first plan consisted of punishing herself for not performing a desired behavior by depriving herself of one of the few things in her life that she enjoyed. She had somehow managed to keep two hours free every Friday afternoon, and she always used them to go to the beach with a close friend. In her plan, she proposed to punish excessive eating by giving up this weekly pleasure. We strongly disagreed with that idea. Her life needed enrichment, not a further impoverishment of positive reinforcers. We suggested that she reward dieting by adding another social activity—if necessary, at the expense of her quite adequate study time. To lose her one weekly contact with a friend would have made her even more dependent on her only other real pleasure—food. Besides, her overall happiness required a broader spectrum of pleasant events. Punishment would have restricted her life and would also have made dieting less likely.

The third reason for not including punishment in your plan is that you will be less likely to carry out your plan. In a course in behavioral self-control, Worthington (1979) found that only one-third of the students actually inflicted self-punishment when their plans called for it.

When you perform some undesired behavior, you should positively reinforce an incompatible behavior instead of punishing the undesired behavior. Reinforce nail grooming instead of punishing nail biting. Before you decide to use punishment, search for an incompatible behavior that you can positively reinforce instead.

The Loss of Positive Events as Punishment

If you insist on using punishment, it should involve giving up something pleasant. This is better than using an aversive stimulus as punishment (Kazdin, 1973). Here are some examples of punishment in the form of giving up usual pleasures. One person might not allow herself to take a customary bath if she has not studied enough. Another might not allow himself to eat certain preferred foods if he has performed some undesired behavior. If you are accustomed to going to a movie on Saturday night, you could punish yourself for your nonperformance of a target behavior by staying home. Many people use the general category of "things I do for fun" to require themselves to perform some target behavior before they allow themselves to engage in the "fun" activities. Another student, who was in love with a man in another state, used the daily letters she received from him. Each day she handed the unopened letter to a friend. If she performed her target behavior, she got the letter back unopened. If she did not perform the target behavior, her friend was instructed to open and read the love letter.

A few of our students have had success with such plans, but a better strategy is to combine positive reinforcement with punishment so that you lose *additional* rewards, not customary ones. A plan to increase studying could call for an extra movie per week, but only if your goal is met.

A token system can be used for a combination program. Lutzker and Lutzker (1974) reported a program used by a dieter with the help of her husband. She could earn several reinforcers for losing a half-pound or more each week, but the most effective part of the plan involved a "household duties" punishment. Before beginning the plan, she and her husband divided the household chores into "his" and "hers," with the husband taking on more chores than he had before. Each week, after her weigh-in, if she lost weight or stayed even, he continued doing the chores on his list for the next week. If she gained weight, she had to do his chores in addition to her own. She lost weight.

Precommitted Punishment

Precommitment refers to making some arrangement in advance so that you will be more likely to choose behaviors that are in your long-term best interest. *Precommitted punishment*, therefore, means arranging in advance that some particular punishing event will take place if you perform a certain undesired act. Precommitted punishment may be appropriate when the undesired behavior is so reinforcing that no new reinforcers can be found to counter it. A woman who was trying to stop eating late-night snacks would tell her daughter, who lived with her, "If I eat anything after 8:00 P.M., I'll give you $20."

You can arrange advance control of yourself by giving over some kind of forfeit to a helper. For example, you can require yourself to study for 2 hours before going to a movie. To enforce this behavior, you can give a friend $10 and instruct the friend to call you every half-hour from 7:00 to 9:00. If you don't answer the telephone, the friend is to mail the money to your worst enemy (Rachlin, 1974). One of our students wanted to completely eliminate using sugar, no longer adding it to coffee, cereal, or other foods. So she selected a cup from her treasured collection of handmade coffee cups, marked it with a piece of tape on the bottom, and instructed her husband to break it if she used any sugar.

In these precommitment strategies, the trick is to make the penalty so heavy that in fact you never apply it. Precommitment should work as a *deterrent*, not as a *punishment*. In this way, precommitment is consistent with our general recommendation that you should not actually punish yourself. In precommitting, you must arrange for penalties that would be so unpleasant that you simply won't incur them. The woman who offered to pay her daughter if she ate late at night only had to pay once in 6 months. That one time was enough to keep her out of the kitchen.

A heavy forfeit, however, presents problems of its own. The specter of a great loss may create new anxieties, and the helper who holds the forfeit may seem a menace. A middle-aged man was determined to stop smoking. His wife, who had recently stopped, was willing to cooperate to almost any extent. The husband was an avid collector of cacti and other small succulent plants. Over the years, his garden had grown down the wall and into the lawn, and even the kitchen counter often held young plants as a kind of incubator. His precommitment plan arranged that for every cigarette he smoked, his wife was to destroy one young cactus. The precommitment worked, in the sense that he smoked no cigarettes for 7 days. But the threat was intolerable. He prowled the house and garden wondering which plant would be sacrificed if he smoked. And how would they die? Drowned in the toilet or crushed under his wife's heel? After 1 week, he canceled the agreement—and felt at ease with his wife once again.

Any form of self-punishment, even when used as a deterrent, brings about problems and should be approached carefully. Precommitted punishment should be used only temporarily and only when you can quickly bring desirable behavior under the control of positive reinforcement or natural rewards (Rachlin, 1974).

Punishment as a Temporary Solution

Punishment can be a temporary, partial tactic for achieving some goals. But remember, it is only temporary and only partial. There is no point in using self-punishment except when it leads to positive reinforcers.

One form of self-punishment can perhaps be recommended in the early stages of self-direction—the "punishment" of facing up to the negative consequences of a problem behavior. Imagining the real consequences of shoplifting, for example, can be a powerful deterrent: prison, publicity, and the loss of contact with family and friends (Gauthier & Pellerin, 1982). Imagining the continued loneliness and frustration of social withdrawal can provide strong motivation to persevere in building social skills. A systematic plan for reminding yourself of these long-range punishments can keep you from drifting from your goals. Force yourself to read the latest figures on cancer and smoking. Youdin and Hemmes (1978) recommend to dieters that they stare at their naked bodies in the mirror for 60 seconds a day while thinking about overeating. Rosen (1981) reports a successful program for weight loss in which dieters agreed that if they decided to overeat, they would do so while watching themselves in a mirror, with as few clothes on as possible. The dieters found the vision "disgusting" and commonly stopped the eating session. Both of the authors have imagined themselves as pot-gutted and too slow on the tennis court and thus have found strength to push the dessert aside.

Ancient Buddhist systems of thought control have also emphasized that unwanted thoughts can be controlled by considering their consequences.

> If you are burdened with distasteful thoughts, be like young men and women who want to be clean and well dressed, and then find the carcass of a snake or dog around their necks. See the effects on you! Immediately get rid of it! (paraphrased from the translation by de Silva, 1985, p. 439)

Reminding yourself of the negative consequences of some problem behavior can be considered not only as punishment, but also as another way of building and maintaining commitment.

Reinforcement in Plans for Self-Modification

Now we must consider the place of reinforcement in the A-B-C sequence. Powerful as reinforcement may be, it must be organized into a total intervention plan that involves antecedents, behaviors, and consequences. As you read this section, bear in mind the preliminary plans you developed in steps 5 (antecedents) and 6 (developing new behaviors) of your own self-direction project. By adding reinforcing contingencies to these plans, you will bring them to full potential.

For example, as you adopt self-reinforcement plans and carry them out, then when observing the improvements include new self-statements about the reinforcement. Tell yourself, "I did it," and "I can control it." Increasing your felt ability at self-directed reinforcement will have its own good effects on your behavior change.

Reinforcement and Antecedent Control

In Chapter 5, we described several methods for achieving antecedent control: avoiding antecedents, narrowing them, and building new ones by performing the desired behavior in new situations. Each of these tactics involves a behavior change that should also be reinforced.

For example, avoiding old antecedents was recommended as a first tactic for reducing undesirable consummatory responses. Thus, avoiding the morning cup of coffee can reduce the temptation to smoke; avoiding parties, at least for a while, can help bring overeating, pot smoking, or drinking under control. But this tactic involves a sharp decrease in reinforcement because old reinforcers are lost. Therefore, new reinforcement is needed—reinforcement gained for avoiding the old antecedents.

The dieter who refused dinner invitations for a month arranged with his wife that they would go to a movie on the nights when the parties were held. A student wanting to stop smoking marijuana reinforced her avoidance of pot parties by having a long telephone chat with a friend the next morning. The young man who avoided excessive masturbation by choosing a busier restroom carried a paperback mystery with him and read it only while using the new facility. Each of these plans replaced the lost reinforcement with a new one, made contingent on avoiding problematic antecedent.

The same principle applies to behaviors performed in the presence of new antecedents: Reinforcement should follow.

Reinforcement and the Development of New Behaviors

The necessity of reinforcing most new behaviors is a general principle, which we will illustrate with a discussion of two topics: *imagined rehearsal* and *shaping.*

Imagined rehearsal. Imagined (covert) rehearsals influence real performances. In rehearsing a desired behavior in your imagination, it is useful to follow it with an imagined reinforcement (Kazdin, 1974a).

Cautela (1972, 1973) gives several examples of imagined reinforcers, such as swimming on a hot day and hearing good music. Suppose you are a dieter who wants to practice control of overeating. Sometime during the day, wherever you happen to be, you imagine you are "sitting at home watching TV. . . . You say to yourself 'I think I'll have a piece of pie.' You get up to go to the pantry. Then you say, 'This is stupid. I don't want to be a fat pig.'" You should follow this imagined scene with the imagined reinforcement—the swim or the music. Here is another scene you can rehearse in imagination: "You are at home eating steak. You are just about to reach for your second piece, and you stop and say to yourself, 'Who needs it, anyway?'" (Cautela, 1972, p. 213) and then imagine your reinforcer.

Imagined rehearsal can be a way of practicing when your own behaviors are not yet firm enough to earn reinforcement in the real world. A young man who had almost no experience or skills in approaching young women was taught to imagine the following scene and to self-reinforce it with imagined swimming in a warm river.

> Say to yourself "I think I'll call Jane for a date." As soon as you have this scene clearly, switch quickly to the reinforcement. As soon as you have the reinforcement vividly, hold it for 2 seconds. Then imagine that you walk to the phone and start to dial (reinforcement). You finish dialing. She answers. You say hello and ask her if she is free Saturday night. You tell her that you would like to go out with her. . . . Now do the whole sequence again. Make sure that the image is vivid. You can see the kitchen, feel the telephone. This time try to imagine that you are comfortable and confident as you call. (Cautela, 1973, p. 30)

A similar example, adapted from Kazdin (1974a), is for the person who wants to become more assertive:

- Imagine that you are eating in a restaurant with friends. You order a steak and tell the waiter you would like it rare. When the food arrives, you begin to eat and notice that it is overcooked.
- Imagine that you immediately signal the waiter. When he arrives, you say, "I ordered this steak rare, and this one is medium. Please take it back and bring me one that is rare."
- Imagine that in a few minutes the waiter brings another steak, rare, and says he is very sorry this has happened.

When imagining assertiveness—saying no when a person asks for a favor you really don't want to do, protesting against being shortchanged, objecting when someone cuts in front of you in a line, sending an undercooked steak back—let the positive reinforcement grow naturally out of the rehearsed behavior: You get the steak you want! If you are rehearsing in your imagination how to deal with a persistent door-to-door salesperson, you can follow your imagined firmness by imagining the person leaving quickly and your own feelings of competence and self-assurance. Whenever possible, use a desirable "natural outcome" as your reinforcer. The advantage of using brief, independent scenes is that you can reinforce the various stages along the way.

Shaping. The technique of shaping also illustrates the necessity of reinforcing all new behaviors: Each step must be reinforced.

The definition of each shaping step is actually a standard or criterion. For example:

Step 1: 2000 calories per day
Step 2: 1800 calories per day
Reinforcer: 1 hour of television per evening

For step 1, the reinforcer is taken when the standard for that step is met (2000 calories). For step 2, the standard becomes 1800 calories daily, and only then will television be watched.

Shaping steps are no different from any other behavior. If their natural consequences are not yet strong enough, they require arranged reinforcement. The case of Linda (Chapter 6), who feared birds, is a good illustration. As she built a schedule of steps closer and closer to the birds she feared, she didn't use any extra reinforcement at first because she received quite enough from her pride in mastering the fear. But when her schedule brought her quite close to the birds, she got stuck. At this point, Linda introduced a token system. For each step in her shaping schedule, she earned points that she could turn in at the end of the day to "buy" certain privileges, such as allowing herself extra dates, doing "idiot" reading, and so on. Her goal was to increase her total positive reinforcements so that she would gain something for getting really close to the birds. In Linda's case, two separate forms of reinforcement were employed. One was the formal token system. The earlier, less obvious reinforcement was the presence of her boyfriend. She originally elected to include him because his presence made her feel more relaxed. But his walking beside her also had reinforcing value for the approach behavior.

Cheating. Taking the reinforcer without having performed the target behavior is a fairly common occurrence in self-modification. Almost everyone does it sometimes. You should watch yourself very carefully, however, because cheating more than occasionally—say, more than 10% of the time—indicates a shaping problem. In that case, you should redesign your shaping schedule so that you will be reinforced for performing at some level that you find realistic. As long as you are able to provide a contingent reinforcement, you are building toward the final goal, no matter how small the steps are or how low you begin. If you cheat, don't abandon the project—redesign it.

A young man whose final goal was to save $7 each week began by requiring himself to save 50¢ each day (he put it in a piggy bank), even though he had almost never saved any money before. He used the reinforcer of eating supper only after he put the money in his piggy bank. After 3 days, he skipped his saving for one day but went ahead and ate supper anyway. This was the beginning of a 2-week period during which he skipped more often than he saved but ate his supper anyway. He realized that this kind of cheating was caused by a problem in his shaping program. So he wrote a new contract in which he required himself to save only 25¢ each day—a more realistic place to begin, in his case, in order to gain the reinforcer.

When to Include Self-Reinforcement in Your Intervention Plan

Now that we have discussed methods for adding reinforcement to self-change projects, both for antecedent control and for developing new behaviors, the questions to be answered are: When should self-reinforcement be included in the project? When can it be omitted?

We suggest the following rule of thumb: During the process of learning, make sure that any new behavior is followed promptly by some reinforcement. Some behaviors will be reinforced naturally and immediately, merely by being performed, and require no contrived reinforcement. For example, a tennis player who coaches herself with self-instructions will be reinforced by the swift consequences of her improved play. In social interactions, the game is also swift, and improved behaviors are likely to produce their own rewards. In such situations, inserting self-reinforcement after each performance of the behavior can be distracting.

And for many new behaviors natural reinforcement can be a long time coming for the dieter, the beginning exerciser, the fearful, the shy, or the academically disadvantaged student who is just beginning to learn study skills (Green, 1982). Therefore, our rule of thumb: New behavior should be followed by some reinforcement. This may not always be necessary. But don't exclude reinforcement unless you are confident that the environment itself will provide the necessary immediate reinforcement.

Box 7-5
Overjustification? Or an Unjustified Concept?

A considerable amount of research has been conducted on the so-called *over-justification effect*, whereby extra rewards for behaviors that people already perform well and enjoy are presumed to cause a reduction of motivation (see Condry, 1977). So "overjustifying" reading, for example, by rewarding people who enjoy reading, would cause them to want to read less. "Overjustification" formed a rallying cry for antibehaviorists such as Kohn (1993), whose book *Punished by Reward* passionately and vehemently condemns all forms of reward/reinforcement in schools and industry, including gold stars, incentive plans, grades, praise, "and other bribes." Though primarily polemical, and not competently scientific, this and other similar attacks on reward have influenced the popular press, and the view that "reward reduces motivation and performance" is creeping in the public mind toward the status of a fact.

Energized by this threat, psychologists have vigorously reexamined the accumulated research evidence (Cameron, Banko, & Pierce, 2001), conducted new more detailed investigations (Carton & Nowicki, 1998; Reitman, 1998), and exploded the myth of "overjustification." The research facts are clear. Decrease of motivation following reward occurs only when the reward is solely for engagement in the task; when reward is made contingent on task completion or on some performance standard, motivation does *not* decrease. And performance improves.

Implications for self-reinforcement are clear, and completely consistent with our message. Set standards for each shaping step. Make reinforcement contingent. For any behaviors that require shaping, and for those that need strengthening, self-reinforcement remains a strong, reliable technique.

Objections to Self-Reinforcement

If you are encountering the idea of control through consequences for the first time, you probably find it peculiar. Some students object. They don't believe that a desired behavior should be deliberately self-rewarded. Virtue should be its own reward. We agree. The goal is to make your desired behavior so smooth and successful that the natural consequences of daily life will sustain it. When you reach that stage, self-reinforcement (and all the rest of your plan) can go underground: Only your skill will be left showing. Self-reinforcement is a temporary strategy, like verbal self-control, to be used only until behaviors have become automated in their settings. But, like talking to yourself, reinforcing your behaviors will continue to be a useful, temporary device whenever virtue again fails to reward itself enough.

Some of our students have continued to object. "Even if we grant that point," they say, "you can't learn—really learn—under these conditions of self-bribery. It's all an act, not real behavior." Well, we reply, bribery is reinforcement for *inappropriate*, not desirable, behavior. Further, what is real, and what is an act? If you could put on an act of playing tennis well enough to win real matches, would you feel embarrassed because "it's just

Box 7-6
Krista Is Crying in Prague: A Continuing Case

When we left Krista in Chapter 6, she had made good progress in understanding the cues that triggered her crying "accidents," and had worked out some procedures for preparing alternate behaviors. She had refined her goal to speaking directly and firmly about her feelings and thoughts, rather than withdrawing into tears.

Krista writes:

> Concerning consequences, in my opinion asking somebody (your friends or family) for help or for reinforcement isn't very good. For them it is normal that adult people don't cry and can solve their own problems. And they think it must be easy to stop doing this thing. Usually they don't even mention when I change. So I recommend to do this change on your own.
>
> So I just use talking to myself. I'm saying, "You will have to stop it some day, so why don't you stop it now. Can you imagine the faces of your (potential) children or the face of your boss in your future job? I need to stop this behavior!" I also tried self-reinforcement with some tangible rewards. I gave myself a set of herbs; it was fine, but it wasn't necessary. But that is just my opinion; for somebody else maybe another technique is good.
>
> The biggest consequence for me is my own conscience and I have to say that it works. When I break my plan I don't feel so good after. My conscience nags me. The best way is to write down all your troubling situations, even if you are lazy to do it, and even if you think it is not useful, because it will be useful when you read it a few days later. Now my crying episodes have almost vanished. Now I need some punishment. I thought for a long time, and then I decided that the best punishment will be to read my structured diary. And it is, really!!!
>
> I have some ideas for my future projects, but I will do them when I will be sure that my current problem is OK. (And I shouldn't be wholly perfect, it wouldn't look well ☺.)

First, technical comments: Rereading her notebook wasn't really a punishment for Krista, it was a reward—reminding her of how far she had come, and increasing her commitment to keep the gains she had made. Also, we are unsure whether Krista really understood that she was actually using self-instructions accompanied by reflection on long-term consequences, by saying to herself, "You will have to stop it some day, so why don't you stop it now." And we continue to believe that a supportive friend could have been helpful in providing practice in speaking out.

Nevertheless, as for "speaking out," those comments from her final report are a perfect example of progress: Not cheeky, but directly and clearly, Krista spoke her own mind on matters her professor surely disagrees with. We suspect Krista wrote that without one sniffle.

And her English was improving, too.

SOURCE: Our thanks again to Professor Karen Budd, DePaul University, for sending us this case. Reprinted with permission.

an act"? Skill is a real thing, however you learn it. But if you mean that "self-bribed" behavior cannot sustain itself, you have a point. If you are motivated to perform your new behavior only by the artificial reinforcers in your plan, you probably won't continue once you tire of playing the game. Remember that we cautioned you to select a behavior-change project you really value. If your changed behavior will bring greater self-respect and a happier life, then these rewarding consequences will sustain you over the long haul. Self-reinforcement is to be used only now and at those times in the future when a stronger push is needed to get you rolling again.

And remember this: You did it. The plan, the self-reinforcement, the changed behavior—you did it all. Take credit, take pride. High five.

Tips for Typical Topics

Anxiety and Stress

Two basic strategies for using consequences in reducing anxieties and stress reactions are (1) avoiding reinforcement for escape, and (2) adding reinforcement for your emerging coping reactions.

By escaping a stressful situation, people stop that punishment, but the learning that results has serious disadvantages: New, successful coping skills are not learned, and new life opportunities are lost. Escaping stress by leaving social situations, by not trying out for a play, or by not attempting to join in class discussions is "self-reinforcing" in the sense that it reduces anxiety. Unfortunately, these escapes also become habitual. To escape anxiety through drinks, drugs, or food creates a short-term advantage with disastrous long-term results. How can this strategy of escape and avoidance be interrupted?

From previous chapters, you have learned how to gain better control over the antecedents of anxiety and stress and how to make your new behaviors more competent and better organized. Now it is time to consider the careful reinforcement of these new behaviors. Provide reinforcement for your new coping skills, and you will be less likely to seek reward in the old escape and avoidance.

Reinforcement should be part of every plan for coping with and mastery of feared situations or for reducing the hassles of daily life. Use shaping schedules backed up by a selection from your menu of reinforcements. Particularly when dealing with anxieties and stresses, follow every instance of your new behaviors with the covert reinforcement of self-encouragement, positive statements of praise, and positive images of your new, more competent self. These quick, private thoughts and images can provide the bridges from moment-to-moment coping to the longer-term reinforcements of the earned movie or mystery book; and those reinforcements from your menu can provide the bridges to the longer-term rewards of a happier and richer life.

Assertion

Most nonassertive people suffer from the unreasonable expectation that some awful consequence will necessarily follow from their attempts to assert themselves: "If I do, he won't be my friend anymore." Instead, use imagined positive reinforcement and anticipate favorable outcomes. If you assert yourself early, moderately, and politely, the actual consequences are likely to be pleasant. But be realistic. If you expect to be punished by someone for asserting yourself (for example, by a hostile waiter who doesn't want to take your steak back), you can take steps to minimize the effects of that punishment. Practice assertion in your imagination, by relaxing and by concentrating on the positive consequences of your behavior (Shelton, 1979).

Use shaping and reinforcement, beginning with assertive behaviors that are likely to produce success. As you risk more, you may feel guilty or hurt after having been assertive. If these feelings persist, they will decrease your chances of maintaining the gains you have made. Try to eliminate those feelings by using thought substitution and by concentrating on the positive consequences of your newly learned assertiveness.

Some of our students abandoned improving assertion as their goal because others punished them for being too "aggressive." Women in particular sometimes meet with disapproval for behavior that is interpreted as "aggressive" (Leviton, 1979), so you may want to tailor your behavior to the situation. The line between assertiveness and abrasiveness is different for every person, depending on his or her own values and the values of friends and associates.

Our advice is to use your A-B-C journal analysis. Think over the A-B-C elements of the situations in which you felt too passive. Then reconstruct those situations as you wish you had behaved. Anticipate the consequences as they are likely to occur in your real social world, and take those into account when establishing goals. For whatever goals you choose, reinforce those gradually practiced behaviors in the ways this chapter suggests. Anticipate that others will respond to you differently. If their response is unfavorable, think again. Have you gone too far? Or is it their responsibility to change?

Depression and Low Self-Esteem

Use self-reinforcement to increase the frequency of your desired behaviors. Your plan should have this general form:

1. *Schedule* pleasant activities frequently.
2. *Reinforce* yourself for engaging in the activities. Be very liberal. Reinforce only on contingency, but begin with shaping steps that you can meet (Fuchs & Rehm, 1977). The goal is to increase pleasant events, not to squeeze even more pleasure out of your life. Do not make your reinforcement plans too severe, complicated, or difficult (Kornblith, Rehm, O'Hara, & Lamparski, 1983). Reward yourself!
3. *Replace* denigrating self-speech with realistic self-praise. Be sure to include verbal self-reinforcement for each desired behavior.

An effective technique for increasing the number of pleasant events in your life is to make sure you notice the ones that do occur. Keeping daily records of pleasant events is a reliable way to bring them to your attention. These may include such things as seeing a rainbow, talking with friends, receiving a smile from someone of the opposite sex, savoring the taste of an excellent olive.

You are almost certainly receiving less reinforcement than you need from other people. To increase those rewards, you will probably have to build new habits—making yourself more available to others or being more skillful in your interactions. Therefore, some problem solving and social-skill building should be a part of your overall plan (Lewinsohn, Sullivan, & Grosscup, 1980).

When a positive event occurs—a success, meeting a goal—be expressive about it. The effect of pleasant emotional states is extended by capitalizing on them, by telling others about successes, by celebrating, by marking them. This makes pleasant events more memorable, more significant, and raises the general level of good feeling (Langston, 1994).

Exercise and Athletics

Reinforcement of your new exercise patterns will help make them solid. You can use all forms of reinforcement: pleasant activities made contingent on completing the shaping steps, material things as reinforcers, and especially the covert reinforcement of self-praise and imagined scenes. Sato (1986) showed that joggers who self-reinforced increased their mileage. Her runners used such self-statements as the following:

- I am doing something really good for this body!
- I am happier and more alert after running.
- Sweat means burning calories and building strength!
- My lover is going to love my good mood!

The following punishing self-statements were to be avoided:

- I'm sweaty and sore.
- My husband is going to bitch about my running.
- I'm conspicuous.

Reinforcers such as clothing have been shown to improve regularity of aerobic dance class attendance. Reinforcement effects are positive whether they are given individually, or whether groups work together to gain group reinforcement (Kravitz & Furst, 1991). Reinforcement is vital, especially in the earlier stages of exercise development, when soreness and tiredness can provide automatic punishment. For successful exercisers, soreness and tiredness actually become positive reinforcers. This is more likely when a coach, class leader, or friend is present to help you identify these feelings and help you associate them with the improvement they represent (Lees & Dygdon, 1988). Participation in group exercise programs, either in formal "classes" or with informal groups of friends, can provide mutual reinforcement and the increase in motivation associated with public goal setting.

Attending carefully to one's performance and comparing it with a standard makes performance more skillful. These benefits can be strengthened by the use of videotapes or mirrors (Johnston-O'Connor & Kirschenbaum, 1986).

Relations with Others: Social Anxieties, Social Skills, and Dating

Imagined rehearsal and reinforcement are particularly appropriate for practicing the early stages of approach—making conversation and asking for dates. Use the logical imagined reinforcement of friendliness and acceptance by the other person. The natural reinforcements offered by the opposite sex are strong enough to maintain behavior once you have achieved confidence and skill.

For problematic relationships, reinforce yourself for doing what is needed to improve the relationships, and be sure to reinforce the others involved: "Hey, that was really nice. We sat and talked about our problem without anyone blowing up. I really appreciate the effort you are making."

Very often, interpersonal problems develop because one person starts punishing the other. Being punished often incites people to revenge, and a vicious circle is established. This, in turn, leads to more punishment, and so on, until the relationship is destroyed. One way of breaking this vicious circle is to realize that you can reinforce someone else by paying attention or making some pleasant statement.

Ask yourself, "How can I reinforce desired behavior?" Your intervention plan might involve paying attention to the "good" things the other person does and acknowledging the person for them. You then reinforce yourself for reinforcing the other. In a book on how to achieve a good marriage, Knox (1971) suggests keeping records like this:

The husband records:

| Wife's desirable behavior | Wife's undesirable behavior | Husband's response to wife's behavior |

The wife records:

| Husband's desirable behavior | Husband's undesirable behavior | Wife's response to husband's behavior |

SOURCE: *Marriage Happiness: A Behavioral Approach to Counseling* by D. Knox, 1971, Champaign, IL: Research Press. Copyright © 1971 by Research Press. Reprinted by permission.

Comparing the two records allows you to see if you are in fact trying to punish your spouse's undesired behavior instead of trying to reinforce his or her desirable acts. This record can also show how your spouse's behavior represents an antecedent for your behavior, and vice versa. It indicates what changes you should ask of your spouse and what changes you should try to make in yourself.

Two people working together to improve their relationship can develop specific agreements: You give up this, and I'll give up that; you do this, and I'll do that. Because certain changes in another person to whom you are close can be a strong incentive for you to change, this kind of mutual agreement is a powerful technique.

Smoking, Drinking, and Drugs

Abstinence from alcohol or drugs often brings surprising and immediate reinforcement, if you attend to it. For instance, many habitual drinkers or dopers attribute their social pleasures to the substance, whereas these pleasures (relaxation, flirtation, good humor) are actually consequences of social gatherings and a playful atmosphere. Notice that many of the pleasures are still there, even without the drugs or drink.

Other advantages are also immediate—think about them. For example, giving up tobacco brings three immediate benefits: immediate clearance of smoke from your lungs, clearance of carbon monoxide from your blood, and reduced risk of sudden death (Pechacek & Danaher, 1979). Remind yourself of the immediate benefits of giving up alcohol or drugs. Better mood and feelings of pride are reinforcers you should notice even in the earliest stages of abstaining. Attend to these feelings, and use them as self-reinforcement.

Cognitive strategies are probably the most effective for abstinence. Tell yourself, "I don't need a cigarette." Remind yourself of the commitment to abstinence. These strategies, and the use of self-reinforcement by positive self-statements, are strongly associated with success in stopping smoking. Use positive statements, such as, "Think of the good example I'm going to set by stopping smoking."

Don't neglect material reinforcers. Use at least the money saved by abstinence. Even for serious cocaine and alcohol problems, adding retail items or cash prizes increases abstinence over standard outpatient treatment alone (Higgins, Wong, Badger, Ogden, & Dantona, 2000; Petry, Martin, Cooney, & Kranzler, 2000).

By all means involve yourself in some form of social support—family, friends, or partners. Persuade your partner that you need to be reinforced for quitting and that you need understanding, listening, and help with developing alternate behaviors to smoking (Coppotelli & Orleans, 1985). "High self-efficacy and the benefits of social support from family, friends, coworkers, and spouses, regardless of their smoking status, were found in this analysis to be among the factors with the strongest positive influence" (Hill et al., 1994, p. 165). The positive effects of social support on smoking cessation continue to be verified, decade after decade (McMahon & Jason, 2000; Wagner, Burg, & Sirois, 2004).

Studying and Time Management

Reinforcement is highly important in studying and time scheduling— much more important than unsuccessful students believe. In fact, successful students tend to develop self-reinforcement techniques on their own without a course or a book like this one (Heffernan & Richards, 1981; Perri & Richards, 1977). The use of reinforcement for studying is especially important if your study habits have not yet been well developed in high school or early college courses (Green, 1982). One of the advantages that competent students have over "disadvantaged" students is that the advantaged already reinforce themselves for studying.

But there are times of "blocking" and distraction when studying and writing will not come, even for competent students, even for professors. Even for seasoned academic writers who were temporarily "blocked," programs of reinforcement have proven effective in increasing productivity (Boice, 1982).

Often reinforcement can be obtained by a simple rearrangement. For example, use pleasant occupations (leisure or hobbies) to reinforce the more difficult ones, such as studying, so that one is directly tied to the other and reinforces it. In drawing up your time-management plan, make sure a pleasant block of time follows any particularly difficult one, and follow the rule that you must complete the difficult activity before you move to the pleasant one.

Whenever you can't arrange your activities as described above, use other reinforcers, however arbitrary—movies, candy, cash, tokens. Your basic plan should (1) be based on a firm schedule, (2) include enough pleasant activities, and (3) provide reinforcement for following the schedule.

Studying behaviors are also more likely to improve when you arrange for some social support. The use of mediators should be explored. Arranging study groups, with group standards, feedback, and reinforcement, is desirable. Publicly announcing your goals and progress is also recommended (Hayes et al., 1985).

Weight Loss and Overeating

All behavioral programs for weight loss have contingency-management features. Reinforcement is a vital element in your plan. Reinforce yourself for avoiding the situations that cue excessive consumption. Use reinforcement to strengthen all the behaviors your self-control requires, such as recording all the food you eat, resisting urges, exercising, making graphs, and avoiding temptation. *Reinforce these behaviors. Do not make reinforcement contingent on weight.* Daily fluctuations in weight can be very deceiving. If you perform the correct eating and exercise behaviors, weight loss will follow.

Do not use food as a reward. As often as possible, use the natural reinforcement that your long-range self-control will bring. Consider the benefits of your diet: Do you feel better, happier, more alive? Remind yourself of the numerous rewards. One of the benefits of weight loss is lowered depression (Wing, Marcus, Epstein, & Kupfer, 1983), and better mood and feelings of pride are reinforcers that you should notice even in the earliest stages of dieting. Attend to these feelings, and use them as self-reinforcement. When dieting, look at your body in the mirror. Enjoy your improved appearance (Owusu-Bempah & Howitt, 1983).

If you are on the verge of violating your rules, say, "Stop!" to yourself, breathe deeply, relax, and reinforce yourself with a pleasant imagined scene.

Odds are that you will continue to need other forms of reinforcement to replace the consummatory behaviors. Reinforce alternatives and arrange for reinforcement from others. Successful weight losers received positive feedback from several external sources, such as parents and peers (Perri & Richards, 1977).

The evidence is convincing that the use of significant others as mediators will help your plan. Read the text material on pages 211–215 carefully, and include mediators in some way. Finding a group of dieters who are willing to commit themselves to good eating habits and who agree to use group reinforcement can provide strong and pleasant motivation (Jeffery, Gerber, Rosenthal, & Lindquist, 1983).

If you are a binge eater, attend also to this research finding: Disordered eating is strongly associated with very restricted self-nurturance (Lehman & Rodin, 1989). This means that binge eaters are not nice enough to themselves in other ways; they have insufficient amounts of self-reward, relaxation, and self-praise. It is highly important that you establish a richer program of noncontingent self-reinforcement, both verbal and material. Otherwise you may continue to nurture yourself only with eating binges.

Chapter Summary

The most basic formula in self-modification is to arrange that reinforcement follow desired behaviors.

Bridging Between Immediate Contingencies and Long-Delayed Consequences

Your self-management plan will require three strategies: first, through envisioning and reminders, to bring delayed goals forward in time; second, through avoiding problematic antecedents, to reduce the frequency of undesired behavior; and third, by using new and powerful immediate reinforcement, to strengthen alternate, desirable behaviors.

Discovering and Selecting Reinforcers

Your A-B-C records may reveal the reinforcers that are maintaining undesirable behavior. The simplest plan is to arrange for these same reinforcers to follow your new goal behavior. This is not possible with indulgent behaviors because the act consumes the reinforcer. Therefore, some other reward must be used to reinforce nonindulgence.

Intermittent reinforcement and avoidance behaviors make discovery of reinforcement difficult. Here, too, you must identify reinforcers that are available and controllable.

A wide variety of possible rewards can be used as reinforcers, including preferred things and preferred activities. The nature of the reward is not important as long as your plan makes it contingent on the desired behavior and reinforces the desired behavior.

Using Others to Dispense Reinforcers

The use of mediators as dispensers of contingent reinforcers is a highly desirable feature of self-modification. Research evidence overwhelmingly supports the power of this strategy in changing behavior. The use of mediators is advisable in every case in which it can be arranged, particularly in maintaining gains. Praise by mediators is probably even more important than material reinforcement. Attention should be paid to the mediators; their cooperative behavior will also need reinforcement. Sharing reinforcers with the mediator or another partner can help provide motivation, but care should be taken to make sure your partner shares your goals.

Self-Administered Consequences

Vigorous debate surrounds the question of whether self-reward acts as a reinforcer or serves only to call attention to the behavior. Various evidence has been presented and critiqued, but the debate goes on. Virtually every psychologist agrees, however, that self-administered consequences do affect behavior.

Techniques of Self-Reinforcement

Contingent reinforcement should follow desired behavior as rapidly as possible. This can often be achieved by using a point system or other form of token reinforcement. Points are gained as soon as the behavior is performed and then are exchanged later for real reinforcers.

Imagined reinforcers can also be delivered rapidly. In this technique, a reinforcer from your list is imagined immediately after the behavior occurs. Especially useful is imagining the long-range eventual outcome of your self-modification program.

Verbal self-reinforcement—praising yourself—following desired behavior is an effective technique that should be included in every self-change program.

Good plans will add to the total of pleasant events in your daily schedule.

Self-Punishment and Extinction

Neither extinction nor self-punishment teaches any new behaviors. Most intervention plans that rely solely on self-punishment don't succeed. In some situations, self-punishment may be necessary—if, for example, no positive reinforcers are available, or if the undesired behavior is so strongly reinforcing in itself that a direct, counteracting consequence is required for not performing it. Indulgent behaviors are typical examples of this situation.

If you do decide to use punishment, you should follow these rules:

1. Remove something positive instead of adding something negative. (Always try to figure out a way to increase behavior by adding something positive.)

2. Use punishment only if it leads to more positive reinforcement.
3. Devise a plan that combines punishment with positive reinforcement.
4. You may use precommitted punishment as a deterrent strategy, but only temporarily until the desired behavior can be supported by positive consequences.

The only recommended form of "punishment" is the systematic facing of the negative long-term consequences of a problem behavior. This helps build commitment.

Reinforcement in Plans for Self-Modification

Reinforcers need to be integrated into plans for controlling antecedents (Chapter 5) and developing new behaviors (Chapter 6). For example, reinforcement can be added to imagined rehearsal and to shaping. The general point is that reinforcement should follow all new behaviors in a self-modification plan. If the natural environment does not provide it, arrange specific reinforcement to be delivered by yourself or your mediators.

Your Own Self-Direction Project: Step 7

Review the previous versions of your plan, which included elements of antecedent control and development of new behaviors, in light of what you have just learned about rearrangement of consequences. Plan to follow new behaviors with reinforcement. Be sure to include verbal self-reinforcement, as well as at least one other technique. The result may well be your final plan. Before implementing it, however, read the next chapter, which will help you combine A, B, and C elements into a comprehensive package.

Chapter 8

Developing
a Successful Plan

Outline and Learning Objectives

Combining A, B, and C Elements

1. Explain how record keeping and A, B, and C elements are combined in a single plan.
2. Describe in detail the two-step process for dealing with high-risk situations. What are steps 1 and 2?
3. How can unwanted stimulus control by various situations be gradually eliminated?
4. How can the two-stage process be used in any kind of project?
5. Explain how developing options can help you deal with high-risk situations.

The Elements of a Good Plan

6. What are the five features of a good plan?
7. How are rules used in self-modification?
8. Explain how goals and subgoals are used.
9. Why is it important to gather feedback? How is feedback compared to goals and subgoals?
10. When do you make adjustments in your plan?
11. Explain the idea of learning from mistakes.
12. Explain the idea of skills for dealing with mistakes. What steps can you take to learn these skills?
13. What are the major techniques in the checklist that you should use for your project?
14. How can you brainstorm to generate more ideas on how to carry out self-change?
15. Do you ever change your target behavior? When?
    a. Should you have a baseline for any new target behavior?
    b. What about new, incompatible responses?

Evaluating Your Plan for Change

16. How can you use an average to see if you are progressing?
17. How can you use a percentage to see if you are progressing?
18. How would you make a graph of your personal records during your self-change project?
    a. What goes on the horizontal axis?
    b. What goes on the vertical axis?

Tips for Typical Topics

Chapter Summary

Your Own Self-Direction Project: Step 8

So far we have treated each technique and principle in isolation, but an effective plan for change integrates all these techniques and principles. A good plan combines record keeping with Antecedent, Behavior, and Consequence (A-B-C) elements—from Chapters 3, 5, 6, and 7. The goal of this chapter is to help you design a complete plan, then evaluate its effectiveness and look for trouble spots.

Combining A, B, and C Elements

Two sample projects illustrate how A, B, and C elements are combined in an effective plan for self-modification.

Two Sample Cases

The student. Paul wrote:

> There are several reasons why I would like to study more. I think I will develop a sense of achievement if I get all As this semester, and it will improve my chances of getting into seminary. I will also learn discipline and build my self-esteem.

For 3 weeks, Paul kept a record of how much he studied. Then he formulated a systematic self-modification plan.

> In the first week I studied quite a bit just because I was keeping records, but by the second and third weeks my average had dropped way off, and I ended up averaging under 10 hours per week. Then I began a full-blown self-modification plan.
>
> I wrote a self-contract. I specified several things to do to change: I scheduled study hours, I gradually built up the amount of time I studied at one sitting, I planned where I would study, I gave myself instructions, and I worked out rewards for studying. When problems came up, I changed my plan to cope with them.

Paul listed all these elements of the plan in his self-contract, along with three escape clauses: He would keep 4:30 to 6:30 as a time to relax; he would devote all day Sunday to church work; and he would not study more than 20 hours a week. Then Paul signed the contract and posted it in his room.

Let's analyze the different parts of Paul's plan from the point of view of antecedents, targets, and consequences.

Antecedents: Paul scheduled specific hours that he would study—for example, Tuesday night, 6:30 to 8:30—and the exact places where he would do it—my desk at home, "college library," or "the local public library." He set certain rules: "I will study at the times designated on my schedule. I will study at least 1 hour before I take a break." After typing out the entire set of rules, he put this contract with himself into his record keeping notebook. Just before each study session, he gave himself instructions:

> Here's another opportunity to get those As. I must study now—I scheduled it. Sit down, look over the assignment, then concentrate on the reading and the note taking. If my attention begins to wander, take up another assignment. Read for 1 hour, and then reward myself.

Behaviors: Paul used shaping to gradually increase how many hours per day he scheduled for studying. First he set $1\frac{1}{2}$, then 2, then $2\frac{1}{2}$, then increased the time by quarter hours up to $3\frac{1}{2}$ hours. He started by requiring himself to study for 1 hour without a break, then increased this by 10-minute segments until his study periods were up to 2 continuous hours.

Consequences: Paul worked out a token system, earning 1 token for every hour of studying. Each token was worth a half hour of TV watching. Seven tokens were enough to earn his three favorite programs. If he earned 10 tokens, he earned a bonus. He would take off from studying all day Saturday. At a later stage, he raised the cost of the bonus to 15 tokens.

Problems: Paul ran into two sets of problems in trying to change his study habits:

> First, I'd get a strong urge not to study, even though it was a scheduled study time. Then, while I was studying, my mind would wander. Sometimes I would think, "This is pointless. I'll never make all As anyway." These thoughts were obviously going to keep me from reaching my goal, so I used thought substitution and told myself, "You can do this. You are an able student, and you have good self-discipline."
>
> A second problem was that I always got hungry while I was studying, and I would take a break to eat. So I started having a snack just before my study time, and then I'd give myself reminders not to eat any more once I started studying.

Toward the end of the semester, Paul nearly reached his goal of 20 hours of studying per week, but after one particularly difficult exam he felt he needed a break, so he didn't study for 2 days. After that it was hard to get back to his schedule. But by this time, the end of the first term had arrived, and Paul found that the biggest reinforcer of all was a gigantic improvement in his grades. "Frankly, I was stunned. I actually made all As! I really *can* sit down and study for 2 hours straight, and doing it regularly has a terrific effect on my GPA."

The putdown artist. Edgar's problem was that he put down his friends. "When I had the chance, I put people down without even thinking about it." He began his self-change program by counting the number of putdowns per week and kept records for several weeks. Edgar then worked out a plan for changing and continued to make observations about his putdowns of his friends.

Antecedents: "I put down my friends as a joke. When we're horsing around, everyone is joking about something or other, and I use these putdowns as my kind of joke. I know I am only joking, but my friends don't like it. So I need to be careful in that kind of situation. I also asked my friends to tell me if I was putting them down. Sometimes I didn't even realize I was doing it."

Behaviors: "Each week I tried to reduce the number of putdowns I did—shaping. I also did relaxation exercises, so I could relax more in those horsing-around times. I tried modeling other people who had good interpersonal manners. I did mental practice for about 3 minutes each day, imagining myself saying nice things to people. I also tried to pause before saying something, so I could ask myself if what I was going to say was a putdown. Instead of putting people down, I tried to compliment them."

Note the large number of different things Edgar is doing: relaxing, pausing, modeling, practicing, and substituting positive remarks for negative ones.

Consequences: "My primary reward for not putting people down was allowing myself to talk on the phone with my friends for a certain number of minutes. I worked out a table to relate the number of putdowns to how long I could talk on the phone:

Number of Putdowns	Number of Minutes Allowed on the Phone
20	10
17	15
15	30
10	45
5	indefinite

"As the weeks went by, I changed the ratio of putdowns to time on the telephone: I had to use fewer putdowns in order to talk on the phone for the same amount of time. After about 3 months, I stopped keeping records, but I still perform the mental rehearsals. Even though I still put people down sometimes, it is not to the extent it was before."

Two-Stage Process for High-Risk Situations

Stage 1. Avoiding high-risk situations. In Chapter 5, we suggested that undesired consummatory behaviors such as drinking, smoking, or overeating can be reduced by a two-stage process. *In stage 1, avoid the antecedent.* Avoid high-risk situations. For example, don't go to parties where you will be strongly tempted to smoke, or don't confront yourself with high-calorie food. Your plan should include reinforcement for this avoidance and a way of substituting other pleasant activities. For example, a young woman, Lisa, who knew she drank too much alcohol when she went out drinking with her friends after work simply gave up that activity for several weeks and tried to spend the time with her boyfriend, who drank only moderately (Sobell & Sobell, 1995b).

Stage 2. Building new behaviors. Few situations can be avoided permanently, however. Eventually you want to return to parties, go out with your friends, walk into a bakery, or go back to your morning cup of coffee without having a cigarette. In stage 2, build new behaviors so that you can be in tempting situations but not perform the overindulging or addictive behavior.

In stage 1, practice avoiding the tempting antecedent situation. In stage 2, practice performing a new, desired situation in the problematic situation.

Larry, a man who had tried unsuccessfully several times to quit smoking, analyzed the situations in which he returned to smoking after having quit for a few days. Taking a coffee break or eating lunch with his colleagues (several of whom smoked) was the most likely time for backsliding. Smoking seemed such a pleasure under those circumstances that he didn't resist. In stage 1 of his plan, Larry avoided these high-risk situations for 2 weeks, explaining to his friends what he was doing and reinforcing himself for successful avoidance. He was not tempted so much on the weekends because he spent them with his wife, who didn't smoke. After he had been off cigarettes for several weeks, he entered stage 2, in which he rewarded himself specifically for not smoking with his friends at lunch. After this had worked for a week, he returned to coffee breaks in his daily schedule and reinforced himself specifically for not smoking at coffee breaks. Now Larry's task was to remain vigilant for tempting antecedents and to reinforce himself for not smoking when they occurred.

Rehearsal in imagination is a good technique for this kind of situation. Several times a day, Larry imagined himself in a situation in which he was tempted to smoke—concentrating on imagining all the details, including his own craving for a cigarette—and he imagined himself not giving in.

Drugs, alcohol, tobacco, and food are taken in response to several particular antecedents—watching TV, reading, being with a person who causes tension, feeling bored, depressed, angry, or excited. After discovering your problem antecedents, divide them into physical and emotional events. First eliminate the stimulus control of the physical events—for example, eating while watching TV—and later eliminate the control of the emotional events—for example, drinking when depressed. For many people, physical events are easier to control than emotional ones because they are more obvious. Start with the easier situations, and gradually work up to the harder ones.

The idea of eliminating stimulus control over unwanted behaviors is not part of commonsense psychology. People tend not to examine their environment to see where it may be controlling their behaviors. You need to learn to spot those situations and to gain control over the situational antecedents that govern your unwanted behaviors. For example, you may overeat in response to the sight of food, to being in Mom's kitchen, to driving past a particular fast-food store—all situational antecedents that control overeating.

Developing options. Develop several different plans for coping with high-risk situations, so that if one doesn't work, you won't necessarily fall back into your old, bad habits. Linda and Mark Sobell (1995b) reported the case of Lisa, who wanted to control her drinking. Lisa was concerned because, as she said, "When I play darts at the pub, I drink until I'm drunk." Under the Sobell's guidance, Lisa developed options to cope with the high-risk situation.

Stage 1, Avoiding the high risk antecedent. Rule: "Don't go to the pub to play darts." Lisa used this stage 1 strategy for several weeks. Her drinking was greatly reduced, but she missed playing darts with her friends.

Stage 2, Developing new behaviors. Option 1: "Go play darts, but don't drink." She thought she would feel strange doing this, but it did have the advantage of seeing her friends and enjoying playing darts. Option 2: "Reduce my drinking so I don't get drunk." This would give her exactly what she really wanted, fun at the pub but staying sober. But could she exercise the self-control to do it?

Lisa chose to attempt option 2, but she had other options ready, should she need them—either option 1, or a return to stage 1.

To make option 2 work, Lisa developed eight rules to make pub drinking moderate. These rules each involved the building of a new behavior into the high-risk situation:

1. Plan beforehand what time I will leave the pub, and leave at that time, so I won't be tempted to drink more.
2. Alternate my drinks—have an alcoholic drink followed by a nonalcoholic drink (juice, pop).
3. Sip rather than gulp my drinks, and drink no faster than one alcoholic drink per hour.
4. Don't drink more than three drinks in an evening.
5. Tell those friends I am comfortable with that I am trying to reduce my drinking.
6. Keep some kind of drink in front of me so my friends won't offer me a drink.
7. Don't let anyone refill my glass before it is finished, so I will know how much I drink.
8. Leave if I don't feel I can manage the situation. (Sobell & Sobell, 1995b)

For your own plan, follow a similar pattern, and work out options for dealing with high-risk situations. Step 1 is to avoid the situation, but the next options should allow you to enter the situation and try to develop new behaviors in them. Chapter 2 has ideas on dealing with temptations.

The Two-Stage Process Applied to Other Problems

The two-stage process is appropriate for more than consummatory behaviors. Many projects can profit from a stage 1 of avoidance.

Leslie and Helen worked together, and over the years their relationship deteriorated. Having to deal with each other in their jobs was extremely unpleasant. When they did talk, the usual result was anger and hurt feelings. The obvious solution—avoiding each other—was impossible, since they had to work in the same room day after day. Leslie decided to try a two-stage intervention program.

Stage 1. Leslie instituted a cooling-off period, in which she didn't talk with Helen except when it was absolutely necessary. When she did talk, she confined her remarks to business topics and tried to be either neutral or mildly pleasant. This was reasonably effective. After a couple of weeks, they settled down to occasional brief and relatively calm interactions. Most important, anger seemed to disappear from the picture.

This first stage of Leslie's program is an example of avoiding the controlling antecedent—in this case, talking with the other person—long enough to begin developing other more desirable reactions. *It is very important to develop the new and more desirable behaviors.* In the case of these two women, for example, if no new behavior had been developed, the cooling-off period would have ended in failure. Eventually their work would have required them to have more substantial conversations, and they would gradually have returned to their old, angry behavior.

Stage 2. Leslie then went into a second stage, which included three elements: (1) She did not respond to annoying remarks from Helen. Thus, if Helen said, "I'm not sure you're doing a good job," Leslie ignored her. (2) She positively reinforced Helen for pleasant remarks. Thus if Helen said, "That seemed to work out very well," Leslie would say, "Why, thanks very much. It's kind of you to say that." (3) She praised Helen for her good work and refrained from criticizing her. She continued this for several months and was able to develop a new, more neutral relationship.

The Elements of a Good Plan

There is no such thing as one best plan for attaining a goal. Several different plans for the same goal could be designed, any one of which might be successful. But successful plans all have certain elements in common.

A Theoretical Overview of a Good Plan

A successful plan includes these features:

1. Rules that state the kinds of behaviors and techniques for change to use in specific situations;
2. Goals and subgoals;
3. Feedback on your behavior, derived from your self-observations;
4. A comparison of feedback to your subgoals and goals in order to measure progress; and
5. Adjustments in the plan as conditions change.

Rules. Self-modification involves setting rules for oneself in order to reach one's goals (cf. Hayes, 1989). If some behavior is not a problem for you, you follow your own rules without paying much attention to them. But if you are not meeting a particular goal, you need to set clear, explicit rules to guide your behavior until that behavior becomes habitual. That's the whole purpose of rules—to make desired behaviors more likely (Malott, 1989).

In your plan for self-change, the rules are statements of the thoughts, behaviors, and techniques for change you will use in specific situations. Here are several examples of rules that people have included in their self-change plans:

- Every night, between 7:00 and 9:00, I will practice relaxation exercises for 20 minutes.
- I will not eat foods that have more than two grams of fat per serving.
- I will exercise for 20 minutes on Monday, Wednesday, and Friday while watching TV.
- I will drink no more than one drink per hour, no matter what the others are doing.
- I will talk to at least one woman each day, for at least 3 minutes.
- I will go to the library to study at least three times per week.

A typical plan will have more than one rule. For example:

1. Each day in my art history class, I will make at least one comment.
2. Every evening for at least 15 minutes I will study either art history or English.

3. I will keep records of both these.
4. I will allow myself to go to parties on the weekend only if I have followed these two rules.

Goals and subgoals. Making goals and subgoals explicit is vital to the success of any plan. The writing of novels, for example, might seem dependent on the rush of inspiration and the caprice of the muse. Not so. Firm, daily work goals—in terms of number of pages (or even words) written—have been used by novelists as diverse as Anthony Trollope, Arnold Bennett, Ernest Hemingway, and Irving Wallace. Each of these writers counted his output daily and compared it to his daily goal (Wallace & Pear, 1977). Jack London required himself to write 1000 words a day before he visited his local saloon (Bandura, 1981).

Each subgoal has to be formulated precisely enough for you to be able to compare it with your performance and know whether or not you have achieved your subgoal. Each subgoal has its own rules, as illustrated in this plan for improving job interview performance:

Rules for subgoal 1: "Each day I will practice the relaxation exercises (at first I'll do this 20 minutes per day), until I can relax without going through all the muscle tension release steps."

After this subgoal is reached, a new one is substituted. The long-range goal here is relaxation in certain situations, but it is reached by carefully stating a series of subgoals and reaching them one at a time.

Rules for subgoal 2: "Each day I will spend at least 10 minutes rehearsing in my imagination applying for a job, until I can think about it with a tension rating no greater than mild."

As each step is achieved, the next step begins with new rules and new subgoals. The goal at each step is the level of performance needed to advance to the next step.

Feedback. Any effective plan must incorporate a system for gathering information about your progress. If you are learning to serve a tennis ball, you don't hit the ball and then close your eyes. You follow the path of the ball, noting its speed, twist, and whether it lands in the proper court or not. Your standard for success is *ball in the court.* If your feedback tells you that it is out, you can perform some operation to correct your behavior. Without feedback, you aren't likely to improve—and if you did, you wouldn't know it.

All goal-oriented behavior is governed by this cybernetic principle. Without some information about your performance (feedback), you cannot correct yourself, whether your goal is to be a better student, a better lover, or a better tennis player. *For this reason, your plan must include a system for collecting data.* Of course you are already doing that for baseline purposes, as outlined in Chapter 3. But you must continue to self-record for the duration of your plan so that self-correction can occur.

Comparison of feedback to goals and subgoals. The next step in your plan is to compare the feedback to your subgoal. How are you doing? The answer may be, "Terrific!" You're studying enough, you're making new friends, or you're exercising more.

But sometimes things are not satisfactory, and you see that you are off your ideal standard. Then you make adjustments, and some improvement occurs. Whether these adjustments are major or minor, you won't be sure that they are the right ones—or even that they are needed—unless you record your self-observations and compare them to your goal.

This process of comparing feedback to goals and subgoals may require a short, deliberate period of taking stock. For example, a woman who was very successful losing weight using this book told us that she made an appointment with herself for 30 minutes to an hour each week, on weigh-in day, to review the week's eating and exercise records, judge progress, make necessary adjustments, collect her weekly reward, praise herself for successes, give herself some self-instructions, and make a weekly summary record in a journal.

Adjustments in the plan. You should expect to adjust your plans from week to week. New goals require new tactics. Sometimes as you progress in your plan you learn new things and have to somewhat change the focus of your plan in order to achieve your goal. One of our students told us:

> My grades were getting to be OK on multiple choice exams, but still not so good on my written papers. Then you gave that little lecture on improving our writing in which you talked about the way poor writers give too much attention to things like grammar and punctuation and not enough to questions like, "Am I getting my ideas across?" or "Do I need to include more information?" or "What can I do to make the whole presentation better?" So I changed the focus of my efforts: I reminded myself with those questions and went back later to clean up grammar and spelling. That was much better; so were my grades.

We're not surprised it worked, incidentally, as research has shown that this kind of change particularly helps poor writers (Watkins, 1991).

Although any new plan will include different techniques, it will have the same elements that characterize all successful plans: explicit rules, precise goals, gathering of feedback, comparison of feedback to goals, and adjustments as the plan continues.

Brainstorming an Effective Plan

Once you have reviewed procedures for each of the A, B, and C elements, you are ready to design your final plan. It's good to pause for a moment and ask, "Do I have the best plan? Have I thought of the best ideas to conquer my problem?" Before settling on a final plan, be creative. Try brainstorming. The goal of brainstorming is to generate as many ideas as possible, quickly and uncritically.

1. Try for quantity of ideas.
2. Don't criticize your ideas; don't even evaluate them. You will do that later.
3. Try to think of unusual ideas.
4. Try to combine ideas to create new ones.

Jim, who had a bad case of acne in high school, had developed the habit of picking at his face. He wanted to stop this habit, because it tended to inflame his sensitive skin, produced infections, and made his face look terrible. But it was an automatic habit, and he was having trouble thinking of ways to stop it. After going through the four steps, Jim brainstormed solutions:

> I have to stop. Let's see. I could . . . slap my face every time I do it. No, that's dumb. [Long pause, no ideas.] Oh, yeah, I was criticizing the idea. Don't do that now. Just

produce a lot of ideas, evaluate them later. OK. So, I could slap my face every time I do it. I could ask Lois to tell me to stop whenever I do it. I could ask my parents to tell me, too. I could rub my face instead of picking it. I could pull out my hair instead. Ha! I could suck my thumb, or—I could pick my nose. Ha! No criticism now! I could say to myself, "I want to stop picking my face, so I won't do it now." I could do that and rub my face instead of picking. I could remind myself that it might get red or infected. Since I do it when I'm watching TV, I could put a sign on the TV reminding me not to do it. Ditto for studying. Put a sign on my desk. I could report to Lois every day about how much I did it the previous day, and show her that I was cutting down. Ditto my parents. Every day I could cut down a little more over the day before. If I didn't, then I wouldn't get to watch TV that day; but if I did, I'd put aside some money for something—for some clothes or a CD. I could force myself to do it for hours at a time until I got so sick of it I'd never do it again. I could . . .

That's how the brainstorming process works. After writing down these ideas, Jim selected the best ones, designed a tentative plan, and examined it to make sure that it was in accord with the principles he had learned.

Improving Ongoing Plans

Learn from mistakes. You will make mistakes as you try to bring some troublesome behavior under control. But you can learn from these mistakes.

A tennis player has just lost a match and is talking to his coach. The coach says, "What happened?"

"He beat me. I lost."

"Yeah, I know he beat you. But why?" The coach is thinking ahead to what needs to be done next.

"Well, for one thing, his backhand was better than mine."

"True," says the coach. "Specifically, what was it about your backhand that was weak?"

"Uh, well, I held it too high at the beginning of the swing, I turned toward the net too soon, so I didn't follow through correctly, and I hit the ball too close to my body."

"Right," says the coach, "Now let's get to work to be sure that doesn't happen again."

Can you see what the coach has done? Instead of just thinking, "I lost and don't know what to do about it," the player can now think of very specific things that he has to do to make his game more competitive.

You will lose a few games on the way to better self-management. *Each loss is merely information about skills that need work.* Remember to hold a skills development attitude, discussed in Chapter 2. If you slipped and had a cigarette while drinking coffee, you need to work on your antismoking skills when faced with coffee. If you intended to study all evening but were distracted by a phone call, you need a plan to deal with phone calls. If you wanted to be assertive but were intimidated by the other person's frown, you need to develop your skill in response to frowns.

The skill of dealing with mistakes. When we make mistakes we can feel frustrated, unhappy, even angry. If you are surprised by this frustration, you may be tempted to quit your self-change project. Your thoughts may discourage you—"Damn, I messed up again.

Man, I'll never get this right!"—and that can lead to quitting your attempts to change. You need to take steps to change your frustrated thoughts, so they won't tempt you to quit.

There is a skill to dealing with mistakes (Kanfer & Ackerman, 1995). No one ever avoids all error, but some people do learn to minimize frustration and avoid negative thoughts. In one experiment subjects who were going to practice a difficult skill were forewarned that it would be frustrating and that they would have negative thoughts, and these subjects did better than those who were not forewarned (Kanfer & Ackerman, 1990). Forewarn yourself. Try these techniques to minimize frustration, anger, and unhappiness:

1. Control your attention:
   - Don't let your attention focus on the frustration or negative emotion; distract yourself.
   - Focus on the next subgoal, the one you really can reach soon. Don't attend exclusively to the distant goal. Someday you'll have a higher GPA, but today just think about meeting today's study goal.
   - Don't compare yourself with other people. Don't focus on how the genius sitting next to you is doing. That's discouraging. Take the skills development approach in which you compare your progress only to yourself.
2. Speak to yourself as your best friend:
   - Remind yourself of the progress you have made so far. Remind yourself of how good you will feel when you reach your target goal.
   - Remind yourself, "I'm developing a skill. That takes time, and mistakes are a part of it."
   - Remind yourself, too, that these skills of dealing with mistakes also need to be learned.

Changing Targets and the Effect on Your Record Keeping

During the course of a plan, the actual target behavior may change. For example, Ben planned to increase his studying, but soon concluded that one of the reasons he didn't study enough was because he felt stressed by events in his life. He changed his plan and worked to reduce his stress.

When you change your target behavior, should you have a new baseline period? When the changes you make in your target behavior are substantial and abrupt, such as Ben's switching from "increasing studying" to "coping with stress," it is best to establish a new baseline. Basically, he was beginning a new plan.

Sometimes you will add something to an ongoing plan, as Sally does in this case. Sally was very shy and withdrawn, especially in groups. She decided that if she smiled more, she would appear less withdrawn. Her original goal (plan 1) was to increase smiling behavior by making a note on a card each time she smiled at someone. She worked out a plan in which she earned tokens (to be applied later to the purchase of elegant clothes) by smiling at people. She also gave herself instructions to smile, and enlisted the help of her roommates.

At first Sally improved just because she was keeping records. Figure 8-1 presents part of her data. She was quite pleased. But around day 11 or 12, Sally began rethinking her problem.

"I started to realize," she later wrote in her report, "that although I was smiling more at people, I still appeared withdrawn. This was because I was not looking at them.

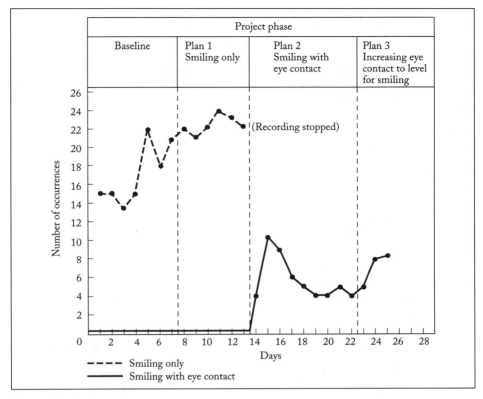

Figure 8-1 Smiling and eye contact

I was smiling but looking down at the ground. Most people feel that looking into some-one's eyes is a sign of interest, so I decided that just smiling at others wasn't enough. I had to smile, and I had to make eye contact."

Sally changed her definition of the target, broadening it. In plan 2, she counted not only smiling but also eye contacts that lasted several seconds. She began plan 2 on day 14. In this revised plan, she earned her tokens for smiling and maintaining about 3 seconds of eye contact, and she gave herself instructions to do both.

Whenever you change your target behavior, you must begin to record the new target to see what your baseline is and to notice small changes as they begin to occur. For example, you might start out with "dieting" as your target and, after a few weeks, decide to add "exercising" to your plan. In that case you would now record both your dieting behaviors and your exercise.

If your initial target for change was some undesired behavior, you might have begun by recording it. But your plan for change will probably involve substituting some new behavior to do instead of the undesired, so be sure to keep a record of the new, to-be-increased actions.

If the new, incompatible behavior is one that you intend to continue permanently, then you will want to keep good records for it—for example, deciding to increase "reading good books" as a behavior incompatible with "wasting time." If you don't intend to continue the incompatible behavior—for example, slapping your hand instead of cracking your knuckles—then it is not necessary to get a separate count of the incompatible behavior as long as you are keeping a good record of the undesired target behavior.

Stopping to Think and Learn

You have read a lot of information about changing yourself and are ready to get on with the show. Box 8-1 contains a checklist you can use, so your self-modification plan gives you the greatest possible chance of success. We also present a final sample plan in its full detail, to demonstrate the process of gradually refining the target behaviors, making adjustments, changing the techniques used, and achieving final success.

A Sample Plan

This is the plan of a young woman who wanted to reduce her anxiety about speaking to her professors. The plan eventually worked well, after several adjustments.

Plan 1: In her report, Laurel wrote:

I almost never talk with my professors. They scare me. Sometimes I have questions. At other times I would just like to talk with them. But I have spoken only to one, Prof A., all year, and it was only a few sentences at a time. My goal is to increase talking with my professors.

I will develop my behavior gradually, on a shaping schedule. I have to start really low, because my baseline is nearly zero. This is my shaping schedule:

Step 1. Say hello to a professor.
Step 2. Talk with a professor for 15 seconds.
Step 3. Talk with a professor for 30 seconds.
Step 4. Talk for 1 minute.
Step 5. Talk for 2 minutes.

Our analysis: So far, Laurel's plan is generally satisfactory. She should specify how many times she will rehearse each step before moving to the next.

Collecting feedback: "My wristwatch has a sweep–second hand. If I turn the band, the watch will be on my wrist facing up. I can sort of look down to check the time without being too obvious. As soon as the conversation is over, I'll write down notes—how many seconds, the professor's name, where we were, and so forth. On the inside front cover of my notebook, I'll write my shaping schedule. Then I can check whether or not I have met my goals."

Techniques: "I've decided to use a combination of Premack and food reinforcers. Since I eat lunch every day at school, I'll set a rule that I won't eat lunch until I have performed whatever step is required by my schedule."

Our analysis: Selecting eating lunch as the reinforcer seems drastic, but since her schedule is reasonable and develops slowly, she probably won't need to go without food. At the same time, she gains the reinforcing effect of eating lunch.

But there are a few problems with the plan. Other techniques should be included, principally self-instructions before the conversation and self-praise after it. It would also

Box 8-1
A Checklist for Your Plan

The major reason people fail in self-modification is because they do not use the techniques they have read about. They don't remember all they have learned (Ley, 1986). Or they don't think these technical steps are necessary, and so they fail (Startup & Edmonds, 1994). Let's review the most important issues presented in the preceding chapters. These issues can be formulated as a series of questions. Write yes or no for each.

I. Begin with ideas from Chapter 2 on *anticipating obstacles and setting goals:*

_____ Have you specified the target behaviors clearly?

_____ Are you taking steps to cope with temptation?

_____ Have you worked on your self-efficacy and optimism beliefs?

_____ Have you dealt with your ambivalence about changing, or any conflicts between long- and short-term goals?

_____ Have you set clear goals and subgoals?

_____ Did you write a self-contract?

II. Questions from Chapter 3, *dealing with self-observation:*

_____ Have you worked out a self-observation system you can use when the problem behavior occurs?

_____ Do you make the records as soon as the behavior occurs? Do you keep written records?

_____ Have you made changes in the way you specified the target as your self-understanding increased?

_____ Are you recording successes as well as failures?

_____ Can you use negative practice?

III. Here's a checklist of the steps involved in *controlling antecedents:*

_____ If your goal is to decrease some unwanted behavior, have you taken steps to discover and eliminate the antecedents of that behavior?

_____ Have you developed a plan to change thoughts that are the antecedents of the behavior?

_____ Have you examined your beliefs to see whether they are contributing to your problem behavior? Have you made plans to restructure them?

_____ Have you developed a plan to cope with the physical antecedents of the behavior?

(continued)

Box 8-1 *(continued)*

_____ Have you worked out a plan to deal with the social and emotional antecedents of the behavior?

_____ Have you taken steps to provide antecedents that will encourage your new, desired behavior?

_____ Have you developed some thoughts you can use as antecedents of the new behavior?

_____ Does your plan include specific self-instructions?

_____ Have you planned for physical antecedents to become cues?

_____ Have you asked others to encourage you or structured your social environment to provide helpful antecedents?

IV. Next, consider the issues involved in *developing new behaviors:*

_____ As you try to develop new behaviors, do you use some form of shaping?

_____ If your goal is to decrease an unwanted behavior, are you planning to use some incompatible behavior as a substitute?

_____ If your problem involves anxiety or tension, are you practicing relaxation?

_____ Are you practicing any new behavior you want to develop?

_____ Does your plan call for imagined rehearsal?

_____ Have you made provisions to practice in the real world?

V. Finally, here is a checklist of issues relating to *reinforcement:*

_____ Have you discovered through self-observation what may be reinforcing your unwanted behaviors? If so, have you developed a plan for using that same reinforcement, or an alternate reward, to strengthen a desired behavior instead?

_____ Have you developed a reinforcement plan in which you are rewarded if you take appropriate steps in your plan for self-change?

_____ Does your plan include a token system?

_____ Does your plan include Premack-type reinforcers? Does your plan include verbal self-reinforcement? Does it include reminders of the reinforcement you will receive if you stick to each step of your plan?

_____ Does your plan include any form of precommitted punishment?

_____ Does your plan include an arrangement ensuring that you will be reinforced in the real world for any changes you make in your behavior?

This box packs a lot of information and ideas into a small place. Use it several times to check your plans as they evolve.

help if Laurel learned relaxation and then relaxed herself before approaching the professor. The plan sounds a bit too simple.

Results: "This plan didn't work. I could do steps 1 and 2 okay. But at step 3 I got into trouble because the professor wouldn't quit talking to me, and suddenly I was involved in a complex conversation and became quite nervous. So I worked out a second plan."

Our analysis: Good! Plans should be changed if they don't work.

Plan 2: Here is Laurel's second plan:

The reason the first plan failed was that the professor carried me too far up the schedule. Looking back, it seems inevitable that this would happen. I might have gotten up to 3 minutes, or something like that, but at some point some professor would have just continued talking to me, and I'd be in trouble. I decided to enlist the aid of one particular teacher.

I wrote my self-change project paper early in the semester and handed it in to Prof A., who was teaching the course. In the paper, I explained why my first plan had failed and asked for his help. I included my new schedule:

Step 1. Talk with Prof A. in the hall for 15 seconds.
Step 2. Talk with him for 30 seconds.
Step 3. Talk for 1 minute.
Step 4. Talk for 90 seconds.
Step 5. Increase 30 seconds at a time, up to 5 minutes.

I was going to do each step three times before going on to the next one. There were two parts to this plan. First, I was going to do the talking in the hall. Then, after I got pretty far up the schedule, I was going to repeat the entire sequence in his office, because it was more scary to talk with him in his office than in the hall. After I got to step 4 for talking in the hall, I started step 1 for talking in the office. Even that was too hard, so I put in some new steps:

Step 1a. Just stick my head in and say hello.
Step 1b. Talk for 5 seconds in the office.
Step 1c. Talk for 10 seconds in the office.

Then I went back to the old schedule. Prof A. agreed not to force me to talk longer than I was supposed to. Reinforcer, feedback, and comparison were all the same as before.

Our analysis: The rules are clear, though somewhat complicated. Goals are present, and feedback and record keeping seem adequate. The double shaping plan is complex but sensible. Still no self-instruction, self-praise, or relaxation in the plan.

Plan 3: Again, Laurel revised her plan.

Plan 2 works better. Prof A. and I are now talking up to 3 minutes in the hall and 2 minutes in his office. But I need to be able to generalize from Prof A. to other professors. I have decided to use Prof A. again. Here is my new schedule:

Step 1. Go up to Prof A. while he is talking with another professor and say hello to both of them.
Step 2. Go up and talk to Prof A. while he is talking with another professor. Say at least a sentence to the other one.

Step 3. Talk with the other one for 5 seconds.

Step 4. Talk with the other one for 10 seconds.

Step 5. Talk with the other one for 15 seconds.

Step 6. Talk with the other one for 30 seconds, then on up from there by 15 second jumps.

Prof A. has agreed to cooperate. He'll know where I am in the schedule and will bail me out whenever I complete my time for that particular step. Also, some professors seem unfriendly to me, and others are pretty good, so I will go up to Prof A. only when he is talking with one of the friendly ones.

Our analysis: This is a critical step, for Laurel is building the new behavior so she can use it in a variety of situations. Also, she has realized that an unfriendly professor is a different antecedent situation than a friendly one, and she has decided to deal with the easier antecedent, the friendly professor.

Plan 3 was apparently successful. By semester's end, Laurel was able to talk with several friendly professors, which she considered a significant improvement. She was wise to change plans when the first plan didn't work. Her plans were generally explicit. Her rules were clear. Her goals were divided into subgoals, and the standards for advancing were made explicit in plans 2 and 3. Her data collection was careful.

We spoke with her several months after the course ended and asked her why she hadn't included relaxation in her plan. She said she really didn't know, but pointed out she could always have backed up and used it if all else had failed. "Besides, I was right, wasn't I? Must have been—I'm talking to you!"

Make Your Plan a Contract

Once you have chosen your plan and decided on each of its elements, write it out and sign it (Kanfer, 1975). This written plan becomes a contract with yourself. The contract should list your rules as well as your goals and subgoals, and it should specify how you will collect feedback. This is not just a fanciful idea: A formal contract increases your chances of success (Griffin & Watson, 1978; Seidner, 1973).

Display your contract. Keep it in your notebook or on your mirror. Make it clear and explicit. When it becomes necessary to change the plan, rewrite the contract, and sign the new one.

Evaluating Your Plan for Change

Does your plan work? This seems like a simple question, and sometimes you can answer it with a clear yes or no. The person who never smokes again, the man who has a female friend for the first time in his life, the overweight person who drops 10 pounds and keeps them off—all these self-modifiers know they are succeeding. They don't need elaborate techniques for assessing their progress.

Often, however, progress is gradual rather than dramatic. Because the change is slow, people misjudge their progress, and underrate the progress they are making. Those who don't rely on their data may be tempted to stop a plan even though it is succeeding, simply because they believe that it is failing.

It is crucial that you record your behavior throughout the operation of your plan, because recording gives you the data you need to know if the plan is having the desired effect. To organize your data to view your progress, you can

- calculate an average,
- calculate percentages, or
- use a graph.

Finding Averages

Weekly averages smooth out the record and usually provide a more reliable picture than daily fluctuations. They can clarify a confusing set of numbers.

Sidney's goal was to reduce his anxiety about talking to women, with the long-term goal of finding a girlfriend. He began a plan that required him to telephone some female acquaintance each evening and talk to her for at least 5 minutes. He used several techniques to aid him in this, and rated on a 5-point scale the degree of anxiety he felt during each phone call. A rating of 1 indicated he was perfectly calm, while 5 meant he was near panic; 3 was "somewhat tense." For the first week, his ratings were: 2, 3, 4, 2, 3, 3, 2. For the second week, they were: 2, 3, 2, 3, 2, 2, 2. Was he making progress?

To compute the average—or mean—amount of anxiety he felt each week, Sidney added the scores for that week and divided by 7, the number of days in the week. For the first week, the total was 19, which divided by 7 gives 2.7. For the second week, the total was 16, which divided by 7 is 2.3. Sid could see that he was making some progress.

Finding Percentages

Tamara began dieting by keeping careful records of the situations in which she ate too much or ate inappropriately. She realized that she ate too fast, too often ate junk food while at work, ate too much at supper, and often had a late-night snack. Each of these situations called for some self-control technique, such as pausing for 2 minutes during a meal. But, Tamara reported, she was using the techniques on only a hit-or-miss basis. So she began keeping records of the number of times an opportunity to use a technique came up, as well as the number of times she actually used one. "That way, I could know the percentage of time I was doing what I needed to do in order to lose weight, and I could try to gradually increase the percentage of time I was coping."

During the first week, Tamara counted 28 opportunities to use some self-control technique in connection with her eating. She actually used a technique 8 times. To compute the percentage of times she used a technique when she could, she divided 8 by 28, which gave her 28.6%. Now her goal was to increase the percentage of times she used a technique when the chance arose.

To compute a percentage, divide the number of times an event occurred by the total number of times it could have occurred. If you were assertive 3 times last week, and there were 6 times when you could have been assertive, your percentage is 3 divided by 6, or 50%.

Percentages can be examined across periods of time to see if you are changing. We recommend using average weekly comparisons rather than daily.

Making Graphs

Each day you gather your observations, and by the end of a few weeks you have so many pieces of information that interpreting them can become difficult. By putting them all together on a graph, you can see your progress or lack of it.

Box 8-2
Working in Groups

Some people like to work with others who are also carrying out self-change projects, and sometimes an instructor will assign students to groups to consult with each other. Working with others can be very helpful—two or more heads being better than one—especially if the people working together follow a few rules on being helpful.

On being a good listener. If you are going to be helpful to others, or get help yourself, you have to listen to them. This means observing these principles:

Listen so that if you were suddenly asked what the person was saying, you could paraphrase it. Really pay attention. Later people will pay attention to you.

Try not to interrupt.

Ask for information. The more you know the easier it is to help by producing new ideas.

Encourage others to continue giving information with comments like, "Mmm hmm," or "Tell me more about that." Don't jump right in with something to say; give the speaker a chance to continue after a moment's pause.

When you do offer an idea, be very considerate of the other person's feelings. Avoid giving directions by saying things like, "You should do this or that. . . ." Instead try, "Have you considered . . . ," or "What works for me is . . ." Putting the other down by saying things like, "Boy, how can you be so dumb! You've never done the steps at the end of the chapters! No wonder you're failing!" only alienates the listener. Messages are only effective if the other person is willing to listen to them calmly.

On being a good helper. If a person is having problems with the self-change project, it is because some of the principles in this book are not being followed. As a helper, you are looking for principles that might be followed, but are not. Focus on the stumbling block, and try to think of techniques you have read about here to deal with it.

First, find out if the person has done the steps at the end of each chapter. If not, that's where to begin.

Second, use Box 8-1 to get ideas for the person to use. For example, if a student wants to increase his assertiveness, but is not using shaping, you might suggest that shaping is a good idea and discuss specifically how to do it.

Third, don't just lay out your ideas. Try to brainstorm with the person, thinking of many ways of dealing with problems.

Fourth, offer any ideas you have in terms of specifics, not abstractions. "I think you ought to use verbal self-reinforcement when you are successful," is more effective than, "You've got to get hold of yourself."

Fifth, don't just look for problems. Don't just be negative. People will have partial successes, and it helps them if you notice that. Try to comment on the successful parts of the person's plan.

Some computer programs will make graphs for you; all you have to do is type in the numbers. Just in case you do not have access to such a program, here are step-by-step instructions on how to do it manually.

Marlene wants to increase her studying. For one semester, she has kept a record of how many hours she studied each week. Here is her record for the semester: 8, $9^{1}/_{4}$, $9^{3}/_{4}$, $9^{1}/_{2}$, $9^{1}/_{2}$, $10^{1}/_{4}$, $10^{3}/_{4}$, $10^{3}/_{4}$, 8, $9^{1}/_{2}$, $10^{1}/_{4}$, 11, $8^{1}/_{4}$, $12^{1}/_{4}$, $10^{1}/_{4}$. With that long string of numbers, it's hard to see whether or not there is an upward progression. With the help of a graph, Marlene can see quite easily whether there is any upward movement over the semester.

On graph paper, Marlene draws the *horizontal axis,* near the bottom of the page, and divides it into 16 marks, one for each week of the semester. Then, beginning at the zero point on the horizontal axis, she draws a vertical line up and marks off 14 equally spaced points on it, one for each hour per week she might have studied. (Her maximum goal was 14 hours.) This is called the *vertical axis.*

Always put the passage of time—minutes, days, weeks—on the horizontal axis and the goal—records of the target behaviors—on the vertical axis. The point where the two lines meet should be the zero point for both lines. Figure 8-2 shows Marlene's graph.

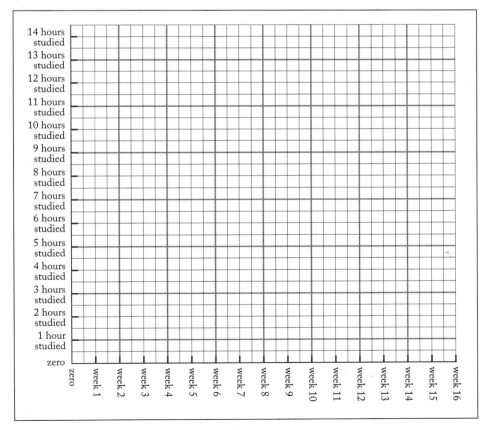

Figure 8-2 The horizontal and vertical axes of a graph

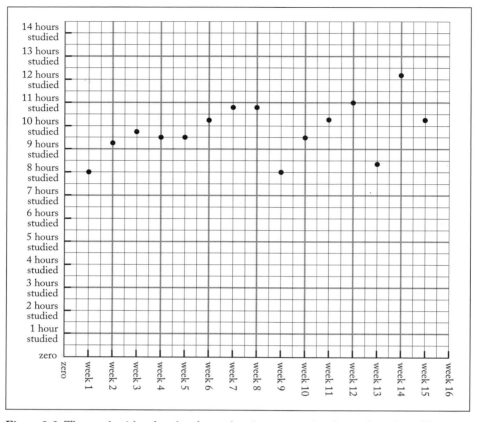

Figure 8-3 The graph with a dot placed at each point representing the total number of hours studied that week

Marlene has a record of the total number of hours she studied each week for 15 of the 16 weeks of the semester. For week 1, the total number of hours was 8. She goes up in a straight line from the spot for week 1 on the horizontal axis, until that line is opposite "8 hours studied." Where the two lines on the graph paper intersect, Marlene makes a dot. She repeats this process for each of the 15 weeks for which she has data, each time connecting the week—for example, week 8—with the total number of hours she studied that week—for example, 10¾. Figure 8-3 shows her graph with all the dots in place.

To make her progress (or lack of it) even clearer, Marlene connects each point on the graph to the next one, moving from left to right. That gives her a finished graph, illustrated in Figure 8-4. On this graph, each point on the horizontal and vertical lines is numbered, and the whole line is labeled "weeks of the semester" or "hours studied."

The custom is to write only the numbers along each axis and to use labels underneath and at the side to describe what the numbers stand for, as in Figures 8-5 and 8-6.

Sometimes it is unnecessary to include all the numbers on the vertical line. Suppose you are working on losing weight, and your weekly weight varies between 148 and 135 pounds over a semester. It would be silly to start the vertical line at 0 pounds and

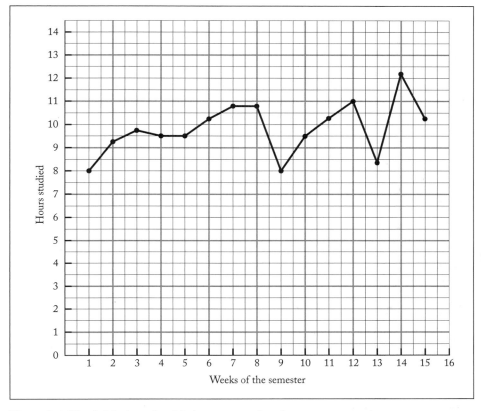

Figure 8-4 The finished graph, with dots connected to show pattern over time

mark off 135 pounds on it before you got to one you would use in making the graph. Instead, break the line to indicate that you are not starting at 0 (see Figure 8-5).

Using the Graph

By inspecting her graph, Marlene could see her data quite clearly. Her pattern was one of general progress, slow and steady, with minor fluctuations, except for weeks 9 and 13. She reviewed her daily logs for those weeks and found that during both she had been ill for several days. Marlene concluded that her time-management plan was working rather well. She resolved to continue it for the following semester.

More than one behavior can be recorded on the same graph, illustrated by the following student's records. Tom wanted to increase the number of comments he made in his classes. He found it difficult to speak in public because he was afraid others would think that his comments were silly or trivial. This fear was particularly acute in large classes, in which he felt that whatever he wanted to say had to be good enough to justify taking the time of so many people.

Tom decided to begin by practicing in small classes and then, if that worked, trying it in larger classes. His goal was to speak at least once per day in a class. "My reinforcer was playing in my rock group. This is a very powerful reinforcer for me in two

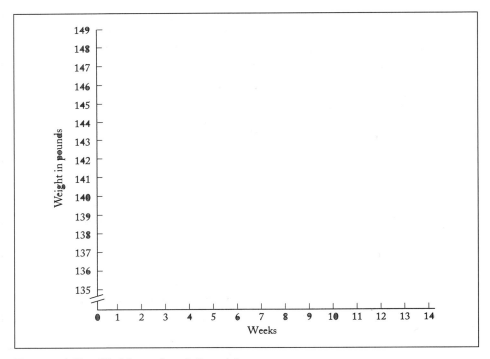

Figure 8-5 Simplified form of graph for weight

ways: I really enjoy playing guitar; and if I didn't show up for a gig, five other guys would wring my neck."

Figure 8-6 is a graph of Tom's data. Notice that in making his graph he counted only school days, so each week has only 5 days. He always had his notebook with him when he went to class, so it was easy for him to make a simple check on a sheet of paper every time he spoke up.

Tom's graph shows a rapid improvement in his speaking behavior in small classes. Beginning on the first day of his plan, he spoke up in class, and within 4 days he was engaging in what he called "constant participation." Most people progress at a slower rate, as Tom himself did when he went into the second stage of his plan—speaking in large classes. You can see from the graph that he did make some progress, but his improvements were interspersed with setbacks—days on which he didn't talk at all. This is the kind of situation in which a graph is particularly helpful, for it shows that you are making some progress.

Tips for Typical Topics

Look up your particular goal in the Subject Index at the back of the book, and read each section of the book in which that kind of goal or problem is discussed. This will give you ideas for your plan or remind you of anything you have forgotten. Remember that most

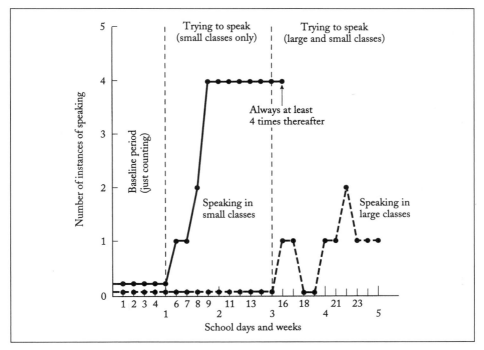

Figure 8-6 Speaking in class

plans fail because people forget to use the techniques, so reminding yourself of them is a good idea.

Chapter Summary

Combining A, B, and C Elements

Good plans for change must include record keeping and elements of antecedent control, the development of new behaviors, and control of consequences.

You should expect that problems will arise, and you need to be prepared to use more than one approach. For example, you may need to approach the problem in two stages or more.

Use a two-stage process for dealing with high-risk situations. First, avoid the controlling antecedents. Second, develop new behaviors to be performed in response to the old cue. Like any new behaviors, these will have to be shaped, practiced, and reinforced. You should develop options to put into action when you have to deal with risky situations and work out plans to put the options into action.

The Elements of a Good Plan

Good plans have:

1. Rules that state the techniques to use in specific situations;
2. Goals and subgoals;

3. Feedback about your behavior based on your self-observations;
4. A comparison of the feedback to your goals and subgoals to see if you are progressing; and
5. Adjustments in the plan as conditions change.

You should try to learn from your mistakes and try to develop skills to deal with the frustrations you will feel when you make mistakes. Sometimes you will want to begin again with a new target, rethinking each aspect of the plan for possible change.

Before designing your final plan, review the checklist of important elements to consider and be sure that you can answer yes to most of the questions. Be creative in designing your plan; use the brainstorming technique to generate more ideas.

Evaluating Your Plan for Change

The data you collect through your observations will lead you to certain decisions about your plan. Your record can be in the form of averages, percentages, or a graph.

Your Own Self-Direction Project: Step 8

1. State your goal. If it is a complex goal or one that will take a long time to achieve, state the first short-term goal. State your current level of performance. Your baseline records provide you with information to use in setting your subgoals.
2. State specific rules for each subgoal. What behaviors will you have to perform in each situation to achieve the subgoal? Examine the three preliminary plans you prepared in Chapters 5, 6, and 7, and consider various alternatives. You may select features from only one of your preliminary plans or combine elements from all of them.
3. Be sure to get accurate self-observations and feedback all along the way, and compare your performance to your goals.
4. Fill out the checklist in Box 8-1 about the plan you are considering. Incorporate as many different techniques as you can. Write out your plan in detail, following the steps described above. Sign your contract, and begin implementing it.

Chapter 9

Problem Solving
and Relapse Prevention

Outline and Learning Objectives

Problem Solving

1. Explain the tinkering strategy for dealing with self-change projects.
2. What are the four steps in problem solving? How can they be applied to your project?
3. Describe the research on the value of problem solving.
4. How do failures in self-observation contribute to failure in self-modification?
5. What are four reasons people have problems with their attention to the target problem?
6. What are the causes of self-control fatigue? What can you do to combat it?
7. What are common obstacles or goals to self-change? What can be done to cope with each?

Relapse Prevention

8. Outline fully the relapse process. What is the difference between a lapse and relapse?
9. Explain the abstinence violation effect.
10. What are four common high-risk situations?
11. How can you identify your personal high-risk situations?
12. Explain how to use problem solving for high-risk situations.
13. List the kinds of self-instructions you should prepare for coping with high-risk situations.
14. How can you stop lapses from becoming a relapse?
    a. What should you do as soon as you lapse?
    b. What kind of self-contract and reminder card should you prepare in advance?
15. Explain the idea of consenting to the bad habit. What can you do to counteract consenting?

Chapter Summary

Your Own Self-Direction Project: Step 9

Problem Solving

Problems can occur while you are engaged in self-modification, or they can come up after you are finished. For example, you might move along well with your exercise project for a few weeks but then not be able to make any more progress. Or you might finish a self-change project, such as stopping excessive drinking, only to find to your dismay that the problem behavior has come back. In this chapter, we deal with both kinds of problems: those that come up while you are actively engaged in self-modification and threats of relapse that occur afterward.

It often happens that your first plan is not enough by itself to change the target behavior. After you begin, you discover something that makes it more difficult to manage than you anticipated. We've said this more than once, because if you act on it, your chances of success are much greater: *Expect that there will be problems.*

Tinkering with Your Plan

Start with the best plan you can devise. See what difficulties occur, and then tinker with the plan, making it more effective in dealing with the unexpected problems.

Rebecca wrote:

There was this person I worked with, Jean, whom I really didn't like at all. As a Christian, I know that loving one another is an important command. But I couldn't bring myself to love Jean—not with *agape* [God's love]. She felt the same way, which made it worse.

Rebecca decided to work out a self-change plan with the goal of increasing *agape* for Jean. Her plan seemed sound. She wrote a detailed contract that included six shaping steps for talking to Jean in a friendly way.

Step 1: Smile at Jean at least once a day at work.
Step 2: Smile and say "Hi."
Step 3: Go up and ask her, "How's everything?"
Step 4: Compliment her on something.
Step 5: Talk about upcoming events at work.
Step 6: Talk about anything else.

Rebecca gathered records carefully on a steno tablet. Her reinforcement system used candy as an immediate reward for being nice to Jean and tokens to be used to buy favorite things as longer-term reinforcers.

Results: "The first two steps worked fine, but when I asked Jean, 'How's everything?' I caught her off guard, and she talked so much that I became uncomfortable and wanted to withdraw. While I felt ready to approach her, I wasn't ready for her response. So I revised my plan."

In Rebecca's second plan, she dealt with a problem that she had not foreseen when she devised her first plan. She tinkered with her old plan, changing elements here and there in an effort to make the plan work better.

I shared this new plan with one of my closest friends. He works with me and knows of my problem. I told him that I would let him know when I was planning to talk with Jean and asked him to give me about 2 minutes and then call me to his office. That way I had enough time to exchange friendly greetings with Jean, without feeling uncomfortable.

The reinforcers were the same, and the record keeping continued.

Results: "The 2-minute limit worked really well. If I felt like talking to Jean longer, I'd just ask my friend to please wait until I was finished. Also, I dropped the idea of complimenting Jean so deliberately. I felt this wouldn't be sincere. I decided that if she did something I felt I could honestly compliment, I would do so."

After 7 weeks, Rebecca wrote: "I can honestly say that things are now fine between Jean and me. The plan really helped."

Here's a second example of tinkering with a plan to make it more effective. A 55-year-old man in our class submitted this final report:

My goal: I wanted to build up to running a mile or so every other day. At the time I began, I had never run at all, so my baseline was zero.

Antecedents: What I needed was an antecedent that would get me started! I really don't think I refrained from running because I would get painfully winded or anything. It's just that there always seemed to be something else to do, so I didn't start. Going for a run requires all sorts of behaviors—putting on the shoes and shorts, stretching, then starting to run.

Intervention plan: My first plan was to require myself to run a quarter of a mile or more every day. I intended to gradually increase my running up to a mile or so. My self-contract was that I would get a dollar to spend on anything I wanted for every time I ran.

This plan worked for the first 4 days, but after that I just sort of quit. It became painfully obvious that the plan was not working. So I listed all the reasons why it was not working:

- I've never run a mile, and it seems like a long way to run.
- I'm afraid I might give myself a heart attack.
- I tell myself, "It's too far, and it could be dangerous."
- It seems like a lot of trouble.
- I find all sorts of excuses for not going running.

I decided that I probably wouldn't have a heart attack if I ran really slowly. I made a mental note to ask my doctor about it the next time I had a checkup. I also decided that the main reason I didn't go out was that it just seemed like a long way for a duffer like me to go. I guess the main reason I quit was that I was starting too high. Then I remembered the shaping rule about not starting too high. "Why should I expect to be able to start that high?" I asked myself. And I redesigned my plan as follows:

Stage 1: Put on footwear and clothes, and walk around the house (30 yards).
Stage 2: Walk around the house twice (60 yards).
Stage 3: Walk around the house four times (120 yards).
Stage 4: Walk around the house six times (180 yards).

Stage 5: Once I get to this point, I will run a quarter of a mile. When I can do that, I will try to increase to half a mile, then three-quarters of a mile, and then finally 1 mile.

I did several things to make sure that I stuck to this ridiculously easy shaping schedule.

First, I established the rule that I have to do my "run" before I can have a beer or eat supper. *Second,* I explained the whole thing to my wife and told her that I really wanted to build up exercising this way. I precommitted myself to do it by asking her (1) to remind me to do it, (2) to call me on it if she saw me eating or drinking a beer before I had done my exercise, and (3) to check on my progress by examining the chart I keep posted on the kitchen cupboard on which I record my daily progress. *Third,* I set aside 5 minutes each morning to imagine resisting the temptation to have a beer or eat when I come home. I imagine coming home and saying to myself, "Wow, it's time to relax after another hard day!" I see myself getting a can of beer, and, just as I'm about to pop the top, I practice resisting this urge and saying to myself, "But first, I'll go for a short run."

At the time of this writing, I am able to run a quarter of a mile regularly and hope to be able to increase it.

Several things had interfered with the man's progress: old reinforcers (having a beer as soon as he got home), thoughts (thinking he might have a heart attack), doubts (thinking a mile is too far), and shaping errors (starting too high).

When you are tinkering with a plan that is not working, ask yourself some questions: What makes it difficult to perform the target behavior? Is it some thought I am having? Is it something I have no control over? (Remember the example of Rebecca finding that Jean talked to her too much.) Am I being reinforced for a behavior that makes my desired behavior difficult (such as having a beer and sitting down instead of going for a run)?

Use the ideas of antecedents, behaviors, and consequences to analyze the obstacles to performing your target behavior:

Antecedents: What antecedents make it difficult to perform the target behavior, or what antecedents are lacking that would make it easier to perform?

Behaviors: Have the correct incompatible or alternate behaviors been chosen?

Consequences: Are there still consequences that maintain the old, undesired behavior?

Systematic Problem Solving

Problem solving means thinking about the obstacles to your progress and figuring out how to overcome them. *You need to be able to define the problem clearly, think of solutions, and predict the consequences of various alternatives* (D'Zurilla, 1986; Kelly, Scott, Prue, & Rychtarik, 1985). Learning to solve problems in life allows you more flexibility and independence in coping and gives you confidence for dealing with other problems in the future (Chang, D'Zurilla, & Sanna, 2004; D'Zurilla & Nezu, 1989).

To solve a problem, follow this four-step process (D'Zurilla & Goldfried, 1971; D'Zurilla & Nezu, 1982):

1. List all the details of the problem as concretely as possible.
2. Brainstorm as many solutions as you can without criticizing any of them. (See below for how to do this.)

3. Choose one or more of the solutions.
4. Think of ways to put the solutions into operation, and then check to be sure you are actually implementing them.

In taking these four steps, expect to go back and forth from listing details to listing possible solutions, perhaps through several cycles.

Each step in the process is a skill, and you will get better at each the more you practice it (D'Zurilla, Nezu, & Maydeu-Olivaries, 2004). If you practice problem solving you will see that you gradually get better at solving problems, and this will increase your belief, your self-efficacy, that you can solve problems. It builds self-confidence if you try it.

The following examples illustrate how each of these four steps can be used to overcome obstacles in your self-change program.

Listing the details. Kalani, a college sophomore, was concerned with both his health and appearance. He wrote:

> I've known for years that I overeat. Finally, I began keeping records of when I overeat—at what particular times I go off my diet. I listed these as the details of my problem. They were surprisingly regular. I often ate two or three bowls of popcorn while watching TV. I always overate after exercising on Mondays. I usually ate three or four snacks on Saturdays. So it wasn't that I overate all the time—just in specific situations. I set out to deal with those particular situations.

That is a common experience. A person thinks of some problem in an abstract way—"I overeat"—but when listing the problem's details, specific situations come up, and the problem-solving efforts can be focused directly on those.

This is a liberating idea. When something goes wrong, it's not our personality that is at fault. It's the effect of some specific situation on our behavior. Diagnose the details and you can cope with the problem.

A woman who wanted to give up drinking coffee wrote:

> I made up a plan to stop drinking coffee, but after a few days it ground to a halt. Then I made a new plan, but it also fizzled. So I listed the details of what was happening when I went off my plan. I noticed that I'd be thinking, "I need this coffee for energy." So I started a new plan to give myself some energy when I needed it, using meditation, and after that it was a lot easier to give up coffee.

Remember the old saying, "The devil is in the details." Be ready to consider them more than once: List details, brainstorm a bit, think of more details, begin choosing solutions, think of more details. Each time you are improving your problem solution.

Brainstorming many alternatives. Brainstorming means thinking of as many solutions to a problem as you can, and without criticizing any idea. One of our colleagues brainstormed a list of things to do when she wanted a cigarette: Chew gum, eat mints, do calisthenics, walk, brush teeth, drink coffee, work with plants, cook, pay bills, make a phone call, mend clothing, iron, shop, groom, shower, take a hot bath, clean closets, drink water, fiddle with hands, smell something pleasant, and so on. When she found herself craving a cigarette, she took out her list and did one or more of the things on it.

Brainstorming many solutions to a problem is important because our best ideas are often not the first ones we think of. Remember not to be critical during the brainstorming process. Our colleague mentioned above told us, "At first it seemed crazy that things like cleaning the closet could help distract me from my need for a cigarette, but they really did help me." If you require yourself to think of many solutions you are more likely to think of creative ones and are also able to combine several solutions into a master plan.

Choosing an alternative. Ruby's goal was to engage in race walking three times a week:

> After 2 weeks I had to acknowledge that I was not keeping records because there was nothing to record. I felt I was already too busy, and the plan to race-walk three times a week was just one more thing I had to do. I needed to have some fun, so I made a list of all the things I could do for fun that would also give me some exercise: weight lifting, ice skating, cross-country skiing, stationary biking, using a walking machine, using a step machine. I selected ice skating and set a goal to go skating once or twice weekly.

Putting the new plan into operation and checking to be sure it's working. Ruby continued:

> I had to force myself to make skating a priority, but I succeeded in going once a week for eight weeks. Although I often didn't want to go, I enjoyed it once I got there. I kept a record, making a check mark each week when I did go. After eight weeks, I started going twice a week. Now I have to say, I absolutely love skating!

Here is an example of a full problem-solving approach. Larry's target behavior was to stop drinking so many colas at work. He drank several cans every day. He succeeded in reducing his habit, but then he changed jobs and became a night taxi driver. Within a few weeks, he was back to drinking several cans each night to keep himself awake, but then he had trouble going to sleep later.

Larry listed all the relevant details of the problem:

- It keeps me high.
- There are convenient machine outlets on practically every corner.
- I tell myself that it helps me stay awake.

Then he listed possible solutions:

- Tell myself, "Don't do it, Larry," whenever I approach a vending machine.
- Keep a record in the cab and a total record at home.
- Get another job.
- Substitute some less harmful drink.
- Buy the drink, then throw it in the rubbish.
- Get fully adjusted to working at night, so I don't have to use the drinks to stay awake.
- Keep track of all the money I'm spending on colas.

Larry finally decided to do three things: (1) tell himself, "Don't do it"; (2) keep a record of the money he spent and the number of colas he drank each day; and (3) go to small stores where he could buy fruit juice instead of colas. Results: "It worked very well.

I haven't touched a cola since I started this project. I have become an orange juice freak instead."

Temptations: Use problem solving. Use problem solving to think of ways of dealing with temptations. David goes to a picnic lunch with his own raw vegetables, intending to eat only them, ready to reject the fat-loaded hot dogs. But suddenly there appears his beloved favorite, apple pie! Whoops! He has two pieces. He wasn't prepared for the temptation.

Slips like David's can be reduced through problem solving. Many beginners expect that they "have enough willpower" to guide them through unanticipated tempting situations. David, for example, thought that he would have no trouble at the picnic with cake or muffins. But the apple pie was unanticipated and "willpower" was not enough. He needed a plan specifically for apple pie, which was such a strong stimulus for his eating.

In Chapter 2 you read about constructing if . . . then plans, ideas you would follow if certain conditions come up. Use problem solving to construct these. David, for example, thinks to himself, "Okay, I was taken by surprise by the apple pie and ate too much. It figures. What should I do if this happens again?" He then goes into a problem solving activity: listing the details, thinking of solutions, trying to pick the best solution, and deciding to keep records to be sure he does it when he needs to. "OK, I could have just one piece, have even a small piece, or say, 'No thanks,' or turn away from the pie, or say, 'No, thanks, I'm on a diet.'"

The Value of Problem Solving

People who do not use problem-solving ideas are less likely to succeed in their self-modification efforts (Fitzgibbon & Kirschenbaum, 1992). Richards and Perri (1978), for example, trained students who were concerned about academic underachievement and who wanted to develop better study skills. The researchers trained some of these students to use simple problem-solving strategies when they ran into problems. Others got no such training. There was a rapid deterioration in study skills among the students who used no problem-solving strategies. When they encountered new situations with new problems, they failed to use their new study techniques. By contrast, the students who used problem-solving techniques were able to maintain their improved study skills up to 1 year after completion of their training.

In another study, obese women who were trained to use problem solving to deal with problems in dieting were more likely to lose 10% of their body weight and keep it off than were women who used standard techniques but no problem solving (Perri et al., 2001).

The technique has been so successful that these days it is used to aid in the treatment of anxiety, depression, substance abuse, marital problems, prevention of unwanted pregnancy, poor performance in college, and weight control (Nezu, 2004; Nezu, D'Zurilla, Zwick, & Nezu, 2004). People who learn problem solving are more likely to cope effectively with stress (D'Zurilla, 1990; D'Zurilla & Chang, 1995), and cancer patients and their caretakers who use problem solving reduce the distress associated with the disease (Nezu, Nezu, Felgoise, McClure, & Houts, 2003).

If your first plan falters, notice what parts were successful and for how long. Keep the successful features in your later plans. If you stop smoking for 6 days and then have a cigarette, don't get down on yourself. Instead, ask yourself, "What went wrong on the seventh day?" Use problem solving to deal with that.

A man who successfully completed a project to stop procrastinating reported:

> A year or so later, I started a new project—to increase social skills. It didn't work well. I knew my earlier project had been a real success, so I checked back to see what techniques I had used to stop procrastinating. In all, I had used six different techniques, and I could see that four of them could easily be modified for use in my new project. So I branched out, adding these techniques to my current plan, and now my social-skills plan is working.

Carol, studying this textbook in a night class, demonstrated some excellent problem solving:

> Last year I was trying to manage my time better. I was newly back in college while coping with a divorce at the same time. A lot of the time I was just too stressed to do much about time management, until I finally realized that I should try problem solving. The next time my time management program didn't work I listed the details of the problem, and of course one of the big issues was that I often felt a lot of stress. I'd feel so stressed out I'd freak and blow off my schedule. So I added daily exercise to my program as a way of dealing with the stress, and my time management got a lot better, too.

Dealing with Problems in Self-Modification

Efforts to change are not always successful. Understanding the reasons for failure at self-modification can help you be on guard. What blocks success? What can you do to achieve success?

Self-change requires self-focus. When people fail at self-change, the most common reason is lack of adequate self-observation. When weight watchers, for example, stop keeping track of the food they eat, they are much more likely to stop their good eating habits (Kirschenbaum, 1994). Focus on the behaviors you are trying to build. You are engaged in a very deliberate process, in which you are trying to overcome old, unwanted habits or develop new habits. This requires concentration.

A middle-aged woman wrote:

> After I finished your course, I continued exercising four times a week. It was the first time in my life that I'd ever been able to stick to an exercise schedule, and I kept records for several months to be sure I wouldn't quit. Then my husband and I went on a month's vacation. My daily schedule was completely different than it had been at home, and I quit keeping records. Perhaps that's why I stopped thinking about exercising. By the time the month was over, I had hardly exercised at all. When we returned home, I put my record sheet back up on the refrigerator door, and within 2 weeks I was back to my old aerobic self.

Several factors interfere with continued self-observation:

- stress;
- alcohol; and
- discouragement in your self-change project.

Stress. Stress takes your attention away from self-change. One theory suggests that during stress our attention turns to controlling our emotional frustrations, leaving no focus for other aspects of self-control (Baumeister & Heatherton, 1996; Baumeister, Heatherton, & Tice, 1994). All self-control doesn't break down under stress, but that which requires intense focus suffers because our attention goes elsewhere. Only well practiced, habitual, automatic self-control continues. Lucinda said to us:

> Three years ago, after my boyfriend died, I started eating to comfort myself, and began putting on weight. I tried to go on a diet, but couldn't stick to it. Life was just too hard—what with the grieving, and working, and taking care of the kids. I just couldn't think about dieting. Now I'm a lot better; life is smoother. Maybe now I can think about a reasonable way of eating.

When people are already under stress, it is harder for them to engage in serious self-change projects, and they are more likely to fail (Cohen & Lichtenstein, 1990; Goodall & Halford, 1991; Kirschenbaum, 1987). In these circumstances, the best approach is to develop a self-modification project to cope with the stress itself. Carol, for example, began an exercise program. Once your stress level is lowered, you can work on your other goals for change.

For some people, the target problem is directly connected to stress; for example, drinking to get stress relief. If this is true of you, your first task should be to learn new ways to cope with stress, such as by exercise.

Alcohol. One of the effects of alcohol is to narrow our focus of attention and particularly to take our focus off ourselves (Hull, 1987). In fact, that's why we like alcohol: A drink or two at a party takes away our self-consciousness so we can act in a more relaxed way. But this same distraction of our attention makes it less likely that we will continue to observe the new behaviors we are trying to develop. Smokers are more likely to have a cigarette, weight watchers are more likely to overeat, and people who lose their tempers are more likely to blow up after drinking (Niaura et al., 1988). Any time you're tempted—to overeat, drink too much, tell someone off—you are more likely to give in if you've been drinking. Alcohol is also a depressant, so using it makes it less likely that you will do such things as engage in exercise or work after drinking. A married couple we knew, for example, decided to stop having any drinks when they discussed their marital problems, for they found their self-control slipped destructively after even two glasses of wine, and they said things they later regretted.

Discouragement in your self-change project. If your project is not working, there is a real temptation to stop self-observation because continuing to keep records is embarrassing or humiliating. You don't want to keep records because you hate what the records tell you.

Yet keeping records even when you are not being successful at self-change increases your chances of later success. Good self-observations bring greater understanding of the antecedents and consequences of your behavior.

Originally Vera's complaint was loneliness. But after days of self-observation, she realized that to some degree she was the cause of her loneliness because of her attitude toward casual social exchanges. She wrote:

> I thought I was lonely because there was no one I was close to. I kept looking over the available men in my life, thinking one of them could be my boyfriend, and then

I'd never be lonely anymore. But none of them measured up. So I kept on being lonely. I thought the cause was a general lack of interesting men. I wasn't paying any attention to my own thoughts. When I recorded the thoughts I was having when I dealt with men, it became clear that the thoughts were very negative. I'd meet one of the men I knew and think, "Here goes another dull conversation. God, why are people so dull?"

After keeping records on my thoughts for a few days, I could see that this was a pattern. I want to get right into important, meaningful conversations. So I have these negative thoughts when I get into situations that involve small talk. The trouble is, all social situations involve small talk. You don't just meet somebody and start right off talking about the meaning of life.

So it finally dawned on me that my thoughts were creating the problem. I had to quit being so negative about chatting, because that is how you start to get to know people. That's the project I'm working on now. I think of those conversations as "openers," not "small talk."

Unrealistic goals are another source of discouragement. People who want to lose weight sometimes have an overly optimistic goal, but then become discouraged when they don't reach this (close to impossible) goal. So they give up and regain all they have lost (Polivy & Herman, 2002). For example, Penny started out weighing 190, wanted to get to 120, actually got to 150, looked a lot better and was healthier, but gave up because she wasn't "thin" and regained back up to 195. Don't get discouraged because you haven't attained perfection. It's a lot better to be somewhat better off, even if not perfect, than to still be in your original, unhappy state.

Self-Control Fatigue

Exercising self-control can be tiring, and your level of self-control can become fatigued and decline if you use it continuously (Baumeister, Bratslavsky, Muraven, & Tice, 1998). No one really thinks self-control is a muscle, but sometimes it acts like one, becoming fatigued and not working as well with continued use. If you resist temptation for a long period of time, your chances of continuing to resist go down, as though your self-control is weakened. This has interesting implications.

First, when you are confronted with temptation, it's safest to get out of the situation. If you stay there, continuing to resist, your self-control may weaken and you will give in. Long-term resistance to temptation weakens our strength of resistance. Sitting beside the chocolate cake at a buffet dinner is a recipe for disaster. You may at first resist the cake, but sooner or later you are likely to give in to it.

Second, when you resist one temptation for a long time, you may give in when a second one comes along (Schmeichel & Baumeister, 2004). You resist the cake, but then cave in to the doughnuts. Too many temptations coming too quickly can overcome self-control (Baumeister & Vohs, 2003). Knowing this can put you on guard. If you realize you're confronting a series of temptations, the best thing is to avoid, or flee, the situation. That way, you are still in control.

Third, you are more likely to make bad self-control decisions late in the day (Baumeister & Heatherton, 1996). An interesting research finding of the last few years is that our level or strength of self-control is not the same all day long. It's as if you've been exercising self-control all day, and now are tired, so you go off your diet or smoke a cigarette or lose your tempter. Knowing about this late-in-the-day effect, you can watch out for it, guard against it. "Be careful, it's getting late, and I can fall off the wagon now."

Sometimes people give in to an unwanted urge just because they are tired of exercising self-control all day long (Sayette, 2004). It's as if we think, "Oh, to hell with it. I'm tired of fighting it. I'll just have one." Later, of course, comes the regret. *Use distraction to deal with this problem.* That way, you're not focused on the effortful self-control so much, so you are less likely to be tired and cave in.

For all these problems in self-control, distraction may be the best solution. Instead of fighting temptation face to face, you distract yourself from it. That lessens the tension you feel in controlling yourself, and thus decreases the chance of self-control fatigue.

Increasing your positive mood also helps. When we feel negative we are less likely to exercise the self-control we want (Tice, Baumeister, & Zhang, 2004), but feeling positive increases the staying power of our self-control attempts. So put on a happy face. If you are feeling negative, realize this increases the chances you will give in to temptation, so first focus on improving your mood to keep your self-control alive.

Common Problems in Designing a Better Plan

In Chapter 2 we dealt with a series of obstacles to change. Let's now consider these issues again, in the light of your experience in designing and trying out your self-change efforts.

You don't believe the techniques will help you, so you don't use them. More than 220 people who were trying to stop smoking were asked how they coped with temptations to smoke. Helpful techniques were: distracting themselves, escaping from the situation, physical activity, thinking of the health consequences, delaying, and eating or drinking. They also listed two "techniques" that did *not* help: self-punishment for smoking and trying simply to exert willpower to resist temptation (Shiffman, 1984). Yet some people persist in the belief that the best way to gain self-control is through self-punishment or by simple force of willpower.

If you don't use the techniques, you won't change. In one research study, people who used no self-change techniques were "least successful" in their attempts to lose weight, while people who used techniques such as increasing activity, planning for change, and positive self-talk were "most successful" (Head & Brookhart, 1997).

If you are not sure what to do, try these steps to increase your efforts (Tompkins, 2003). Reread Chapter 1, where we describe the success rate for self-modification. Why do you think you would be the exception, the failure? If you don't think you can reach your goal, reread Chapter 2, where we talk about increasing your self-efficacy and using subgoals. If you still aren't sure what to do, reread Chapters 5, 6, and 7, where we outline the steps you can take. If your project is too difficult, for example, use shaping to make the steps easier. If emotions get in your way, first deal with them.

Try the techniques; then evaluate them. If you don't try, then of course they won't work.

You don't believe you can attain the goal you want. Your belief that you can cope with the problem affects how hard you try to overcome it, and that in turn affects your success. You may have lost confidence in your ability to change because you have been observing only your failures (Candiotte & Lichtenstein, 1981). Don't record only negative information. Record the successes you have. The successes may be small at first, but this is all the more reason to record them and celebrate them. You learn from them, and try to increase them. What led to the success; what were it's antecedents or consequences?

Some people take credit for their failures but not for their successes (Dweck, 1975). "When I fail, it's my fault; when I succeed, it's luck." Monitor your thinking. Focus on your successes, and realize that you are responsible for the positive things that have happened so far: "When I fail, it's because I didn't try hard enough. When I succeed, it's because I did try hard enough."

You really don't want to change. If you feel ambivalent about changing—"Do I really want to study more each day?"—then recheck the list of advantages and disadvantages of changing that you filled out in Chapter 2. Fill it out again. Perhaps you have changed your mind. If you are sincerely satisfied with your present adjustment, then of course don't try to change.

Other people are discouraging your use of the techniques. Others may hold beliefs such as those described above—it won't work, it's silly, you just need willpower—and may encourage you not to bother (Shelton & Levy, 1981). Tell them you're going to try the techniques and then decide whether or not they work.

People may also place temptation in your way. "Go ahead, have a cigarette. One won't hurt." Some people may be inconvenienced or made uncomfortable by your efforts to change and may sabotage your plan. They may even do it out of politeness, as when a host at a party urges food on someone who is dieting.

Sometimes people actually punish your attempts to change. This can be true for people who are trying to be assertive. Your behavior may make people uncomfortable; a new, assertive you rocks the boat. A student told us that all her life she had done whatever her older sister suggested. When she asserted herself, her sister complained that she was becoming "pushy." This student eventually gained her sister's cooperation by explaining her goals and the reasons for them. But this is not always possible. You may have to choose: Are your new goals worth some opposition from friends or family?

Incidentally, you should know that most people like appropriately assertive women more than unassertive ones and think they are more competent (Levin & Gross, 1984).

You started off with some success but then became discouraged. Dana's project was to make more friends. At first, he only kept records of how often he talked with others. He showed some success almost immediately, probably because just keeping the records encouraged him to talk more. But he didn't use any other techniques. After a few days, the novelty of record keeping wore off, and he slipped back into his old, reclusive ways. He gave up his self-change project, saying that it wasn't working.

There is a skill in keeping yourself motivated to continue when you're in the slow process of developing a new habit (Kanfer & Ackerman, 1995). When you are first developing a skill, progress can be rapid and exciting. But this first, easy stage passes. The early, large strides are behind you, and your concentration, your attention, will begin to wander. The quick improvements are gone, and now you have to deal with the harder issues, one at a time.

First, simply be aware that you have to keep your attention focused on coping or you will begin to show slippage. That's what happened to Dana, above: He let his attention lapse after his first success and ended with no success at all. Developing a new habit can take time, and you have to stay focused on your goal by continuing to self-observe.

Second, use a finer-grained list of subgoals. Dana's overarching, long-term goal was to make more friends, but he should have started with shorter-term steps, such as increasing his acquaintances, increasing the number of conversations he had, talking on the telephone or the Internet, generally having social interactions. A short-term goal such as a minimum of one exchange on the Internet each day is easily attainable, and Dana would have felt he was making some progress. He also should have kept records of his successes at reaching short-term goals.

Relapse Prevention

Jeb took up smoking when he was 15. When he turned 25, he decided it was time to quit. He gave himself a date: "On August 1, I will quit smoking." As the date drew near, he worried about his ability to just quit, but he wanted to try. He woke up that fateful morning, fixed his coffee, reached for a cigarette, said, "No," and threw all his cigarettes, matches, and ashtrays into the garbage. During the next 10 days, he did not smoke at all.

Other things were changing for Jeb during this time. He and his girlfriend were having increasing difficulties. She wanted to break up, but Jeb didn't. Finally, she told Jeb she wouldn't see him anymore. This depressed him considerably, as he had thought she was the one. His depression lingered, made worse by the fact that his grades on his most recent tests were unexpectedly low.

That weekend, to cheer himself up, Jeb went to a local singles bar. He wasn't cheered, however. The sight of all those strangers trying to make a good impression on each other just depressed him more. It also seemed as though everyone was going outside to smoke. "I feel rotten," he thought. "A cigarette would sure cheer me up right now." When a casual friend said, "Want to go outside and have a smoke?" Jeb accepted. A few minutes later, he went to the corner store and bought a pack of his favorite brand. He ordered another drink, felt his spirits lift, and lit up.

The next day Jeb woke up, poured his coffee, and had a cigarette. A year later, he is still smoking. "I was never sure that I could quit, anyway. When I went back that night, it just proved it. I'm addicted. I can't quit."

Jeb's story contains several elements that may help you prevent a relapse—whether your problem is overeating, smoking, drinking, abuse of substances, or any other kind of situation in which relapse is a possibility.

First, let's define lapse and relapse. A *lapse* is a slip or a mistake. When a lapse occurs, you perform a behavior you are trying to avoid: You smoke a few smokes; you go back to being rude to your friends. A *relapse* means going back to your full-blown pattern of unwanted behavior. Jeb's first cigarette after quitting need not have precipitated a relapse: It was only a slip, a lapse. The fact is, on the way to greater self-control, many people lapse, and many lapse many times. But one swallow doesn't make a summer. Expect that you will have lapses. *The trick is to keep them from becoming a relapse, a full-blown return of the unwanted, problem behavior.*

Marlatt's Model of the Relapse Process

Psychologically, what was going on when Jeb went back to smoking? He was emotionally upset: His girlfriend had left him; his grades were low. He went into a risky situation—a singles bar where many people were smoking. Jeb doubted his ability to quit. Jeb was unprepared when the friend offered him a cigarette, and he accepted it. He believed that a cigarette would make him feel better, and in fact it seemed to do so. Afterwards, he felt that he had relapsed and that the relapse was caused by conditions within himself—his addiction, his inability to quit, his lack of willpower. The implication was that there was no point in trying to quit again.

There are several models of the relapse process (Laws, 1995). One of the best comes from G. Alan Marlatt and his co-workers (Marlatt & George, 1990; Marlatt & Gordon, 1985). This model is diagrammed in Figure 9-1. See also Witkiewitz & Marlatt (2004).

The relapse model applies not just to situations involving addictions, such as smoking or drinking. It applies to any self-change project in which there is danger that you will fall back into your old, unwanted ways. A relapse into depression, for example,

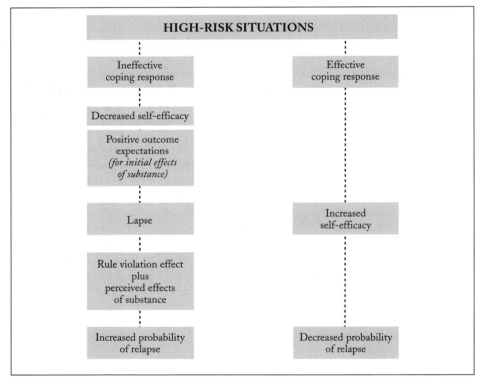

Figure 9-1 Marlatt's original cognitive-behavioral model of the relapse process. Marlatt and Witkiewitz presented a more dynamic, complicated model in 2004, elements of which will be presented in the text as we discuss the original model.

SOURCE: *Relapse Prevention: Maintenance Strategies in the Treatment of Addictive Behaviors,* edited by G. A. Marlatt and J. R. Gordon, 1985, New York: The Guilford Press. Copyright © 1985. Reprinted with permission.

often begins with some disappointment, leading to a bad mood (Teasdale, Moore, Hayhurst, Pope, & Segal, 2002) in which the old self-statements begin to reappear: "I'm a loser. After all this time, I still can't handle it." When this lapse into such self-statements begins, cut it off immediately. Use thought substitution and relaxation.

People whose problems involve gambling, exercising, overeating, studying, depression, unwanted sexual behaviors, and so on, will all benefit from learning about this model (Brownell, Marlatt, Lichtenstein, & Wilson, 1986). For addictive behaviors, such as smoking, drinking, and using drugs, it is absolutely essential that you use the ideas in this section to be successful in your efforts to change (Glasgow & Lichtenstein, 1987).

We can use Jeb's experience to follow through the model in Figure 9-1.

A high-risk situation is one that presents a greater than usual temptation to lapse into the unwanted behavior. Jeb's high-risk situations were that he was upset and depressed, in a negative emotional state. He felt as though everyone else in the bar was smoking, so he felt some social pressure to smoke. Someone surprised him by offering him a cigarette.

What makes a situation high-risk depends to some degree on your individual learning history. Your Aunt Jenny's rhubarb pie may be an irresistible temptation to you, but not to everyone. There are, however, common patterns to high-risk situations, which Jeb's case illustrates.

Jeb might have coped effectively with the risk. He could have noted that he was very upset, realized that a lapse was likely, and done something about it. That would have routed him through the right path of the model, where coping in the face of a high-risk situation leads to increased self-efficacy—and to increased skill through practice of the coping behavior. This, in turn, lessens the probability of relapse.

Unfortunately for Jeb, his behavior followed the left path of the model. Either he did not recognize that he was in a high-risk situation, or any coping that he attempted was ineffective. He chose his old, destructive way of dealing with depression—smoking.

Jeb could have gotten up the next morning and gone right back to nonsmoking. But the combination of factors—not coping effectively with a high-risk situation, the belief that the indulgent behavior will make him feel better, and the belief that he probably can't give up the substance anyway—greatly increases the probability of an initial lapse turning into a relapse (Marlatt & Gordon, 1985).

Jeb also experienced what is called the *abstinence violation effect*. In this situation, the person establishes a rule of total abstinence. The gambler takes a pledge never to gamble again; the smoker takes a pledge never to have another cigarette; the overweight person will never binge again. The person believes that there is no gray area: Any lapse into the prohibited behavior leads to total disaster. But we all make mistakes when we are trying to change. When people backslide, they feel guilty, blame themselves for the lapse, and feel there is nothing they can do about it (Curry, Marlatt, & Gordon, 1987; Grilo & Shiffman, 1994).

But the belief ignores reality, for many people lapse now and then while developing greater control, no matter what behaviors or addictions they strive against. The best way to cope with this problem is to be aware of it and try to avoid thinking that way (Roberts & Marlatt, 1998).

Once he had smoked in the bar, Jeb felt that his behavior demonstrated what he had always believed—that he could not quit smoking. He ignored the transient nature of the situation that had caused his behavior—his low mood, being in the bar, being offered a cigarette—and focused instead on his own personal characteristics. Ignoring the effects of the situation in causing our behavior is a common, erroneous pattern in human thinking (Nisbett & Ross, 1980). In Jeb's case, it led to real problems.

In the original model the process through the steps is linear, but in the newer model the theorists realized that things might not be so simple, and they offered a more dynamic theory in which there can be several causes of relapse, some occurring at the time of relapse while others lie in the past but have an influence on the current situation (Witkiewitz & Marlatt, 2004). For example, factors outside the current situation, such as family history or the amount of social support a person has, can affect whether a lapse becomes a relapse, and current factors such as the degree of craving for a substance or the motivation to control one's actions all have an affect. Some of these, of course, you can do nothing to change.

One of the best ways to keep lapses from becoming relapses is to use lots of social support for changing so that, when you do lapse, you don't relapse because others help you avoid it (Stanton, 2005). Suppose, on the day after his lapse, Jeb had had a friend who had said, "Oh, no! Don't go back to smoking! Hey, let's go for a jog. It'll help you get your mind off it. Come on, you can do this."

Remember, the chances are very high that you will lapse. You'll overeat or smoke or do something else you want to quit doing. The trick is to stop it then and there. What can you do to lessen the chances that your lapses will turn into relapse? There are three steps:

1. Recognize your own high-risk situations.
2. Cope with them when you meet them.
3. Prevent any lapse that occurs from becoming a relapse.

Recognizing High-Risk Situations

People often think that relapse into an unwanted behavior like smoking, drug use, or overeating is due to a terrific craving, one that cannot be ignored, but it's not actually a craving by itself that drives people into relapse. Some ex-smokers, for example, crave cigarettes for years after they quit, but they still don't relapse. So it's not the craving itself that causes relapse. What is it, then?

Actually, high-risk situations for behaviors like smoking, compulsive gambling, drug use, drinking, or overeating are fairly predictable (Baumeister, Heatherton, & Tice, 1994; Marlatt & George, 1990; Velicer, DiClemente, Rossi, & Prochaska, 1990). Here are the four main culprits:

1. Being emotionally upset;
2. Social settings in which you are tempted;
3. Drinking; and
4. Unexpectedly encountering the to-be-avoided objects.

1. Being emotionally upset. Feeling depressed, angry, frustrated, bored, or anxious is a high-risk situation for everyone. For example, having a fight with your loved one is dangerous for your self-control because it upsets you. Being upset is the most dangerous of all risky situations, the one most likely to push you back into your unwanted behaviors (Hodgkins, el-Guebaly, & Armstrong, 1995; Shiffman & Waters, 2004). This is true especially for eating problems and smoking.

In the past, you may have used your unwanted behavior—smoking, drinking, overeating, watching TV, or whatever—as a way of lightening your mood. Lapses are often an attempt to regulate a negative mood, to lighten up (Sayette, 2004). You smoke or binge eat because it makes you feel better.

A father said to us, "I've tried three times in the past 2 weeks to stop smoking. Each time, an argument with my teenage son got me back to smoking. He's in a rebellious period, and his actions upset me a lot. I take a walk to cool off—and invariably end up down at the corner store buying a pack of cigarettes."

If you are lapsing because you are using your unwanted habit to control your mood, reread our section on emotional control in Chapter 6 to think of other, less problematic ways of controlling mood.

2. Dangerous social settings. These are settings in which other people are engaging in the behavior you want to stop, or even encouraging you to join in. Just going to a party where people are drinking, smoking, and overeating can be problematic. It's much harder to stop smoking, for example, if you socialize a lot with people who smoke (Mermelstein, Cohen, Lichtenstein, Baer, & Kamarck, 1986). If you want to exercise every day at 5:00 P.M., don't spend that time with people who hate exercise. If you want to increase your studying in the evening, don't schedule that time to be with people who are into goofing off every evening.

You can even get social pressure from others to engage in your unwanted behavior. You want to quit overeating, but your Aunt Jenny bakes her special rhubarb pie and brings it over to your house. Her feelings will be hurt if you don't eat some of it. Or your old drinking buddy encourages you to drop your attempts to stop drinking. After all, he doesn't want to lose his drinking buddy. Or your friends offer you the foods they know you like, because they want to be hospitable and friendly.

3. Drinking. The risk of backsliding from any goal is greater when you are drinking, because you are paying less attention to yourself. Recall that alcohol makes us less self-aware (Hull, 1987). You are less on guard against old, bad habits. Therefore, you are more likely to smoke, overeat, be rude, or whatever else it is that you're trying to stop. One of our students said to us, "I've stopped having discussions—arguments, really—with my husband when I've been drinking. I know I fall back on my old, mean ways of talking to him then."

4. Unexpected encounters with temptation. Suddenly encountering the object that in the past has led to unwanted behavior can control your behavior as an antecedent before you even think.

It is important to learn to recognize and cope with these tempting situations. People who do something to cope with high-risk situations are more likely to be successful than people who just trust luck (Grilo, Shiffman, & Wing, 1989; Shiffman, 1982). And the more competently you cope with high-risk situations, the better your chances are of avoiding relapse (Davis & Glaros, 1986). Different kinds of situations call for different kinds of coping. You need to learn new ways to relax and to recognize when you're feeling social pressure to engage in your old, unwanted behavior (Lichtenstein et al., 1986).

Your personal high-risk situations can be learned from self-observation. This is why it is so important to continue keeping records when your plan for self-modification is failing. Your self-observations will tell you about the situations that are high-risk for you—being in a singles bar, in social situations, at a dinner party, or your own thoughts. The father who wanted to quit smoking made accurate self-observations. Then he was in a position to do something effective: He gave himself instructions not to react so strongly to what his son did, and he practiced relaxation when he got upset. He also went for longer walks, and didn't let himself pass the store that sold cigarettes on the way.

What constitutes a high-risk situation is different for different kinds of problem behaviors. People struggling with too much gambling, for example, are likely to relapse into unwanted gambling when they are worrying about their personal finances (Hodgkins & el-Guebaly, 2004). Being in a bad mood and the abstinence violation effect was a strong force leading to relapse in dieters (Carels, Douglass, Cacciapaglia, & O'Brien, 2004). And a low self-efficacy belief that one could stop smoking had a strong effect on smokers' ability to avoid relapse (Gwaltney et al., 2002).

Keep records of your thoughts when you are upset and have a lapse. "I'm upset. I'd feel better if I ate." "A cigarette would sure relax me now." "I need to lighten up. Have a little drink." "I've been under a lot of stress. I owe myself a drink." If you believe that nice things will happen as a result of lapsing, you'll tell yourself, "Go ahead. It would feel good." You are tempting yourself with these thoughts.

It's even possible that you may choose, "unthinkingly," to put yourself into a high-risk situation (George & Marlatt, 1986; Laws, 1995). Goal ambivalence can lead to a seemingly irrelevant decision—to stop at the shopping center on the way home (where that fantastic bakery is), to go get a newspaper (where they also sell cigarettes)—and then you may find yourself in a situation that leads to a lapse. Ask yourself, "Am I tempting myself? Are I making some apparently unimportant decisions—to go home one way instead of another—that later get me into high-risk situations? Do I want to do that?"

Effective Coping with High-Risk Situations

The first step is to recognize risky situations, and the second step is to develop skills to cope with them. By learning such skills, you increase your chances of dealing successfully with high-risk situations when they arise (Irvin, Bowers, Dunn, & Wang, 1999; Sobell & Sobell, 1993).

The easiest way to cope with high-risk situations is to avoid them. In Chapters 5 and 8, we discussed the idea of deliberately staying away from situations in which you have performed the problem behavior in the past. This is particularly important if you are trying to get rid of some addiction, such as smoking, drinking, or drugs. When you have been used to satisfying your addiction in certain situations—always drinking with the same friends in the same place, for example—your addictive reaction is actually conditioned to that situation (Leavitt, 1982). This means that mere exposure to the situation leads to physical withdrawal symptoms now that you are trying to stop the addictive behavior. If you go back to the place where you used to indulge, you're going to experience the pain of withdrawal again and be tempted to reduce it by lapsing into the old, unwanted behavior. If you stay away, you'll not only feel better, but you'll be less likely to lapse.

This means that smokers should stay away from the old situations in which they used to enjoy smoking—the after-work TGIFs, for example. Drinkers should stay away from bars, and drug users should avoid the places and people with whom they used to indulge.

Some kinds of situations can be avoided forever. "I've spent way too much money gambling, but now I'm going to stop. No more gambling of any kind. No poker, no bets, no LOTTO, nothing."

But some kinds of risky situations cannot always be avoided. You can't give up eating, for example, even if you want to control your overeating, and you don't want to give up socializing, even if you have a tendency to drink too much when socializing. *When you can't avoid them, use problem-solving skills to deal with high-risk situations* (Marlatt & Gordon, 1985).

Listing the details of situations in which you are tempted to lapse will suggest specific problems. Instead of thinking, "I drink too much," or "I eat too much," substitute "I drink (or eat) when I am really upset and alcohol (or food) is present." Your problem is more specific, and your attack on the problem can focus more closely on the real issues.

Sherwin, for example, gave up excessive drinking, but was still tempted now and then. He wrote:

> I listed the details of situations in which I drank. One was when I needed to relax. Another was when I was with a bunch of people. Sometimes I had liquor in the house that was left there after a party. I worked out alternative ways of dealing with those situations. To get myself to relax, I tried meditating and exercising. I made lists of self-instructions to use when I was with other people. I decided to pour out all liquor that was left after a party.

Work out instructions to give yourself as soon as you realize that you are in a high risk situation. Sherwin continued:

> One Friday after work, the whole office decided to go out for a beer. I wanted to go, to be with them and have some fun, but I knew it was risky. I told myself, "Be careful. This is a high-risk situation. Order ginger ale. If someone says, 'Come on, have a beer,' I will say, 'No, thanks, I prefer ginger ale.'"

He was warning himself, and also telling himself what to do and how to cope with social pressure to lapse, an if . . . then rule that worked for him.

Recognize that you may want to give in to the temptation, and give yourself instructions to cope with the rationalizations you make to yourself. Sherwin says to himself, "When I get there, I may say to myself, 'I'll just have one beer.' But I won't have one, I'll have several, and I really don't want to do that. So don't have the first one."

Remind yourself of the advantages of changing your old, unwanted behavior. Sherwin tells himself:

> I'm tempted to drink now, but I really want to stop drinking, because it will make me feel better. I'll be healthier, look better, be better for my work, and improve my social life. The advantages outweigh the disadvantages, so I won't drink.

Distract yourself, or switch from hot to cool thoughts about the object of your desire. Instead of thinking, "Man, a beer would sure taste good now," Sherwin switches to thinking, "The beer looks like a urine specimen." It's important *not* to continue having hot thoughts about the tempting substance, for you are more likely to give in and lapse if you have those thoughts.

Try taking a detached view of your craving for a tempting substance (George & Marlatt, 1986). This lowers the emotional impact of your thoughts. Instead of thinking,

"Oh, I really gotta have a beer right now," a thought with emotional overtones, Sherwin calmly tells himself, "I am experiencing an urge to drink now." Or he could think, "I feel it coming from a distance, trying to build up, but it's not too awful. If I wait just a couple of minutes, it will pass. I'm going to surf right through this urge." A man who said he felt "irresistible" hunger and urges to eat found that if he simply drank water and waited a few minutes, the hunger passed. Cravings do pass fairly quickly. Remind yourself of this.

Perhaps the most important aspect of resisting an urge is your belief that you can resist. If you believe you can deal with a lapse, you are more likely to be successful dealing with it (Haaga & Stewart, 1992; Velicer, DiClemente, Rossi, & Prochaska, 1990).

You will increase your belief that you can resist only if you notice your successes at resisting. They may be small at first, but if you notice them, you will increase them. Laura, who was trying to hold her drinking to one drink per hour, wrote in her final report: "I was in this bar for about 4 hours. For the first 3 hours I actually held my drinks to one an hour. In the final hour I screwed up and had three. Later I realized, hey, at least I showed I can do it for a while. Maybe I can build on that."

Prepare in advance some self-instructions and ready other coping skills so that you will have them available when you meet a high-risk situation. Practice these in your imagination before you get into high-risk situations, so you will have them available when the time comes.

1. Warn yourself, "Danger!"
2. Give yourself instructions on what behaviors to perform: Relax, be mildly assertive, leave, or whatever.
3. Remind yourself of rationalizations you may make, and remind yourself you don't want to indulge.
4. Remind yourself of the advantages of changing.
5. Cope with feelings of wanting to indulge: Distract yourself; switch from hot to cool thoughts about the substance.
6. Take a detached view of any craving you feel, remind yourself that it will pass, and tell yourself what to do until it does pass.
7. Remind yourself of successes you've had in the past coping with urges.

Remember that mistakes are very common. In one study of a large group of people who had *successfully* stayed away from cigarettes for over 6 months, one-quarter had slipped at some point in the process but had successfully reinstated their anti-smoking plans (Hughes et al., 1992).

Putting on the Brakes: Stopping Lapses from Becoming Relapses

Suppose you make a mistake and lapse. You smoke, you drink, you overeat, you gamble, or whatever. What now? A plan for coping with lapses—for putting on the brakes before you totally relapse—is essential. Jeb, after a night of lapses, got up the next morning and went right back to smoking as though he'd never stopped. One of his mistakes was having no plan to cope with lapses. A study compared people who lapsed but eventually stopped smoking with those who lapsed and stayed relapsed. Of the eventual successes, 100% said they had some plan for coping following a lapse. Only half of those who failed had any plan (Candiotte & Lichtenstein, 1981). In another study, people who relapsed and stopped exercising usually had very few plans for coping with lapses, but people who lapsed and then went back to exercising had several plans for coping with that kind of problem (Simkin & Gross, 1994).

Often when people lapse, they become upset by the lapse and stop self-observation. If you have not been self-monitoring, reinstate it. If you do so, you are much more likely to reinstate a full-blown plan for self-modification.

The second step is to make out a full-scale self-change plan for what you will do if you lapse. If you have not been using a full plan—for example, you are no longer counting, you aren't self-reinforcing, you aren't thinking about antecedents, and so on—go back to a full plan: antecedent control for wanted behavior, shaping, reinforcement, imaginary rehearsal, relaxation, and so on. Write out a self-contract: "I promise myself that if I lapse, I will immediately begin counting my lapses. I will continue to count as long as I am lapsing. Also, I will reinstate a full self-modification project to cope with my problem behavior." Sign this, and keep it in your wallet.

Make out a reminder card to carry with you. Here is the reminder card used in a study with smokers who wanted to quit:

> A slip is not all that unusual. It does not mean that you have failed or that you have lost control over your behavior. You will probably feel guilty about what you have done, and will blame yourself for having slipped. This feeling is to be expected. . . . There is no reason why you have to give in to this feeling and continue to smoke. Look upon the slip as a learning experience. What were the elements of the high-risk situation that led to the slip? What coping response could you have used to get around the situation?
>
> Remember the old saying: One swallow doesn't make a summer. Well, one slip doesn't make a relapse, either. Just because you slipped once does not mean that you are a failure, that you have no willpower, or that you are a hopeless addict. Look upon the slip as a single, independent event, something that can be avoided in the future with an alternative coping response. (adapted from Marlatt, 1982, pp. 359–360)

Blame the situation instead of your personality. The lapse doesn't mean you can't change, it means you need a plan to cope with the situation that led to the lapse. If you think, "Well, that lapse was due to the particular circumstances I was in," rather than, "I lapsed because I just don't have enough willpower," then you are more likely to persist in your efforts to change (Kernis, Zuckerman, Cohen, & Spadafora, 1982).

Consenting to your unwanted habit. Sometimes after a slip, a mistake, or a lapse people abandon self-control and furiously engage in the behaviors they have been trying to stop. They give up the goal of controlling the unwanted behavior and spiral out of control. For example, a man who wants to quit smoking has three cigarettes at a party and then seems to say, "What the hell," and goes back to smoking 30 the next day. A woman overeats the appetizer, then goes whole hog at the table, eating everything in reach.

Is this an "irresistible impulse," something you just cannot refrain from doing? Usually not. Rather, it involves actively cooperating with the lapse. Failure at self-control is "not so much something that happens to you as something that you allow to happen" (Baumeister, Heatherton, & Tice, 1994, p. 248). People who lapse and abandon self-control appear to be saying to themselves, "I was trying not to do this, but since I've slipped, what the hell, I might as well go all the way!" They consent. Why?

Several theoretical answers have been suggested for this pattern, called *acquiescence* (cf. Baumeister, Heatherton, & Tice, 1994; Karoly, 1995; Kirschenbaum, 1994; Rachlin, 1995). Acquiescence involves three elements. First, there are some short-term rewards for undesired behavior: It feels good; there is an immediate rush. So, having made a mistake, you continue, enjoying the short-term rewards. Second, acquiescence results from focusing on the short-term rewards and withdrawing attention from your long-term goals. Notice when you are in the process of acquiescing to the bad habit how intensely you are focused on it, how little you are paying attention to anything else but the food, the drug, the sex. (Until later!)

A third reason for acquiescence is that it comes in a tightly organized chain of events, and once you have started it, enormous attention is required to interrupt that chain. Habits are organized in chains or packages of behaviors, and once the package is well practiced, interruption is unlikely. When you have habitually performed certain acts in certain situations, you will feel awkward and uncomfortable not doing them. For example, Lisa wanted to cut down on her drinking, but noted that it would "feel strange" to go to a bar to see her friends, play darts, and not drink. It was all part of a chain that had to be disconnected, one link at a time.

What can be done about acquiescence? First, don't feel guilty when you slip. Don't think, "I'm weak," or "I'm evil," or "I'm stupid." Realize that the reason this bad habit is a problem for you is precisely because it is a habit, something that runs on automatic pilot. Also, it is a behavior that at some level you actually enjoy doing. Therefore, changing it is not going to be easy. It is no disgrace to make mistakes, and it does not reflect on your total worth. Just keep trying.

What should you try? Observe your behavior. Remember that one advantage to consenting to the bad habit is that it takes your attention off yourself as you concentrate on doing it. So *keep making records: This keeps your attention focused where you want it.* If you continue to keep records even when you are out of control, you will gradually learn to bring the unwanted behavior under control.

This is what we suggested in the box, "The Mindful Diet," in Chapter 3: Keep your attention focused on the problem, and gradually you will bring it under control.

A man who took over a year to decrease his drinking told us:

> I was working very hard and had a difficult time sticking to my prescribed number of drinks. I really expected to get high because some days that seemed about the only reward I got. But I also knew I wanted to stop drinking so much. So I made a plan: I would continue to keep a record of my drinking even when I was drinking too much. That got me through. I felt I was somewhat in control and figured that when I got time I could deal with my problem.

If you force yourself to continue recording what you are doing, even when it embarrasses you, you will come to a position long advocated by transpersonal psychologists. You will "own" your own behavior. That is, you will take responsibility for it (cf. Weinder, 1995). Oprah Winfrey explains how she was able to lose weight and keep it off once she took responsibility for her own behavior:

> For years I'd been saying on my show that you are so damned responsible for your life. You can't keep blaming somebody else for your dysfunction. . . . Then as I entered my 40th year, I realized that this belief applied to me, too. So I asked myself, if you want it so much, then why are you still fat? (Reynolds, 1995, p. 17)

She realized that the only way to reach her goals was to take responsibility for reaching them, which meant keeping her attention focused on them even when she didn't want to.

Chapter Summary

Problem Solving

Start off with your best plan for change, and observe what interferes with it. Then revise the plan, taking into consideration the sources of interference. Analyze your mistakes, and learn from them.

Using formal problem solving increases your chances of success, particularly if you run into difficulties. The four steps in problem solving are:

1. List the concrete details of the problem.
2. Think of as many solutions as possible.
3. Choose one or more to implement.
4. Check to be sure you are carrying out the solution.

Lack of continued self-observation is the biggest reason for failure in self-modification. Self-focused attention is necessary to achieve change. Three events interfere with this: stress, alcohol, and failure at self-modification. People sometimes fail because of problems with obstacles or goals.

Self-control fatigue occurs when we resist temptation for a long period, or later in the day, and can lead to giving in.

Relapse Prevention

A lapse is one slip into old, unwanted behavior and a relapse means fully returning to the unwanted pattern. When a person encounters a high-risk situation he or she might cope with the temptation to return to the unwanted act, or might not, and lapse into it.

To lessen the chances of a lapse becoming a relapse:

1. Learn to recognize your own high-risk situations.
2. Cope with them when you meet them. Don't assume that any violation of the rule of abstinence means failure.
3. Take steps to prevent any lapse that occurs from becoming a relapse.

Common high-risk situations are:

- Being emotionally upset;
- Social settings in which you are tempted;
- Drinking; and
- Unexpectedly encountering the to-be-avoided objects.

Through self-observation you can learn about your own personal high-risk situations. To cope with lapses, and to keep them from becoming relapses, first try to avoid high risk situations; when that is not possible, work out instructions to guide yourself through the situations. Practice coping with the situation in your imagination.

Have a plan for dealing with lapses. Reinstate self-observation immediately, work out a new full-blown self-change plan, and use reminders of the difference between lapses and relapses. If you find you are consenting to a return of the old, unwanted behavior, force yourself to continue keeping records until you finally "own" your own behavior.

Your Own Self-Direction Project: Step 9

Solving Problems
What makes it difficult to perform the target behavior? How can the plan be made more effective? To increase the adequacy of your self-change plan, answer these questions:

Are you using enough techniques?
Are you increasing a behavior to replace an unwanted one?
Are you taking full advantage of the ideas on how to deal with problem antecedents?
Are you practicing the wanted behavior?
Are you being reinforced for the wanted behavior?

The most common reason for failure in self-modification is lack of continued self-observation. Are you still keeping records? If not, what interferes with it? Use problem solving to get yourself to continue record keeping, even if all else fails.

Preventing Relapse
Keep records of your lapses and learn from them. Find out what your personal high-risk situations are. Use problem-solving techniques to cope with high-risk situations. Do this work now, before you are involved in the situation. List the details of your personal high-risk situations, think of as many solutions as you can, select solutions to use, and be sure you are using the solutions.

Prepare now the self-statements you will use when you meet a high-risk situation:

1. Use a warning statement.
2. Prepare self-instructions on what behaviors to perform.
3. Remind yourself of any rationalizations you may make.
4. Make a list of the advantages of not giving in to the urge to lapse.
5. Make plans on how to distract yourself and how to switch from hot to cool thoughts.

Once you have made up the self-instructions, use imaginary rehearsal to practice them. Set aside periods in which you imagine suddenly being in a high-risk situation. Give yourself a warning, tell yourself what behaviors to perform, and give yourself the self-instructions. Imagine yourself being reinforced by feelings of pride and self-efficacy.

Make out a relapse-prevention contract now. This will include plans (1) to resume self-observation immediately after any lapse and (2) to resume a full self-change project. Sign this contract, and keep it with you.

Take all these steps now, before you run into a high-risk situation. If you meet a high-risk situation unprepared, you are more likely to lapse—and relapse.

Chapter 10

Termination and Beyond

Outline and Learning Objectives

Planning to Maintain Gains
1. Explain the goals of maintenance and transfer of a newly learned behavior.
2. How can you evolve natural reinforcements for a new behavior?
3. Explain how to use thinning.
4. How should you deal with lack of reinforcement from others?
5. How can you get social support for new behaviors?
6. How confident are you that you can maintain your new behaviors? How is this measured?
7. Why should you continue to keep records?
8. How do you program for transfer to new settings?
9. How important is practice in developing new behaviors? What does it mean to say, "Practice of perfect—not practice makes perfect"?

Beyond the Ending
10. How can you increase the chances that you will use self-change techniques when needed in the future?
11. Do people ever carry out lifelong self-modification projects? When might this be necessary?
12. When should you seek professional help?
13. What happens in psychotherapy?
14. How should you choose a therapist?

Self-Directed Happiness
15. What are the three elements of happiness?
16. What three factors affect our level of happiness?
17. Name nine of Fordyce's happiness fundamentals.
18. What emotional and pro-social steps can you take to increase happiness?
19. Name four categories of behavior that lead to life satisfaction.
20. Having filled out the happiness checklist, what self-change projects should you begin?

Chapter Summary

Your Own Self-Direction Project: Step 10

Sometimes you have to pay as much attention to the ending of the self-change plan as you did while you were carrying it out. New gains are tentative. Anyone who has lost weight knows how easy it is to regain it. People who lose weight have to remain vigilant that their old, weight-adding behaviors don't come back (Westover & Lanyon, 1990). Smokers sometimes show a pattern of vigilant coping early in their antismoking campaign, but then relax their guard and stop coping after a few successes. Then they relapse and are smoking again (Shiffman & Jarvik, 1987). Even for nonconsummatory behaviors, such as mood improvement or increasing studying, you may find that after a few weeks of stability at your new goal, you begin drifting back.

Maintaining your new, positive behaviors is a process that you may have to repeat, cycling through several times in order to be sure you keep the new, desired acts (Wing, 2000). Remember that these are *new* behaviors. Because they are not well practiced, they can be lost, and the old, unwanted habits may reappear.

Planning to Maintain Gains

At this point, you have two goals:

1. To maintain gains; and
2. To make sure that any newly learned behavior transfers to new situations.

Suppose you have increased your studying to a new, satisfying level, but after a few months notice that it is dropping back toward the old level. That is a *maintenance* problem; your level of work hasn't stayed where you want it. On the other hand, suppose you have developed good study habits for certain courses, but still don't seem to be studying well for other courses. You study well for science, but not for English. That is a *transfer* problem. Either way, you are not performing the desired behavior at the level you want.

There are several things you can do to be sure you maintain your gains and to help them transfer to new situations. If you work out a plan for maintenance and transfer, you are much more likely to keep your new gains (Perri, McAllister, Gange, Jordan, McAdoo, & Nezu, 1988).

Evolving Natural Reinforcements

In the early stages of terminating a self-change project, it's a good idea to remind yourself of the rewards that bolster your behavior. A woman who lost many pounds was delighted to discover that other people found her more attractive. She had many more dates. When she stopped the formal reinforcement for weight loss, she posted a reminder on the refrigerator door: "Dieting keeps the telephone ringing!"

Besides reminding yourself, *be sure you will be reinforced for new behaviors you have developed.* Suppose you successfully improved your study habits after a lifetime of being a poor student. Now you should plan natural situations that will reinforce your new competence without punishing you for skills you still lack (Stokes & Osnes, 1989). Where will your studying be reinforced? If there is an advanced course, for example, with prerequisites—courses that earlier you did poorly in—then your new study behaviors won't be well rewarded, because you lack background in that course. Choose courses in which you are getting a fresh start. This way you are much more likely to be reinforced for the new, good study habits that you have learned.

Elizabeth, who had learned through her self-change project to talk comfortably with men, wrote: "I'm still careful in striking up conversations. I look for guys who seem easy to get to know and stay away from the stuck-up ones." She is very sensibly putting herself into situations where she can reasonably expect to be rewarded.

Jack felt awkward in small peer groups, alternating between strained silence and sarcastic remarks. When he was assigned to a six-person team project in one of his courses, he decided to take the opportunity to change his behavior. Jack reinforced friendly and task-related statements he made to other group members, using as a reinforcement the amount of time he allowed himself to spend surfing each week. He improved his performance and his comfort, but because he was still not satisfied with his level of improvement when the course was over, he looked for another situation in which to practice. From among several possibilities, he chose to attend evening meetings of the Writers' Club. This was a good choice because he was interested in writing and had much to say on the subject. Furthermore, lapses into his more aggressive behavior wouldn't be punished too severely, since criticism of other members' work was part of the club's function. In short, this group was one into which he could bring his newly acquired abilities and from which he could expect enjoyment and relative lack of punishment. The situation reinforced and increased the kind of participation he wanted.

Ask other people to reinforce your new behaviors (Goldstein & Martens, 2000). "How'd you think I handled the group today?" "Do you like this dress on me?" "Did that feel better?" "What do you think about the way I dealt with him?" Soliciting reinforcement is not bragging; it's asking for feedback, and the more of it you get, the better you are able to guide your own behavior. "Did you notice that I skipped dessert?" You're actually seeking social support for your new changes, and that's a very good idea, as it increases the chances you will stick with the new behavior. Don't be shy; ask for feedback.

Thinning: Building Resistance to Extinction

In your self-modification plan, you probably get reinforced every time you perform some desired behavior. That's the way you produce the fastest change. But out in the world, reinforcement isn't so predictable. Once you start thinking about transferring to naturally occurring reinforcers, you should take steps to ensure that your newly gained behaviors are not lost because of extinction. This is necessary because a behavior that has been reinforced continuously is most likely to extinguish when reinforcements do not continue to occur.

Therefore, don't stop self-modification abruptly. The best way to guard against extinction is to use an intermittent reinforcement schedule.

Odette had been working to be more assertive in certain situations—such as when other people made unreasonable requests. Every time she performed an act of assertion, she gave herself one token. Later she used these tokens to select from a menu of favorite foods. After several weeks, she felt she was now being assertive when it was called for.

At this point, instead of stopping her reinforcement system, she started preparing for the fact that the world out there couldn't be counted on to reinforce her behavior. She prepared by thinning her reinforcement schedule, moving to an intermittent schedule of reinforcement. She began thinning in the simplest way, by not getting a token every time. At first she cut down so that she got tokens 75% of the time. She then reduced further, to one every other time, 50%, and later to only 25%. She did this over several days, slowly, to guard against extinction of her newly learned behavior.

In thinning, continue to count the frequency of the target behavior. It may decline. Some drop from your upper goal might be acceptable, but you'll want to know if there has been a drop and, if so, how much. If it drops too low, go back to 100% reinforcement.

Dealing with Lack of Reinforcement from Others

Rick took a short course in how to increase open communication in marriage and carried out a self-change project toward this goal. But his wife, Roberta, was irritated by Rick's efforts to change their mode of communication. Obviously, he was not going to be reinforced by her for his new behavior. Rick then started a plan in which he would invite Roberta to cooperate and try to get her to discuss why she was opposed to his attempts to improve their communication. He praised her for her participation in this kind of discussion and also reminded himself to be patient and not to expect her to change too quickly. He realized that, in the long run, he might be reinforced for his changes—when Roberta, too, had changed—but, meanwhile, he continued reinforcing himself and keeping records of his new behavior, because he felt that it would drop away from lack of reinforcement if he did not.

When you change yourself, you may affect others, but they may not reinforce your new behavior (Lichtenstein, Glasgow, & Abrams, 1986). In these kinds of situations, you must notice your own gains and benefits and remind yourself of your goals. Also, try reinforcing others for behavior that cooperates with your goals as Rick did.

Confidence, Record Keeping, and Challenging Situations

Confidence. One of our pessimistic students said, "You know, I've been using all these techniques you teach, and I have successfully changed. But I bet when I finish this course—which is really like a crutch—I'll flop right back to my old behaviors."

"Yeah, you're right," we agreed.

"What?" he said, surprised. "I thought you said these techniques work."

"They do. But only if you take credit for the control you've gained. It's you who has done the work, not the course. You're giving it all the credit. You don't seem to think that you personally have control over the behavior. So you probably won't try to control it, and therefore you won't."

You have to understand that the new behavior is under your personal control if you are to have a good chance of maintaining it (Katz & Vinciguerra, 1982). As your behavior changes, you should deliberately notice that it is coming more and more under *your own control*. If you do so, you increase the chances that you will maintain the behavior (Sonne & Janoff, 1982). For example, if ex-smokers think their quitting was due to something other than their own self-control, they are less able to stay away from cigarettes (Harackiewicz, Sansone, Blair, Epstein, & Manderlink, 1987), but if they do see that they are controlling the behavior, they are more able to avoid relapse.

In fact, you are better equipped than you've ever been before, for research has shown that taking a course like this increases your strength to resist relapse. You have developed skills that really do give you greater self-control (Glasgow & Lichtenstein, 1987; Hall, Rugg, Tunstall, & Jones, 1984).

Before you stop your formal self-modification plan, rate your ability to maintain the new behavior without the plan. Stop and think before completing this statement:

My estimation of my ability to control my behaviors without my self-modification plan is . . .

1	2	3	4	5
no chance at all				total certainty

If your rating is below 4, then it's not yet time to stop formal self-modification (see Baer, Holt, & Lichtenstein, 1986). Continue practicing. And ask yourself, "Why isn't my confidence level higher?" The answer to that may tell you what you need to work on next. Rebeq, for example, noted that his confidence about weight control was low "because every now and then I blow it and overeat." He realized that if he could bring that under better control his confidence in continuing to control his eating would increase, so he focused his self-change on controlling occasional pig-outs.

Record keeping. Some people find that they need to continue only one part of their old plan, their record keeping (Hall, 1980). If you are not yet sure about stopping, give yourself a trial period while continuing careful record keeping.

Remember that the surest way to scuttle your plan is to stop keeping records. If you stop record keeping you are much more likely to stop the new, desired actions because there will no longer be feedback indicating that you are living up to your own values (Baumeister, Heatherton, & Tice, 1994).

Once you have changed, continued recording makes it easier to maintain the change. For example, a man who had to use a fairly complicated schedule of manipulating antecedents for problem drinking found that once his drinking problem had lessened, he could keep himself on the straight and narrow by keeping records of his alcohol intake. Another man who had been drinking seven to eight cups of coffee each day cut down to only two or three, but he continued keeping records to be sure he didn't gradually move back up. A woman who had become a long-distance runner reported that she no longer needed to use a complicated self-change program to get herself to run, but she did need to keep records of her running to avoid slacking off. "If I keep the records of my exercise posted in the closet, I run three times a week, but if I stop keeping the records, down it goes."

Challenging situations. Your newly learned ability to control your behavior will vary from one situation to another. Here is a list of different kinds of situations smokers have to cope with (Colletti, Supnick, & Payne, 1985):

1. Feeling stressed, due to various things such as poor performance on an exam, being stood up by a date, or an argument with friend.
2. Feeling good, as when relaxed at the end of an evening, watching TV, or reading a novel.
3. In social situations in which others are smoking.
4. Drinking coffee and after a meal.

To be sure they stay off cigarettes, quitting smokers need to prepare ways of coping with each of those tempting situations.

Whatever your target problem, make a list of the different kinds of situations in which you will be tempted to relapse. Rate your confidence in each situation. If you know the situations in which you feel least confident, be sure to use self-control techniques in those situations.

Programming for Transfer to New Situations

When a behavior is first developing into a habit, it is tied to particular situations. When new situations occur, the behavior may or may not transfer to them. For example, a student who learned to control his depression during the fall was surprised to see his mood collapse with the arrival of the holidays—and the loss of pleasant, school-related activities. In an experiment, school children were trained to behave well when the teacher was out of the room, but they tended to misbehave when they were unsupervised in the hallways. They only behaved in the halls when they were taught to transfer their good behavior from the classroom to the hallways (Ninness, Fuerst, Rutherford, & Glenn, 1991).

Some people have difficulty believing that transferring newly learned behavior is a problem, because they believe that we carry our personality around with us and project it onto situations. (This is discussed in Chapter 1.) If, on the other hand, you think of personality as sets of different behaviors we perform in different situations, then it is easy to see why we might not transfer a newly learned behavior from the situation in which we learned it to other situations. All the research on transfer supports this second point of view, which means that newly learned behaviors will not automatically transfer. Just learning some new behavior and hoping it will transfer to a novel situation is a recipe for disaster.

This problem of transfer is not widely understood in areas such as education. Teachers often teach and then assume the ideas will transfer. But they don't. For example, many of us took a course in serious literature while we were in college, but how many of us read serious literature today? We didn't transfer the learning from a college classroom to our everyday lives.

Transfer is only likely to occur if you specifically train yourself for transfer (McKeough, Lupart, & Marini, 1995). To avoid losing a new behavior through lack of transfer to new situations, program for transfer. For example, a group of clients who had "shy bladder" problems—inability to urinate in public restrooms when anyone was around—were taught to relax in public restrooms, with the result that the time required for them to urinate decreased markedly. Half these clients were also trained to practice using different restrooms, under varying conditions. This gave them experience in transferring the newly learned ability to relax. The other half received no such treatment. Then all were tested under severe conditions, using a crowded public restroom at a sports event. The clients who were trained to transfer their relaxation were able to relax and use the facilities, but the clients who were not trained for transfer were unable to relax in the press of a crowded arena restroom (Shelton, 1981). The behavior they had learned under one condition did not transfer to the new because they had not practiced transfer.

Principles of Transfer

1. *Your new behavior may not transfer to new situations if you don't make a conscious effort to make it transfer* (Patrick, 1992). You have to do the work in this

chapter, or you may very well lose the benefits of all the work you've done so far. If you are aware of the problem of transfer, you increase the chances that a newly learned behavior will transfer to a new situation (Perkins & Saloman, 1996).

2. *Transfer effects can be very specific to situations.* Newly learned behaviors do sometimes transfer, but whether they do or not depends on at least nine separate variables (Barnett & Ceci, 2002). You want your newly learned behavior to transfer to all the situations in which you need it, but it is difficult to predict the exact situations to which some newly learned behavior will transfer. It is prudent, therefore, not to expect automatic transfer, but instead to deliberately build it in. One of our students spent an entire semester trying to avoid overeating at breakfast and lunch. But he never tried to transfer what he had learned to the supper situation and made no progress at all. He expected automatic transfer from one meal to another, but it didn't happen.

3. *Obstacles to transfer often occur.* So often, in fact, that you should expect them. When the obstacles occur, use your problem solving skills to think of solutions. Using problem solving and relapse prevention techniques, in fact, may increase the chances that you will get transfer of your new behavior when you need it (Milne, Westerman, & Hanner, 2002).

Carlo wrote:

> I had lost about 10 pounds: Then a whole series of dinners out came along, and I drifted off my weight-loss program. I wasn't gaining, but I wasn't losing either. I realized I had been successful in the past because I hadn't had to cope with eating out very often. So I had to go back to the drawing board and figure out how to cope with eating out.

Carlo used problem solving, began self-observation again, and worked out a new plan.

4. *To transfer your new skills, you need to practice.* Look for opportunities to practice your newly learned acts. Remind yourself to practice them. In new situations, give yourself instructions to practice. "Whoa! I've never had to be assertive in this kind of situation. Better I know what to do. Now, remember . . ."

At some point, a behavior will "take hold." It becomes easy to do, automatic, a habit. This take-hold point is directly related to the number of times the behavior is practiced. John Shelton (1979) writes: "Regardless of the particular methods chosen to promote transfer, practice is crucial. Recall that individuals lose 50% of what they learn during the day following the learning trial. . . . Practice is the one way to overcome this" (p. 238).

You should not terminate your program as soon as you reach your goal. Many years ago George Mandler (1954) trained people at a task until they were able to perform it without error 0, 10, 30, 50, or 100 times. Practicing beyond the level of errors is called *overlearning.* The more overlearning the people had, the more easily they transferred their training to new situations. Plan to overlearn. "The guiding rule should not be practice makes perfect (implying simply practice until one gets it right, and then move on), but practice of perfect (implying numerous overlearning trials of correct responses after the initial success)" (Goldstein, Lopez, & Greenleaf, 1979, p. 14).

How many overlearning trials should you use? The more, the better. Try the target behavior in new situations, and continue keeping records. If the target behavior drops alarmingly as soon as you try the new situation, you know that you haven't practiced enough. Go back to practicing with a formal self-change plan.

Beyond the Ending

Long-Term Self-Modification

Some goals can be achieved only through long-term effort, like Crystal's battle with anorexia detailed in Box 10-1. Once you have been a heavy smoker, for example, you may have to maintain vigilance for years to stay off cigarettes and reactivate self-change plans if you slip back into smoking. Successful dieters or exercisers must continue to be vigilant after they have learned their new eating or exercising skills (Westover & Lanyon, 1990). The most honestly titled book on weight loss is Kirschenbaum's (1994) *Weight Loss Through Persistence*. Because such acts have been heavily developed as habits in the past, they return easily. Research shows that formerly obese people who lose a large amount of weight and keep it off for years continue watching what they eat throughout their lives (Fletcher, 2003).

There is a general rule for the return of lapses: Expect that the old habit may return, design a plan for it in advance, and institute the plan immediately when the problem returns. Follow the steps for relapse prevention. Learn from your mistakes.

Suppose you quit smoking but after 3 months say to yourself, "Well, I can smoke just a couple at this party." Two weeks later, you're back to a pack a day. Learn from that. The next time you quit, be prepared to deal with parties. It would be a mistake to conclude that you have no willpower. Instead, conclude that you must attend carefully to the particular situations that tempt you.

Don't give up because you have not reached perfection. Throughout this book we have urged you to be persistent, not to give up, to keep trying and continue learning, but now we have to say: *Sometimes you have to settle for less than perfect.* If you weigh 190, but want to weigh 120, and manage to get down to 140, it's really foolish to give up the whole project and let yourself drift back up to 190. Yet lots of people do just that (Rothman, Baldwin, & Hertel, 2004). They have great expectations, but become so disappointed when they are not reached that they give up the whole project (Wadden et al., 2003). It would be lots smarter to continue doing whatever let you get down to 140. Small losses can make a considerable difference in your level of health. Keep on trying, at least keep on maintaining records, and over the long run you may come closer to your perfect goal.

Lifelong Projects

Some goals require nearly lifelong attention to records and self-change techniques. See "The Mindful Diet" in Chapter 3 for how one of us has struggled with overeating. Malott (2005) presents a wonderfully amusing case history of a young professor (surely not himself) who struggles throughout an entire, successful career with trouble starting his professional writing. He keeps on procrastinating, rationalizing, pulling his hair—which is graying—but continues to pour out excellent writings because he keeps on self-modifying. Sometimes lifelong self-modification is necessary, but think of what would happen if you didn't do it: Your bad habits would win.

Box 10-1
Conquering Anorexia: A Teenager Invents
Self-Modification to Change Her Life

Crystal, one of our best students, told us how as a 14-year-old she struggled with anorexia and bulimia and conquered them by independently inventing some of the techniques of self-modification that we suggest in this book.

At first I handled my diet sensibly. I began by reducing portions of my food and exercising a few days a week, but soon my weight became an obsession. I'm a perfectionist, and I wanted to be perfect. As I continued my diet, I noticed that the less I ate, the less I weighed. I ate less and less, and at the end was eating maybe one orange a day. By the end of the summer of the year I was 14, I had lost 40 pounds, going from 142 to 102. [She is 5'5" and weighs 125 now, and is slim and athletic.] I looked like one of those Ethiopian refugees. If someone hugged me all they could feel were my bones with a paper-thin covering of skin. I stopped menstruating for about a year.

When I returned to school that fall everyone raved about how thin I looked and how pretty I had become. This reinforced my new, anorectic pattern of eating. Someone would say, "You look nice today," but I would think, "Oh, no, I don't. I need to lose more weight."

At first no one seemed to realize that I was wasting away, both physically and emotionally, although later my Dad would beg me to eat. To please him I would eat a little, but as soon as he wasn't paying attention I would go to the bathroom and throw it all up.

One night I looked into my bedroom mirror and saw the hollow skeleton I had become. This reflection made me realize the damage I was doing to myself. I had heard of anorexia, but never thought it would affect me. I never told anyone what I was doing, and I never sought professional help. I made it all on my own, but the road back was long and hard.

After my realization I decided to gather as much information as possible about eating disorders. I searched for books, articles, shows, any information to help me uncover the mysteries of my disorder. As I became more knowledgeable I found ways that assisted in my recovery to a healthy lifestyle.

The first step was to monitor and eventually learn to alter my thoughts and behavior patterns about eating. I did this for many months. I kept a record of everything I ate. I also kept a diary of the day's activities, writing down my feelings and reactions, and began recognizing the patterns that led to my anorectic behavior. For example, I noticed that after an argument or confrontation with someone I would relieve my tension by exercising excessively while continuing to eat nothing.

By tracking my feelings and my eating I was eventually able to alter both. I learned to control my unrealistic thoughts about how I looked. I wore a loose rubber band around my wrist and snapped it lightly whenever a negative

(continued)

Box 10-1 *(continued)*

thought entered my mind. Also, whenever I had a negative thought, I forced myself to have two positive thoughts.

To change my eating patterns, I first gathered information about nutrition. I learned which foods were more healthful. Instead of starving all day and then eating a Dairy Queen Blizzard—whenever I did eat much, it was mostly sweets—I began eating whole wheat cereal for breakfast, a low-fat chicken sandwich for lunch, and a grilled chicken dinner, all for the same amount of fat as the Blizzard. I questioned myself about my eating: Was I eating enough to sustain my body, or was I eating like a bird because I was afraid of "ruining" my unrealistically thin figure?

I learned to use imagery to practice how I would handle situations. I practiced how I would handle a buffet line. I imagined arriving at a party and talking with friends. Then the host would invite us to eat. I imagined approaching the buffet and taking small portions of healthy food. These practice sessions helped me to relax in the real situations.

It's been 7 years since my anorexia was at its worst. I was able to overcome my eating disorder, but it is still difficult at times, and to win the struggle I have to remind myself that I want a happy, healthy, family life.

Crystal's plan contained several crucial aspects. First, she used self-observation over a long period of time, keeping track of her eating and her thoughts and feelings, and finally seeing the relation between these. This provided her with rich details to use in her problem solving. She planned seriously and used many techniques. These included changing her thinking, mildly punishing the negative thoughts, and substituting positive ones. She developed new behaviors—eating healthful foods. She provided lots of imagined practice in eating well. Last, she never gave up.

Note that 7 years after her worst problem Crystal still uses relapse prevention: She sometimes reminds herself to eat well and occasionally fights against unrealistic thoughts.

This is a remarkable case of invention by a very young person. Her plan deviated from the principles described in this book in only two respects, and these errors were outgrowths of her tendencies to be excessively private and excessively hard on herself. We would have counseled against snapping herself with the rubber band, and we would have urged her to involve others to increase reinforcement. But her extraordinary success is a demonstration of how closely her unassisted invention corresponded to the discoveries and recommendations of scientific psychology. Crystal, we hope you are celebrating your success with many friends. You are fantastic!

As you terminate your self-change project, what lies ahead? Blue skies and cloudless days, with no problems to darken the horizon? We wish you well, but we predict that sooner or later something in your life will benefit from another systematic application of self-change techniques.

You have learned these techniques by using them on one personal problem. Will you think to use them 2 years from now, when a new problem comes into your life? You can increase the chances that you will continue to use the techniques if you make a plan now for another self-change project (Barone, 1982).

Anticipating problems and thinking of ways of using self-change techniques in dealing with them may also increase your chances of remembering them when the time comes. For example:

> I know I spend my money unwisely. So far it hasn't made much difference, but it's just a matter of time until I am on my own, and then it's going to matter a lot. When that happens, I could keep records, set rules, and state those rules as self-instructions.

Or another example: "Everybody says that the job interviews for graduates are very difficult and competitive. Well, I could practice relaxation beforehand."

Stop for a minute now and think about problems you are likely to encounter in the next couple of years. How will you cope with them?

B. F. Skinner, one of the fathers of modern scientific psychology and perhaps the most influential applied psychologist of all time, was an unusually productive and happy man. Skinner invented and used many of the techniques recommended in this book long before we knew about them (Epstein, 1997). For example, he actively sought out reinforcements and enjoyed them with great gusto. He scheduled fun things into his life, but also scheduled work. He kept many records of things he was doing. He consciously controlled his environment to encourage the behaviors he wanted to perform. For example, he wanted to write about psychology, so he scheduled daily writing and used an office with no distractions in which he did nothing but write. Throughout his life he thought about how his life was going and made changes and adjustments whenever necessary. In old age, for example, he worked out social behaviors and physical cues to deal with his failing memory.

Skinner's attitude was that our lives need to be directed. Use self-management to direct your own life. When you run into problems that require self-direction, remember the techniques you have learned.

Seeking Professional Help

Sometimes our own efforts at change are not enough. There are at least four conditions that limit the usefulness of a self-modification project:

1. Your personal goals may not be clear enough to permit the choice of goal behaviors.
2. The technical problems of designing a plan may be greater than the skills that can be acquired by reading this book.
3. The natural environment itself may be too chaotic or unyielding to allow a plan to succeed.
4. Your emotions may be so strong that you can't plan enough to reach goals on your own.

Under any of these circumstances, professional advice may be helpful.

What do professionals do? Although they may take different approaches, they all employ one general strategy: They help establish situations that encourage the development of new behaviors and emotions. They help you help yourself.

Thus, even if you choose professional help, you will still find yourself engaged in building personal skills of self-direction (Showers, Limke, & Zeigler-Hill, 2004). Professionals don't solve the problems. They help you solve them. They do this by helping you create an environment that fosters your own efforts to change.

If you consider professional help, consider several points: Shop around for someone with whom you think you can work. Use the initial interview with a therapist to make your decision. You need to feel confident and comfortable with your counselor and free to talk about your problems, but whether or not you like the person is not especially important. Do some comparison shopping. Search for a good price. More expensive doesn't mean better help.

It's important to ask, as well, if the kind of therapy offered has been shown by research to be effective. Some therapies have been empirically shown to work, others have not been researched, and it is wise to select an approach that you know has worked for others.

Many groups suggest that therapist and client have a written contract specifying the goals and techniques of the process. The contract should spell out goals, costs, and time involved. For example, you may feel you want someone with whom you can discuss your uncertainty about career goals or your fears about your upcoming marriage. The contract should be flexible, allowing you to change goals during the course of therapy. Its goals may also be achieved by verbal agreement.

Self-Directed Happiness

"There is no duty we so much underrate as the duty of being happy. By being happy we sow anonymous benefits upon the world."

—Robert Louis Stevenson (1850–1894)
Scottish author

The nature of happiness has in the past been an issue that primarily philosophers discussed, but in the last few years scientific psychologists have begun to do research on happiness. It's a new area of research, so most of the conclusions are tentative, but we know enough that we can say that if you do certain things you increase the chances that you will be happy.

Happiness comes from attaining pleasure and avoiding pain, plus a feeling that life has meaning (Ryan & Deci, 2001). Happiness consists of three elements: having frequent positive emotions, having infrequent negative emotions, and feeling satisfied with your life (Diener, Lucas, & Oishi, 2002). The first element is the pleasure we all know as part of happiness, and the second element is the absence of gloom, anxiety, or pain. The third element, life satisfaction, expresses the idea that the most satisfying life is not simple amusement. We must feel satisfied with our lives to feel deeply happy. A Peace Corps volunteer living in miserable conditions in some third world country might feel a great amount of personal satisfaction, and thus say she was very happy living there in mud and squalor. A student enduring a difficult, boring, stressful course might nevertheless be happy because it will lead to a wonderful career.

If you fill out the questionnaire in Box 10-2, you'll find how you currently rate on life satisfaction. Fortunately, only a few people fall at the very low end of happiness scales, and about 20% fall at the high end (Myers, 2000). Twenty percent is good, but it

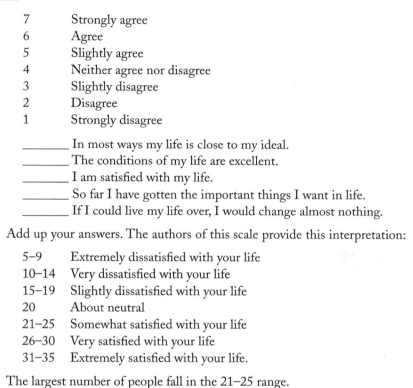

Box 10-2
Measuring Life Satisfaction

How satisfying is your life? Here are five statements you may agree or disagree with. Use the 1–7 scale below to indicate your degree of agreement with each item.

7	Strongly agree
6	Agree
5	Slightly agree
4	Neither agree nor disagree
3	Slightly disagree
2	Disagree
1	Strongly disagree

_____ In most ways my life is close to my ideal.

_____ The conditions of my life are excellent.

_____ I am satisfied with my life.

_____ So far I have gotten the important things I want in life.

_____ If I could live my life over, I would change almost nothing.

Add up your answers. The authors of this scale provide this interpretation:

5–9	Extremely dissatisfied with your life
10–14	Very dissatisfied with your life
15–19	Slightly dissatisfied with your life
20	About neutral
21–25	Somewhat satisfied with your life
26–30	Very satisfied with your life
31–35	Extremely satisfied with your life.

The largest number of people fall in the 21–25 range.

SOURCE: Adapted from "Subjective Well-Being," by E. Diener, R. E. Lucas, & S. Oishi. In *Handbook of Positive Psychology* (p. 70), C. R. Snyder & S. J. Lopez (Eds.), 2002, Oxford: Oxford University Press.

means that, for most of us, there is room for improvement. It's nice to be somewhat happy, but it's great to be very happy.

If you wanted to improve your general level of happiness, what would you do? To answer this, we need to know what causes happiness. The analysis needs to be based in data, not just theory.

The best current, research-based analysis suggests that there are three primary factors that influence happiness (Lyubomirsky, Sheldon, & Schkade, 2005). The first is heredity. Identical twins, for example, tend to have about the same levels of happiness just as they tend to have the same height, hair color, and facial features. Current theory is that people inherit a happiness set point, a point around which their happiness fluctuates throughout life. Events may take them up or down for a while, but they return to their base range of happiness.

Life circumstances are the second determinant of happiness. On the negative side, experiencing a severe childhood trauma, falling prey to a crippling disease, being born into poverty, or on the positive side, having a wonderful childhood, earning a really good salary, or having several good friends, are all circumstances that affect your level of happiness.

Heredity and life circumstances account for about 60% of the variation between people in their level of happiness. That is, if you ask what affects the differences between people in their level of happiness, these two factors account for just over half.

What accounts for the other 40%? *Our own behavior; our own activities.* You can be in a wheelchair, but if you do the things that lead to happiness, you have a good chance of being happy. You can be rich and beautiful, but if you do things that make you miserable, you have little chance of happiness.

The most effective thing we can do to increase our happiness is perform the behaviors that lead to happiness. What you do affects your happiness and life satisfaction. You can't control your heredity, and it can be difficult or impossible to control your circumstances, but we can all control our behavior.

Can you actually increase your level of happiness? Yes, if you know what to focus on and adapt your behavior to focus on that.

As early as 1977, Michael Fordyce (1977, 1983) showed that a training program in which students were taught and encouraged to practice fourteen "happiness fundamentals"—specific behaviors—actually led to increased happiness, and the effects were still present 28 months later. Research in this field languished for years, but in 2005 it was shown that encouraging three specific actions—performing acts of kindness, pausing to count one's blessings, and expressing gratitude once a week—led to increased happiness over a 6-week period (Lyubomirsky, Sheldon, & Schkade, 2005). Another study designed to increase happiness by noticing what went well every day for a week and using our character strengths in novel ways for a week, produced increases in happiness that lasted several months (Seligman, Steen, Park, & Peterson, 2005). Engaging in certain specific activities increases your happiness.

Happiness Fundamentals

Fordyce's original idea was to discover what happy people did, then teach that to everyone. For example, if the research showed that happy people tend to have more active social lives than unhappy folks—and it does—one should try to have a more active social life. Here are some of his happiness fundamentals (1981) with our comments:

1. *Be more active.* People who exercise tend to have higher levels of subjective well-being.
2. *Spend more time socializing.* Other people make us happy. If this is not always true for you, work on relaxing with others, eliminating negative thoughts about the interaction, and developing social skills such as listening.
3. *Be productive at meaningful work.* See our section on life's meaning below.
4. *Get organized.* Happy people tend to be well organized.
5. *Stop worrying.* If worrying is a problem for you, start a self-change program to reduce it by changing the focus of your thoughts.
6. *Think optimistically.* Pessimism is an emotional downer.

7. *Orient yourself to the present.* Don't dwell in the past or in a fantasy future.
8. *Eliminate negative feelings.* There are paragraphs on this below.
9. *Develop and nurture close relationships.* They are one of the main sources of happiness.

If you wanted to try for some of these goals, what would you do? Use the techniques of self-change. For example, you might put a reminder on your TV set, where you usually end up the day, "Remember to think of three good things from today." You might keep a record in a notebook: "Something I am grateful for this week." You might decide to deliberately practice switching from a negative thought to a positive one, or from a pessimistic thought to an optimistic one. You might start a self-change program to get better organized or to increase your social interactions or to exercise more.

Just thinking about this may make you feel happier for a few days (Seligman et al., 2005) but that effect will not last unless you take active steps to incorporate happiness fundamentals into your daily life. *The more you do the suggested activities, the stronger the happiness inducing effect is* (Seligman et al., 2005). Of course, the effects won't work for everyone, and you may be doubtful. But try it; then evaluate it.

Activities to Increase Happiness

Where should you start? You could start with one of Fordyce's ideas. Or try one of these.

Reduce negative emotions. An important part of happiness is absence of negative emotions, so a good place to start increasing your happiness is to focus on reducing the negatives in your thoughts and activities. Learn to meditate to reduce nervousness, exercise for the same effect, or do both. Work up a list of positive thoughts and practice substituting them for negative ones. Watch out for excessive negative thinking and rumination, in which you go over and over a problem, worrying about it, but doing nothing to solve it (Nolen-Hoeksema, 2000). One of our students said, "I used to ruminate a lot. I'd go over and over a problem, all the negative aspects of it, worrying over each aspect. I almost thought it was my duty: I had the problem; I had to worry about it. Then I realized, 'Wait, I don't have to do this. I can use problem solving and come up with some solution.' So that's what I did, and I didn't let myself worry anymore."

Count your blessings. One effective technique for reducing negative emotion is to pause each day to count your blessings. In one study participants were asked to write down three things that had gone well for them that day and to think about the causes of this (Seligman et al., 2005). They did this each night for a week. It increased their happiness scores. If you are depressed, this is a particularly good exercise to do.

Can't think of a blessing? We are not talking about major events such as winning a lot of money or getting promoted at work or falling in love. We mean minor blessings that can occur every day. Barbara Ann Kipfer (1990), who must be a really happy person, wrote *14,000 Things to Be Happy About*, in which she suggests remembering things like clean windows, the uncurling of a fern leaf, stamp machines, and polliwogs. Start your own list.

Don't think of the same things every day. If every day the blessing you remember is Newman's Own mint chocolate candy bar, pretty soon its positive emotional value will diminish. This is called *adaptation*. You get used to the effect, and it no longer has an emotional impact. Do the activity in different ways each day. One day, for example, think of good things at work, the next day at school, the next day in a friendship.

Prosocial behaviors. Performing several different prosocial behaviors has been shown to increase happiness. Not the happiness of the recipient of the good deed, please note, but the happiness of the actor. If you are kind to a stranger, the stranger might feel good, but you, too, will feel happier. In one study (Lyubomirsky et al., 2005) students were asked to perform five acts of kindness per week for 6 weeks. They might donate blood, visit a sick relative, help a friend do something, write a thank you note, or anything else that was kind. Many did small acts such as complimenting someone on looking good or helping someone move furniture. Compared to a group that did not practice kindness, these students were happier at the end of the 6 weeks. If your kind acts are small ones, it seems to be better to do them all in one day. You get more emotional punch that way.

If you wanted to implement this strategy into your life, you might benefit from keeping a record of your kind acts and using reminders to encourage yourself to be kind.

Expressing gratitude increases our level of happiness. Being grateful is good for you, and may even affect your health (Emmons & Shelton, 2002). We are not speaking of some Pollyannaish feeling—"Oh, the world is so wonderful!"—but of sincere gratitude to someone who has benefited you in some way. In one study students were encouraged to express gratitude once a week (Emmons & Shelton, 2002) and in another they were asked to pay a gratitude visit and personally thank someone who had benefited them and whom they had never personally thanked (Seligman et al., 2005). In both cases the happiness level of the grateful person increased. The research seems to indicate that to get a long-term effect gratitude needs to be repeated now and then.

You probably can't express major gratitude every week—not that many people have been extremely kind to you!—but you can express it in minor ways, such as thanking someone sincerely for some aid. And it has been shown that if you practice being grateful, you get "better" at it; it becomes easier to do (Seligman et al., 2005).

Forgiving people, the other side of gratitude, also increases our happiness (McCullough & Witvliet, 2002). Forgiveness means letting go of resentment, forgoing revenge, not holding negative emotions. You don't have to tell the person you forgive them. You just do this in your own mind. Why forgive? Because it hurts us to hold anger, resentment, and obsessive rumination about a transgression against us. The transgression is done, whatever damage has been done, and holding on to a negative state only injures us more. Besides, the best revenge is living a happy life.

Forgiveness comes easier if (1) you see that being unforgiving has a negative emotional impact on your life, and (2) you try to understand why the person acted as he or she did (Enright, Freedman, & Rique, 1998). This doesn't mean that you think the action was justified, but simply that you can see why it might have happened. "She was really a jerk to do that, but, you know, she had a miserable childhood, and her view of things is probably warped." If you can see that holding on to resentment injures you, you are ready to forgive. It's good for you.

Making Meaning in Your Life

Why would a Peace Corps volunteer living in mud and squalor in some third world jungle be happy? The pursuit of pleasure and the avoidance of pain are two parts of happiness, but being satisfied with your life is an important third part. Here is an irony: "Happiness is most often a by-product of participating in worthwhile projects and activities that do not have as the primary goal the attainment of happiness" (Emmons, 2003, p. 106). *Striving for important personal goals or devoting time to personally meaning-ful causes produces happiness* (Lyubomirsky et al., 2005).

Feeling competent with respect to valued goals leads to a feeling of well-being (Ryan & Deci, 2001). This applies whether your goal is to be a great dog breeder, a world adventurer and traveler, a gardener, a writer, a sailor, a scientist, an artist, a wonderful mother, a great husband, healthy, whatever. Don't think only of goals that involve some kind of reward, such as getting a college degree. Being a loving grandfather is just as important. The question is, "What goals should you seek?"

In terms of behavior, there are two tasks: (1) decide your personal goals, and then (2) pursue them with vitality and planfulness.

Deciding on goals could be your first self-direction project leading to high life sat-isfaction. Developing your character strengths, for example, would be a worthy goal. We all have strengths, but many don't know theirs. Are you good at patience? At hopeful-ness? At creativity or love of learning or kindness or leadership or bravery? A recent book lists these and several others and suggests that each can have a positive effect on our lives (Peterson & Seligman, 2004). Have a look at www.authentichappiness.org, a website that provides a questionnaire to discover your own personal character strengths. Once discovered, your goal might be to use your strengths more, which can lead to increased happiness.

Several researchers have converged on four categories of behavior that produce a meaningful life (Emmons, 2003). The four categories describe the areas in which people typically seek to make their life meaningful. The four are:

1. The life work dimension, in which we are committed to our work and feel it gives our life meaning;
2. The spiritual dimension, which can involve conventional religion or a spiritual feeling for something else, such as the environment, and which usually involves joining a community of the like-minded;
3. The relationship dimension, in which our life with others and intimacy with them gives us meaning; and
4. A social dimension in which one transcends self-interest and has an impact on society, leaving something behind.

Even people with chronic, debilitating diseases such as postpolio syndrome can lead happy lives if they are strong on these four dimensions (Emmons, 2003).

Notice that having a lot of money is not one of the dimensions that leads to hap-piness. Is money irrelevant to happiness? No. Wealthy people tend to be happier than poor people, and increasing income for poor people makes them happier, probably be-cause it allows them to buy life's necessities (Diener & Seligman, 2004). If you don't have enough for the kids' medicines, you are not happy, and getting enough will make you happier. But once you get to an acceptable level of income, more money does not lead to more happiness (Diener & Biswas-Diener, 2002). In the United States, increasing in-come from a very low level leads to more happiness, but as one's income gets into the middle-class range the impact of more money is less and less, and at the high end more money has little effect on happiness (Diener & Seligman, 2004).

Summary: A Happiness Checklist

Performing these activities will over time increase your happiness. If you practice them they become easier and easier to do. We suggest choosing at least two, one that is easy for you and one you have not been doing but would like to do. Then practice them for a month or more.

_____ Improve your life circumstances to increase your happiness. What, exactly, would this be?

_____ Increase your activity level.

_____ Spend more time socializing.

_____ Be better organized.

_____ Stop worrying.

_____ Think optimistically.

_____ Be oriented to the present.

_____ Try to reduce negative thoughts and feelings.

_____ Count your blessings daily.

_____ Practice kindness daily.

_____ Express gratitude when appropriate.

_____ Forgive people.

_____ Select important goals to work toward.

_____ Devote your time to meaningful causes.

_____ Be willing to invest effort in these goals and causes.

_____ Discover and develop your character strengths.

_____ Develop meaningful work.

_____ Develop your spiritual side.

_____ Develop close relationships.

_____ Transcend self-interest; give back.

Try a self-direction plan for happiness and meaning. Keep records of your efforts. Can you initiate a project, and can you keep it going? Use problem solving when difficulties arise: What keeps you from making progress? Expect lapses in your pursuit of perfection. Keep on trying; never give up. If it's not working, maybe you are pursuing goals that don't work for you, or not trying hard enough.

Happiness and life satisfaction are wonderful goals. Use the ideas in this book to reach them. We wish you the pursuit of happiness.

Chapter Summary

Planning to Maintain Gains

Your newly developed behaviors will require special attention if they are to be maintained over time and transferred to additional situations. Maintenance and transfer can be strengthened by planning for natural reinforcements to occur—that is, by seeking out situations in which the new behavior will be valued or successful. Simultaneously, resistance to extinction can be increased by thinning self-administered reinforcement to an intermittent schedule.

Find social support for new, desirable behaviors, and rate your estimation of your ability to control the new behaviors without a formal self-modification plan.

Some important principles of transfer of new learning:

- Transfer will occur only if you try for it.
- Transfer effects can be very specific to situations.
- Obstacles to transfer often occur.
- Transfer of your new skills means practice, often and in many situations.

Program for transfer of new behaviors to new, unexpected situations by practicing the behavior in a variety of situations, practicing the behavior well past the first point of learning it, continuing to keep records of your behavior, and using problem-solving techniques.

Beyond the Ending

Even after formal termination, your life conditions may change in ways that cause your new habits to lapse. This is not unusual and can be countered by the quick application of relapse prevention. Learn from those conditions that bring about lapses.

Self-direction is a lifelong practice. Use the techniques you have learned in a variety of situations. Have them ready when needed.

Professional help in changing may be needed if your goals are confused, if the technical problems of designing a plan are too great, if your natural environment is too chaotic or unyielding to support your change efforts, or if you are too emotional to be effectively planful. Professionals can assist you to change, but they do not do it for you. Select a professional carefully. Inquire about the techniques and goals that the professional offers. Make sure that there is clear agreement over the goals, techniques, and costs.

Self-Directed Happiness

Happiness has three elements: frequent positive emotions, infrequent negative emotions, and a feeling of life satisfaction. In turn, three primary factors influence happiness: heredity, circumstances, and our own behavior. The most effective thing to do to increase our happiness is to change our behaviors.

Fordyce (1983) suggested several happiness fundamentals, behaviors one should perform to induce happiness. Other researchers have shown that reducing negative emotions such as by counting our blessings, and increasing prosocial behaviors such as expressing gratitude, being kind, and forgiving trespassers increase happiness.

Life satisfaction comes from striving for goals and devoting time to meaningful activities. Four categories of behavior appear to lead to life satisfaction: meaningful life work, spirituality, close relationships, and transcending self-interest.

Your Own Self-Direction Project: Step 10

As you consider termination, follow these procedures:

1. Make a list of opportunities for practicing your newly learned behavior. Rate these opportunities in terms of how likely you are to be naturally reinforced for the new behavior.

2. If you suspect that your new behavior will not be naturally reinforced, continue reinforcing yourself or arrange for reinforcement from others.
3. Find social support for the new behavior.
4. Rate your ability to control the new behavior without a self-modification plan.
5. Program and test for transfer. Practice the behavior in a variety of situations. Continue keeping records.
6. Use problem-solving steps to deal with new difficulties.
7. Practice the new behavior until it is perfect, then practice doing it perfectly. The more you practice after you have reached your goal level, the more likely it is that your behavior will persist.
8. For long-term projects, be ready to reinstate a plan as soon as an unwanted behavior reappears.

Start a happiness project. Select at least two items from the happiness checklist, one easy and one not so, and start planning to make changes.

References

Aaronson, N. K., Ershoff, D. H., & Danaher, B. G. (1985). Smoking cessation in pregnancy: A self-help approach. *Addictive Behaviors, 10,* 103–108.

Ackerman, R., & DeRubeis, R. J. (1991). Is depressive realism real? *Clinical Psychology Review, 11,* 565–584.

Adams, J. A. (1987). Historical review and appraisal of research on the learning, retention and transfer of human motor skills. *Psychological Bulletin, 101,* 41–74.

Agran, M., & Martella, R. C. (1991). Teaching self-instructional skills to persons with mental retardation: A descriptive and experimental analysis. In M. Hersen, R. M. Eisler, & P. M. Miller (Eds.), *Progress in behavior modification* (Vol. 27, pp. 36–55). Newbury Park, CA: Sage.

Agran, M., & Martin, J. E. (1987). Applying a technology of self-control in community environments for individuals who are mentally retarded. In M. Hersen, R. M. Eisler, & P. M. Miller (Eds.), *Progress in behavior modification* (Vol. 21, pp. 108–151). Newbury Park, CA: Sage.

Agras, W. S. (1987). *Eating disorders: Management of obesity, bulimia and anorexia nervosa.* New York: Pergamon Press.

Ainslee, G. (1975). Specious reward: A behavioral theory of impulsiveness and impulse control. *Psychological Bulletin, 82,* 463–496.

Ainslee, G. (1992). *Picoeconomics: The strategic interaction of successive motivational states within the person.* New York: Cambridge University Press.

Ainslee, G. (2001). *Breakdown of will.* New York: Cambridge University Press.

Ajzen, I. (1991). The theory of planned behavior. *Organizational Behavior and Human Decision Processes, 50,* 179–211.

Ajzen, I., & Fishbein, M. (1980). *Understanding attitudes and predicting social behavior.* Englewood Cliffs, NJ: Prentice-Hall.

Altmaier, E., Ross, S., Leary, M., & Thornbookrough, M. (1982). Matching stress inoculations treatment components to clients' anxiety mode. *Journal of Counseling Psychology, 29,* 331–334.

Antony, M. M. (2001). *10 simple solutions to shyness: How to overcome shyness, social anxiety & fear of public speaking.* Oakland, CA: New Harbinger Publications, Inc.

Antony, M. M., & McCabe, R. E. (2005). *Overcoming animal & insect phobias: How to conquer fear of dogs, snakes, rodents, bees, spiders & more.* Oakland, CA: New Harbinger Publications.

Arnkoff, D. B., & Smith, R. J. (1988). Cognitive processes in test anxiety: An analysis of two assessment procedures in an actual test. *Cognitive therapy and research (Historical archive), 12*(5), 425–439.

Arntz, A., Lavy, E., van den Berg, G., & van Rijsoort, S. (1993). Negative beliefs of spider phobics: A psychometric evaluation of the spider phobia beliefs questionnaire. *Behaviour Research and Therapy, 15,* 257–277.

Ascher, L. M. (1973). An experimental analog study of covert positive reinforcement. In R. D. Rubin, J. P. Brady, & J. D. Henderson (Eds.), *Advances in behavior therapy* (Vol. 4, pp. 127–138). New York: Academic Press.

Axelrod, S., & Apsche, J. (Eds.). (1983). *The effects of punishment on human behavior.* New York: Academic Press.

Ayduk, O., Mendoza-Denton, R., Mischel, W., Downey, G., Peake, P., & Rodriguea, M. I. (2000). Regulating the interpersonal self: Strategic self-regulation for coping with rejection sensitivity. *Journal of Personality and Social Psychology, 79,* 776–792.

Azrin, N. H., Donohue, B., Besalel, V. A., Kogan, E. S., & Acierno, R. (1994). Youth drug abuse treatment: A controlled outcome study. *Journal of Child & Adolescent Substance Abuse, 3,* 1–15.

Azrin, N. H., Hake, D. F., Holz, W. C., & Hutchinson, R. R. (1965). Motivational aspects of escape from punishment. *Journal of the Experimental Analysis of Behavior, 8,* 31–44.

Azrin, N. H., & Nunn, R. G. (1973). Habit reversal: A method of eliminating nervous habits and tics. *Behavior Research and Therapy, 11,* 619–628.

Baer, J. S., Holt, C. S., & Lichtenstein, E. (1986). Self-efficacy and smoking reexamined: Construct validity and clinical utility. *Journal of Consulting and Clinical Psychology, 54,* 846–852.

Baird, S., & Nelson-Gray, R. O. (1999). Direct observation and self-monitoring. In S. C. Hayes, D. H. Barlow, & R. O. Nelson-Gray (Eds.), *The scientist practitioner* (pp. 535–586). Boston: Allyn Bacon.

Baker, R. C., & Kirschenbaum, D. S. (1993). Self-monitoring may be necessary for successful weight control. *Behavior Therapy, 24,* 377–394.

Baker, R. C., & Kirschenbaum, D. S. (1998). Weight control during the holidays: Highly consistent self-monitoring as a potentially useful coping mechanism. *Health Psychology, 17,* 367–370.

Bandura, A. (1971). Vicarious and self-reinforcement processes. In R. Glaser (Ed.), *The nature of reinforcement* (pp. 228–278). New York: Academic Press.

Bandura, A. (1981). In search of pure unidirectional determinants. *Behavior Therapy, 12,* 30–40.

Bandura, A. (1986). *Social foundations of thought and action: A social-cognitive theory.* Englewood Cliffs, NJ: Prentice-Hall.

Bandura, A. (1992). Exercise of personal agency through the self-efficacy mechanism. In R. Schwarzer (Ed.), *Self-Efficacy: Thought Control of Action* (pp. 3–37). Washington, DC: Hemisphere.

Bandura, A. (1994). Self-efficacy. In V. S. Ramachaudran (Ed.), *Encyclopedia of human behavior* (Vol. 4, pp. 71–81). New York: Academic Press.

Bandura, A. (1997). *Self-Efficacy.* New York: W. H. Freeman.

Bandura, A. (2004). Health promotion by social cognitive means. *Health Education and Behavior, 31,* 143–164.

Bandura, A., Jeffery, R. W., & Gajdos, E. (1975). Generalizing change through participant modeling with self-directed mastery. *Behaviour Research and Therapy, 13,* 141–152.

Bandura, A., & Locke, E. A. (2003). Negative self-efficacy and goal effects revisited. *Journal of Abnormal Behavior, 88*(1), 87–99.

Bandura, A., & Mahoney, M. J. (1974). Maintenance and transfer of self-reinforcement functions. *Behaviour Research and Therapy, 12,* 89–97.

Bandura, A., Reese, L., & Adams, N. E. (1982). Microanalysis of action and fear arousal as a function of differential levels of perceived self-efficacy. *Journal of Personality and Social Psychology, 43,* 5–21.

Bargh, J. A. (1997). The automaticity of everyday life. In R. S. Wyer (Ed.), *The automaticity of everyday life* (pp. 1–61). Mahwah, NJ: Erlbaum.

Barlow, D. (1988). *Anxiety and its disorders: The nature and treatment of anxiety and panic.* New York: Guilford Press.

Barnett, S. M., & Ceci, S. J. (2002). When and where do we apply what we learn? A taxonomy for far transfer. *Psychological Bulletin, 128,* 612–637.

Barone, D. F. (1982). Instigating additional self-modification projects after a personal adjustment course. *Teaching of Psychology, 9,* 111.

Barrera, M., & Glasgow, R. (1976). Design and evaluation of a personalized instruction course in behavioral self-control. *Teaching of Psychology, 3,* 81–83.

Barrios, B. A., & Shigetomi, C. C. (1979). Coping skills training for the management of anxiety: A critical review. *Behavior Therapy, 10,* 491–522.

Barrios, B. A., & Shigetomi, C. C. (1980). Coping skills training: Potential for prevention of fears and anxieties. *Behavior Therapy, 11,* 431–439.

Barrios, F. X. (1985). A comparison of global and specific estimates of self-control. *Cognitive Therapy and Research, 9,* 455–469.

Baumeister, R. F., Bratslavsky, E., Muraven, M., & Tice, D. M. (1998). Ego depletion: Is the active self a limited resource? *Journal of personality and social psychology, 74,* 1252–1265.

Baumeister, R. F., Heatherton, T. F., & Tice, D. M. (1994). *Losing control. How and why people fail at self-regulation.* San Diego, CA: Academic Press.

Baumeister, R. F., & Vohs, K. D. (2003). Self-regulation and the executive function of the self. In M. R. Leary & J. P. Tanguey (Eds.), *Handbook of self and identity* (pp. 197–217). New York: Guilford Press.

Baumeister, R. F., & Vohs, K. D. (2004). *Handbook of self-regulation.* New York: Guilford Press.

Baumeister, R. R., & Heatherton, T. F. (1996). Self-regulation failure: An overview. *Psychological Inquiry, 7,* 1–15.

Beck, A. T., & Emery, G. (1985). *Anxiety and phobias: A cognitive perspective.* New York: Basic Books.

Beck, F. M., Kaul, T. J., & Russell, R. K. (1978). Treatment of dental anxiety by cue-controlled relaxation. *Journal of Counseling Psychology, 25,* 591–594.

Becker, M. H., & Green, L. W. (1975). A family approach to compliance with medical treatment. *International Journal of Health Education, 18,* 175–182.

Bell, S. L., & Higa, W. R. (1995). Personal communication.

Bellack, A. S., Rozensky, R., & Schwartz, J. (1974). A comparison of two forms of self-monitoring in a behavioral weight reduction program. *Behavior Therapy, 5,* 523–530.

Bennet-Levy, J., Turner, F., Beaty, T., Smith, M., Paterson, B., & Farmer, S. (2001). The value of self-practice of cognitive therapy techniques and self-reflection in the training of cognitive therapists. *Behavioural and Cognitive Psychotherapy, 29,* 203–220.

Berk, L. E. (1986). Relationship of elementary school children's private speech to behavioral accompaniment to task, attention, and task performance. *Developmental Psychology, 22,* 671–680.

Biglan, A., & Campbell, D. R. (1981). Depression. In J. L. Shelton, R. L. Levy, & contributors, *Behavioral assignments and treatment compliance: A handbook of clinical strategies* (pp. 111–146). Champaign, IL: Research Press.

Blackwell, B. (1979). Treatment adherence: A contemporary overview. *Psychosomatics, 20,* 27–35.

Blanchard, E. B. (1970). Relative contributions of modeling, informational influences, and physical contact in extinction of phobic behavior. *Journal of Abnormal Psychology, 76,* 55–61.

Boice, R. (1982). Increasing the writing productivity of "blocked" academicians. *Behaviour Research and Therapy, 20,* 197–207.

Bootzin, R. R., & Nicassio, P. M. (1979). Behavioral treatments for insomnia. In M. Hersen, R. Eisler, & P. Miller (Eds.), *Progress in behavioral modification* (Vol. 6, pp. 1–45). New York: Academic Press.

Borkovec, T. D., Wilkinson, L., Folensbee, R., & Lerman, C. (1983). Stimulus control applications to the treatment of worry. *Behaviour Research and Therapy, 21,* 247–251.

Bornstein, P. H., Hamilton, S. B., & Bornstein, M. T. (1985). Self-monitoring procedures. In A. R. Ciminero, K. S. Calhoun, & H. E. Adams (Eds.), *Handbook of behavioral assessment* (2nd ed., pp. 176–222). New York: Wiley.

Boudreau, L. (1972). Transcendental meditation and yoga as reciprocal inhibitors. *Journal of Behavior Therapy and Experimental Psychiatry, 3,* 97–98.

Boutelle, K. N., Baker, R. C., Kirschenbaum, D. S., & Mitchell, M. E. (1999). How can obese weight controllers minimize weight gain during the high risk holiday season? By self-monitoring very consistently. *Health Psychology, 18,* 364–368.

Brandon, T. H. (1994). Negative affect as motivation to smoke. *Current Directions in Psychological Science, 3*(2), 33.

Brigham, T. A. (1982). Self-management: A radical behavioral perspective. In P. Karoly & F. H. Kanfer (Eds.), *Self-management and behavior*

change. *From theory to practice* (pp. 32–59). New York: Pergamon Press.

Brigham, T. A. (1989). *Self management for adolescents.* New York: Guilford Press.

Brigham, T. A., Donahoe, P., Gilbert, B. J., Thomas, N., Zemke, S., Koonce, D., & Horn, P. (2002). Psychology and AIDS education: Reducing high risk sexual behavior. *Behavior and Social Issues, 12,* 10–18.

Brigham, T. A., Moseley, S. A., Sneed, S., & Fisher, M. (1994). Excel: An intensive and structured program of advising and academic support to assist minority freshmen to succeed at a large state university. *Journal of Behavioral Education, 4,* 227–242.

Britt, E., & Singh, N. H. (1985). Reduction of rapid eating by normal adults. *Behavior Modification, 9,* 116–125.

Broman-Fulks, J. J., Berman, M. E., Rabian, B. A., & Webster, M. J. (2004). *Behaviour Research and Therapy, 42,* 125–136.

Brown, G. (1978). Self-administered desensitization of a cemetery phobia using sexual arousal to inhibit anxiety. *Journal of Behavior Therapy and Experimental Psychiatry, 9,* 73–74.

Brown, G. P., Hammen, C. L., Craske, M. G., & Wickens, T. D. (1995). Dimensions of dysfunctional attitudes as vulnerabilities to depressive symptoms. *Journal of Abnormal Psychology, 104,* 431–435.

Brown, J. D. (1991). Accuracy and bias in self-knowledge. In C. R. Snyder & D. R. Forsyth (Eds.), *Handbook of social and clinical psychology.* New York: Pergamon Press.

Brown, S. A., Stetson, B. A., & Beatty, P. A. (1989). Cognitive and behavioral features of adolescent coping in high-risk drinking situations. *Addictive Behaviors, 14,* 43–52.

Brownell, K. (2000). *The LEARN® program for weight management 2000.* Dallas, TX: The American Health Publishing Co.

Brownell, K. D., Heckerman, C. L., Westlake, R. J., Hayes, S. C., & Monti, P. M. (1978). The effect of couples training and partner cooperativeness in the behavioral treatment of obesity. *Behaviour Research and Therapy, 16,* 323–333.

Brownell, K. D., Marlatt, G. A., Lichtenstein, E., & Wilson, G. T. (1986). Understanding and preventing relapse. *American Psychologist, 41,* 765–782.

Brownlee, A. (1978). The family and health care: Explorations in cross-cultural settings. *Social Work in Health Care, 4,* 179–198.

Burnette, M. M., Koehn, K. A., Kenyon-Jump, R., Hutton, K., & Stark, C. (1991). Control of genital herpes recurrences using progressive muscle relaxation. *Behavior Therapy, 22,* 237–247.

Buss, A. H. (1980). *Self-consciousness and social anxiety.* San Francisco: W. H. Freeman.

Cameron, J., Banko, K. M., & Pierce, D. (2001). Pervasive negative effects of rewards on intrinsic motivation: the myth continues. *The Behavior analyst, 24,* 1–44.

Campbell, D. R., Bender, C., Bennett, N., & Donnelly, J. (1981). Obesity. In J. L. Shelton, R. L. Levy, & contributors, *Behavioral assignments and treatment compliance: A handbook of clinical strategies* (pp. 187–221). Champaign, IL: Research Press.

Candiotte, M. M., & Lichtenstein, E. (1981). Self-efficacy and relapse in smoking cessation programs. *Journal of Consulting and Clinical Psychology, 49,* 648–658.

Cannon, D. S., Leeka, J. K., Patterson, E. T., & Baker, T. B. (1990). Principal components analysis of the inventory of drinking situations: Empirical categories of drinking by alcoholics. *Addictive Behaviors, 15,* 265–269.

Cantor, N., Mischel, W., & Schwartz, J. (1982). Social knowledge: Structure, content, use, and abuse. In A. H. Hastorf & A. M. Isen (Eds.), *Cognitive social psychology* (pp. 33–72). New York: Elsevier/North Holland.

Cappe, R. F., & Alden, L. E. (1986). A comparison of treatment strategies for clients functionally impaired by extreme shyness and social avoidance. *Journal of Consulting and Clinical Psychology, 54,* 796–801.

Carels, R. A., Douglass, O. M., Cacciapaglia, H. M., & O'Brien, W. H. (2004). An ecological momentary assessment of relapse crises in dieting. *Journal of Consulting and Clinical Psychology, 72,* 341–348.

Carey, M. P., Snel, D. L., Carey, K. B., & Richards, C. S. (1989). Self-initiated smoking cessation: A review of the empirical literature from a stress and coping perspective. *Cognitive Therapy and Research, 13,* 323–341.

Carlbring, P., Westling, B. E., Ljungstrand, P., Ekselius, L., & Anderson, G. (2001). Treatment of panic disorder via the Internet: A randomized trial of a self-help program. *Behavior Therapy, 32,* 751–764.

Carter, J. C., & Fairburn, C. G. (1998). Cognitive-behavioral self-help for binge eating disorder: A controlled effectiveness study. *Journal of Consulting and Clinical Psychology, 66,* 616–623.

Carton, J. S., & Nowicki, S. L., Jr. (1998). Should behavior therapists stop using reinforcement? A reexamination of the undermining effect of reinforcement on intrinsic motivation. *Behavior Therapy, 29,* 65–86.

Carver, C. S. (2003). Self awareness. In M. R. Leary & J. P. Tanguen (Eds.), *Handbook of self and identity* (pp. 179–196). New York: Guilford Press.

Carver, C. S. (2004). Self-regulation of action and affect. In R. F. Baumeister & K. D. Vuhs (Eds.), *Handbook of self-regulation.* New York: Guilford Press.

Carver, C. S., & Ganellen, R. J. (1983). Depression and components of self-punitiveness: High standards, self-criticism, and overgeneralization. *Journal of Abnormal Psychology, 92,* 330–337.

Carver, C. S., & Scheier, M. F. (1982). Control theory: A useful conceptual framework for personality—social, clinical, and health psychology. *Psychological Bulletin, 92,* 111–135.

Carver, C. S., & Scheier, M. F. (1986). Analyzing shyness: A specific application of broader self-regulatory principles. In W. H. Jones, J. M. Cheek, & S. R. Briggs (Eds.), *Shyness: Perspectives on research and treatment* (pp. 173–185). New York: Plenum.

Carver, C. S., & Scheier, M. F. (2001). On the structure of behavioral self-regulation. In M. Boekaets, P. R. Pintrich, & M. Zeidner (Eds.), *Handbook of self-regulation: Theory, research, applications.* San Diego: Academic Press.

Carver, C. S., & Scheier, M. F. (2002). Optimism. In C. R. Snyder & S. J. Lopper (Eds.), *Handbook of Positive Psychology* (pp. 231–243). New York: Oxford University Press.

Cash, T. F., & Hicks, K. L. (1990). Being fat versus thinking fat: Relationships with body image, eating behaviors, and well-being. *Cognitive Therapy and Research, 14,* 327–341.

Castro, F. (1987, August). *Concurrent changes on nontargeted health behaviors in a 28-day behavior change trial.* Paper presented at the meeting of the American Psychological Association, New York.

Castro, L., de Perez, G. C., de Albanchez, D. B., & de Leon, E. P. (1983). Feedback properties of "self-reinforcement": Further evidence. *Behavior Therapy, 14,* 672–681.

Castro, L., & Rachlin, H. (1980). Self-reward, self-monitoring, and self-punishment as feedback in weight control. *Behavior Therapy, 11,* 38–48.

Catania, A. C. (1975). The myth of self-reinforcement. *Behaviorism, 3,* 192–199.

Catania, A. C., Matthews, B. A., & Shimoff, E. H. (1990). Properties of rule-governed behavior and their implications. In D. E. Blackman & H. Lejune (Eds.), *Behavior analysis in theory and practice: Contributions and controversies* (pp. 215–230). Hillsdale, NJ: Erlbaum.

Catanzaro, S. J., Wasch, H. H., Kirsch, I., & Mearns, J. (2000). Coping-related expectancies and dispositions as prospective predictors of coping responses and symptoms. *Journal of Personality, 68*(4), 757–788.

Cautela, J. R. (1966). A behavior therapy treatment of pervasive anxiety. *Behaviour Research and Therapy, 4,* 99–109.

Cautela, J. R. (1972). The treatment of overeating by covert conditioning. *Psychotherapy: Theory, Research and Practice, 9,* 211–216.

Cautela, J. R. (1973). Covert processes and behavior modification. *Journal of Nervous and Mental Disease, 157,* 27–36.

Cautela, J. R. (1983). The self-control triad: Description and clinical applications. *Behavior Modification, 7,* 299–315.

Cautela, J. R., & Baron, M. G. (1993). Consequence training: A behaviorological strategy for self-management. *Behaviorology, 2,* 31–46.

Cautela, J. R., & Kearney, A. J. (1986). *The covert conditioning handbook.* New York: Springer.

Cautela, J. R., & Samdperil, L. (1989). Imagaletics: The application of covert conditioning to athletic performance. *Applied Sport Psychology, 1,* 82–97.

Cepeda-Benito, A., Reynoso, J. T., & Erath, S. (2004). Meta-analysis of the efficacy of nicotine replacement therapy for smoking cessation: Differences between men and women. *Journal of Consulting and Clinical Psychology, 72*(4), 712–722.

Cervone, D. (1989). Effects of envisioning future activities on self-efficacy judgments and motivations: An availability heuristic interpretation. *Cognitive Therapy and Research, 13,* 247–261.

Cervone, D. (2000). Thinking about self-efficacy. *Behavior Modification, 24,* 30–56.

Cervone, D. (2004). The architecture of personality. *Psychological Review, 111,* 183–204.

Cervone, D., Jiwani, N., & Wood, R. (1991). Goal setting and the differential influence of self-regulatory processes on complex decision-making performance. *Journal of Personality and Social Psychology, 61,* 257–266.

Cervone, D., & Scott, W. D. (1995). Self-efficacy theory of behavioral change: Foundations, conceptual issues and therapeutic implications. In W. O'Donohue & L. Krasner (Eds.), *Theories of behavior therapy: Exploring behavior change.* Washington, DC: American Psychological Association.

Chang, E. C., D'Zurilla, T. J., & Sanna, L. J. (Eds.). (2004). *Social problem solving.* Washington, DC: American Psychological Association.

Chedd-Angier Productions (Producer). (1994, Nov. 2). About all you can eat. *Scientific American Frontiers.* Hartford, CT: Connecticut Public Television.

Christian, L., & Poling, A. (1997). Using self-management procedures to improve the productivity of adults with developmental disabilities in a competitive employment setting. *Journal of Applied Behavior Analysis, 30,* 169–172.

Clark, D. M., Ball, S., & Paper, D. (1991). An experimental investigation of thought suppression. *Behaviour Research and Therapy, 29,* 253–257.

Clements, C. B., & Beidleman, W. B. (1981). Undergraduate self-management projects: A technique for teaching behavioral principles. *Academic Psychology Bulletin, 3,* 451–461.

Clum, G. A., & Curtin, L. (1993). Validity and reactivity of a system of self-monitoring suicide ideation. *Journal of Psychopathology and Behavioral Assessment, 15,* 375–385.

Cognition, behavior and causality: A broad exchange of views stemming from the debate on the causal efficacy of human thought. (1995, September). *Journal of Behaviour Therapy and Experimental Psychiatry, 26*(3) [Special Issue].

Cohen, R., De James, P., Nocera, B., & Ramberger, M. (1980). Application of a simple, self-instruction procedure on adults' exercise and studying: Two case reports. *Psychological Reports, 46,* 443–451.

Cohen, S., & Lichtenstein, E. (1990). Perceived stress, quitting smoking and smoking relapse. *Health Psychology, 9,* 466–478.

Cohen, S., Lichtenstein, E., Prochaska, J. O., Rossi, J. S., Gritz, E. R., Carr, C. R., Orleans, C. T., Schoenbach, V. J., Biener, L., Abrams, D., DiClemente, C., Curry, S., Marlatt, G. A., Cummings, K. M., Emont, S. L., Giovino, G., & Osspi-Klein, D. (1989). Debunking myths about self-quitting: Evidence from ten prospective studies of persons who attempt to quit smoking by themselves. *American Psychologist, 44,* 1355–1365.

Colletti, G., Supnick, J. A., & Payne, T. J. (1985). The Smoking Self-Efficacy Questionnaire (SSEQ): Preliminary scale development and validation. *Behavioral Assessment, 7,* 249–260.

Collins, K. W., Dansereau, D. F., Garland, J. C., Holley, C. D., & McDonald, B. A. (1981). Control of concentration during academic tasks. *Journal of Educational Psychology, 73,* 122–128.

Condry, J. (1977). Enemies of exploration: Self-initiated versus other-initiated learning. *Journal of Personality and Social Psychology, 35,* 459–477.

Coppotelli, H. C., & Orleans, C. T. (1985). Partner support and other determinants of smoking cessation maintenance among women. *Journal of Consulting and Clinical Psychology, 53,* 455–460.

Craighead, L. W., & Blum, M. D. (1989). Supervised exercise in behavioral treatment for moderate obesity. *Behavior Therapy, 20,* 49–59.

Creer, T. L. (2000). Self-management of chronic illness. In M. Boekaerts, P. R. Pintrich, & M. Zeidner (Eds.), *Handbook of self-regulation* (pp. 601–630). San Diego: Academic Press.

Critchfield, T. A., & Vargas, E. A. (1991). Self-recording, instructions and public self-graphing. *Behavior modification, 15,* 95–112.

Cummings, C., Gordon, J. R., & Marlatt, G. A. (1980). Relapse: Prevention and prediction.

In W. R. Miller (Ed.), *The addictive behaviors* (pp. 291–321). Oxford: Pergamon Press.

Curry, S. (1993). Self-help interventions for smoking cessation. *Journal of Consulting and Clinical Psychology, 61,* 790–803.

Curry, S., Wagner, E. H., & Grothaus, L. C. (1990). Intrinsic and extrinsic motivation for smoking cessation. *Journal of Consulting and Clinical Psychology, 58,* 310–316.

Curry, S. G., & Marlatt, A. (1987). Building self-confidence, self-efficacy and self-control. In W. M. Cox (Ed.), *Treatment and prevention of alcohol problems* (pp. 117–137). New York: Academic Press.

Curry, S., Marlatt, G. A., & Gordon, J. (1987). Abstinence violation effect: Validation of an attributional construct with smoking cessation. *Journal of Consulting and Clinical Psychology, 55*(2), 145–149.

Davidson, A., Denney, D. R., & Elliott, C. H. (1980). Suppression and substitution in the treatment of nail biting. *Behaviour Research and Therapy, 18,* 1–9.

Davies, M. I., & Clark, D. M. (1998). Thought suppression produces a rebound effect with analogue post-traumatic intrusions. *Behaviour Research and Therapy, 36*(6), 571–572.

Davis, J. R., & Glaros, A. G. (1986). Relapse prevention and smoking cessation. *Addictive Behaviors, 11,* 105–114.

deBortali-Tregerthan, G. (1984). *Self-change and attribution-change training: Implications for primary prevention.* Unpublished doctoral dissertation, University of Hawaii, Honolulu, HI.

Deffenbacher, J. L. (1981). Anxiety. In J. L. Shelton, R. L. Levy, & contributors, *Behavioral assignments and treatment compliance: A handbook of clinical strategies* (pp. 93–109). Champaign, IL: Research Press.

Deffenbacher, J. L., & Hahnloser, R. M. (1981). Cognitive and relaxation coping skills in stress inoculation. *Cognitive Therapy and Research, 5,* 211–215.

Deffenbacher, J. L., McNamara, K., Stark, R. S., & Sabadell, P. M. (1990). A combination of cognitive, relaxation, and behavioral coping skills in the reduction of general anger. *Journal of College Student Development, 31,* 351–358.

Deffenbacher, J. L., & Michaels, A. C. (1981). Anxiety management training and self-control desensitization—fifteen months later. *Journal of Counseling Psychology, 28,* 459–462.

Deffenbacher, J. L., & Shepard, J. M. (1989). Evaluating a seminar on stress management. *Teaching of Psychology, 16,* 79–81.

Deffenbacher, J. L., & Suinn, R. M. (1982). The self-control of anxiety. In P. Karoly & F. H. Kanfer (Eds.), *Self-management and behavior change: From theory to practice* (pp. 393–442). New York: Pergamon Press.

de Jong, P. J., Andrea, H., & Muris, P. (1997). Spider phobia in children: Disgust and fear before and after treatment. *Behavior research and therapy, 35*(6), 559–562.

de Jong, P. J., Vorage, I., & van den Hout, M. A. (2000). Counterconditioning in the treatment of spider phobia: Effects on disgust, fear and valence. *Behavior Research and Therapy, 38,* 1055–1069.

Delmonte, M. M. (1985). Meditation and anxiety reduction: A literature review. *Clinical Psychology Review, 5,* 91–102.

Denney, D. R. (1980). Self-control approaches to the treatment of test anxiety. In I. G. Sarason (Ed.), *Test anxiety: Theory, research, and applications* (pp. 209–243). Hillsdale, NJ: Erlbaum.

de Silva, P. (1985). Early Buddhist and modern behavioral strategies for the control of unwanted intrusive cognitions. *The Psychological Record, 35,* 437–443.

DiCara, L. (1970, January). Learning in the autonomic nervous system. *Scientific American,* 30–39.

Dickson-Parnell, B. E., & Zeichner, A. (1985). Effects of a short-term exercise program on caloric consumption. *Health Psychology, 4,* 437–448.

DiClemente, C. C. (1994). If behaviors change, can personality be far behind? In T. F. Heatherton & J. L. Weinberger (Eds.), *Can personality change?* (pp. 175–198). Washington, DC: American Psychological Association.

DiClemente, C. C., & Proschaska, J. O. (1998). Toward a comprehensive, transtheoretical model of change: Stages of change and addictive behaviors. In H. R. Miller & N. Heather (Eds.), *Treating addictive behaviors* (2nd ed., pp. 3–24). Albuquerque: University of New Mexico Press.

Diener, E., & Biswas-Diener, R. (2002). Will money increase subjective well-being? A literature review and guide to needed research. *Social Indicators Research, 57,* 119–169.

Diener, E., Lucas, R. E., & Oishi, S. (2002). Subjective well-being: The science of happiness and life satisfaction. In C. R. Snyder & S. J. Lopez (Eds.), *Handbook of positive psychology* (pp. 63–73). Oxford: Oxford University Press.

Diener, E., & Seligman, M. E. P. (2004). Beyond money: Toward an economy of well-being. *Psychological Science in the Public Interest, 5*(1).

Dixon, W. A., Heppner, P. P., Burnett, J. W., Anderson, W. P., & Wood, P. K. (1993). Distinguishing among antecedents, concomitants, and consequences of problem-solving appraisal and depressive symptoms. *Journal of Counseling Psychology, 40,* 357–364.

Dodd, D. K. (1986). Teaching behavioral self-change: A course model. *Teaching of Psychology, 13,* 82–85.

Doerfler, L. A., & Richards, C. S. (1981). Self-initiated attempts to cope with depression. *Cognitive Therapy and Research, 5,* 367–371.

Doerfler, L. A., & Richards, C. S. (1983). College women coping with depression. *Behavioral Research Therapy, 21,* 221–224.

Dollard, J., & Miller, N. E. (1950). *Personality and psychotherapy.* New York: McGraw-Hill.

Doyne, E. J., Ossip-Klein, D. J., Bowman, E. D., Osborn, K. M., McDougall-Wilson, I. B., & Neimeyer, R. A. (1987). Running versus weight lifting in the treatment of depression. *Journal of Consulting and Clinical Psychology, 55,* 748–754.

Dubbert, P. M., Martin, J. E., & Epstein, L. H. (1986). Exercise. In K. A. Holroyd & T. L. Creer (Eds.), *Self-management of chronic disease* (pp. 127–162). New York: Academic Press.

Dubbert, P. M., Martin, J. E., Raczynski, J., & Smith, P. O. (1982, March). *The effects of cognitive-behavioral strategies in the maintenance of exercise.* Paper presented at the third annual meeting of the Society of Behavioral Medicine, Chicago.

Dunning, D., Heath, C., & Suls, J. (2004). Flawed self-assessment. *Psychological science in the public interest, 5*(3).

Dunning, D., Johnson, K., Ehrlinger, J., & Kruger, J. (2003). Why people fail to recognize their own incompetence. *Current directions in psychological science, 12,* 83–87.

Dush, D. M., Hirt, M. L., & Schroeder, H. (1983). Self-statement modification with adults: A meta-analysis. *Psychological Bulletin, 94,* 408–422.

Dweck, C. S. (1975). The role of expectations and attributions in the alleviation of learned helplessness. *Journal of Personality and Social Psychology, 31,* 674–685.

Dweck, C. S. (1999). *Self-theories: Their role in motivation, personality and development.* Philadelphia: Taylor & Francis.

D'Zurilla, T. J. (1990). Problem solving training for effective stress management and prevention. *Journal of Cognitive Psychotherapy, 4,* 327–354.

D'Zurilla, T. J., & Chang, E. C. (1995). The relationship between problem solving and coping. *Cognitive Therapy and Research, 19,* 547–562.

D'Zurilla, T. J., & Goldfried, M. R. (1971). Problem solving and behavior modification. *Journal of Abnormal Psychology, 78,* 107–126.

D'Zurilla, T. J., & Nezu, A. (1982). Social problem solving in adults. In P. C. Kendall (Ed.), *Advances in cognitive-behavioral research and therapy* (Vol. 1, pp. 201–274). New York: Academic Press.

D'Zurilla, T. J., & Nezu, A. M. (1989). Clinical stress management. In A. M. Nezu & C. M. Nezu (Eds.), *Clinical decision making in behavior therapy—A problem solving perspective* (pp. 371–400). Champaign, IL: Research Press.

D'Zurilla, T. J., Nezu, A. M., & Maydeu-Okivaries, A. (2004). Social problem solving. In E. C. Chang, D. J. D'Zurilla, & L. D. Sanna (Eds.), *Social problem solving* (pp. 11–27). Washington, DC: American Psychological Association.

Egan, G. (1977). *You and me: The skills of communicating and relating to others.* Pacific Grove, CA: Brooks/Cole.

Eich, E. (1995). Searching for mood dependent memory. *Psychological Science, 6,* 67–75.

Eich, E., Rachman, S., & Lopatka, C. (1990). Affect, pain and autobiographical memory. *Journal of Abnormal Psychology, 99,* 174–178.

Eifert, G. H., Craill, L., Carey, E., & O'Conner, C. (1988). Affect modification through evaluative conditioning with music. *Behaviour Research and Therapy, 26,* 321–330.

Eisenberger, R., & Adornetto, M. (1986). Generalized self-control of delay and effort. *Journal of Personality and Social Psychology, 51,* 1020–1031.

Ekkekakis, P., Hall, E. E., VanLanduyt, L. M., & Petruzzello, S. J. (2000). Walking in (affective) circles: can short walks enhance affect? *Journal of Behavioral Medicine, 23*(3), 245–275.

Emmelkamp, P. M. G. (1990). Anxiety and fear. In A. S. Bellack, M. Hersen, & A. E. Kazdin (Eds.), *International handbook of behavior modification and therapy* (pp. 283–306). New York: Plenum Press.

Emmons, R. A. (2003). Personal goals, life meaning, and virtue: Wellsprings of a positive life. In C. L. M. Keyes & J. Haidt (Eds.), *Flourishing: positive psychology and the life well lived* (pp. 105–128). Washington, DC: American Psychological Association.

Emmons, R. A., & Shelton, C. M. (2002). Gratitude and the science of positive psychology. In C. R. Snyder & S. J. Lopez (Eds.), *Handbook of positive psychology* (pp. 459–471). Oxford: Oxford University Press.

Endler, N. S., & Kocovski, N. L. (2000). Self-regulation and distress in clinical psychology. In M. Boedaerts, P. R. Pintrich, & M. Zeidner (Eds.), *Handbook of self-regulation* (pp. 569–599). San Diego: Academic Press.

Enright, R. D., Freedman, S., & Rique, J. (1998). The psychology of interpersonal forgiveness. In R. D. Enright & J. North (Eds.), *Exploring forgiveness* (pp. 46–62). Madison, WI: University of Wisconsin Press.

Epstein, L. H., Miller, P. M., & Webster, J. S. (1976). The effects of reinforcing concurrent behavior on self-monitoring. *Behavior Therapy, 7,* 89–95.

Epstein, L. H., Webster, J. S., & Miller, P. M. (1975). Accuracy and controlling effects of self-monitoring as a function of concurrent responding and reinforcement. *Behavior Therapy, 6,* 654–666.

Epstein, R. (1997). Skinner as self-manager. *Journal of Applied Behavior Analysis, 30,* 545–568.

Epstein, S. (1992). Coping ability, negative self-evaluation, and overgeneralization: Experiment and theory. *Journal of Personality and Social Psychology, 62,* 826–836.

Erber, R., & Tesser, A. (1992). Task effort and the regulation of mood: The absorption hypothesis. *Journal of Experimental Social Psychology, 28,* 339–359.

Ericsson, K. A., & Charness, N. (1994). Expert performance: Its structure and acquisition. *American Psychologist, 49,* 725–747.

Ericsson, K. A., Krampe, R., & Tesch-Romer, C. (1993). The role of deliberate practice in the acquisition of expert performance. *Psychological Review, 100*(3), 361–406.

Ernst, F. A. (1973). Self-recording and counter-conditioning of a self-mutilative compulsion. *Behavior Therapy, 4,* 144–146.

Fanning, P. (1990). *Lifetime weight control.* Oakland, CA: New Harbinger.

Fantuzzo, J. W., Rohrbeck, C. A., & Azar, S. T. (1987). A component analysis of behavioral self-management interventions with elementary school children. *Child and Family Behavior Therapy, 9,* 33–43.

Farber, B. (1987). *Making people talk.* New York: William Morrow.

Farmer, R., & Nelson-Gray, R. (1990). The accuracy of counting versus estimating event frequencies in behavioral assessment: The effects of behavior frequency, number of behaviors monitored, and time delay. *Behavioral Assessment, 12,* 425–442.

Febbraro, G. A. R., & Clum, G. A. (1998). Meta-analytic investigation of the effectiveness of self-regulatory components in the treatment of adult problem behaviors. *Clinical Psychology Review, 18,* 143–161.

Febbraro, G. A. R., Clum, G. A., Roodman, A. A., & Wright, J. H. (1999). The limits of bibliotherapy: A study of the differential effectiveness of self-administered interventions in individuals with panic attacks. *Behavior Therapy, 30,* 209–222.

Ferguson, J. M. (1975). *Learning to eat.* Palo Alto, CA: Bell.

Ferrari, J. R. (1991). Compulsive procrastination: Some self-reported characteristics. *Psychological Reports, 68,* 455–458.

Ferster, C. B., Nurnberger, J. I., & Levitt, E. G. (1962). The control of eating. *Journal of Mathematics, 1,* 87–109.

Fischer, K. W. (1980). A theory of cognitive development: The control and construction of hierarchies of skills. *Psychological Review, 87,* 477–531.

Fisher, E. B., Jr., Levenkron, J. C., Lowe, M. R., Loro, A. D., & Green, L. (1982). Self-initiated self-control in risk reduction. In R. Stuart (Ed.), Adherence, compliance, and generalization in behavioral medicine (pp. 145–168). New York: Brunner/Mazel.

Fisher, E. B., Jr., Lowe, M. R., Levenkron, J. C., & Newman, A. (1982). Reinforcement and structural support of maintained risk reduction. In R. B. Stuart (Ed.), *Adherence, compliance and generalization in behavioral medicine* (pp. 169–192). New York: Brunner/Mazel.

Fitzgibbon, M. L., & Kirschenbaum, D. S. (1992). Who succeeds in losing weight? In Y. Klar, J. D. Fisher, J. M. Chinsky, & A. Nadler (Eds.), *Self change: Social, psychological and clinical perspectives.* New York: Springer-Verlag.

Fixen, D. L., Phillips, E. L., & Wolf, M. M. (1972). Achievement place: The reliability of self-reporting and peer-reporting and their effects on behavior. *Journal of Applied Behavior Analysis, 5,* 19–30.

Flannery, R. F., Jr. (1972). A laboratory analogue of two covert reinforcement procedures. *Journal of Behavior Therapy and Experimental Psychiatry, 3,* 171–177.

Flaxman, J. (1978). Quitting smoking now or later: Gradual, abrupt, immediate, and delayed quitting. *Behavior Therapy, 9,* 260–270.

Fletcher, A. M. (2003). *Thin for life.* Boston: Houghton Mifflin.

Ford, D. H. (1987). *Humans as self-constructing living systems: A developmental perspective on behavior and personality.* Hillsdale, NJ: Erlbaum.

Ford, E. E. (1989). Fostering self-control: Comments of a counselor. In W. Hershberger (Ed.), *Volitional action: Conation and control.* Amsterdam: North Holland.

Ford, M. E. (1992). *Motivating humans.* Newbury Park, CA: Sage.

Fordyce, M. W. (1977). Development of a program to increase personal happiness. *Journal of Counseling Psychlogy, 24,* 511–521.

Fordyce, M. W. (1981). *The psychology of happiness: A brief version of the fourteen fundamentals.* Ft. Myers, FL: Cypress Lake Media.

Fordyce, M. W. (1983). A program to increase happiness: Further studies. *Journal of Counseling Psychology, 30,* 483–498.

Foreyt, J. P., & Goodrick, K. (1994). Attributes of successful approaches to weight loss and control. *Applied and Preventive Psychology, 3,* 209–215.

Forsterling, F., & Morgenstern, M. (2002). Accuracy of self-assessment and task performance: Does it pay to know the truth? *Journal of Educational Psychology, 94,* 576–585.

Fortmann, S. P., & Killen, J. D. (1995). Nicotine gum and self-help behavioral treatment for smoking relapse prevention: Results from a trial using population-based recruitment. *Journal of Consulting and Clinical Psychology, 63,* 460–468.

Frankel, A. J. (1975). Beyond the simple functional analysis—The chain: A conceptual framework for assessment with a case study example. *Behavior Therapy, 6,* 254–260.

Freeman, A., & Zaken-Greenburg, F. (1989). Cognitive family therapy. In C. Figley (Ed.), *Psychological stress.* New York: Brunner/Mazel.

Fritzler, B. K., Hecker, J. E., & Losee, M. C. (1997). Self-directed treatment with minimal therapist contact: preliminary findings for obsessive-compulsive disorder. *Behavior Research and Therapy, 35,* 627–631.

Fuchs, C. Z., & Rehm, L. P. (1977). A self-control behavior therapy program for depression. *Journal of Consulting and Clinical Psychology, 45,* 206–215.

Gable, S. L., Reis, H. T., Impett, E. A., & Asher, E. R. (2004). What do you do when things go right? The intrapersonal and interpersonal benefits of sharing positive events. *Journal of Personality and Social Psychology, 87*(2), 228–245.

Gambrill, E., & Richey, C. (1985). *Taking charge of your social life.* Belmont, CA: Wadsworth.

Gauthier, J., & Pellerin, D. (1982). Management of compulsive shoplifting through covert sensitization. *Journal of Behavior Therapy and Experimental Psychiatry, 13,* 73–75.

Gauthier, J., Pellerin, D., & Renaud, P. (1983). The enhancement of self-esteem: A comparison of two cognitive strategies. *Cognitive Therapy and Research, 7,* 389–398.

George, W. H., & Marlatt, G. A. (1986). Problem drinking. In K. A. Holroyd & T. L. Creer (Eds.), *Self-management of chronic disease* (pp. 59–98). New York: Academic Press.

Gershman, L., & Stedman, J. M. (1971). Oriental defense exercises as reciprocal inhibitors of anxiety. *Journal of Behavior Therapy and Experimental Psychiatry, 2,* 117–119.

Gilchrist, L. D., Schinke, S. P., Bobo, J. K., & Snow, W. H. (1986). Self-control skills for preventing smoking. *Addictive Behaviors, 11,* 169–174.

Gilovich, T. (1991). *How we know what isn't so.* New York: Free Press.

Ginsberg, D., Hall, S. M., & Rosinski, M. (1991). Partner interaction and smoking cessation: A pilot study. *Addictive Behaviors, 16,* 195–201.

Glasgow, R. E., & Lichtenstein, E. (1987). Long-term effects of behavioral smoking cessation interventions. *Behavior Therapy, 18,* 297–324.

Glynn, S. M., & Ruderman, A. J. (1986). The development and validation of an eating self-efficacy scale. *Cognitive Therapy and Research, 10,* 403–420.

Godat, L. M., & Brigham, T. A. (1999). The effect of a self-management training program on employees of a mid-sized organization. *Journal of Organizational Behavior Management, 19,* 65–82.

Goldfried, M. R. (1971). Systematic desensitization as training in self-control. *Journal of Consulting and Clinical Psychology, 37,* 228–234.

Goldfried, M. R. (1977). The use of relaxation and cognitive relabelling as coping skills. In R. B. Stuart (Ed.), *Behavioral self-management: Strategies, techniques and outcomes* (pp. 82–116). New York: Brunner/Mazel.

Goldfried, M. R. (1979). Anxiety reduction through cognitive-behavioral intervention. In P. C. Kendall & S. D. Hollon (Eds.), *Cognitive-behavioral interventions: Theory, research, and procedures* (pp. 117–152). New York: Academic Press.

Goldfried, M. R. (1988). Application of rational restructuring to anxiety disorders. *The Counseling Psychologist, 16,* 50–68.

Goldfried, M. R., & Goldfried, A. P. (1977). Importance of hierarchy content in the self-control of anxiety. *Journal of Consulting and Clinical Psychology, 45,* 124–131.

Goldfried, M. R., & Robins, C. (1982). On the facilitation of self-efficacy. *Cognitive Therapy and Research, 6,* 361–380.

Goldfried, M. R., & Trier, C. S. (1974). Effectiveness of relaxation as an active coping skill. *Journal of Abnormal Psychology, 83,* 348–355.

Goldiamond, I. (1965). Self-control procedures in personal behavior problems. *Psychological Reports, 17,* 851–868.

Goldstein, A. P., & Kanfer, F. H. (Eds.). (1979). *Maximizing treatment gains: Transfer enhancement in psychotherapy.* New York: Academic Press.

Goldstein, A. P., Lopez, M., & Greenleaf, D. O. (1979). Introduction. In A. P. Goldstein & F. H. Kanfer (Eds.), *Maximizing treatment gains: Transfer enhancement in psychotherapy* (pp. 1–22). New York: Academic Press.

Goldstein, A., & Martens, B. K. (2000). *Lasting change.* Champaign, IL: Research Press.

Goldstein, A. P., Sprafkin, R. P., & Gershaw, N. J. (1979). *I know what's wrong, but I don't know what to do about it.* Englewood Cliffs, NJ: Prentice-Hall.

Gollwitzer, P. M., Fujita, K., & Oettingen, G. (2004). Planning and the implementation of goals. In R. R. Baumeister & K. D. Vohs (Eds.), *Handbook of Self-Regulation: Research, Theory, and Applications* (pp. 211–228). New York: Guilford Press.

Goodall, T. A., & Halford, W. K. (1991). Self-management of diabetes mellitus: A critical review. *Health Psychology, 10*(1), 1–8.

Gould, R. A., & Clum, G. A. (1993). A meta-analysis of self-help treatment approaches. *Clinical Psychology Review, 13,* 169–186.

Gould, R. A., & Clum, G. A. (1995). Self-help plus minimal therapist contact in the treatment of panic disorder: A replication and extension. *Behavior Therapy, 26,* 533–546.

Gould, R. A., Clum, G. A., & Shapiro, D. (1993). The use of bibliotherapy in the treatment of panic: A preliminary investigation. *Behavior Therapy, 24,* 241–252.

Grant, H., & Dweck, C. (1999). Content versus structure in motivation and self-regulation. In R. S. Wyer (Ed.), *Perspectives on behavioral self-regulation* (pp. 161–174). Mahwah, NJ: Erlbaum.

Graziano, A. M. (1975). Futurants, coverants, and operants. *Behavior Therapy, 6,* 421–422.

Gredler, M. E., & Schwartz, L. S. (1997). Factorial structure of the self-efficacy for self-regulated learning scale. *Psychological Reports, 81,* 51–57.

Green, L. (1982). Minority students' self-control of procrastination. *Journal of Counseling Psychology, 29,* 636–644.

Griffin, D. E., & Watson, D. L. (1978). A written, personal commitment from the student encourages better course work. *Teaching of Psychology, 5,* 155.

Grilo, C. M., & Shiffman, S. (1994). Longitudinal investigation of the abstinence violation effect in binge eaters. *Journal of Consulting and Clinical Psychology, 62,* 611–610.

Grilo, C. M., Shiffman, S., & Wing, R. R. (1989). Relapse crises and coping among dieters. *Journal of Consulting and Clinical Psychology, 57,* 488–495.

Gross, A. M., & Drabman, R. S. (1982). Teaching self-recording, self-evaluation, and self-reward to nonclinic children and adolescents. In P. Karoly & F. H. Kanfer (Eds.), *Self-management and behavior change: From theory to practice* (pp. 285–315). New York: Pergamon Press.

Gustafson, R. (1992). Treating insomnia with a self-administered muscle relaxation training program: A follow-up. *Psychological Reports, 70,* 124–126.

Gwaltney, C. J., Shiffman, S., Paty, J. A., Liu, K. S., Kassel, J. D., Gnys, M., & Hickcox, M. (2002). Using self-efficacy judgments to predict characteristics of lapses to smoking. *Journal of Consulting and Clinical Psychology, 70,* 1140–1149.

Haaga, D. A. F., & Stewart, B. L. (1992). Self-efficacy for recovery from a lapse after smoking cessation. *Journal of Consulting and Clinical Psychology, 60,* 24–28.

Halford, W. K., Sanders, M. R., & Behrens, B. C. (1994). Self-regulation in behavioral couple's therapy. *Behavior Therapy, 25,* 431–452.

Hall, S. M. (1980). Self-management and therapeutic maintenance: Theory and research. In P. Karoly & J. Steffen (Eds.), *Improving the long-term effects of psychotherapy* (pp. 263–300). New York: Gardner Press.

Hall, S. M., Rugg, D., Tunstall, C., & Jones, R. T. (1984). Preventing relapse to cigarette smoking by behavioral skill training. *Journal of Consulting and Clinical Psychology, 52,* 372–382.

Hamilton, S. B. (1980). Instructionally based training in self-control: Behavior-specific and generalized outcomes resulting from student-implemented self-modification projects. *Teaching of Psychology, 7,* 140–145.

Hamilton, S. B., & Waldman, D. A. (1983). Self-modification of depression via cognitive-behavioral intervention strategies: A time series analysis. *Cognitive Therapy and Research, 7,* 99–106.

Harackiewicz, J. M., Sansone, C., Blair, L. W., Epstein, J. A., & Manderlink, G. (1987). Attributional processes in behavior change and maintenance: Smoking cessation and continued abstinence. *Journal of Consulting and Clinical Psychology, 55,* 372–378.

Harris, K. R., & Graham, S. (1996). *Making the writing process work.* Cambridge, MA: Brookline Books.

Harris, G. M., & Johnson, S. B. (1980). Comparison of individualized covert modeling, self-control desensitization, and study-skills training for alleviation of test anxiety. *Journal of Consulting and Clinical Psychology, 48,* 186–194.

Harris, G. M., & Johnson, S. B. (1983). Coping imagery and relaxation instructions in a covert modeling treatment for test anxiety. *Behavior Therapy, 14,* 144–157.

Hayes, S. C. (Ed.). (1989). *Rule governed behavior: Cognition, contingencies, and instructional control.* New York: Plenum.

Hayes, S. C., & Nelson, R. O. (1986). Assessing the effects of therapeutic interventions. In R. O. Nelson & S. C. Hayes (Eds.), *Conceptual foundations of behavioral assessment.* New York: Guilford Press.

Hayes, S. C., Rosenfarb, I., Wulfert, E., Munt, E. D., Korn, Z., & Zettle, R. D. (1985). Self-reinforcement effects: An artifact of social standard setting? *Journal of Applied Behavior Analysis, 18,* 201–214.

Head, S., & Brookhart, A. (1997). Lifestyle modification and relapse prevention training during treatment for weight loss. *Behavior Therapy, 28,* 307–321.

Heatherton, T. F., & Baumeister, R. F. (1991). Binge eating as escape from self-awareness. *Psychological Bulletin, 110,* 86–108.

Heffernan, T., & Richards, C. S. (1981). Self-control of study behavior: Identification and evaluation of natural methods. *Journal of Counseling Psychology, 28,* 361–364.

Heiby, E. M. (1981). Depression and frequency of self-reinforcement. *Behavior Therapy, 12,* 549–555.

Heiby, E. M. (1983a). Depression as a function of the interaction of self- and environmentally controlled reinforcement. *Behavior Therapy, 14,* 430–433.

Heiby, E. M. (1983b). Toward the prediction of mood change. *Behavior Therapy, 14,* 110–115.

Heiby, E. M. (1986). Social versus self-control skills deficits in four cases of depression. *Behavior Therapy, 17, 158–169.*

Heiby, E. M. (1987, August). *Toward the unification of the psychology of depression: Contributions from a paradigmatic behavioral theory.* Paper presented at the meeting of the American Psychological Association, New York.

Heiby, E. M., Ozaki, M., & Campos, P. E. (1984). The effects of training in self-reinforcement and reward: Implications for depression. *Behavior Therapy, 15,* 544–549.

Heinrichsen, H., & Clark, D. M. (2003). Anticipatory processing in social anxiety: Two pilot studies. *Journal of Behavior Therapy and Experimental Psychiatry, 34,* 205–218.

Heins, E. D., Lloyd, J. W., & Hallahan, D. P. (1986). Cued and noncued self-recording of attention to task. *Behavior Modification, 10,* 235–254.

Heinzelman, E., & Bagley, R. W. (1970). Response to physical activity programs and their effects on health behavior. *Public Health Reports, 85,* 905–911.

Herman, C. P., & Polivy, J. (2004). The self-regulation of eating. In R. F. Baumeister & K. D. Vohs (Eds.), *Handbook of self-regulation* (pp. 492–508). New York: Guilford Press.

Herman, C. P., Roth, D. A., & Polivy, J. (2003). Effects of the presence of others on food intake: A normative interpretation. *Psychological Bulletin, 129*(6), 873–886.

Herren, C. M. (1989). A self-monitoring technique for increasing productivity in multiple media. *Journal of Behavior Therapy and Experimental Psychiatry, 20,* 69–72.

Hiebert, B., & Fox, E. E. (1981). Reactive effects of self-monitoring anxiety. *Journal of Counseling Psychology, 28,* 187–193.

Higgins, R. L., Frisch, M. B., & Smith, D. (1983). A comparison of role-played and natural responses to identical circumstances. *Behavior Therapy, 14,* 158–169.

Higgins, R. L., Wong, C. J., Badger, G. J., Ogden, D. E. H., & Dantona, R. L. (2000). Contingent reinforcement increases cocaine abstinence during outpatient treatment and 1 year of follow-up. *Journal of Consulting and Clinical Psychology, 68,* 64–72.

Hill, H. A., Schoenbach, V. J., Kleinbaum, D. G., Strecher, V. J., Orleans, C. T., Gebski, V. J., & Kaplan, B. H. (1994). A longitudinal analysis of predictors of quitting smoking among participants in a self-help intervention trial. *Addictive Behaviors, 19,* 159–173.

Hodgkins, D. C., & el-Guebaly, N. (2004). Retrospective and prospective reports of precipitants to relapse in pathological gambling. *Journal of Consulting and Clinical Psychology, 72*(1), 72–80.

Hodgkins, D. C., el-Guebaly, N., & Armstrong, S. (1995). Prospective and retrospective reports of mood states before relapse to substance use. *Journal of Consulting and Clinical Psychology, 63,* 400–407.

Hofer, R. K., & Yu, S. L. (2003). Teaching self-regulated learning through a "Learning to Learn" course. *Teaching of Psychology, 30,* 30–33.

Holden, A. E., O'Brien, G. T., Barlow, D. H., Stetson, D., & Infantino, A. (1983). Self-help manual for agoraphobia: A preliminary report of effectiveness. *Behavior Therapy, 14,* 545–556.

Hollon, S. D., & Beck, A. T. (1979). Cognitive therapy of depression. In P. C. Kendall & S. D. Hollon (Eds.), *Cognitive-behavioral interventions: Theory, research, and procedures* (pp. 153–203). New York: Academic Press.

Holman, J., & Baer, D. M. (1979). Facilitating generalization of on-task behavior through self-monitoring of academic tasks. *Journal of Autism and Developmental Disorders, 9,* 429–446.

Hope, D. A., Rapee, R. M., Heimberg, R. G., & Dombeck, M. J. (1990). Representations of the self in social phobia: Vulnerability to social threat. *Cognitive Therapy and Research, 14*(2), 177–189.

Hopko, D. R., Armento, M. E. A., Cantu, M. S., Chambers, L. L., & Lejuez, C. W. (2003). The use of daily diaries to assess the relations among mood state, overt behavior, and reward value of activities. *Behaviour Research and Therapy 41,* pp. 1137–1148.

Horan, J. J., Baker, S. B., Hoffman, A. M., & Shute, R. E. (1975). Weight loss through variations in the coverant control paradigm. *Journal of Consulting and Clinical Psychology, 43,* 68–72.

Horan, J. J., & Johnson, R. G. (1971). Coverant conditioning through a self-management application of the Premack Principle: Its effect on weight reduction. *Journal of Behavior Therapy and Experimental Psychiatry, 2,* 243–249.

Horn, D. (1972). Determinants of change. In R. G. Richardson (Ed.), *The second world conference on smoking and health* (pp. 58–74). London: Pitman Medical.

Horn, P. A., & Brigham, T. A. (1996). A self-management approach to reducing AIDS risk in sexually active heterosexual college students. *Behavior and Social Issues, 6*(1), 3–61.

Hughes, C. A., & Schumaker, J. (1991). Test-taking strategy instruction for adolescents with learning disabilities. *Exceptionality, 2,* 205–221.

Hughes, J. R. (1992). Tobacco withdrawal in self-quitters. *Journal of Consulting and Clinical Psychology, 60,* 689–697.

Hughes, J. R., Gulliver, S. B., Fenwick, J. W., Valliere, W. A., Cruser, K., Pepper, S., Shea, P., Solomon, L. J., & Flynn, B. S. (1992). Smoking cessation among self-quitters. *Health Psychology, 11,* 331–334.

Hull, J. (1987). Self-awareness model. In H. Blaine & K. Leonard (Eds.), *Psychological theories of drinking and alcoholism.* New York: Guilford Press.

Irvin, J. E., Bowers, C. A., Dunn, M. E., & Wang, M. C. (1999). Efficacy of relapse prevention: A meta-analytic review. *Journal of Consulting and Clinical Psychology, 67,* 561–570.

Israel, A. C., & Saccone, A. J. (1979). Follow-up of effects of choice of mediator and target of reinforcement on weight loss. *Behavior Therapy, 10,* 260–265.

Jamison, C., & Scogin, F. (1995). The outcome of cognitive bibliotherapy with depressed adults. *Journal of Consulting and Clinical Psychology, 63,* 644–650.

Janis, I. L. (Ed.). (1982). *Counseling on personal decisions: Theory and research on short-term helping relationships.* New Haven, CT: Yale University Press.

Jeffery, R. W., French, S. A., & Schmid, T. L. (1990). Attributions for dietary failures: Problems reported by participants in the hypertension prevention trial. *Health Psychology, 9,* 315–329.

Jeffery, R. W., Gerber, W. M., Rosenthal, B. S., & Lindquist, R. A. (1983). Monetary contracts in weight control: Effectiveness of group and individual contracts of varying size. *Journal of Consulting and Clinical Psychology, 51,* 242–248.

Jeffery, R. W., Hellerstedt, W. L., & Schmid, T. L. (1990). Correspondence programs for smoking cessation and weight control: A comparison of two strategies in the Minnesota Heart Health Program. *Health Psychology, 9,* 585–598.

Johnsgard, K. W. (1989). *The exercise prescription for depression and anxiety.* New York: Plenum Press.

Johnson, D. J., & Rusbult, C. E. (1989). Resisting temptation: Devaluation of alternative partners as a means of maintaining commitment in close relationships. *Journal of Personality and Social Psychology, 57,* 967–980.

Johnson, W. G. (1971). Some applications of Homme's covarant control therapy: Two case reports. *Behavior Therapy, 2,* 240–248.

Johnstone, K. A., & Page, A. C. (2004). Attention to phobic stimuli during exposure: the effect of distraction on anxiety reduction, self-efficacy and perceived control. *Behaviour Research and Therapy, 42,* 249–275.

Johnston-O'Connor, E. J., & Kirschenbaum, D. S. (1986). Something succeeds like success: Positive self-monitoring for unskilled golfers. *Cognitive Therapy and Research, 10,* 123–136.

Jones, D. N., Schroeder, J. R., & Moolchan, E. T. (2004). Time spent with friends who smoke and quit attempts among teen smokers. *Addictive Behaviors, 29*(4), 723–729.

Jones, M. K., & Menzies, R. G. (2000). Danger expectancies, self-efficacy and insight in spider phobia. *Behaviour Research and Therapy, 38,* 585–600.

Jorgensen, R. S., & Richards, C. S. (1989). Negative affect and the reporting of physical symptoms among college students. *Journal of Counseling Psychology, 36,* 501–504.

Kagan, N. I., Kagan, H., & Watson, M. G. (1995). Stress reduction in the workplace: The effectiveness of psychoeducational programs. *Journal of Counseling Psychology, 42,* 71–78.

Kamarck, T. W., & Lichtenstein, E. (1988). Program adherence and coping strategies as predictors of success in a smoking treatment program. *Health Psychology, 7*(6), 557–574.

Kanfer, F. H. (1975). Self-management methods. In F. H. Kanfer & A. P Goldstein (Eds.), *Helping people change: A textbook of methods* (pp. 334–389). New York: Pergamon Press.

Kanfer, F. H. (1984). Self-management in clinical and social interventions. In R. P. McGlynn, J. E. Maddux, C. D. Stoltenberg, & J. H. Harvey (Eds.), *Social perception in clinical and counseling psychology* (pp. 141–163). Lubbock, TX: Texas Tech University Press.

Kanfer, E. H., & Karoly, P. (1972). Self-control: A behavioristic excursion into the lion's den. *Behavior Therapy, 3,* 398–416.

Kanfer, F. H., & Schefft, B. K. (1987). Self-management therapy in clinical practice. In J. S. Jacobson (Ed.), *Psychotherapists in clinical practice: Cognitive and behavioral perspectives.* New York: Guilford Press.

Kanfer, F. H., & Stevenson, M. K. (1985). The effects of self-regulation on concurrent cognitive processing. *Cognitive Therapy and Research, 9,* 667–684.

Kanfer, R., & Ackerman, P. L. (1990). *Ability and metacognitive determinants of skill acquisition and transfer.* Air Force Office of Scientific Research Final Report, Minneapolis, MN.

Kanfer, R., & Ackerman, P. L. (1995). A self-regulatory skills approach to reducing cognitive interference. In I. G. Sarason, G. R. Pierce, & B. R. Sarason (Eds.), *Cognitive interference: Theories, methods and findings* (pp. 153–171). Hillsdale, NJ: Erlbaum.

Kanter, N. J., & Goldfried, M. R. (1979). Relative effectiveness of rational restructuring and self-control desensitization in the reduction of interpersonal anxiety. *Behavior Therapy, 10,* 472–490.

Karoly, P. (1991). Self-management in health care and illness prevention. In C. R. Snyder & D. R. Forsyth (Eds.), *Handbook of social and clinical psychology* (pp. 579–608). New York: Pergamon Press

Karoly, P. (1993). Mechanisms of self-regulation: A systems view. In L. W. Porter & M. R. Rosenzweig (Eds.), *Annual review of psychology, 44,* (pp. 23–51). Palo Alto, CA: Annual Reviews.

Karoly, P. (1995). Self-control theory. In W. O'Donohue & L. Krasner (Eds.), *Theories of behavior therapy: Exploring behavior change* (pp. 259–285). Washington, DC: American Psychological Association.

Karoly, P. (2005). Self-monitoring. In M. Hersen & J. Rosqvist (Eds.), *Encyclopeida of behavior modification and cognitive behavior therapy* (Vol. 1, pp. 521–525). Thousand Oaks, CA: Sage.

Karoly, P., & Kanfer, F. H. (Eds.). (1982). *Self-management and behavior change: From theory to practice.* New York: Pergamon Press.

Karoly, P., Ruehlman, L. S., Okun, M. A., Lutz, R. S., Newton, C., & Fairholme, C. (2005). Perceived self-regulation of exercise goals and interfering goals among regular and irregular exercises: a life space analysis. *Psychology of Sport and Exercise, 1–16.*

Katz, R. C., & Vinciguerra, P. (1982). On the neglected art of "thinning" reinforcers. *Behavior Therapist, 5,* 21–22.

Kau, M. L., & Fischer, J. (1974). Self-modification of exercise behavior. *Journal of Behavior Therapy and Experimental Psychiatry, 5,* 213–214.

Kazdin, A. E. (1973). The effect of response cost and aversive stimulation in suppressing punished and non-punished speech disfluencies. *Behavior Therapy, 4,* 73–82.

Kazdin, A. E. (1974a). Effects of covert modeling and model reinforcement on assertive behavior. *Journal of Abnormal Psychology, 83,* 240–252.

Kazdin, A. E. (1974b). Self-monitoring and behavior change. In M. J. Mahoney & C. E. Thoresen (Eds.), *Self-control: Power to the person* (pp. 218–246). Pacific Grove, CA: Brooks/Cole.

Kazdin, A. E. (1982). The separate and combined effects of covert and overt rehearsal in developing assertive behavior. *Behaviour Research and Therapy, 20,* 17–25.

Kazdin, A. E. (1984). Covert modeling. In P. C. Kendall (Ed.), *Advances in cognitive-behavioral research and therapy* (Vol. 3, pp. 103–129). New York: Academic Press.

Kazdin, A. E. (1993). Evaluation in clinical practice: Clinically sensitive and systematic methods of treatment delivery. *Behavior Therapy, 24,* 11–45.

Keeley, J., Williams, C., & Shapiro, D. A. (2002). A United Kingdom survey of accredited cognitive behaviour therapists' attitudes towards and use of structured self-help materials. *Behavioural and Cognitive Psychotherapy, 30,* 193–203.

Kelly, M. L., Scott, W. O. M., Prue, D. M., & Rychtarik, R. G. (1985). A component analysis

of problem solving training. *Cognitive Therapy and Research, 9,* 429–441.

Kendall, P. C., Haaga, D. A., Ellis, A., Bernard, M., DiGiuseppe, R., & Kassinove, H. (1995). Rational-emotive therapy in the 1990s and beyond: Current status, recent revisions, and research questions. *Clinical Psychology Review, 15,* 169–185.

Kendall, P. C., Stark, K. D., & Adam, T. (1990). Cognitive deficit or cognitive distortion in childhood depression. *Journal of Abnormal Child Psychology, 18,* 255–270.

Kernis, M. H., Zuckerman, M., Cohen, A., & Spadafora, S. (1982). Persistence following failure: The interactive role of self-awareness and the attributional basis for negative expectancies. *Journal of Personality and Social Psychology, 43,* 1184–1191.

Killen, J. D., Fortmann, S. P., Davis, L., & Varady, A. (1997). Nicotine patch and self-help video for cigarette smoking cessation. *Journal of Consulting and Clinical Psychology 65*(4) 663–672.

Kipfer, B. A. (1990). *14,000 Things to Be Happy About.* New York: Workman Publishing Company.

Kirby, K. C., Fowler, S. A., & Baer, D. M. (1991). Reactivity in self-recording: Obtrusiveness of recording procedure and peer comments. *Journal of Applied Behavior Analysis, 24,* 487–498.

Kirk, J. (1989). Cognitive-behavioural assessment. In K. Hawton, P. M. Salkovakis, J. Kirk, & D. M. Clark (Eds.), *Cognitive behavior therapy for psychiatric problems: A practical guide.* Oxford: Oxford University Press.

Kirschenbaum, D. S. (1984). Self-regulation and sport psychology: Nurturing an emerging symbiosis. *Journal of Sport Psychology, 6,* 159–183.

Kirschenbaum, D. S. (1985). Proximity and specificity of planning: A position paper. *Cognitive Therapy and Research, 9,* 489–506.

Kirschenbaum, D. S. (1987). Self-regulatory failure: A review with clinical implications. *Clinical Psychology Review, 7,* 77–104.

Kirschenbaum, D. S. (1994). *Weight loss through persistence.* Oakland, CA: New Harbinger.

Kirschenbaum, D. S., & Flanery, R. C. (1984). Toward a psychology of behavioral contracting. *Clinical Psychology Review, 4,* 597–618.

Kirschenbaum, D. S., & Perri, M. G. (1982). Improving academic competence in adults: A review of recent research. *Journal of Counseling Psychology, 29,* 76–94.

Kirschenbaum, D. S., & Tomarken, A. J. (1982). On facing the generalization problem: The study of self-regulatory failure. In P. C. Kendall (Ed.), *Advances in cognitive-behavioral research and therapy* (Vol. 1, pp. 119–200). New York: Academic Press.

Kirschenberg, D. (1994). *Weight loss through persistence: Making science work for you.* Oakland, CA: New Harbinger.

Kleinke, C. L., Peterson, T. R., & Rutledge, T. R. (1998). Effects of self-generated facial expressions on mood. *Journal of Personality and Social Psychology, 74,* 272–279.

Klesges, R. C., Eck, L. J., & Ray, J. W. (1995). Who underreports intake in a dietary recall? Evidence from the second national health and nutrition examination survey. *Journal of Consulting and Clinical Psychology, 63,* 438–444.

Knapp, T., & Shodahl, S. (1974). Ben Franklin as a behavior modifier: A note. *Behavior Therapy, 5,* 656–660.

Knowlton, G. E., & Harris, W. (1987, November). *A comparison of two treatment components of an anxiety management program to improve the free-throw performance on a women's collegiate basketball team.* Paper presented at the annual meeting of the Association for the Advancement of Behavior Therapy, Boston.

Knox, D. (1971). *Marriage happiness: A behavioral approach to counseling.* Champaign, IL: Research Press.

Koegel, L. K., Koegel, R. L., Hurley, C., & Frea, W. D. (1992). Improving social skills and disruptive behavior in children with autism through self-management. *Journal of Applied Behavior Analysis, 25,* 341–353.

Kohn, A. (1993). *Punished by reward.* Boston: Houghton Mifflin.

Kohn, P. M., Lafreniere, K., & Gurevich, M. (1991). Hassles, health and personality. *Journal of Personality and Social Psychology, 61,* 478–482.

Kornblith, S. J., Rehm, L. P, O'Hara, M. W., & Lamparski, D. M. (1983). The contribution of self-reinforcement training and behavioral assignments to the efficacy of self-control therapy for depression. *Cognitive Therapy and Research, 7,* 499–528.

Kravitz, L., & Furst, D. (1991). Influence of reward and social support on exercise adherence in aerobic dance classes. *Psychological Reports, 69,* 423–426.

Krop, H., Calhoon, B., & Verrier, R. (1971). Modification of the "self-concept" of emotionally disturbed children by covert reinforcement. *Behavior Therapy, 2,* 201–204.

Kuiper, N. A., & Olinger, L. J. (1986). Dysfunctional attitudes and a self-worth contingency model of depression. In P. C. Kendall (Ed.), *Advances in cognitive-behavioral research and therapy* (Vol. 5, pp. 115–142). New York: Academic Press.

Lacks, P., Bertelson, A. D., Gans, L., & Kunkel, J. (1983). The effectiveness of three behavioral treatments for different degrees of sleep onset insomnia. *Behavior Therapy, 14,* 593–605.

Lan, W. Y. (1980). Teaching self-monitoring skills in statistics. In D. H. Schunk & B. J. Zimmerman (Eds.), *Self-regulated learning* (pp. 86–105). New York: Guilford Press.

Lange, A., Richard, R., Gest, A., de Vries, M., & Lodder. L. (1998). The effects of positive self-instruction: A controlled trial. *Cognitive Therapy and Research 22*(3), 225–236.

Langston, C. A. (1994). Capitalizing on and coping with daily-life events: Expressive responses to positive events. *Journal of Personality and Social Science, 67,* 1112–1125.

Larsen, R. J., & Prizmic, Z. (2004). Affect regulation. In R. F. Baumeister & K. D. Vohs (Eds.), *Handbook of self-regulation* (pp. 40–59). New York: Guilford Press.

Lascelles, M. A., Cunningham, S. J., McGrath, P., & Sullivan, M. J. L. (1989). Teaching coping strategies to adolescents with migraine. *Journal of Pain and Symptom Management, 4,* 135–145.

Lasure, L. C., & Mikulas, W. L. (1996). Biblical behavior modification. *Behavior Research and Therapy, 34,* 563–566.

Latner, J. D., & Wilson, G. T. (2002). Self-monitoring and the assessment of binge eating. *Behavior Therapy, 33,* 465–477.

Laws, D. R. (1995). A theory of relapse prevention. In W. O'Donohue & L. Krasner (Eds.), *Theories of behavior therapy: Exploring behavior change.* Washington, DC: American Psychological Association.

Lawson, D. M., & Rhodes, E. C. (1981, November). *Behavioral self-control and maintenance of aerobic exercise: A retrospective study of self-initiated attempts to improve physical fitness.* Paper presented at the meeting of the Association for the Advancement of Behavior Therapy, Toronto.

Layden, M. A. (1982). Attributional style therapy. In C. Antaki & C. Brewin (Eds.), *Attributions and psychological change* (pp. 63–82). London: Academic Press.

Lazarus, A. (1971). *Behavior therapy and beyond.* New York: McGraw-Hill.

Leavitt, F. (1982). *Drugs and behavior* (2nd ed.). New York: Wiley.

LeBow, M. D. (1981). *Weight control. The behavioral strategies.* New York: Wiley.

Lees, L. A., & Dygdon, J. A. (1988). The initiation and maintenance of exercise behavior: A learning theory conceptualization. *Clinical Psychology Review, 8,* 345–353.

Lehman, A. K., & Rodin, J. (1989). Styles of self-nurturance and disordered eating. *Journal of Consulting and Clinical Psychology, 57,* 117–122.

Leith, K. P., & Baumeister, R. F. (1996). Why do bad moods increase self-defeating behavior? Emotion, risk taking, and self-regulation. *Journal of Personality and Social Psychology, 71,* 1250–1267.

Leon, G. R. (1979). Cognitive-behavior therapy for eating disturbances. In P. C. Kendall & S. D. Hollon (Eds.), *Cognitive-behavioral interventions: Theory, research, and procedures* (pp. 357–388). New York: Academic Press.

Levendusky, P., & Pankratz, L. (1975). Self-control techniques as an alternative to pain medication. *Journal of Abnormal Psychology, 84,* 165–168.

Levin, R. B., & Gross, A. M. (1984). Reactions to assertive versus nonassertive behavior: Females in commendatory and refusal situations. *Behavior Modification, 8,* 581–592.

Leviton, L. C. (1979). Observer's reactions to assertive behavior. *Dissertation Abstracts International, 39*(11-B), 5652.

Lewinsohn, P. M., Sullivan, J. M., & Grosscup, S. J. (1980). Changing reinforcing events: An approach to the treatment of depression. *Psychotherapy: Theory, Research and Practice, 17,* 322–334.

Lewis, L. E., Biglan, A., & Steinbock, E. (1978). Self-administered relaxation: Training and money deposits in the treatment of recurrent anxiety. *Journal of Consulting and Clinical Psychology, 46,* 1274–1283.

Ley, P. (1986). Cognitive variables and noncompliance. *The Journal of Compliance in Health Care, 1,* 171–188.

Libby, L. K., Eibach, R. P., & Gilovich, T. (2005). Here's looking at me: The effect of memory perspective on assessments of personal change. *Journal of personality and social psychology, 88,* 50–62.

Lichtenstein, E., Glasgow, R. E., & Abrams, D. B. (1986). Social support in smoking cessation: In search of effective interventions. *Behavior Therapy, 17,* 607–619.

Lichtenstein, E., Weiss, S. M., Hitchcock, J. L., Leveton, L. B., O'Connell, K. A., & Prochaska, J. O. (1986). Task force 3: Patterns of smoking relapse. *Health Psychology, 5*(Suppl.), 29–40.

Linehan, M. M. (1979). Structural cognitive behavioral treatment of assertion problems. In P. C. Kendall & S. D. Hollon (Eds.), *Cognitive behavioral interventions: Theory, research, and procedures* (pp. 205–240). New York: Academic Press.

Lipinski, D., Black, J. D., Nelson, R. O., & Ciminero, A. R. (1975). Influence of motivational variables on the reactivity and reliability of self-recording. *Journal of Consulting and Clinical Psychology, 43*(5), 637–646.

Lipton, D. N., & Nelson, R. O. (1980). The contribution of initiation behaviors to dating frequency. *Behavior Therapy, 11,* 59–67.

Littell, J. H., & Girvin, H. (2002). Stages of change: A critique. *Behavior Modification, 26,* 223–273.

Locke, E. A., & Latham, G. P. (1990). Work motivation and satisfaction: Light at the end of the tunnel. *Psychological Science, 1,* 240–246.

Locke, E. A., & Latham, G. P. (1994). Goal setting theory. In H. F. O'Neil & M. Drillings (Eds.), *Motivation: Theory and research* (pp. 13–29). Hillside, NJ: Erlbaum.

Locke, E. A., & Latham, G. P. (2002). Building a practically useful theory of goal setting and task motivation. *American Psychologist, 57,* 705–717.

Loeb, K. L., Wilson, G. T., Gilbert, J. S., & Labouvie, E. (2000). Guided and unguided self-help for binge eating. *Behavior Research and Therapy, 38,* 259–272.

Loftus, E. F. (2004). Memories of things unknown. *Current directions in psychological science, 13,* 145–147.

Logue, A. W. (1995). *Self-Control: Waiting until tomorrow for what you want today.* Englewood Cliffs, NJ: Prentice-Hall.

Logue, A. W. (1998). Laboratory research on self-control: Applications to administration. *Review of General Psychology, 2,* 221–238.

Logue, A. W. (2004). The psychology of eating and drinking. Philadelphia: Brunner-Routledge.

Long, B. C., & Haney, C. J. (1988). Coping strategies for working women: Aerobic exercise and relaxation interventions. *Behavior Therapy, 19,* 75–83.

Lucic, K. S., Steffen, J. J., Harrigan, J. A., & Stuebing, R. C. (1991). Progressive relaxation training: Muscle contraction before relaxation? *Behavior Therapy, 22,* 249–256.

Luria, A. (1961). *The role of speech in the regulation of normal and abnormal behaviors.* New York: Liveright.

Lutzker, S. Z., & Lutzker, J. R. (1974, April). *A two dimensional marital contract: Weight loss and household responsibility performance.* Paper presented at the meeting of the Western Psychological Association, San Francisco.

Lydon, J. E., & Zanna, M. P. (1990). Commitment in the face of adversity: A value-affirmation approach. *Journal of Personality and Social Psychology, 58,* 1040–1047.

Lyubomirsky, S., & Nolen-Hoeksema, S. (1993). Self-perpetuating properties of dysphoric rumination. *Journal of Personality and Social Psychology, 65,* 339–349.

Lyubomirsky, S., Sheldon, K. M., & Schkade, D. (2005). Pursuing happiness: The architecture of sustainable change. *Review of General Psychology, 9,* 132–142.

Mace, F. C., & Kratochwill, T. R. (1985). Theories of reactivity in self-monitoring. *Behavior Modification, 9,* 323–343.

MacPhillamy, D. J., & Lewinsohn, P. M. (1982). The Pleasant Events Schedule: Studies on reliability, validity, and scale intercorrelation. *Journal of Consulting and Clinical Psychology, 50,* 363–380.

Maddux, J. E. (1991). Self-efficacy. In C. R. Snyder & D. R. Forsyth (Eds.), *Handbook of social and clinical psychology* (pp. 57–78). New York: Pergamon Press.

Maddux, J. E. (2002). Self-efficacy. In C. R. Snyder & S. J. Lopez (Eds.), *Handbook of Positive Psychology* (pp. 277–298). New York: Oxford University Press.

Maddux, J. E., & Gosselin, J. T. (2003). Self-efficacy. In M. R. Leary & J. P. Tanguey (Eds.), *Handbook of self and identity*. New York: Guilford Press.

Maes, S., & Karoly, P. (2005). Self-regulation assessment and intervention in physical health and Illness: A review. *Applied Psychology: An international review, 54*, 245–277.

Maher, C. A. (Ed.). (1985). *Professional self-management Techniques for special services providers*. Baltimore: Paul H. Brooks.

Maletzky, B. M. (1974). Behavior recording as treatment: A brief note. *Behavior Therapy, 5*, 107–111.

Malle, B. F., & Horowitx, L. M. (1995). The puzzle of negative self-views: An explanation using the schema concept. *Journal of Personality and Social Psychology, 68*, 470–484.

Malott, R. W. (1989). The achievement of evasive goals: Control by rules describing contingencies that are not direct acting. In S. C. Hayes (Ed.), *Rule governed behavior* (pp. 269–322). New York: Plenum.

Malott, R. W. (2005). Self management. In M. Hersen & J. Rosquist (Eds.), *Encyclopedia of behavior modification and cognitive behavior therapy* (pp. 519–521). Thousand Oaks, CA: Sage.

Mandler, G. (1954). Transfer of training as a function of degree of response overlearning. *Journal of Experimental Psychology, 47*, 411–417.

Marcus, B. H., Rakowski, W., & Rossi, J. S. (1992). Assessing motivational readiness and decision making for exercise. *Health Psychology, 11*(4): 257–261.

Marks, I. (1994). Behavior therapy as an aid to self-care. *Current Directions in Psychological Science, 3*, 19–22.

Marlatt, G. A. (1982). Relapse prevention: A self-control program for the treatment of addictive behaviors. In R. B. Stuart (Ed.), *Adherence, compliance, and generalization in behavioral medicine* (pp. 329–378). New York: Brunner/Mazel.

Marlatt, G. A., & George, W. H. (1990). Relapse prevention and the maintenance of optimal health. In S. Schumaker, E. Schron, & J. K. Ockene (Eds.), *The handbook of health behavior change* (pp. 44–63). New York: Springer.

Marlatt, G. A., & Gordon, J. R. (1985). *Relapse prevention: Maintenance strategies for addictive behavior change*. New York: Guilford Press.

Marlatt, G. A., & Marques, J. K. (1977). Meditation, self-control and alcohol use. In R. B. Stuart (Ed.), *Behavioral self-management: Strategies, techniques, and outcomes* (pp. 117–153). New York: Brunner/Mazel.

Marlatt, G. A., & Parks, G. A. (1982). Self-management of addictive disorders. In P. Karoly & F. H. Kanfer (Eds.), *Self-management and behavior change: From theory to practice* (pp. 443–488). New York: Pergamon Press.

Martin, J. E., Dubbert, P. M., Katell, A. D., Thompson, J. K., Raczynski, J. R., Lake, M., Smith, P. O., Webster, J. S., Sikora, T., & Cohen, R. E. (1984). Behavioral control of exercise in sedentary adults: Studies one through six. *Journal of Consulting and Clinical Psychology, 52*, 795–811.

Martin, L. L., & Tesser, A. (Eds.). (1996). *Striving and feeling: Interactions among goals, affect and self-regulation*. Mahwah, NJ: Erlbaum.

Masters, J. C., Burrish, T. C., Hollon, S. D., & Rimm, D. C. (1987). *Behavior therapy: Techniques and empirical findings* (3rd ed.). New York: Harcourt Brace Jovanovich.

Masterson, J. F., & Vaux, A. C. (1982). The use of a token economy to regulate household behaviours. *Behavioural Psychotherapy, 10*, 65–78.

Matson, J. L. (1977). Social reinforcement by the spouse in weight control: A case study. *Journal of Behavior Therapy and Experimental Psychiatry, 8*, 327–328.

Mayer, J. (1968). *Overweight*. Englewood Cliffs, NJ: Prentice-Hall.

Mayo, L. L., & Norton, G. R. (1980). The use of problem solving to reduce examination and interpersonal anxiety. *Journal of Behavior Therapy and Experimental Psychiatry, 11*, 287–289.

McBride, C. M., & Pirie, P. L. (1990). Postpartum smoking relapse. *Addictive Behaviors, 15*, 165–168.

McCann, I. L., & Holmes, D. S. (1984). Influence of aerobic exercise on depression. *Journal of Personality and Social Psychology, 46*, 1142–1147.

McCullough, M. E., & Snyder, C. R. (2000). Classical sources of human strength: Revisiting an old home and building a new one. *Journal of Social and Clinical Psychology, 19*, 1–10.

McCullough, M. F., & Witvliet, C. V. (2002). The psychology of forgiveness. In C. R. Snyder & S. J. Lopez (Eds.), *Handbook of positive psychology* (pp. 446–458). Oxford: Oxford University Press.

McGlynn, F. D., Kinjo, K., & Doherty, G. (1978). Effects of cue-controlled relaxation, a placebo treatment, and no treatment on changes in self-reported anxiety among college students. *Journal of Clinical Psychology, 34*, 707–714.

McGlynn, F. D., Moore, P. M., Lawyer, S., & Karg, R. (1999). Relaxation training inhibits fear and arousal during in vivo exposure to phobia-cue stimuli. *Journal of Behavior Therapy and Experimental Psychiatry, 30,* 155–168.

McKeough, A., Lupart, J., & Marini, A. (1995). *Teaching for transfer.* Mahwah, NJ: Erlbaum.

McKnight, D. L., Nelson, R. O., Hayes, S. C., & Jarrett, R. B. (1984). Importance of treating individually assessed response classes in the amelioration of depression. *Behavior Therapy, 15,* 315–335.

McLeod, A. K. (1994). Worry and explanation-based pessimism. In G. C. I. Davey & F. Tallis (Eds.), *Worrying: Perspectives on theory, assessment and treatment* (pp. 115–134). New York: Wiley.

McMahon, S. D., & Jason, L. A. (2000). Social support in a worksite smoking intervention: A test of theoretical models. *Behavior Modification, 24*(2), 184–201.

Meichenbaum, D. (1985). *Stress inoculation training.* New York: Pergamon Press.

Meichenbaum, D., & Turk, D. C. (1987). *Facilitating treatment adherence: A practitioners guidebook.* New York: Plenum.

Meichenbaum, D. H. (1977). *Cognitive behavior modification: An integrative approach.* New York: Plenum.

Mendoza-Denton, R., Ayduk, O., Mischel, W., Shoda, Y., & Testa, A. (2001). Person X situation interactionism in self-encoding (I am . . . When I . . .): Implications for affect regulation and social information processing. *Journal of Personality and social Psychology, 80,* 533–544.

Menges, R. J., & Dobroski, B. J. (1977). Behavioral self-modification in instructional settings: A review. *Teaching of Psychology, 4,* 168–174.

Merckelbach, H., Arntz, A., Arrindell, W. A., & de Jong, P. J. (1992). Pathways to spider phobia. *Behaviour Research and Therapy, 30*(5), 543–546.

Mercklebach, H., de Jong, P. J., Arntz, A., & Schouten, E. (1993). The role of evaluative learning and disgust sensitivity in the etiology and treatment of spider phobia. *Behaviour Research and Therapy, 15,* 243–255.

Merckelbach, H., & Muris, P. (1997). The etiology of childhood spider phobia. *Behaviour Research and Therapy, 35*(11), 1031–1034.

Mermelstein, R., Cohen, S., Lichtenstein, E., Baer, J., & Kamarck, T. (1986). Social support and smoking cessation and maintenance. *Journal of Consulting and Clinical Psychology, 54,* 447–453.

Mezo, P. G., & Heiby, E. M. (2004). Self-management skills as a mediator of schizotypy and life satisfaction. Poster presented at the 16th annual meeting of the American Psychological Society, Chicago.

Mikulas, W. L., Coffman, M. G., Dayton, D., Frayne, C., & Maier, P. L. (1986). Behavioral bibliotherapy and games for treating fear of the dark. *Child and Family Behavior Therapy, 7,* 1–7.

Miller, G. A., Galanter, E., & Pribram, K. H. (1960). *Plans and the structure of behavior.* New York: Holt, Rinehart, & Winston.

Miller, N. E. (1969, January). Learning of visceral and glandular responses. *Science,* 434–445.

Miller, R. K., & Bornstein, P. H. (1977). Thirty minute relaxation: A comparison of some methods. *Journal of Behavior Therapy and Experimental Psychiatry, 8,* 291–294.

Miller, W. R., & Rollnick, S. (1991). *Motivational interviewing.* New York: Guilford Press.

Milne, D., Westerman, C., & Hanner, S. (2002). Can a "relapse prevention" module facilitate the transfer of training? *Behavioural and Cognitive Psychotherapy, 30,* 361–364.

Miltenberger, R. G. (2001). *Behavior modification* (2nd ed.). Belmont, CA: Wadsworth.

Miltenberger, R. G., Fuqua, R. W., & Woods, D. W. (1998). Applying behavior analysis to clinical problems: Review and analysis of habit reversal. *Journal of Applied Behavior Analysis, 31,* 447–469.

Mischel, W. (1981). Metacognition and the rules of delay. In J. H. Flavell & L. Ross (Eds.), *Social cognitive development: Frontiers and possible futures* (pp. 240–271). Cambridge: Cambridge University Press.

Mischel, W., & Ayduk, O. (2004). Willpower in a cognitive-affective processing system: The dynamics of delay of gratification. In R. F. Baumeister & K. D. Vohs (Eds.), *Handbook of self-regulation.* New York: Guilford Press.

Mischel, W., & Shoda, Y. (1995). A cognitive-affective system theory of personality: Reconceptualizing situations, dispositions, dynamics, and invariances in personality structure. *Psychological Review, 102,* 246–268.

Mithaug, D. E. (1993). *Self-regulation theory: How optimal adjustment maximizes gain.* Westport, CT: Praeger.

Mithaug, D. D., Agran, M., Martin, J. E., & Wehmeyer, M. L. (2003). Self-determined learning theory. Mahwah, NJ: Erlbaum.

Mizes, J. S., Morgan, G. D., & Buder, J. (1987, November). *Global versus specific cognitive measures and their relationship to assertion deficits.* Paper presented at the meeting of the Association for the Advancement of Behavior Therapy, Boston.

Moon, J. R., & Eisler, R. M. (1983). Anger control: An experimental comparison of three behavioral treatments. *Behavior Therapy, 14,* 493–505.

Mor, N., & Winquist, J. (2002). Self-focused attention and negative affect: A meta-analysis. *Psychological Bulletin, 128,* 638–662.

Moss, M. K., & Arend, R. A. (1977). Self-directed contact desensitization. *Journal of Consulting and Clinical Psychology, 45,* 730–738.

Mulkens, S. A. N., de Jong, P. J., & Merckelbach, H. (1996). Disgust and spider phobia. *Journal of Abnormal Psychology 105*(3), 464–468.

Muris, P., Merckelbach, H., Horselenberg, R., Susenaar, M., & Leeuw, I. (1997). Thought suppression in spider phobia. *Behaviour Research and Therapy 35*(8), 769–774.

Murphy, T. J., Pagano, R. R., & Marlatt, G. A. (1986). Lifestyle modification with heavy alcohol drinkers: Effects of aerobic exercise and meditation. *Addictive Behaviors, 11,* 175–186.

Myers, D. G. (2000). The funds, friends and faith of happy people. *American Psychologist, 55,* 56–67.

Neimeyer, R. A., & Feixas, G. (1990). The role of homework and skill acquisition in the outcome of group cognitive therapy for depression. *Behavior Therapy, 21,* 281–292.

Nelson, R. O. (1977). Methodological issues in assessment via self-monitoring. In J. D. Cone & R. P. Hawkins (Eds.), *Behavioral assessment: New directions in clinical psychology* (pp. 217–240). New York: Brunner/Mazel.

Nelson, R. O., Hayes, S. C., Spong, R. T, Jarrett, R. B., & McKnight, D. L. (1983). Self-reinforcement: Appealing misnomer or effective mechanism? *Behaviour Research and Therapy, 21,* 557–566.

Nelson-Gray, R. O., Herbert, D. L., Herbert, J. D., Farmer, R., Badawi, I., & Lin, K. (1990). The accuracy of frequency estimation as compared with actual counting in behavioral assessment. *Behavioral Assessment, 12,* 157–178.

Newman, A., & Bloom, R. (1981a). Self-control of smoking—I. Effects of experience with imposed, increasing, decreasing, and random delays. *Behaviour Research and Therapy, 19,* 187–192.

Newman, A., & Bloom, R. (1981b). Self-control of smoking—II. Effects of cue salience and source of delay imposition on the effectiveness of training under increasing delay. *Behaviour Research and Therapy, 19,* 193–200.

Nezlek, J. B. (2001). Daily psychological adjustment and the planfulness of day-to-day behavior. *Journal of Social and Clinical Psychology, 20*(4), 452–474.

Nezu, A. M. (2004). Problem solving and behavior therapy revisited. *Behavior therapy, 35,* 1–33.

Nezu, A. M., D'Zurilla, T. J., Zwick, M. L., & Nezu, C. M. (2004). Problem solving therapy for adults. In E. C. Chang, T. J. D'Zurilla, & L. J. Sanna (Eds.), *Social problem solving.* Washington, DC: American Psychological Association.

Nezu, A. M., Nezu, C. M., Felgoise, S. H., McClure, K. S., & Houts, P. S. (2003). Project Genesis: Assessing the efficacy of problem solving therapy for distressed adult cancer patients. *Journal of counseling and clinical psychology 71,* 1036–1048.

Niaura, R. S., Rohsenow, D. J., Binkoff, J. A., Monti, P. M., Pedraza, M., & Abrams, D. B. (1988). Relevance of cue reactivity to understanding alcohol and smoking relapse. *Journal of Abnormal Psychology, 97,* 133–152.

Nicki, R. M., Remington, R. E., & MacDonald, G. A. (1984). Self-efficacy, nicotine-fading/self-monitoring and cigarette-smoking behaviour. *Behaviour Research and Therapy, 22,* 477–485.

Ninness, H. A. C., Fuerst, J., Rutherford, R. D., & Glenn, S. S. (1991). Effects of self-management training and reinforcement on the transfer of improved conduct in the absence of supervision. *Journal of Applied Behavior Analysis, 24,* 499–508.

Nisbett, R. E., & Ross, L. (1980). *Human inference: Strategies and shortcomings of social judgment.* Englewood Cliffs, NJ: Prentice-Hall.

Noel, R. (1980). The effect of visuo-motor behavior rehearsal on tennis performance. *Journal of Sport Psychology, 2,* 221–226.

Nolan, J. D. (1968). Self-control procedures in the modification of smoking behavior. *Journal of Consulting and Clinical Psychology, 32,* 92–93.

Nolen-Hoeksema, S. (2000). The role of rumination in depressive disorders and mixed anxiety/depressive disorders. *Journal of abnormal psychology, 109,* 504–511.

Norcross, J. C., Santrock, J. W., Campbell, L. F., Smith, T. P., Sommer, R., & Zuckerman, E. L. (2003). *Authoritative guide to self-help resources in mental health* (Rev. Ed.). New York: Guilford Press.

O'Banion, D., Armstrong, B. K., & Ellis, J. (1980). Conquered urge as a means of self-control. *Addictive Behaviors, 5,* 101–106.

O'Connor, K. P., & Stravynski, A. (1982). Evaluation of a smoking typology by use of a specific behavioural substitution method of self-control. *Behaviour Research and Therapy, 20,* 279–288.

Okwumabua, T. M., Meyers, A. W., Schleser, R., & Cooke, C. J. (1983). Cognitive strategies and running performance: An exploratory study. *Cognitive Therapy and Research, 7,* 363–370.

Ollendick, T. H., & King, N. J. (1991). Origins of childhood fears: An evaluation of Rachman's theory of fear acquisition. *Behaviour Research and Therapy, 29,* 117–123.

Olympia, D. E., Sheridan, S. M., Jenson, W. R., & Andrews, D. (1994). Using student-managed interventions to increase homework completion and accuracy. *Journal of Applied Behavior Analysis, 27,* 85–99.

O'Neill, H. K., Sandgren, A. K., McCaul, K. D., & Glasgow, R. E. (1987). Self-control strategies and maintenance of a dental hygiene regimen. *The Journal of Compliance in Health Care, 2,* 85–89.

Öst, L.-G. (1987). Applied relaxation: Description of a coping technique and review of controlled studies. *Behaviour Research and Therapy, 25,* 397–409.

Öst, L.-G. (1989). One-session treatment for specific phobias. *Behavior Research and Therapy, 27,* 1–7.

Öst, L.-G., Stridh, B. M., & Wolf, M. (1998). A clinical study of spider phobia: Prediction of outcome after self-help and therapist directed treatments. *Behavior Research and Therapy, 36,* 17–35.

Owusu-Bempah, J., & Howitt, D. L. (1983). Self-modeling and weight control. *British Journal of Medical Psychology, 56,* 157–165.

Ozer, E. M., & Bandura, A. (1990). Mechanisms governing empowerment effects: A self-efficacy analysis. *Journal of Personality and Social Psychology, 58,* 472–486.

Passman, R. (1977). The reduction of procrastinative behaviors in a college student despite the "contingency fullfillment problem": The use of external control in self-management techniques. *Behavior Therapy, 8,* 95–96.

Patrick, J. (1992). *Training: research and practice.* London: Academic Press. Adapted from G. L. Paul (1966). *Insight vs. desensitization in psychotherapy.* Palo Alto, CA: Stanford University Press.

Pawlicki, R., & Galotti, N. (1978). A tic-like behavior case study emanating from a self-directed behavior modification course. *Behavior Therapy, 9,* 671–672.

Payne, P. A., & Woudenberg, R. A. (1978). Helping others and helping yourself. An evaluation of two training modules in a college course. *Teaching of Psychology, 5,* 131–134.

Pechacek, T. F., & Danaher, B. G. (1979). How and why people quit smoking: A cognitive-behavioral analysis. In P. C. Kendall & S. D. Hollon (Eds.), *Cognitive behavioral interventions: Theory, research, and procedures* (pp. 389–422). New York: Academic Press.

Perkins, D., & Perkins, F. (1976). *Nail biting and cuticle biting.* Dallas: Self-Control Press.

Perkins, D. N., & Saloman, G. (1996). Learning transfer. In E. DeCorte & F. Weinert (Eds.), *International handbook of developmental and instructional psychology* (pp. 483–487). Oxford: Pergamon Press.

Perri, M. G., McAllister, D. A., Gange, J. J., Jordan, R. C., McAdoo, W. G., & Nezu, A. M. (1988). Effects of four maintenance programs on the long-term management of obesity. *Journal of Consulting and Clinical Psychology, 56,* 529–534.

Perri, M. G., Nezu, A. M., McKelvey, W. F., Shermer, R. L., Renjilian, D. A., & Viegener, B. J. (2001). Relapse prevention training and problem-solving therapy in the long-term management of obesity. *Journal of Consulting and Clinical Psychology, 69,* 722–726.

Perri, M. G., & Richards, C. S. (1977). An investigation of naturally occurring episodes of self-controlled behaviors. *Journal of Counseling Psychology, 24,* 178–183.

Perri, M. G., Richards, C. S., & Schultheis, K. (1977). Behavioral self-control and smoking reduction: A study of self-initiated attempts to reduce smoking. Behavior Therapy, 8, 360–365.

Peterson, C., & Seligman, M. E. P. (2004). *Character strengths and virtues: A handbook and classification.* Oxford: Oxford University Press.

Peterson, L. (1983). Failure in self-control. In E. B. Foa & P. M. G. Emmelkamp (Eds.), Failures in Behavior Therapy (pp. 172–196). New York: Wiley.

Petrie, K. J., Broadbent, D., & Meechan, G. (2003). Self-regulatory interventions for improving the management of chronic illness. In. L. D. Carmeron & H. Leventhal (Eds.). *The self-regulation of health and illness behavior* (pp. 257–275). London: Routledge.

Petry, N. M., Martin, B., Cooney, J. L., & Kranzler, H. R. (2000). Give them prizes, and they will come: Contingency management for treatment of alcohol dependence. *Journal of Consulting and Clinical Psychology, 68,* 250–257.

Pintrich, P. R. (2000). The role of goal-orientation in self-regulated learning. In M. Boekaerts, P. R. Pintrich, & M. Zeidner (Eds.), *Handbook of Self-Regulation* (pp. 452–502). San Diego: Academic Press.

Pintrich, P. R., McKeachie, W. J., & Yin, Y.-G. (1987). Teaching a course in learning to learn. *Teaching of Psychology, 14* (2), 81–86.

Polivy, J., & Herman, C. P. (2000). The false hope syndrome: Unfulfilled expectations of self-change. *Current Directions in Psychological Science, 9,* 128–131.

Polivy, J., & Herman, C. P. (2002). If at first you don't succeed: False hopes of self-change. *American Psychologist, 57,* 677–689.

Poulton, R., & Menzies, R. G. (2002). Non-associative fear acquisition: a review of the evidence from retrospective and longitudinal research. *Behaviour Research and Therapy, 40,* 127–149.

Prochaska, J. O. (1983). Self-changers versus therapy changers versus Schachter. *American Psychologist, 38,* 853–854.

Prochaska, J. O., & DiClemente, C. C. (1984). *The transtheoretical approach: Crossing traditional boundaries of therapy.* Homewood, IL: Dow Jones-Irwin.

Prochaska, J. O., & DiClemente, C. C. (1992). Stages of change in the modification of problem behaviors. In M. Herzen, R. M. Eisler, & P. M. Miller (Eds.), *Progress in behavior modification* (Vol. 28, pp. 183–218). Sycamore, IL: Sycamore Publishing Company.

Prochaska, J. O., DiClemente, C. C., & Norcross, J. C. (1992). In search of the structure of change. In Y. Klar, J. D. Fisher, J. M. Chinsky, & A. Nadler (Eds.), *Self-change: Social psychological and clinical perspectives* (pp. 87–114). New York: Springer Verlag.

Propst, L. R. (1980). The comparative efficacy of religious and nonreligious imagery for the treatment of mild depression in religious individuals. *Cognitive Therapy and Research, 4,* 167–178.

Putnam, D. E., Finney, J. W., Barkely, P. L., & Bonner, M. J. (1994). Enhancing commitment improves adherence to a medical regimen. *Journal of Consulting and Clinical Psychology, 62,* 191–194.

Rachlin, H. (1974). Self-control. *Behaviorism, 2,* 94–107.

Rachlin, H. (1995). Self-control: Beyond commitment. *Behavioral and brain sciences, 18,* 109–159. With Open Peer Commentary (many authors), 122–159.

Rachlin, H. (2000). *The science of self-control.* Cambridge, MA: Harvard University Press.

Rachman, S. (1977). The conditioning theory of fear acquisition: A critical examination. *Behaviour Research and Therapy, 15,* 375–387.

Raineri, A., & Rachlin, H. (1993). The effect of temporal constraints on the value of money and other commodities. *Journal of Behavioral Decision Making, 6,* 77–94.

Rakos, R. F. (1991). *Assertive behavior: Theory, research, and training.* London & New York: Routledge.

Rakos, R. F., & Grodek, M. V. (1984). An empirical evaluation of a behavioral self-management course in a college setting. *Teaching of Psychology, 11,* 157–162.

Rehm, L. P. (1982). Self-management in depression. In P. Karoly & F. H. Kanfer (Eds.), *Self-management and behavior change: From theory to practice* (pp. 522–567). New York: Pergamon Press.

Rehm, L. P. (1988). Self-management and cognitive processes in depression. In L. B. Alloy (Ed.), *Cognitive processes in depression* (pp. 143–176). New York: Guilford Press.

Rehm, L. P., Kaslow, N. J., & Rabin, A. S. (1987). Cognitive and behavioral targets in a self-control therapy program for depression. *Journal of Consulting and Clinical Psychology, 55,* 60–67.

Rehm, L. P., & Marston, A. R. (1968). Reduction of social anxiety through modification of self-reinforcement: An instigation therapy technique. *Journal of Consulting and Clinical Psychology, 32,* 565–574.

Reich, J. W., & Zautra, A. (1981). Life events and personal causation: Some relationships with satisfaction and distress. *Journal of Personality and Social Psychology, 41,* 1002–1012.

Reitman, D. (1998). The real and imagined harmful effects of rewards: Implications for clinical practice. *Journal of Behavior Therapy and Experimental Psychiatry, 29,* 101–113.

Rescorla, R. A. (1988). Pavlovian conditioning: It's not what you think it is. *American Psychologist, 43,* 151–160.

Reynolds, G. (1995, January 7). A year to remember: Oprah grows up. *TV Guide.*

Richards, C. S. (1976). Improving study behaviors through self-control techniques. In J. D. Krumboltz & C. E. Thoresen (Eds.), *Counseling methods* (pp. 462–467). New York: Holt, Rinehart & Winston.

Richards, C. S. (1985). Work and study problems. In M. Hersen & A. S. Bellack (Eds.), *Handbook of clinical behavior therapy with adults.* New York: Plenum.

Richards, C. S., & Perri, M. G. (1978). Do self-control treatments last? An evaluation of behavioral problem solving and faded counselor contact as treatment maintenance strategies. *Journal of Counseling Psychology, 25,* 376–383.

Rickard-Figueroa, K., & Zeichner, A. (1985). Assessment of smoking urge and its concomitants under an environmental smoking cue manipulation. *Addictive Behaviors, 10,* 249–256.

Rimm, D. C., & Masters, J. C. (1979). *Behavior therapy: Techniques and empirical findings.* New York: Academic Press.

Roberts, L. J., & Marlatt, G. A. (1998). Guidelines for relapse prevention. In G. P. Koocher, J. C. Norcross, & S. S. Hill (Eds.), *Psychologists' desk reference* (pp. 243–247). New York: Oxford University Press.

Robins, R. W., & John, O. P. (1997). The quest for self-insight: Theory and research on accuracy and bias in self-perception. In R. Hogan, J. Johnson, & S. Briggs (Eds.), *Handbook of personality psychology* (pp. 649–679). New York: Academic Press.

Robinson, F. P. (1970). *Effective study* (4th ed.). New York: Harper & Row.

Rodgers, W. M., & Sullivan, M. J. L. (2001). Task, coping and scheduling self-efficacy in relation to frequency of physical activity. *Journal of Applied Social Psychology, 31,* 741–753.

Rogoff, B. (1982). Integrating context and cognitive development. In M. E. Lamb & A. L. Brown (Eds.), *Advances in developmental psychology* (Vol. 2, pp. 125–170). Hillsdale, NJ: Erlbaum.

Rogoff, B., & Lave, J. (Eds.). (1984). *Everyday cognition: Its development in social contexts.* Cambridge, MA: Harvard University Press.

Rohde, P., Lewinsohn, P. M., & Seeley, J. R. (1990). Are people changed by the experience of having an episode of depression? A further test of the scar hypothesis. *Journal of Abnormal Psychology, 99,* 266–271.

Rokke, P. D., Tomhave, J. A., & Jocic, Z. (2000). Self-management therapy and educational group therapy for depressed elders. *Cognitive Therapy and Research, 24,* 99–119.

Rosen, G. M., Glasgow, R. E., & Moore, T. E. (2002). Self-help therapy: The science and business of giving psychology away. In S. O. Lilienfeld, J. M. Lohr, & S. J. Lynn (Eds.), *Science and pseudoscience in contemporary clinical psychology.* New York: Guilford Press.

Rosen, L. W. (1981). Self-control program in the treatment of obesity. *Journal of Behavior Therapy and Experimental Psychiatry, 12,* 163–166.

Rosenbaum, M. (1983). Learned resourcefulness as a behavioral repertoire for the self-regulation of internal events: Issues and speculations. In M. Rosenbaum, C. M. Franks, & Y. Jaffe (Eds.), *Perspectives on behavior therapy in the eighties* (pp. 54–73). New York: Springer.

Rosenbaum, M. (1988). A model for research on self-regulation: Reducing the schism between behaviorism and general psychology. In I. M. Evans (Ed.), *Paradigmatic behavior therapy: Critical perspectives on applied social behaviorism.* New York: Springer.

Ross, M., & Conway, M. (1986). Remembering one's own past: The construction of personal histories. In R. M. Sorrentino & E. T. Higgins (Eds.), *Handbook of motivation and cognition* (pp. 122–144). New York: Guilford Press.

Rothman, A. J., Baldwin, A. S., & Hertel, A. W. (2004). Self-regulation and behavior change: Disentangling behavioral initiation and behavioral maintenance. In R. F. Baumeister & K. D. Vohs (Eds.), *Handbook of self-regulation* (pp. 130–150). New York: The Guilford Press.

Rozensky, R. H. (1974). The effect of timing of self-monitoring behavior on reducing cigarette consumption. *Journal of Behavior Therapy and Experimental Psychiatry, 5,* 301–303.

Russell, R. K., & Lent, R. W. (1982). Cue-controlled relaxation and systematic desensitization versus nonspecific factors in treating test anxiety. *Journal of Counseling Psychology, 29,* 100–103.

Russell, R. K., Miller, D. E., & June, L. N. (1975). A comparison between group systematic desensitization and cue-controlled relaxation in the treatment of test anxiety. *Behavior Therapy, 6,* 172–177.

Russell, R. K., & Sipich, J. F. (1974). Treatment of test anxiety by cue-controlled relaxation. *Behavior Therapy, 5,* 673–676.

Russell, R. K., Wise, F., & Stratoudakis, J. P. (1976). Treatment of test anxiety by cue-controlled relaxation and systematic desensitization. *Journal of Counseling Psychology, 3,* 563–566.

Ryan, R. M., & Deci, E. L. (2001). On happiness and human potentials: A review of research on hedonic and eudaimonic well-being. *Annual Review of Psychology, 52,* 141–166.

Saccone, A. J., & Israel, A. C. (1978). Effects of experimenter versus significant other-controlled reinforcement and choice of target behavior on weight loss. *Behavior Therapy, 9,* 271–278.

Saelens, B. E., Gehrman, C. A., Sallis, J. F., Calfas, K. J., Sarkin, J. A., & Caparosa, S. (2000). Use of self-mangement strategies in a 2-year cognitive-behavioral intervention to promote physical activity. *Behavior therapy, 31,* 365–379.

Samoilov, A., & Goldfried, M. R. (2000). Role of Emotion in cognitive-havavior therapy. *Clinical psychology: Science and practice, 1,* 373–385.

Sandifer, B. A., & Buchanan, W. L. (1983). Relationship between adherence and weight loss in a behavioral weight reduction program. *Behavior Therapy, 14,* 682–688.

Sarason, I. G. (Ed.). (1980). *Test anxiety: Theory, research and applications.* Hillsdale, NJ: Erlbaum.

Sarason, I. G., Pierce, G. R., & Sarason, B. R. (Eds.). (1996). *Cognitive interference: Theories, methods and findings.* Mahway, NJ: Erlbaum.

Sato, R. A. (1986). *Increasing exercise adherence among Honolulu Marathon Clinic participants.* Unpublished master's thesis, University of Hawaii, Honolulu, HI.

Sayette, M. A. (2004). Self-regulatory failure and addiction. In R. F. Baumeister & K. D. Vohs (Eds.), *Handbook of self-regulation* (pp. 447–465). New York: Guilford Press.

Schafer, W. (1992). *Stress management for wellness* (2nd ed.). Fort Worth, TX: Harcourt Brace Jovanovich.

Scheier, M. F., & Carver, C. S. (1993). On the power of positive thinking: The benefits of being optimistic. *Current Directions in Psychological Science, 2,* 26–30.

Schmeichel, B. J., & Baumeister, R. F. (2004). Self-regulatory strength. In R. F. Baumeister & K. D. Vohs (Eds.), *Handbook of self-regulation* (pp. 84–94). New York: Guilford Press.

Schuele, J. G., & Wiesenfeld, A. R. (1983). Autonomic response to self-critical thought. *Cognitive Therapy and Research, 7,* 189–194.

Schunk, D. H., & Ertmer, P. A. (2000). Self-regulation and academic learning: Self-efficacy enhancing interventions. In M. Boekaerts,

P. R. Pintrich, & M. Zeidner (Eds.), *Handbook of self-regulation* (pp. 631–650). San Diego: Academic Press.

Schwartz, S. H., & Inbar-Saban, N. (1988). Value self-confrontation as a method to aid in weight loss. *Journal of Personality and Social Psychology, 54,* 396–404.

Scruggs, T. E., & Mastropierri, M. A. (1992). Cambridge, MA: Brookline Books.

Seidner, M. L. (1973). Behavior change contract: Prior information about study habits treatment and statements of intention as related to initial effort in treatment. Unpublished doctoral dissertation, University of Cincinnati.

Selby, V. C., DiLorenzo, T. M., & Steinkamp, C. A. (1987, November). *An examination of the behaviors and characteristics distinguishing exercisers, non exercisers, and drop-outs.* Paper presented at the meeting of the Association for the Advancement of Behavior Therapy, Boston.

Self-control: Beyond commitment. (1995). *Behavior and Brain Science 18*(1) [Special Issue].

Seligman, M. E. P. (1971). Phobias and preparedness. *Behavior Therapy, 2,* 307–320.

Seligman, M. E. P. (1991). *Learned optimism.* New York: Knopf.

Seligman, M. E. P. (1994). *What you can change and what you can't.* New York: Knopf.

Seligman, M. E. P., Steen, T. A., Park, N., & Peterson, C. (2005). Positive psychology progress: Empirical validation of interventions. *American Psychologist, 60,* 410–421.

Severson, H. H., Akers, L., Andrews, J. A., Lichtenstein, E., & Jerome, A. (2000). Evaluating two self-help interventions for smokeless tobacco cessation. *Addictive Behaviors, 25,* 465–470.

Sewitch, T. S., & Kirsch, I. (1984). The cognitive content of anxiety: Naturalistic evidence for the predominance of threat-related thoughts. *Cognitive Therapy and Research, 8,* 49–58.

Shapiro, D. H., & Walsh, R. (Eds.). (1980). *The science of meditation: Theory, research and experience.* Hawthorne, NY: Aldine.

Shelton, J. L. (1979). Instigation therapy: Using therapeutic homework to promote treatment gains. In A. P. Goldstein & F. H. Kanfer (Eds.), *Maximizing treatment gains: Transfer enhancement in psychotherapy* (pp. 225–245). New York: Academic Press.

Shelton, J. L. (1981). The use of behavioral assignments in clinical practice. In J. L. Shelton, R. L. Levy, & contributors, *Behavioral assignments and treatment compliance: A handbook of clinical strategies* (pp. 1–19). Champaign, IL: Research Press.

Shelton, J. L., Levy, R. L., & contributors. (1981). *Behavioral assignments and treatment compliance: A handbook of clinical strategies.* Champaign, IL: Research Press.

Sherman, A. R. (1972). Real-life exposure as a primary therapeutic factor in the desensitization treatment for fear. *Journal of Abnormal Psychology, 79,* 19–28.

Sherman, A. R. (1975). Two-year follow-up of training in relaxation as a behavioral self-management skill. *Behavior Therapy, 6,* 419–420.

Sherman, A. R., & Plummer, I. L. (1973). Training in relaxation as a behavioral self-management skill: An exploratory investigation. *Behavior Therapy, 4,* 543–550.

Sherman, A. R., Turner, R., Levine, M., & Walk, J. (1975, December). *A behavioral self-management program for increasing or decreasing habit responses.* Paper presented at the meeting of the Association for the Advancement of Behavior Therapy, San Francisco.

Shiffman, S. (1982). Relapse following smoking cessation: A situational analysis. *Journal of Consulting and Clinical Psychology, 50,* 71–86.

Shiffman, S. (1984). Coping with temptations to smoke. *Journal of Consulting and Clinical Psychology, 52,* 261–267.

Shiffman, S., & Jarvik, M. E. (1987). Situational determinants of coping in smoking relapse crises. *Journal of Applied Social Psychology, 17,* 3–15.

Shiffman, S., & Waters, A. J. (2004). Negative affect and smoking lapses: A prospective analysis. *Journal of Consulting and Clinical Psychology, 72,* 192–201.

Showers, C. J., Limke, A., & Zeigler-Hill, V. (2004). Self-structure and self-change: Applications to psychological treatment. *Behavior Therapy, 35,* 167–184.

Silvia, P. J., & Duval, T. S. (2004). Self-awareness, self-motives and self-motivation. In R. A. Wright, J. Greenberg, & S. S. Brehm (Eds.), *Motivational analysis of social behavior* (pp. 57–75). Mahwah, NJ: Erlbaum.

Simkin, L. R., & Gross, A. M. (1994). Assessment of coping with high-risk situations for excercise relapse among healthy women. *Health Psychology, 13,* 274–277.

Simons, A. D., McGowan, C. R., Epstein, L. H., Kupfer, D. J., & Robertson, R. J. (1985). Exercise as a treatment for depression: An update. *Clinical Psychology Review, 5,* 553–568.

Skinner, B. F. (1953). *Science and human behavior.* New York: Macmillan.

Smith, J. C. (2005). *Relaxation, meditation, & mindfulness: A mental health practitioner's guide to new and traditional approaches.* New York: Springer Publishing.

Smith, J. C. (1985). *Relaxation dynamics: Nine world approaches to self-relaxation.* Champaign, IL: Research Press.

Smith, K. L., Kirkby, K. C., Montgomery, I. M., & Daniels, B. A. (1997). Computer-delivered modeling of exposure for spider phobia:

Relevant versus irrelevant exposure. *Journal of Anxiety Disorders, 11*(5): 489–497.

Smith, N. M., Floyd, M. R., Scogin, F., & Jamison, C. S. (1997). *Journal of Consulting and Clinical Psychology, 65,* 324–327.

Snyder, A. L., & Deffenbacher, J. L. (1977). Comparison of relaxation as self-control and systematic desensitization in the treatment of test anxiety. *Journal of Consulting and Clinical Psychology, 45,* 1202–1203.

Sobell, L. C., Cunningham, J. A., & Sobell, M. B. (1996). Recovery from alcohol problems with and without treatment: Prevalence in two population surveys. *American Journal of Public Health, 86,* 966–972.

Sobell, L. C., & Sobell, M. B. (1995a, November). Guided self-change: A brief intervention for alcohol and drug abusers. Workshop presented at the Association for the Advancement of Behavior Therapy, Washington, DC.

Sobell, M. B., & Sobell, L. C. (1995b). Controlled drinking after 25 years: How important was the great debate? *Addiction, 90* (9), 1149–1153.

Sobell, M. B., & Sobell, L. C. (1993). *Problem drinkers.* New York: Guilford Press.

Sohn, D., & Lamal, P. A. (1982). Self-reinforcement: Its reinforcing capability and its clinical utility. *Psychological Record, 32,* 179–203.

Sonne, J. L., & Janoff, D. S. (1982). Attributions and the maintenance of behavior change. In C. Antaki & C. Brewin (Eds.), *Attributions and psychological change* (pp. 83–96). New York: Academic Press.

Sowers, J., Verdi, M., Bourbeau, P., & Sheehan, M. (1985). Teaching job independence and flexibility to mentally retarded students through the use of a self-control package. *Journal of Applied Behavior Analysis, 18,* 81–85.

Speidel, G. E., & Tharp, R. G. (1980). What does self-reinforcement reinforce: An empirical analysis of the contingencies in self-determined reinforcement. *Child Behavior Therapy, 2,* 1–22.

Spring, B., Doran, N., Pagoto, S., Schneider, K., Pingitore, R., & Hedeker, D. (2004). Randomized controlled trial for behavioral smoking and weight control treatment: Effect of concurrent versus sequential intervention. *Journal of Consulting and Clinical Psychology, 72*(5), 785–796.

Spurr, J., & Stevens, V. J. (1980). Increasing study time and controlling student guilt: A case study in self-management. *Behavior Therapist, 3,* 17–18.

Spurr, J. M., & Stopa, L. (2002). Self-focused attention in social phobia and social anxiety. *Clinical psychology review, 22,* 947–975.

Staats, A. W. (1968). *Learning, language, and cognition.* New York: Holt, Rinehart & Winston.

Stalonas, P. M., & Kirschenbaum, D. S. (1985). Behavioral treatment for obesity: Eating habits revisited. *Behavior Therapy, 16,* 1–14.

Stanton, M. (2005). Relapse prevention needs more emphasis on interpersonal factors. *American Psychologist, 60*(4), 341–342.

Stark, K. D., Reynolds, W. M., & Kaslow, N. J. (1987). A comparison of the relative efficacy of self-control therapy and a behavioral problem solving therapy for depression in children. *Journal of Abnormal Child Psychology, 15,* 91–113.

Startup, M., & Edmonds, J. (1994). Compliance with homework assignments in cognitive-behavioral psychotherapy for depression: Relation to outcome and methods of enhancement. *Cognitive Therapy and Research, 18,* 567–601.

Steenman, H. F. (1986). *Cognitive coping and chronic pain.* Unpublished doctoral dissertation, University of Hawaii, Honolulu, HI.

Stevenson, H. C., & Fantuzzo, J. W. (1986). The generality and social validity of a competency based self-control training intervention for underachieving students. *Journal of Applied Behavior Analysis, 19,* 269–276.

Stice, E., Cameron, R. P., Killen, J. D., Haywayd, C., & Taylor, C. B. (1999) Naturalistic weight-reduction efforts prospectively predict growth in relative weight and onset of obesity among female adolescents. *Journal of Consulting and Clinical Psychology, 77,* 967–974.

Stock, J., & Cervone, D. (1990). Proximal goal-setting and self-regulatory processes. *Cognitive Therapy and Research, 14,* 483–498.

Stockton, W. (1987, November 16). Just how far, and how fast, for fitness? *New York Times,* p. Y33.

Stokes, T. F., & Baer, D. M. (1977). An implicit technology of generalization. *Journal of Applied Behavior Analysis, 10,* 349–368.

Stokes, T. F., & Osnes, P. G. (1989). An operant pursuit of generalization. *Behavior Therapy, 20,* 337–355.

Strauman, T. J. (1992). Self-guides, autobiographical memory, and anxiety and dysphoria: Toward a cognitive model of vulnerability to emotional distress. *Journal of Abnormal Psychology, 101,* 87–95.

Stuart, R. B. (1967). Behavioral control of overeating. *Behaviour Research and Therapy, 5,* 357–365.

Stuart, R. B. (1977). Self-help group approach to self-management. In R. B. Stuart (Ed.), *Behavioral self-management: Strategies, techniques and outcomes* (pp. 278–305). New York: Brunner/Mazel.

Stuart, R. B., & Davis, B. (1972). *Slim chance in a fat world: Behavioral control of obesity.* Champaign, IL: Research Press.

Stunkard, A. J. (1958). The management of obesity. *New York State Journal of Medicine, 58,* 79–87.

Sudnow, D. (1978). *Ways of the hand. The organization of improvised conduct* (pp. 146–147). Cambridge, MA: Harvard University Press.

Suinn, R. M. (1976, July). Body thinking: Psychology for Olympic champs. *Psychology Today*, 38–40.

Suinn, R. M. (1977). *Manual for anxiety management training (AMT)*. Fort Collins, CO: Rocky Mountain Behavioral Science Institute.

Suinn, R. M. (1983). Imagery and sports. In A. A. Sheikh (Ed.), *Imagery: Current theory, research, and application* (pp. 507–534). New York: Wiley.

Suinn, R. M. (1985). The 1984 Olympics and sport psychology. *Sport Psychology Today, 1*, 321–329.

Suinn, R. M. (1987). Psychological approaches to performance enhancement. In M. Asken & J. May (Eds.), *Sports psychology: The psychological health of the athlete* (pp. 41–57). New York: Spectrum.

Suinn, R. M. (1989). Behavioral intervention for stress management in sports. In D. Hackfort & C. Spielberger (Eds.), *Anxiety in sports: An international perspective* (pp. 203–214). New York: Hemisphere.

Suinn, R. M. (1990). *Anxiety management training: A behavior therapy*. New York: Plenum.

Swann, W. B., Jr., Wenzlaff, R. M., & Tafarodi, R. W. (1992). Depression and the search for negative evaluations: More evidence of the role of self-verification strivings. *Journal of Abnormal Psychology, 101*, 314–317.

Tangney, J. P., Baumeister, R. F., & Boone, A. L. (2004). High self-control predicts good adjustment, less pathology, better grades and interpersonal success. *Journal of Personality, 72*, 273–324.

Taylor, S. E., & Pham, L. B. (1996). Mental stimulation, motivation, and action. In P. M. Gollwitzer & J. A. Bargh (Eds.), *The psychology of action: Linking cognition and motivation to behavior* (pp. 219–235). New York: Guilford Press.

Teasdale, J. D., Moore, R. G., Hayhurst, H., Pope, M., & Segal, Z. V. (2002). Metacognitive awareness and prevention of relapse in depression: Empirical evidence. *Journal of Consulting and Clinical Psychology, 70*(2), 275–287.

Tharp, R. G., Estrada, P., Dalton, S. S., & Yamauchi, L. A. (2000). *Teaching transformed: Achieving excellence, fairness, inclusion and harmony*. Boulder, CO: Westview Press.

Tharp, R. G., & Gallimore, R. (1988). *Rousing minds to life*. New York: Cambridge University Press.

Tharp, R. G., Gallimore, R., & Calkins, R. P. (1984). On the relationship between self-control and control by others. *Avances en Psicologia Clinica Latinoamericana, 3*, 45–58.

Tharp, R. G., Watson, D. L., & Kaya, J. (1974). Self-modification of depression. *Journal of Consulting and Clinical Psychology, 42*, 624. (Extended Report, University of Hawaii).

Tharp, R. G., & Wetzel, R. J. (1969). *Behavior modification in the natural environment*. New York: Academic Press.

Thase, M. E., & Moss, M. K. (1976). The relative efficacy of covert modeling procedures and guided participant modeling on the reduction of avoidance behavior. *Journal of Behavior Therapy and Experimental Psychiatry, 7*, 7–12.

Thayer, R. E. (1989). *The biopsychology of mood and arousal*. New York: Oxford University Press.

Thayer, R. E. (2001). *Calm energy: How people regulate mood with food and exercise*. Oxford: Oxford University Press.

Thayer, R. E., Peters, D. P., Takahashi, P. J., & Birkhead-Flight, A. M. (1993). Mood and behavior (smoking and sugar snacking) following moderate exercise: A partial test of self-regulation theory. *Personality and Individual Differences, 14*, 97–104.

Thompson, S. C. (1991). Intervening to enhance perceptions of control. In C. R. Snyder & D. R. Forsyth (Eds.), *Handbook of social and clinical psychology* (pp. 607–623). New York: Pergamon Press.

Thorpe, G. L., Amatu, H. I., Blakey, R. S., & Burns, L. E. (1976). Contributions of overt instructional rehearsal and "specific insight" to the effectiveness of self-instructional training: A preliminary study. *Behavior Therapy, 7*, 504–511.

Thorpe, S. J., & Salkovskis, P. M. (1997). The effect of one-session treatment for spider phobia on attentional bias and beliefs. *British Journal of Clinical Psychology, 36*, 225–241.

Throll, D. A. (1981). Transcendental meditation and progressive relaxation: Their psychological effects. *Journal of Clinical Psychology, 37*, 776–781.

Tice, D. M., Baumeister, R. F., & Zhang, L. (2004). The Role of emotion in self-regulation: Differing roles of positive and negative emotion. In P. Philippot & R. S. Feldman (Eds.), *The regulation of emotion* (pp. 213–226). Mahwah, NJ: Lawrence Erlbaum Associates.

Timberlake, W. (1995). Reconceptualizing reinforcement: A causal-system approach to reinforcement and behavior change. In W. O'Donohue & L. Krasner (Eds.), *Theories of behavior therapy: Exploring behavior change* (pp. 59–96). Washington, DC: American Psychological Association.

Tinling, D. C. (1972). Cognitive and behavioral aspects of aversive therapy. In R. D. Rubin, H. Fensterheim, J. D. Henderson, & L. P. Ullmann (Eds.), *Advances in behavior therapy* (pp. 73–80). New York: Academic Press.

Todd, F. J. (1972). Covariant control of self-evaluative responses in the treatment of depression: A new use for an old principle. *Behavior Therapy, 3*, 91–94.

Tolin, D. F., Lohr, J. M., Sawchuck, C. N., & Lee, T. C. (1997). Disgust and disgust sensitivity in blood-injection-injury and spider phobia. *Behaviour Research and Therapy*, *35*(10), 949–953.

Tompkins, M. (2003). Effective homework. In R. L. Leahy (Ed.), *Roadblocks in cognitive-behavioral therapy*. New York: Guilford Press.

Tucker, J. S., & Anders, S. L. (2001). Social control of health behaviors in marriage. *Journal of applied social psychology, 31*, 3, 467–485.

Tucker, J. S., & Mueller, J. S. (2000). Spouses' social control of health behaviors: Use and effectiveness of specific strategies. *Personality and Social Psychology Bulletin, 26*(9), 1120–1130.

Turner, R. M. (1986). Behavioral self-control procedures for disorders of initiating and maintaining sleep. *Clinical Psychology Review, 6*, 27–38.

Turner, S. M., Holzman, A., & Jacob, R. G. (1983). Treatment of compulsive looking by imaginal thought-stopping. *Behavior Modifcation, 7*, 576–582.

Upper, D. (1974). Unsuccessful self-treatment of a case of "writer's block." *Journal of Applied Behavior Analysis, 7*, 497.

Van Lankveld, J. J. D. M. (1998). Bibliotherapy in the treatment of sexual dysfunctions: A meta-analysis. *Journal of Consulting and Clinical Psychology, 66*, 702–708.

Velicer, W. F., DiClemente, C. C., Rossi, R. S., & Prochaska, J. O. (1990). Relapse situations and self-efficacy: An integrative model. *Addictive Behaviors, 15*, 271–283.

Vygotsky, L. S. (1965). *Thought and language* (E. Hantmann & G. Vokar, Eds. and Trans.). Cambridge, MA: MIT Press.

Vygotsky, L. S. (1978). *Mind and society.* Cambridge, MA: Harvard University Press.

Wachelka, D., & Katz, R. C. (1999). Reducing test anxiety and improving academic self-esteem in high school and college students with learning disabilities. *Journal of Behavior Therapy and Experimental Psychiatry, 30*, 191–198.

Wadden, T. A., Vogt, R. A., Foster, G. D., & Anderson, D. A. (1998). Exercise and the maintenance of weight loss: 1-year follow-up of a controlled clinical trial. *Journal of Consulting and Clinical Psychology, 66*, 429–433.

Wadden, T. A., Womble, L. G., Sarwer, D. B., Berkowitz, R. I., Clark, V. L., & Foster, G. D. (2003). Great expectations: "I'm losing 25% of my weight no matter what you say." *Journal of Consulting and Clinical Psychology, 71*, 1084–1089.

Wagner, J., Burg, M., & Sirois, B. (2004). Social support and the transtheoretical model: Relationship of social support to smoking cessation stage, decisional balance, process use, and temptation. *Addictive Behaviors, 29*(5), 1039–1043.

Wallace, I., & Pear, J. J. (1977). Self-control techniques of famous novelists. *Journal of Applied Behavior Analysis, 10*, 515–525.

Walters, G. D. (2000). Behavioral self-control training for problem drinkers: A meta-analysis of randomized control studies. *Behavior Therapy, 31*, 135–149.

Ward, P., & Carnes, M. (2002). Effects of posting self-set goals on collegiate football players' skill execution during practice and games. *Journal of Applied Behavior Analysis, 35*, 1–12.

Warda, G., & Bryant, R. A. (1998). Thought control strategies in acute stress disorder. *Behaviour Research and Therapy, 36*, 1171–1175.

Watkins, L. (1991). *The critical standards used by college students in evaluating narrative and argumentative essays.* Unpublished master's thesis, University of Hawaii–Manoa, Honolulu, HI.

Watson, D. L. (2001). *Learning skills for college and life.* Belmont, CA: Wadsworth.

Watson, D. L., & Friend, R. (1969). Measurement of social-evaluative anxiety. *Journal of Consulting and Clinical Psychology, 33*, 448–457.

Watson, D. L., Tharp, R. G., & Krisberg, J. (1972). Case study of self-modification: Suppression of inflammatory scratching while awake and asleep. *Journal of Behavior Therapy and Experimental Psychiatry, 3*, 213–215.

Watson, J. B., & Rayner, R. (1920). Conditioned emotional reactions. *Journal of Experimental Psychology, 3*, 1–14.

Wegner, D. M. (1989). *White bears and other unwanted thoughts.* New York: Viking.

Wegner, D. M., & Guiliano, T. (1983). On sending artifact in search of artifact: Reply to McDonald, Harris, & Maher. *Journal of Personality and Social Psychology, 44*, 290–293.

Wegner, D. M., & Schneider, D. J. (1989). Mental control: The war of the ghosts in the machine. In J. S. Uleman & J. A. Bargh (Eds.), *Unintended thought* (pp. 287–305). New York: Guilford Press.

Wegner, D. M., Schneider, D. J., Knutson, B., & McMahon, S. R. (1991). Polluting the stream of consciousness: The effect of thought suppression on the mind's environment. *Cognitive Theory and Research, 15*, 141–152.

Weinder, B. (1995). *Judgments of responsibility.* New York: Guilford Press.

Weisz, G., & Bucher, B. (1980). Involving husbands in treatment of obesity—effects on weight loss, depression, and marital satisfaction. *Behavior Therapy, 11*, 643–650.

Wenzlaff, R. M., & Wegner, D. M. (2000). Thought suppression. *Annual Review of Psychology, 51*, 59–91.

Wenzlaff, R. M., Wegner, D. M., & Klein, S. B. (1991). The role of thought suppression in the bonding of thought and mood. *Journal of Personality and Social Psychology, 60,* 500–508.

Wenzlaff, R. M., Wegner, D. M., & Roper, D. W. (1988). Depression and mental control: The resurgence of unwanted negative thoughts. *Journal of Personality and Social Psychology, 55,* 882–892.

Westover, S. A., & Lanyon, R. I. (1990). The maintenance of weight loss after behavioral treatment. *Behavior Modification, 14,* 123–137.

Wiener, N. (1948). *Cybernetics: Control and communication in the animal and the machine.* Cambridge, MA: MIT Press.

Wilson, J. K., & Rapee, R. M. (2005). The interpretation of negative social events in social phobia: changes during treatment and relationship to outcome. *Behaviour Research and Therapy, 43*(3), 373–389.

Wilson, T. O., & Dunn, E. W. (2004). Self-knowledge: Its limits, value and potential for improvement. *Annual Review of Psychology, 55,* 493–514.

Wilson, T. O., & LaFleur, S. J. (1995). Knowing what you'll do: Effects of analyzing reasons on self-prediction. *Journal of Personality and Social Psychology, 68,* 21–35.

Wine, J. D. (1980). Cognitive-attentional theory of test anxiety. In I. G. Sarason (Ed.), *Test anxiety: Theory, research, and applications* (pp. 349–385). Hillsdale, NJ: Erlbaum.

Wing, R. R. (2000). Cross-cutting themes in maintenance of behavior change. *Health Psychology, 19,* 84–88.

Wing, R. R., & Jeffery, R. W. (1999). Benefits of recruiting participants with friends and increasing social support for weight loss and maintenance. *Journal of Consulting and Clinical Psychology, 67,* 132–138.

Wing, R. R., & Klem, M. L. (2002). Characteristics of successful weight maintainers. In C. G. Fairburn and K. D. Brownell (Eds.), *Eating disorders and obesity,* (2nd ed., pp. 588–592). New York: Guilford Press.

Wing, R. R., Marcus, M. D., Epstein, L. H., & Kupfer, D. (1983). Mood and weight loss in a behavioral treatment program. *Journal of Consulting and Clinical Psychology, 51,* 153–155.

Wiser, S. L., Goldfried, M. R., Raue, P. J., & Vakoch, D. A. (1995). Cognitive-behavioral and psychodynamic therapies: A comparison of change processes. In W. Dryden (Ed.), *Research in counseling and psychotherapy: Practical applications.* London: Sage.

Wisocki, P. A. (1973). A covert reinforcement program for the treatment of test anxiety: Brief report. *Behavior Therapy, 4,* 264–266.

Witkiewitz, K., & Marlatt, G. A. (2004). Relapse prevention for alcohol and drug problems:

That was Zen this is Tao. *American Psychologist, 59,* 224–235.

Wolko, K. L., Hrycaiko, D. W., & Martin, G. L. (1993). A comparison of two self-management packages to standard coaching for improving practice performance of gymnasts. *Behavior Modfication, 17,* 209–223.

Wolpe, J. (1981). The dichotomy between classically conditioned and cognitively learned anxiety. *Journal of Behavior Therapy and Experimental Psychiatry, 12,* 35–42.

Wood, J. V., Saltzberg, J. A., & Goldsamt, L. A. (1990). Does affect induce self-focused attention? *Journal of Personality and Social Psychology, 58,* 899–908.

Wood, J. V., Saltzberg, J. A., Neale, J. M., Stone, A. A., & Rachmiel, T. B. (1990). Self-focused attention, coping responses, and distressed mood in everyday life. *Journal of Personality and Social Psychology, 58,* 1027–1036.

Woody, S. R., & Rodriquez, B. F. (2000). Self-focused attention and social anxiety in social phobics and normal controls. *Cognitive Therapy and Research, 24,* 473–488.

Woolfolk, R. L., Lehrer, P. M., McCann, B. S., & Rooney, A. J. (1982). Effects of progressive relaxation and meditation on cognitive and somatic manifestations of daily stress. *Behaviour Research and Therapy, 20,* 461–467.

Worthington, E. L. (1979). Behavioral self-control and the contract problem. *Teaching of Psychology, 6,* 91–94.

Wright, S. S. (2000). Looking at the self in a rose-colored mirror: Unrealistically positive self-views and academic performance. *Journal of Social and Clinical Psychology, 19,* 451–462.

Wyer, R. S., Jr. (1997). *The Automaticity of everyday life (Advances in Social Cognition).* Mahwah, NJ: Erlbaum.

Youdin, R., & Hemmes, N. S. (1978). The urge to overeat: The initial link. *Journal of Behavior Therapy and Experimental Psychiatry, 9,* 339–342.

Zemore, R. (1975). Systematic desensitization as a method of teaching a general anxiety-reducing skill. *Journal of Consulting and Clinical Psychology, 43,* 157–161.

Zimmerman, B. J. (1998). *Uses of self-management.* Address at the annual convention of the American Educational Research Association, San Diego.

Zimmerman, B. J., & Kitsantas, A. (1996). Self-regulated learning of a motoric skill: The role of goal setting and self-monitoring. *Journal of Applied Sport Psychology, 8,* 69–84.

Zimmerman, B. J., & Kitsantas, A. (1997). Developmental phases in self-regulation: Shifting from process to outcome goals. *Journal of Educational Psychology, 89,* 29–36.

Zimmerman, B. J., & Pons, M. M. (1986, Winter). Development of a structured interview for assessing student use of self-regulated learning strategies. *American Educational Research Journal, 23*(4), 614–628.

Zimmerman, B. J., & Schunk, D. H. (2001). *Self-regulated learning and academic achievement* (2nd ed.). Mahwah, NJ: Erlbaum.

Zimmerman, B. J., & Schunk, H. (2004). Self-regulating intellectual processes and outcomes: A social cognitive perspective. In D. Y. Dai & R. J. Sternberg (Eds.), *Motivation, emotion and cognition: Integrative perspectives on intellectual function and development* (pp. 323–349). Mahway, NJ: Erlbaum.

Zimmerman, J. (1975). If it's what's inside that counts, why not count it? 1. Self-recording of feelings and treatment by "self-implosion." *Psychological Record, 25,* 3–16.

Zitter, R. E., & Fremouw, W. J. (1978). Individual versus partner consequation for weight loss. *Behavior Therapy, 9,* 808–813.

Name Index

Subject Index

Behaviors (*continued*)
operant, 116
positive and negative reinforcers of, 116–122
prosocial, 310
relaxation, 174–182, 201–202
respondent, 123–127, 133
rule-governed, 115
self-modification of, 8, 11–12
self-regulation of, 2–7, 123–127, 133
shaping, 191–196, 202
stimulus control and automatic, 122–123
structured diary to record, 72–78, 88–89
as thoughts, behaviors, feelings, 74–76, 129–131, 164–203
tips for typical topics related to, 196–201
tracking patterns of, 76–78
Beliefs
benefits of changing negative, 139
expectations as form of, 139–140
lack of, 281–282
phobias and role of, 190
as type of self-directed messages, 138–139
in your ability to resist an urge, 290
"Best Friend technique," 140
Binge eating, 161
Brain-Power Bowling record, 87
Brainstorming
for planning change, 254–255
for problem solving, 275–276
Bulimia, 303–304

"Case of the Worn-Out Student," 38
Case studies. *See* Self-modification cases
"Causal Efficacy of Human Thought, The" (*Journal of Behavior Therapy and Experimental Psychiatry*), 131
Chains of events
controlling antecedents by changing, 143–145, 146–147
family's, 146–147
identifying/modifying antecedents and changing, 159–160, 161
leading to successful change, 54, 147
Challenging situations. *See* High-risk situations
Change. *See also* A-B-Cs of self-change; Self-modification
planning for, 12, 14–17, 24–26
"reality testing" role in plans for, 71
seeking professional help for, 305–306

self-efficacy beliefs and successful, 45–56
self-modification courses for, 17, 20–22
specifying targets for, 32–39, 66–67, 68
spiral process of, 61–62
willingness to work toward, 65
Change plan contract, 262
Change plan elements
brainstorming an effective plan, 254–255
changing targets and effect on record keeping, 256–258
checklist for plan, 259–260
improving ongoing plans, 255–256
plan contract as, 262
sample plan and, 258, 261–262
stopping to think and learn, 258
theoretical overview of good, 252–254
Change plans. *See also* Planning change
combining A-B-C elements in, 247–252, 269
developing options as part of, 250–251
elements of a good, 252–262, 269–270
evaluating, 262–268
to maintain gains, 296–302
tips for typical topics related to, 268–269
two sample cases of, 247–249
two-stage process applied to other problems, 251–252
two-stage process for high-risk situations, 249–251
working in groups, 264
your own self-direction project for, 270
Cheating, 235
Checklist for Happiness, 312
Checklist for Your Plan, 259–260
Children
development of language regulation in, 114–115
language development in, 114
Cognition, 129
Communication. *See also* Language
problems with people and role of, 103
SOLER (body language), 199
Competing exercises, 168
Conditioning
emotional, 125–126
respondent behavior and, 123–127, 133
Confidence
dealing with temptation by borrowing, 42–45
planning termination and maintaining, 298–299
"Conquering Anorexia: A Teenager Invents Self-Modification to

Change Her Life" case study, 303–304
Consequences. *See also* A-B-Cs of self-change; Reinforcers
as A-B-Cs of self-change component, 12
bridging between contingencies and, 206–207, 243
definition of, 11
"Me and My Girls" case on, 26
operant behaviors affected by, 116
operant theory on, 115–121, 132
reinforcers of, 116–121
relationship between antecedents, behavior, and, 10–12, 73
self-administered, 215–219, 244
self-direction project related to, 245
structured diary to record, 72–78, 88–89
as thoughts, behaviors, feelings, 74–76
tips for typical topics related to, 238–243
Contingent consequences
bridging delayed consequences and immediate, 206–207, 243
conditions of, 117
rewards linked to, 206
success of, 219
Continuous reinforcement, 120–121
Coping
with high-risk for relapse situations, 288–290
imagined rehearsal to help with, 183–185
self-control as part of, 8
substitution strategy used for, 171
tactics for coping with temptation, 44
Covert (imagined) reinforcement, 223–226
Cybernetic theory, 110–112

Dating relationship antecedents, 103, 158–159
Dear Helper, 216
Delayed reinforcement, 208
Dental hygiene
self-modification, 21
Depression. *See also* Emotions; Feelings
antecedents of, 157–158
benefits of exercise for, 198
consequences to decrease, 239–240
relieved with incompatible thoughts, 169–170
self-observation of, 101–102
successful self-modification of, 19
tips on new thoughts/behaviors to cope with, 197–198